I0090948

COME HELL OR HIGH WATER

Studies in Critical Social Sciences Book Series

Haymarket Books is proud to be working with Brill Academic Publisher (www.brill.nl) to republish the *Studies in Critical Social Sciences* book series in paperback editions. This peer-reviewed book series offers insights into our current reality by exploring the content and consequences of power relationships under capitalism, and by considering the spaces of opposition and resistance to these changes that have been defining our new age. Our full catalog of *SCSS* volumes can be viewed at www.haymarketbooks.org/category/scss-series.

Series Editor
David Fasenfest, Wayne State University

Editorial Board
Chris Chase-Dunn, University of California–Riverside
G. William Domhoff, University of California–Santa Cruz
Colette Fagan, Manchester University
Martha Gimenez, University of Colorado, Boulder
Heidi Gottfried, Wayne State University
Karin Gottschall, University of Bremen
Bob Jessop, Lancaster University
Rhonda Levine, Colgate University
Jacqueline O'Reilly, University of Brighton
Mary Romero, Arizona State University
Chizuko Ueno, University of Tokyo

COME HELL OR HIGH WATER

Feminism and the Legacy
of Armed Conflict in Central America

TINE DESTROOPER

Haymarket
Books
Chicago, IL

First published in 2014 by Brill Academic Publishers, The Netherlands.
© 2014 Koninklijke Brill NV, Leiden, The Netherlands

Published in paperback in 2015 by
Haymarket Books
P.O. Box 180165
Chicago, IL 60618
773-583-7884
www.haymarketbooks.org

ISBN: 978-1-60846-488-3

Trade distribution:
In the U.S. through Consortium Book Sales, www.cbsd.com
In the UK, Turnaround Publisher Services, www.turnaround-uk.com
In all other countries by Publishers Group Worldwide, www.pgw.com

Cover design by Ragina Johnson.

This book was published with the generous support of Lannan Foundation
and the Wallace Action Fund.

Entered into digital printing November 2022.

Library of Congress Cataloging-in-Publication Data is available.

History is a long process, and if one can muster the patience to understand it, one can derive satisfaction from the small battles that drive it forward. A cause isn't hopeless just because its objectives aren't reached in one's lifetime.

GIOCONDA BELLI, Nicaraguan writer, El Pais Bajo mi Piel, 2002

∴

Contents

Preface and Acknowledgements

One late afternoon mid February 2011 – after she held a long and passionate speech about women's militancy and just before we say goodbye – a Guatemalan feminist activist looks at me and said, "I used to believe that we are as strong as we believe we are, but now I feel that there is something else to it, to some extent, we are as strong as others believe us to be. We need friends, a family, a society who support us and give us the room to take initiative and to manifest ourselves".

These words, spoken in the context of an interview on women's different roads to empowerment, said a lot about the constraints which feminist activists in Central America still face every day, but also about my own process of writing.

This book is the result of a doctoral research project on the influence of wartime and revolutionary mobilization on women's post-conflict mobilization, priorities and activism in Guatemala and Nicaragua. Like the situation of women and feminist activists in these two countries, the project has changed significantly since I moved to Central America in 2010. Being confronted with the daily realities, the hurdles, the resources, the discourses and the priorities of the women whom I talked to, I came to understand that a purely academic approach would not constitute an appropriate strategy to accurately reflect the realities of these women. Confronted with the complexities of daily life, I let go of my initial rigid research design and aimed instead to account as accurately as possible for the societal processes which I witnessed. This resulted in a book which moves from a concern with the impact of wartime activism on women's post-war activism, to an exploration of how different women's organizations have incorporated this legacy differently, and in specific, which alternatives to social activism women are exploring on the basis of their personal histories of mobilization.

This in-depth analysis of how women's wartime experiences have shaped their future activism, and of how this activism is in turn shaping the emancipation process of women, would not have been possible without the openness and accommodating attitudes of my interviewees and of the multitude of women to whom I spoke about these topics on a daily basis during my stay in Central America. This openness was nowhere near undemanding for some women, who recounted their life histories to shed light on their choices; life histories often characterized by trauma, violence and oppression. These personal life histories however are key to understand the evolution of the women's movement and its individual organizations.

My sincere appreciation and gratitude therefore goes to all these women who facilitated a better understanding of women's activism and women's emancipation in Guatemala and Nicaragua. Additionally, I should like to express my specific thanks to women like Claudia Say, whom, through their hospitality and helpfulness, made my daily life in these countries so much easier and richer.

Next to the overwhelming and compelling input from these women, activists and local interviewees, I could also rely on the incessant support and guidance of my doctoral supervisor, professor Pascal Vennesson, who helped me to make sense of the vast amount of information which I gathered during my fieldwork in Guatemala and Nicaragua. His extraordinary capacity to offer me both creative freedom and academic guidance, helped me to produce a work which reflects my own wide and eclectic interest and the daily realities of these women, while at the same time being surveyable and coherent. Also the constructive feedback of members of my doctoral defense panel – Donatella Della Porta, Maxine Molyneux and Marie-Louise Glebbeek – and of several other academics – e.g. Karen Kampwirth and Gerhard Haupt – significantly improved the quality of this book.

Most important however, as the abovementioned interviewee suggested, was the support of my immediate surroundings, and their belief in my ability to finish this project. While their kind gestures and encouragements often went unacknowledged because I was too focused on my writing process, they have been fundamental to the outcome of that same process. Knowing that there was a place to come 'home' to after long periods of fieldwork and traveling, and that this place was populated with some of the most supportive people, reassured me. The casual remarks of these people inspired me, on the one hand, because day-to-day conversations sometimes triggered a new way of looking at things, on the other hand because they made me aware of how universal the topic of this book is.

A commonly heard remark when I mentioned that I was doing research on women's activism in Central America, was 'Ah yes, probably a lot of work remains to be done *there* in terms of women's rights'. Implicit in these statements was the idea that in Western Europe and Northern America, there is no need for women's activism anymore, because, as a society, we have arrived at gender equality. A brief look at statistics on this topic and even at the daily lives of some of my own friends and acquaintances, however immediately reveals the incorrectness of this assumption. Yes, we have formal equality, but what does this mean in practice? What do we see if we look beyond this formal equality? And what do we choose to do with what we see?

My initial interest in the topic of women's mobilization, women's rights and gender equality, was to a large extent an academic one. In the process of researching this topic, I have however become more aware of the striking inequalities that continue to characterize our societies, also closer to home. Writing this book, turned my aspiration to become a neutral observer into an aspiration to become an active participant in the process of reshaping gender norms in a more balanced way. It is my hope that this book contributes both to a better theoretical understanding of women's empowerment, and to the actual process of bringing this empowerment into practice.

List of Illustrations and Tables

Abbreviations

AHPN	Archivo Histórico de la Policía Nacional de Guatemala – Historic Archive of the National Police of Guatemala
AMNLAE	Asociación de Mujeres Nicaragüenses Luisa Amanda Espinoza – Luisa Amanda Espinoza Association of Nicaraguan Women
AMPRONAC	Asociación de Mujeres ante la Problemática Nacional – Association of Women Confronting the National Problem
ASDECO	Asociación para el Desarrollo Comunitario – Community Improvement Association
CCC	Consejo de Comunicación y Ciudadania – Council for Communication and Citizenship
CCPP	Comisiones Permanentes – Permanent Commissions of Guatemalan Refugees in Mexico
CEDAW	Committee on the Elimination of Discrimination against Women
CEH	Comisión para el Esclarecimiento Histórico – Historical Clarification Commission (Guatemala)
CICAM	Centro de Investigación, Capacitación y Apoyo a la Mujer – Centre for Research, Training and Support of Women
COAMUGUA	Coordinadora de Agrupaciones de Mujeres de Guatemala – Coordinator of Guatemalan Women's Groups
CODECOT	Coordinadora Departamental de Comadronas Tradicionales de Quetzaltenango – Departmental Coordination of Traditional Midwives of the Department of Quetzaltenango (Guatemala)
CODEFEM	Colectiva para la Defensa de los Derechos Humanos de las Mujeres en Guatemala – Collective for the Defense of Women's Rights in Guatemala
COMFUITAG	Union of Food and Allied Workers' Associations of Guatemala
CONAPREVI	Coordinadora Nacional para la Prevención de la Violencia Intrafamiliar y contra las Mujeres – Council the Prevention of Domestic Violence and Violence against Women
CONAVIGUA	Coordinadora Nacional de Viudas de Guatemala – National Coordinator of Widows of Guatemala
DEMI	Defensoría de la Mujer Indígena – Indigenous women advocacy group
ECAP	Equipo de Estudios Comunitarios y Acción Psicosocial – Group for Community Studies and Psychosocial Action
FLACSO	Facultad Latinoamericana de Ciencias Sociales – Latin American Faculty of Social Sciences

FSLN	Frente Sandinista de Liberación Nacional – Sandinista National Liberation Front
GAM	Grupo de Apoyo Mutuo – Mutual Support Group (Guatemala)
GDI	Gender development index
GGM	Grupo Guatemalteco de Mujeres – Guatemalan Women's Group
GRUFEPROMEFAM	Grupo Femenino Pro Mejoramiento Familiar – Women's Group for Family Improvement (Guatemala)
IAHCR	Inter-American Commission on Human Rights
IIARS	Instituto Internacional de Aprendizaje para la Reconciliación Social – International Institute for Learning for Social Reconciliation
IMF	International Monetary Fund
INE	Instituto Nacional de Estadísticas – National Statistics Institute
INIM	Instituto Nicaragüense de la Mujer – Nicaraguan Institute for Women
INSSBI	Instituto Nicaragüense de Seguridad y Bienestar – Nicaraguan Institute for Social Security and Well-being
MAM	Movimiento Autónomo de Mujeres – Autonomous Women's movement (Nicaragua)
MRS	Movimiento de Renovación Sandinista – Sandinista Renovation Movement (Nicaragua)
PDDH	Procurador para la Defensa de los Derechos Humanos – Human Rights Prosecutor (Nicaragua)
PEO	Plan de Equidad de Oportunidades – Plan for Equal Opportunities (Guatemala)
PLC	Partido Liberal Constitucionalista – Constitutionalist Liberal Party (Guatemala)
PNPDMG	Plan Nacional de Promoción y Desarrollo de las Mujeres Guatemaltecas – National Plan for the Advancement and Development of Guatemalan women
REDNOV	Red de la No Violencia contra las Mujeres – No to Violence against Women – Network (Guatemala)
REDSALUD	Health network
SEPREM	Secretaria Presidencial de la Mujer – Presidential Secretary for Women (Guatemala)
UNAMG	Unión Nacional de Mujeres Guatemaltecas – National Union of Guatemalan Women
URNG	Unidad Revolucionaria Nacional Guatemalteca – Guatemalan National Revolutionary Unit
USAID	United States Agency for International Development

Introduction

"Come hell or high water". The words were used by a Nicaraguan feminist activist to describe the way in which international actors try to push through their own priorities in negotiations with local women's organizations (Serra Vázquez 2007: 103). Reading the testimony of this activist triggers a number of questions about the relationship between local women's organizations and their international benefactors, and by extension about the development of the Central American women's movement more generally.

While living in Guatemala and Nicaragua to study this issue, I came to understand and experience that the above quote is not only characteristic of the attitude of some financial donors. The words "come hell or high water", more than anything, adequately describe the firmness and determination of women's organizations and activists themselves. This comes to expression in the passion, vigor and drive with which women's activists defend their cause, but sometimes also in the form of a fixation on their own goals, which leans towards a blindness for contextual factors. "Come hell or high water" thus refers to a fervor, a steadfastness, both on the side of the women's movement and on the side of the donor community, which has constructive as well as limiting effects for the development of the women's movement.

This book considers both the cause and consequences of this fervor for the Guatemalan and Nicaraguan women's movement. In specific, I turn to factors directly and indirectly related to the armed conflict to explain the dynamics of women's mobilization today. While women's activism in these two countries has been a major focus of feminist analysis,[1] little thinking has gone into depicting how the work of these activists was influenced by their experience during the armed conflict.[2] Discussions with local feminist activists, who were active as guerrilleras during the armed conflict, challenge us to think about the importance of these revolutionary experiences for their current activism. How has the wartime activism of these women shaped their present-day activism? Three aspects of this question are particularly pertinent. First, how accurate is the assumption that women's participation in revolutionary groups has benefitted their emancipation process and the emergence of a viable women's movement in the post-conflict period? Second, how valid is it to measure women's emancipation process on the basis of their access to the public realm and the installation of legal protection mechanisms? Third, is there an

---

1   For example Suaréz Navaz et al 2008, Chejter 2007, Sternbach et al. 1992.
2   For exceptions see Chinchilla 1990, Kampwirth, 2004, Berger 2006.

inherently depoliticizing dynamic in approaches which do not operate in the public realm to arrive at women's empowerment? In order to introduce these questions, I first set out why the relationship between armed conflict, women's mobilization and gender relations is relevant, before turning to a contextualization of the cases, a definition of core concepts and an overview of the theories and methods of the present volume.

Armed Conflict, Gender Relations and Women's Mobilization

Since the early 1990s, there has been an eruption of writings on the topic of women in war, which underlined both the practical and theoretical relevance of gender relations in post-conflict societies.[3] This volume builds on insights of these authors publishing in the immediate post-conflict period, and asks what has happened to gender relations and women's activism since then. I avoid a disproportional focus on institutions and structures, and instead aim at a concerted analysis of the relation between individual agency, collective action and structural transformation. In doing so, I explore new ways of studying gender relations from a Central American feminist perspective.

Why is this important? Why should the issue of gender relations in countries emerging from civil conflict receive special attention at all? The answer to this question is threefold. Firstly, statistics show that countries emerging from war in general, and Guatemala and Nicaragua in specific, are dealing with high levels of societal violence which can be seen as direct consequences of the civil conflict (Moser et al 2006, Koch 2008, Caliskan and Griese 2006, Kurtenbach 2007, Ayres 1998).[4] Not only do these high levels of societal violence pose structural threats to durable peace, they also have an important gendered component. In the sense that they are linked to gendered power relations (Zuckerman and Greenberg 2004: 73) and affect women and men differently (Fruhling et al 2003: 104).

Next to this obvious negative consequence, armed conflict also relates to the transformation of gender relations in the sense that wartorn societies are dynamic places with plenty of transformative potential (Reilly 2007: 158). Among scholars, there exists widespread acknowledgement that armed conflict is linked to social change, and that the aftermath of large-scale societal

---

3   For example Chinchilla 1990, Light 1992, Hooks 1993, Sternbach et al. 1992.

4   I use the notion *armed conflict* or *civil conflict* rather than *war* when talking about patterns of organized violent armed confrontations, because the connotation of being state-based is not as present in the notion of armed conflict.

conflict can be seen as inducing societal transformation (Widmaier, Blyth and Seabrook 2007, Gilpin 1981, Halperin 2004). However, few societies manage to tap into this transformative potential to challenge, for example, the existence of hegemonic masculinity (Caliskan and Griese 2006, Human Rights Watch 2004).

Furthermore, armed conflict affects the transformation of gender relations because it shapes women's activism in the post-conflict period. A significant proportion of those women active in the women's movement today, were active in the revolutionary units during the civil conflict. This means that in many cases today's activists, had their first experience with sociopolitical activism in a context of armed civil conflict. It was during this revolutionary mobilization that these women developed their worldview and gained the practical skills and experiences on which they built their post-conflict activism. How has this affected their priorities and strategies over time? In addition, one should ask how women's activism was influenced by the priorities and programs of international actors and donors who entered Guatemala and Nicaragua during the period of armed conflict and during the peace-negotiations, since these actors had a strong agenda-setting potential and were crucial for the development of a vocal women's movement. Their effect on women's activism and legitimacy in the long run, needs to be rigorously analyzed however.

From the above it is clear that the factor of time is central in this work. Given the protracted nature of the Nicaraguan and especially the Guatemalan conflict, it would be unintelligible to end any analysis of the relationship between conflict, the transformation of gender relations and women's activism in the immediate post-war period, since we are in many cases looking at individuals whose entire youth was marked not only by violence, but also, in the cases of my interviewees, by the struggle against this violence.

Rather than looking at these interviewees as individuals, my analysis revolves around their role as members of the women's movement. I prioritize the role of the women's movement when studying gender relations both for operational and analytical reasons, and because of several inherent characteristics of the movement.

Firstly, women's organizations are an important factor in determining whether and how new skills and values which women gained during the conflict evolve after the signing of peace treaties. In this sense, women's organizations can be seen as a sort of transmission belt influencing the nature of women's mobilization. Secondly, they are an important voice in the societal re-definition of what constitutes an acceptable gender identity. Flood and Pease (2009: 136) demonstrate the capacity of the women's movement to influence attitudes and values, and define it as 'the social movement with the most impact on community norms regarding violence against women'. They establish both its direct influence (through advocacy) and indirect influence (through impact on gender norms more widely). Moreover, the feminist movement in particular considers itself as a crucial actor for bringing about changes in gender norms in the long run (Aguilar 1997: 13). The movement's efforts to make gender a political issue have increased the legitimacy of female mobilization and attracted much international support for the issue. It is therefore interesting to consider the role which these organizations actually play in reshaping gender norms. A last argument for analyzing the women's movement is that – while it is in itself very diverse with expressions ranging from communal kitchens to women's rights groups to *ad hoc* protest groups – it is a more apprehensible object of analysis than such interesting, but hardly operationalizable, concepts like 'gender norms', 'social climate' or 'social discourse'. At the same time, focusing on women's movements offers a more balanced insight into the domain of gender norms and relations, than does a focus on more narrow indicators such as legal changes, statistical indicators or government actions.

The Cases

Guatemala and Nicaragua share many morphologic, geographic, socio-economic and cultural characteristics. Also with regards to gender norms and women's rights a great number of similarities can be distinguished. So, for example, both countries are characterized by a high degree of hegemonic masculinity, great gender disparities and high levels of violence against women (Ellsberg et al 2000: 1607, Leonard 2002, Lambach 2007, Munck 2008). Moreover, both Guatemala and Nicaragua have experienced armed civil conflict in the 1980s–1990s which were similar in some respects. In both countries, leftist guerrilla groups rose against an authoritarian government, leading to the overthrow of the latter. Moreover, there was considerable international intervention during and after the conflict in both cases. These armed conflicts have regularly been described as the first case of women's mobilization and consciousness (Kampwirth 2004, Berger 2006). However the modalities of this mobilization were different in both countries, especially the attention paid to women's rights differed significantly across the two cases, as did the nature of women's activism. I argue that the modalities of women's mobilization during conflict and the nature of the armed conflict itself (the degree of armed violence, the organization of the opposition, the arrival of international actors, and the polarization of the political landscape), have shaped women's post-conflict activism significantly, and I use the comparison of these two cases to illuminate this dynamic.

Nicaragua

In Nicaragua, leftist FLSN revolutionaries overthrew the Somoza dictatorship in 1979. This was the beginning of a period of more than ten years of FSLN-reign, but also of a bloody conflict between revolutionaries of the Sandinista National Liberation Front (FSLN) on the one hand, and Contras funded by the US on the other hand (Miranda and Ratliff 1993). The conflict (1979–1990) was less violent than the Guatemalan one, but entailed an important degree of popular mobilization, including that of women.

Revolutionary leaders in the Guatemalan conflict addressed women as a distinct group, both in the sense that they called upon women to support the revolutionary cause, and in the sense that they promised gender-specific legal changes (Thayer 1994). As a result, despite a long history of conservative patriarchy in Nicaragua, 'the massive participation of Nicaraguan women in the overthrow of the Somoza dictatorship [in 1979] was unprecedented, not only in the history of Nicaragua, but in the Western hemisphere' (Chinchilla 1990: 374, see also Ramirez Horton 1982). After 1979, women remained active and comprised 30 per cent of the guerrilla forces (Leonard 2002: 117, Randall 1980: 34).[5] This put women in a position – at least formally speaking – to make substantive demands upon the new government. Moreover, the FSLN had previously expressed a commitment to women's issues by explicitly mentioning women's rights on several occasions, and by issuing its declarations of 1969, 1979 and 1987 in a gender-neutral language (Ortega et al 1979). In short, despite persisting patriarchy, a space seemed to open up for progressive gender-politics – even if only through a dynamic of rhetorical entrapment (Schimmelfennig 2001)

This attention to women and women's rights can be explained by the leftist ideology of equality, which envisioned the equality of men and women, and which supported the positive discrimination of women to arrive at this. Also the socio-economic situation of women in the pre-Sandinista period partially explains why women mobilized in the first place, and why the FSLN addressed women as a distinct group. In the Somoza-era, Nicaraguan women played an

---

5 Valdivia (1991: 164) shows that women are proportionally more numerous as leaders (ratio membership-leadership) and that Nicaraguan women have the highest political participation rate in Latin America at that time.

important economic role, but had a low economic position.[6] This made them particularly receptive to the gendered promises of revolutionaries (Valdivia 1991: 157). Moreover, women's activism in organizations such as the Association of Women Confronting the National Crisis (AMPRONAC, later AMNLAE) in the pre-Sandinista period, spearheaded the introduction of women into the national political platform by fostering the idea that women's problems were best solved at the socio-political level (Valdivia 1991: 150–151). This too meant that the FSLN could not ignore women in its propaganda.

The propaganda by the FSLN was however notably patriarchal. In the propaganda women were addressed as mothers or wives. The famous picture of a woman with a riffle in one hand, a baby in the other is the most obvious example thereof. Also in other pamphlets however, women were in the first place addressed as mothers (see illustrations below).

In addition to this, those women who mobilized, were invariably organized in the FSLN's women's organization AMNLAE – often referred to as 'the submissive wife of the FSLN'. In this organization there was little room for maneuver, and women were expected to act as exponents of the FSLN rather than as independently thinking critical individuals (Kampwirth 2004: 29). As one interviewee stated, "We were to toe the line in every way – how we thought, how we acted, was decided from above. Yes, the activism was an eye-opener for many women, but not in the sense that it was our first feminist experience or that it helped us to think about our own emancipation. Not at that point". (Jiménez, former activist and currently member of the MRS).

Also the nature of the proposed legal chances reinforced traditional gender norms. Women were, for example, granted the right to take time off from paid employment to breast-feed children, or could leave work earlier to take care of children (AMNLAE, n.d.). These provisions did not exist for men and thus bolstered women's motherhood roles.

Hence, despite the fact that women were actively recruited and granted gender-specific rights, these rights and the FSLN's propaganda *de facto* often reinforced a patriarchal situation and were frequently dependent on women's loyalty and obedience to the ruling FSLN (Ellsberg et al 1997: 83). Nevertheless, the fact that women were granted sex-specific rights fostered a collective self-awareness amongst women, as well as a vision that women were to be seen as a group with specific gendered needs by policy-makers.

While efforts by Sandinistas in the 1980s were modest, the most serious backlash for women's rights only came with the electoral victory of Violetta Barrios de Chamorro in 1990 (Ellsberg 1997: 83). Her election and consequent

---

6   During the Somoza-regime, 48 per cent of heads of household were female and over 80 per cent of employed women were heads of household (Valdivia 1991: 157).

FIGURE 1   *FSLN campaign poster for the tenth anniversary of the revolution* (1989)
© BUJARD AND WIRPER 2010.

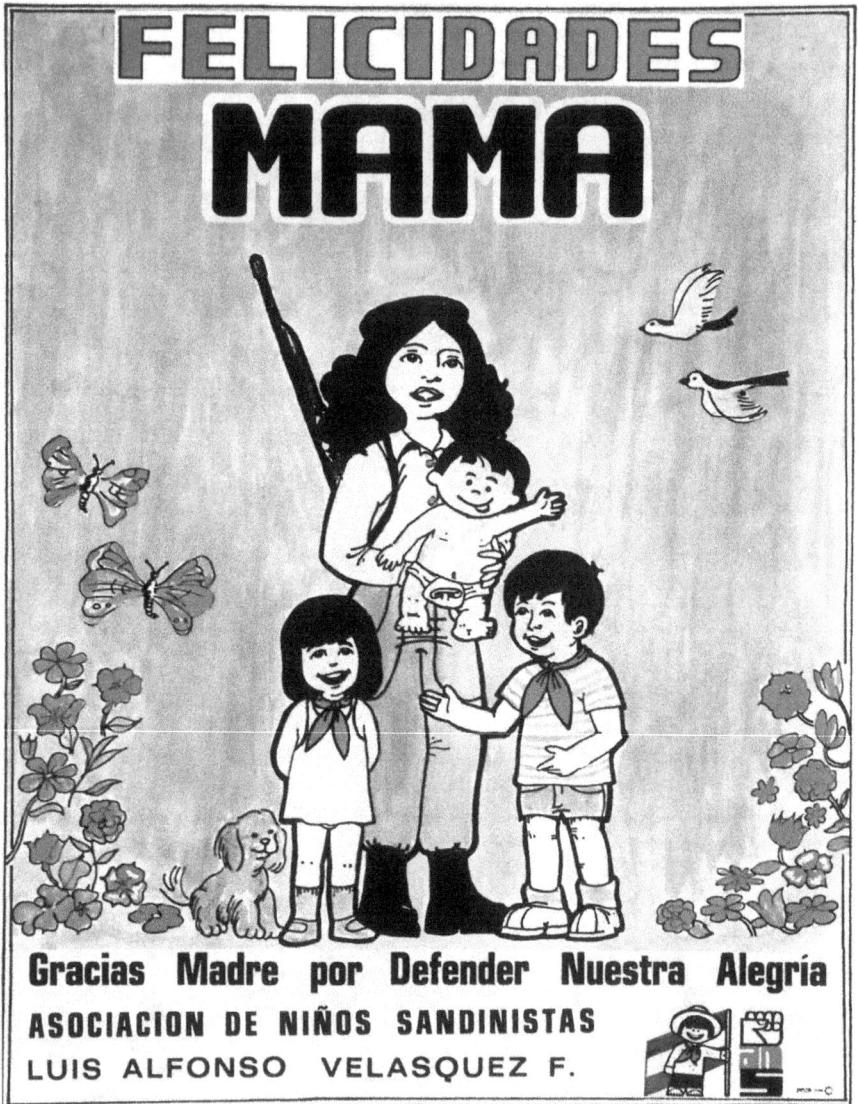

FIGURE 2   *FSLN poster for mother's day emphasizing women's multiple roles (1983)*
            © BUJARD AND WIRPER 2010.

anti-feminist government program, as well as women's absence from the peace
talks, meant that the changes which were hoped for, were not consolidated in
the 1990s (Luciak 2001: 98). In this period, consecutive governments approved
a series of conservative laws regulating sexual behavior, thereby undoing much
of the scope for progress which had been created and setting the stage for a
return to a more patriarchal society.

FIGURE 3   *FSLN poster referring to mothers as heroes (1980)*
© BUJARD AND WIRPER 2010.

Guatemala

Nicaragua was not the only country in Latin America where women's rights were explicitly mentioned during the armed conflict. Attention to women's rights was also prominent in El Salvador, Chiapas (Mexico) and Cuba (Kampwirth, 2004). It was rarer to find a Central American revolution in which there was little or no explicit attention for women's rights and mobilization, than one in which there was. It is interesting to select such a case – like Guatemala – to explore the reasons for, and consequences of, absence of attention for women's rights during conflict.

The class struggle in Guatemala reached the level of armed confrontation at the beginning of the 1960s. This was the start of a 36 year long violent conflict which intensified between 1978 and 1985 (DNSA 2010). Sexual violence and singling out women for femicide was an integral part of the military's counter-insurgency strategy (CEH 1999, Khan 2004, Stetlet and Sharp 2008). While women's rights were breached in structural ways, women had no formal organizations defending them. Propaganda and campaigns by revolutionaries had a blind spot for women and women's issues, as is illustrated by the Declaration of Revolutionary Unity in Guatemala, which makes no reference to women as a separate group at any point (Guatemalan National Revolutionary Unit 1982).

The exceptions to this lack of attention to women were some dispersed efforts to organize women as a group, first by conservative and reactionary organizations – such as the Anticommunist Women of Guatemala created in 1968 and Catholic Women in 1966 (Aguilera and Beverly 1980: 112) – and later by revolutionary organizations such as the Mutual Support Group, GAM (Lupe 1983: 107). Also pamphlets – in the AHPN archive – addressing women are scant and tend to only address women as mothers of soldiers. Like in Nicaragua, women are thus in the first place addressed as a group for pragmatic reason: to foster support for the revolution more efficiently. What is different however, is that, in Guatemala, women are not offered something in return, such as gendered legislation (Nakaya 2003). Luciak (2001) attributes the relative neglect of women by revolutionaries to the extremely violent nature of the Guatemalan conflict, which nourished the idea that male combatants were needed who were able to fight. This allegedly led to the overlooking of women in propaganda.

The post-war reconstruction and peace negotiations of 1996 partially leveled out this neglect of women and their rights. On this occasion, women organized and participated in societal decision-making in organized women's groups or as members of other groups of civil society (Garrard-Burnett 2000). In this period, partially due to the presence of international monitoring, societal conditions were more supportive of women's participation than during conflict. However, in Guatemala, like in Nicaragua, the women's movement had difficulties consolidating the momentum for change (Luciak 2001: 239). Yet, the Guatemalan women's and feminist movement eventually developed in a more balanced way than the Nicaraguan one. In the second chapter, I consider the structured and monitored allocation of international funds, and the respect for local and ethnic dynamics to explain this development.

Comparing Both Cases

In sum, in Nicaragua the civil conflict set the scene for women's mobilization and for attention to women's rights – albeit from a patriarchal perspective. This stagnated in the period following the armed conflict. In Guatemala, on the other hand, the armed conflict did not trigger much attention for women's rights and did not explicitly aim to mobilize women as a group. Yet, in Guatemala, women mobilized around the peace negotiations and claimed their rights in this context. Today, women's rights are increasingly being challenged in both countries, and in both cases, the conditions for female mobilization and activism are becoming more difficult. In neither case was the women's movement really able to live up to the expectations which arose directly after the conflict. The envisioned changes of attitudes and practices with relation to the position of women have not been as profound as hoped for in the transition period. As Luciak writes, 'a general problem [...] has been rising unmet expectations. Former combatants [...] questioned whether their sacrifices had been worth it' (2001: 93). A longitudinal analysis of Human Development Reports and Global Gender Gap reports since 1990 shows that the position of women in Nicaragua has become comparable to that of women in Guatemala in terms of Gender Development Index, socio-economic position and physical security. In the early 2010s a patriarchal political and societal climate prevails in both cases, with more traditional gender norms being reintroduced in most sectors of society (Dore 2006).

Yet, despite these similarities, there are also striking differences between both countries, notably so with relation to the composition, priorities and methods of the women's and feminist movement. While similarities – such as the choice for an organizational model based on NGO's – exist, significant differences can be observed, for example in the degree of polarization. The nature of these differences and the way in which they seem to relate to the armed conflict, makes it particularly pertinent to ask why the women's and feminist movement has evolved in one way in Nicaragua and in another in Guatemala. This leads to the main question of this book, namely, how factors directly related to the armed conflict shaped women's rights activism in post-conflict Guatemala and Nicaragua?

Core Concepts

Before embarking on an exploration of this issue, I lay out the core concepts underlying this research, in order to establish a comprehensible framework for reading this book.

Gender, Gender Relations, Gender Norms
Gender refers to the historically and socially constructed roles of, and relations between, men and women. It can be seen as a 'boundary marker and identity producer' (Polletta and Lee 2006: 51). Gender norms assign specific identities, entitlements and responsibilities to men and women. In most societies, gender relations continue to be characterized by unequal power relations, and gender norms for women perpetuate women's subordination to men (Butler 2004: 55). Two visions on gender are particularly relevant for this book: a social constructivist one and an essentialist one.

Social constructivist feminism can be seen as a form of egalitarian feminism and is closely linked to radical libertarian feminism and liberal feminism. All these forms of feminism problematize and challenge the beliefs which a society holds about the capabilities and roles of women and men respectively (Castro 1990: 45). This strand of feminism believes that – apart from reproductive differences – biological and psychological differences between males and females are limited, and that differences in their roles and behavior can be explained mainly by gendered socialization and historical construction (Deutsch 2007).

Scholars like Judith Butler, challenge traditional gender roles by arguing that they are social constructs. Butler criticizes the way in which the apparently coherent construction of these two categories, establishes the appearance of an essential 'core' gender, which legitimizes differences between men and women to persist (Butler 1993: 5). This, she argues, is limiting for women – and men alike – since it limits their ability to be full persons and make their own decisions (Butler 2004).

Difference feminism on the other hand, like radical cultural feminism, stresses the existence of inherent differences between men and women and presents gender roles as natural. They emphasize ontological, biological and psychological differences between men and women (Weedon 1999). This strand of feminism does not so much reject the idea that these differences exist, but instead denounces the fact that these characteristics are valued differently. This interpretation is especially relevant when studying the Guatemalan case, where the basic assumptions of difference feminism correspond with the indigenous belief in complementarity between men and women. Indigenous feminists posit that there are inherent differences between men and women, but that women should value these, and aim for complementarity rather than equality so as to preserve the characteristics that define them as women (Marcos 2009: 43). Moreover, alleged differences are not seen as absolute or divisive, but as tendencies or inclinations. I consider this interpretation to the extent it can shed light on the activism of Guatemalan indigenous feminists who adhere to the idea of complementarity as presented in Mayan *cosmovision*. This allows for a more culturally embedded assessment of the notion of equality and equal rights.

Next to this debate on the nature of gender differences, it is also relevant to briefly set out the guiding frame on gender needs and interests. The prevailing interpretation in literature, which is also used here, is the framework proposed by Molyneux in 1985. Molyneux – and scholars writing in her tradition, such as Alsop (1993) and Moser (1993) – argue that one should distinguish between women's interests on the one hand, and gender interests on the other hand. Women's interests and needs are those which are based on biological similarities, whereas gender interests and needs are derived from the social position which women take up in specific societies. Gender interests are thus more narrow and cannot be assumed to be primary or universal for all women at all times.

In the category of gender interests and needs, Molyneux further distinguishes between strategic gender interests or needs on the one hand, and practical gender interests or needs on the other. In this framework, strategic gender needs concern the structure and nature of relationships between men and women in general. They are derived from the subordination of women to men, and are determined deductively from the analysis of women's situation of subordination. Structural action is needed to change these, since they cannot be removed by uncoordinated initiatives alone. Practical gender needs and interests on the other hand arise from the specific conditions of women within the gender division of labour, and are in theory formulated by women themselves within their position (Molyneux 1985: 233). Practical gender needs are for example health care programs for pregnant women, suitable working conditions for women, measures to guarantee decent wages for women, etc. Since practical gender needs and interests are an immediately perceived need, they do not *per se* entail a goal like women's emancipation or gender equality.

In practice, strategic gender needs and interests are usually defended by feminist activists, whereas, practical gender needs and interests tend to be defended by women activists in the first place. Alsop visualizes women's different gender needs and interests as follows (1993: 369).

TABLE 1   *The relation between practical and strategic gender needs and interests, based on*
           Molyneux 1985

	Interest	Need
Strategic **An issue or concern** **embedded in or derived** **from the subordination** **of women to men**	Would be: to address the equity balance in gender relations	Would be: to provide women with equipping mechanisms
Practical **An issue or concern** **embedded in or derived** **from the everyday** **situations that women** **find themselves in**	Would be: to identify thematic areas in which women have options for improvement in their status and standard of living	Would be: to intervene at critical points in the existing system

The Women's Movement

Above, I set out the relevance of studying the influence of wartime activism on the post-war women's movement. However, the notion of a "women's movement" is imprecise and has been used to refer to a variety of phenomena. While some scholars only include feminist activism, others include all forms of women's activism in women's organizations as well as in mixed-gender organizations and on an individual basis (Rowbotham 1992, Beckwith 2000: 434). For the purpose of this research, I use Alvarez' (1990: 23) criteria of autonomy and public visibility, i.e. women's organizations are those organizations which aim to improve the situation of women, have a degree of autonomy from other political or social organizations, and are visible social actors.

The women's movement is defined as all the organizational spaces which women create to acknowledge, confront and resolve practical and strategic gender needs and interests of women. Since there is a multiplicity of these organizations and since the scope of issues addressed by these organizations, as well as their working methods, priorities and politics of alliance are so diverse, it would be inaccurate to speak of the women's movement as if this were a unitary actor or to ascribe to it a degree of unity beyond the goal of furthering women's rights.

This fragmentation means that there are many subdivisions within the movement. Organizations with a similar orientation define problems and solutions similarly and are linked by a common identity (Meyers 2008). These like-minded organizations often refer to themselves as 'networks' in the Guatemalan and Nicaraguan context, for example the Network against violence against women (REDNOVI, Guatemala), and the Network for women's health (REDSALUD, Nicaragua). These networks are loose forms of co-operation which usually involve periodic meetings between the members of the network. Most large women's organizations are part of at least one network.

In both countries, the most vocal subsection of the women's movement is the feminist one. Feminist organizations invest considerably in profiling themselves as a group and in influencing the societal debate on women's issues. By feminist organizing, I refer to those organizations which are in the first place dedicated to changing gender relations and gendered divisions of power in a structural way, because they see this as a precondition for improving women's everyday lives. Feminist organizations embark on a project of social transformation inspired by the ideal of equal gender relations. Transforming the roles which society assigns to women is crucial in this view, because feminist activists ascribe gendered injustices to the restriction of women's roles to domestic-reproductive ones (Kampwirth 2004: 8, Aguilar et al, 1997: 23 and 107).

Feminine organizing, on the other hand, refers to 'a way of promoting women's well-being within the context of their traditional roles, without directly challenging the gender division of power' or without aiming to transform the roles society ascribes to women (Kampwirth 2004: 8). Their work can implicitly challenge gender roles or change long-term gender structures, but it is not their first aim (Bayard de Volo 2003).

This duality between feminist and feminine organizing shows strong overlaps with the perceived duality between practical and strategic gender needs and interests (Alvarez 1990). These conceptual dualities were heavily criticized in the mid-1990s however when critics argued that in practice interests and types of activism overlap and that presenting them as different or exclusionary undertakings renders it difficult for activists to work at the intersection of both (Schirmer 1993; Bayard de Volo 2003; Chinchilla 1991). Moreover, according to these critics, distinguishing between feminist and feminine activists, *de facto* sidelines feminine organizing by portraying its potential gains as marginal in comparison to those of – often middle-class – feminists (Stephen 1997; Lind 1992; Alvarez 1990). Several academics furthermore argued that also organizations which do not self-define as feminist, can to some extent further feminist goals, for example by organizing women or through the way they frame issues (Bayard de Volo 2003). Organizations working with women within their traditional gender roles, such as the maternity frame or *marianismo* for example, can – unintentionally – touch upon new layers of this role, which can be a

basis for emancipative and feminist action. Franceschet (2004: 526) for example illustrates how first- and second-wave feminist movements in Chile
employed a maternal framing, but ascribed new meanings to it. She thereby
demonstrated the dynamic and contextual nature of gender framing, and the
potential of incorporating traditional gender constructs in the feminist struggle. Non-feminist organizations can thus politicize women's motherhood role
and use it as a basis for action. Affirming rather than denying these traditional
gender identities and politicizing them, can encourage women from all layers
to mobilize (Alsop 1993).

However, in practice, in the Guatemalan and Nicaraguan context, efforts to
overcome this distinction between feminist and feminine goals and between
work around practical and strategic gender needs prove to be difficult. Biannual
'encuentros' between self-defined feminist and feminine sectors of the Central
American women's movement in the mid-1990s – during which the goal was
precisely to overcome this opposition – were only a short-lived initiative (Ray
and Korteweg 1999: 49). Since the early 2000s, due to several conjectural factors, to which I return below, differences between both strands are once more
being pushed to the limit.

This means that despite the validity of the theoretical critiques to the distinction between practical and strategic gender needs, and between feminist
and feminine organizing, these categories remain relevant in practice. The
debate on the role of feminism in the women's movement today is still virulent
in Guatemala and Nicaragua, and the ideological convergence between both
types of activism of which the above critics speak, is not yet in place in these
two countries. Given the persisting importance of this feminine-feminist identity, and the conscious self-positioning of those involved on either side of the
continuum, the practical effects thereof on the programs are tangible, and the
distinction is therefore used throughout this volume.

The above discussion raises the question whether one can speak of *a* wom-
en's movement – singular – at all in these two countries. There is little unity or
coherence within the women's movement beyond the common goal of improving the situation of women. According to social movement literature, the
extent to which one can speak of *a* movement is therefore doubtful. Escobar
(2008: 96), for example, argues that social movements are often perceived in
terms of 'collective sustained activities of a large number of women organized
under strong leadership, with an effective network of solidarity, procedures,
memberships, mechanisms of framing, communication and publicity'. Other
authors (Polletta 2001, Tarrow 1998, Morris and Mueller 1992) stress the importance of a shared identity between all members of the movement as a precondition for movement mobilization. As the next chapters will show, these

elements are not present in the women's movements in Guatemala and Nicaragua in the early 2010s.

How then should we account for the sum of women's organizing and activism which does not *per se* rely on coherent organizational structures, collective identity or shared procedures and priorities amongst all participants?

I argue that the mere absence of many large collective efforts in which all women's organizations participate is not sufficient reason to turn to the notion of a "non-movement" (Escobar 2008: 111),[7] given the multiplicity of actions, organizations and lobbying which takes places. Chinchilla's notion (1991: 304) of a "pre-movement" is not appropriate here neither, since this implies the normative idea that the organizations should further converge and become one unitary actor. I therefore argue, that while not all the formal characteristics of a social movement are applicable to the variety of women's organizations and women's activism in these two countries, the fact that they share one major goal and an ongoing commitment to achieve this, are sufficient conditions to consider them as a movement in their own right (Munkres 2008: 190). Moreover, as Westwood and Radcliffe (1993: 23) argue, fragmentation can in itself be seen as a profoundly emancipatory feature of social movements, since it allows for dissident voices.

In sum, there is something like a women's movement in both countries – however loosely defined – which is an important actor of civil society. This research considers those elements which have influenced the development of this movement, as well as the influence the movement has on women's lives. In specific, the book revolves around the question of how the history of the Guatemalan and Nicaraguan women's movement influences its approach of women's empowerment. This question arises from several overlapping puzzles. How is it that in two countries with such vocal women's and feminist movements, such high levels of violence against women persist and relatively few changes in gender norms are visible? If women's mobilization during conflict has indeed benefited their post-war social activism, then how come women's organizations remain so dependent on international donors? And what can explain crucial differences between the Guatemalan and Nicaraguan women's movement? Underlying all these issues, is the question of how dynamics related to the armed conflicts influenced the newly emerging women's movements. To understand this, I first present the theoretical and methodological underpinnings of the book.

---

7   The concept of a non-movement is used to frame the idea that every everyday action has a potential political and societal relevance, and that the existence of 'classic' social movements is thus not per se necessary for social change to occur.

Methodological and Theoretical Framework

To quote Michael Quinn Patton (2002: 432), "Qualitative analysis transforms data into findings. No formula exists for that transformation. Guidance, yes. But no recipe. Direction can and will be offered, but the final destination remains unique for each inquirer, known only when – and if – arrived at". Given the nature of the analysis and the scarcity of reliable quantifiable sources, this is not a variable-driven analysis. I refrain from ascribing a greater degree of objectivity to quantitative indicators, because of the risk of a quantitative approach to distort the reality of women, and because such an approach tends to lead to an emphasis on those factors which are easier to quantify, rather than on those having the largest influence on women's daily life. Moreover, there is a legitimate concern with statistics which are kept by non-sociologists and often collected with gender-biased assumptions (Cook and Fonow 1986).

I thus adopt a qualitative approach to analyze the development of the women's movement. This means that I also step away from a dichotomous conceptualization of success and failure in my analysis of the movements. Instead I consider the broader evolution of the movement in various respects. Previous studies have analyzed women's activism on the basis of the output they produced in terms of legal changes, gender development indexes (GDI) or the societal mobilization which they trigger (see for example Turner 1973). This entails two paradoxes however. Firstly, both movement activists and quantitative measures indicate that considerable advances have been made, while women in the street are not equally positive about the extent to which their daily lives have changed in terms of gender equality and gender-based violence. Secondly, there is the paradox that the higher the level of awareness of their own rights amongst women, the higher figures on violence against women are likely to be, because women will be more likely to denounce their perpetrators and talk about the issue in public. This means that these types of indicators offer only a partial picture. I therefore used in-depth interviews and participatory observations within organizations, as well as a discourse analysis of the materials produced by the organizations to analyze the evolution of the movement.

The research contains both a descriptive and an explanatory element. On the one hand, it offers a detailed analysis of where the movement finds itself at present and what its options are in this situation. On the other hand, it turns to the influence of the armed conflict to explain this situation. The aim is thus not to propose blueprints for action, but merely to facilitate reflection on decisions and their effects. This fits the assumption of feminist methodology that 'knowledge must be elicited and analyzed in such a way that it can be used by women to alter the conditions of their existence' (Cook and Fonow 1986: 12–13). Research must therefore be designed to provide a structural picture of the present, as well as a vision of the future. While the boundary with normative claims here is a very thin one, my work is written with the goal of facilitating local ownership based on a theoretical analysis, rather than prescribing new modes of action. Therefore I have also engaged in an elaborate and continuous effort of presenting my findings and interpretations with the women whom I interviewed, or 'talk back' as Cook and Fonow (1986) call this, to take into account their opinion on this and avoid objectification of the subject.

Interviews and Participatory Observation
Critical Discourse Analysis and the Interpretation of Interviews
For the interpretation of the interview data, I used critical discourse analysis (CDA) as a guiding frame. CDA is an interdisciplinary approach to the study of discourse which emphasizes that discourse is a social practice which exposes structures of domination. In CDA, discourse is defined as language use in speech and writing, which has a social function in a certain context, and which can alter social reality (Fairclough and Wodak 1997: 258). Discourse thus refers to the social activity of making meaning through language in a way which is governed by social habits (Wodak 2008: 6). Discourse is more abstract than the texts and speech acts out of which it is made up, and requires a certain degree of cohesion, coherence, intertextuality and intentionality.

Like post-structuralist feminism, CDA also points out the normativeness of a discourse, and how ideology operates through discourse, as well as the way in which norms and ideology are (re-)negotiated in the discourse (Bruner 1991: 15). Analyzing discourses is thus key to understanding the ways in which different material realities are negotiated, constructed, consolidated, defended, drawn upon and learned from (Burr 1995). At the societal level, discourses – rather than top-down implementations – are fundamental in shaping new social realities and institutional structures. It is also in discourse that norms and values are expressed. These norms and values funnel ideas and reconstruct interests (Finnemore and Sikkink 1998: 889). Discourses thus profoundly shape our view of the world and give an insight into how actors define their world and their problems. As Whitehead (2002: 96) posits, the way in which mechanisms of subordination are put into practice is also to a large extent discursive. A critical discourse analysis thus bridges the gap between material and ideational interests and norms, as well as between structural and cultural explanations, since discourse is seen as the sphere in which material, institutional and ideational factors are combined (Polletta and Jasper 2001). It is therefore important to consider both how power is reflected in discourse, as well as how a discourse can consolidate or change existing power relations.

Since discourse refers to an identifiable social practice which systematically forms the object of which it speaks (Abu-Lughod and Lutz 1990: 9), the effects thereof can be analyzed by studying these particular practices. Analyzing discourses thus allows one to also consider subconscious and intangible processes in an operationalizable way (Hajer 2006). An operationalization of discourse which also takes into account the implicit know-how of actors, is an important step in acknowledging implicit mental models and making them explicit (Kim 1993: 44).

CDA is thus instrumental because it allows for a more dynamic interpretation of interview findings in which actors' preferences, interactions, strategies and normative orientations are assessed (Schmidt 2008; 2010). CDA acknowledges the material and path-dependency of discourse as well as the potential of discourse to contribute to change (Jacobsen 1995).

'Rich Data' and Interview Techniques[8]
For the structure of the interviews, I relied on interview techniques proposed by Silverman (2006: 110). In order to obtain rich data – e.g. on life histories – Silverman suggests 'active listening, in which the interviewer allows the interviewee the freedom to talk and ascribe meanings, while bearing in mind the broader aims of the project'. By proceeding in this way, the interview is collaboratively produced and both the interviewer and the interviewee are active participants in the creation of content. My role as an interviewer was to maintain some level of control in the sense of following up and closing different topics.

When using this technique, it is important to be aware of one's role as a researcher, both in terms of how presence and personal characteristics shape the interview and in terms of how one's immersion in the local context shapes the interpretation of research findings.

With regards to the former – how my presence shaped the dynamic of the interview – it should be remarked that the setting of an interview in which questions are asked about the daily operations of the organizations may resemble the situation of an audit (by donors, government, etc.), which potentially triggered a degree of caution on the side of interviewees. This may have kept them from talking freely to some extent. In order to avoid this as much as possible, I clearly introduced myself, my research project and my interests at

---

8 Silverman's use of the notion 'rich data' follows the idea of 'thick description' which allow for a better understanding of social phenomena because a contextualization is provided.

the beginning of each interview and explicitly emphasized the absence of any ties with governmental or non-governmental organizations. Also the fact that most interviewees were selected through snowballing, helped to create a degree of confidence and leveled out a cautious attitude (Silverman 2006: 110). Furthermore, virtually all interviews were conducted in the offices of the respective organizations, meaning that interviewees found themselves in a familiar context. This too is conducive to the creation of a setting in which interviews can talk more freely. Lastly, caution on the side of interviewees was less likely in situations of participatory observation, where my presence was partially blended out by the group dynamic, and by the fact that I was often present for a longer period of time.

With regards to how my participatory observation in the movement and my interactions with my research subject shaped my own frames of reference, it is relevant to remark that interacting on a frequent basis with some interviewees and engaging in long and lively discussions with others, inevitably colored my interpretation of findings. However, awareness of this fact, constant triangulation of interview findings with secondary literature and statements made by other interviewees, coming back to my academic community between two periods of fieldwork, and discussions with other scholars who researched this topic, helped me to keep a necessary distance – without aiming for a completely disconnected observation. On the contrary, my interactions helped me to look beyond the facts and figures and also grasp what women's own take on issues was and how they perceived the concepts which are at the core of this research, such as empowerment, feminism, gender and mobilization. This way the potential bias created by knowing one's subjects of research was dwarfed by the advantage of obtaining thick descriptions of people's own experiences.

Another caution with interviews is warranted. As Silverman (2006: 117) argues, interviews give no direct access to facts or experiences because historical memory is constantly reworked in light of the current situation. Interviews therefore only give us access to representations of people's experiences, not to their experiences directly. I aimed to overcome this lack of stability by conducting a large number of interviews on similar topics and triangulating interviews with documentary resources where possible on the one hand, and by accepting the absence of a stable referent on the other hand. Constructing some version of the world this way acknowledges that different interviewees have different relations to the phenomena they describe and to the situation of the interview itself.

In practice, I invited women to tell me about how they became active members of the women's movement and used this as a starting point for an exploration of how they saw the movement today, how they felt it had changed since they joined, and what they felt were the most important shortcomings and achievements of the women's movement as a whole and of their organization in particular. In most cases, these questions also led to a discussion of the life histories of these people, in which revolutionary mobilization often played an important role.

This strategy of qualitative open-ended interviews allowed for a focus on processes rather than outcomes and provided women with the opportunity to touch upon issues which they found relevant. This often led to interesting deviations from the standard interview design. Moreover, this technique also gave women the opportunity to define which experiences had been most influential in terms of how they perceived their own role and the role of the women's movement today. Probing for this issue by means of open ended questions, rendered overlaps in the answers more significant and also threw light on the process underlying certain developments.

Organization of the Interviews

In total, I conducted 74 in-depth interviews, some with more than one interviewee, and some interviewees were interviewed more than once. Interviewees pertained to local and international women's organizations, governmental bodies working on women's rights and protection, church organizations, or were beneficiaries/participants of these organizations, or had been involved in revolutionary activism during the period of armed conflict.

There is an overrepresentation of Guatemalan interviewees, as compared to Nicaraguan interviewees. This can be explained by the fact that the second part of the book is an in-depth analysis of an approach which was only found in certain Guatemalan women's organizations, and for which an additional number of interviewees were conducted.

Furthermore, there is an overrepresentation of interviewees from organizations based in the capital cities. Next to a practical motivation, the reason for this is twofold. On the one hand, many organizations based in the capital are also active in the rest of the country, and it was particularly interesting to analyze how they use certain concepts in one way when working with middle-class women in the capital and in another way when working with rural women in remote areas. Secondly, the second part of the book focuses on the activities of organizations which self-define as feminist, and these are more active in the capitals. Nevertheless, I also conducted a number of interviews with NGO's and women from the rural areas (nineteen in total, eleven of which with activists of rural women's organizations), to get an insight into how these local organizations – which often organize around practical gender needs – proceed, and how they relate to organizations in the capital. This way, the selection of

interviewees and organizations, reflects the variety in the types of organizations, while at the same time allowing for a profound analysis of a certain type
of women's organization.

All interviews were conducted in Spanish, and English citations in the next
chapters are my own translations. Some interviews were recorded and tran-
scribed. However, due to the nature of the topic, many women wished to
remain anonymous and not to have the interview recorded. The interviews
were conducted in the period March 2010 until March 2011, during which
I spent about six months in both countries conducting fieldwork. In this
period, I also attended several events on women's rights organized by the wom-
en's movements or by governmental actors, and I engaged in many informal
discussions with women and men, on how the position of women in society
had changed since the armed conflict. Like the talks which I had with my interviewees after the formal interview, these discussions were often as insightful
than the actual interviews, since they provided me with an insight into how
women lived out their gender in daily life and how they experienced the
changes which had taken place since the early 1980s. During these discussions
women would also more easily vent their frustrations with the current situation and their desires for a change of strategies. This provided me with insights
which I could not leave untapped, and on the basis of which I conceptualized
the second part of the book. I decided to use this part to shift the focus from an
analysis of how the women's movement was influenced by the civil conflict, to
an exploration of alternative strategies for women's emancipation, because
this seemed to me a plausible way to validate the experiences of the women
I talked to during my fieldwork. Hence, in the first part of the work, I examine
a puzzle collected from social movement theory, whereas the second part is
problem-oriented and deals with issues which became apparent during my
first period of fieldwork.

Document Analysis

Next to interviews, discussions and participation in events and protest
marches, I also conducted a document analysis. In both countries, women's
organizations had a fair amount of historical information on their own organization. I analyzed those publications which my interviewees themselves
considered to be the most important ones. While this information usually
only dealt with those elements which the organizations found relevant to
include in their archives, these documents provide useful information on how
the movement sees its evolution and how its discourse and priorities has
changed. In Guatemala, this documentary evidence was complemented with
documents from the Historic Archive of the National Police of Guatemala

(*Archivo Histórico de la Policía Nacional, AHPN*) which is a secret police archive
of eight kilometers of documents retrieved in 2005 of which about two and a
half million documents had been systematized at the time of writing. One section thereof (about 2000 documents) concerns pamphlets of social and revolutionary movements which the secret forces confiscated. These documents shed
light on how women operated initially as a part of the broader revolutionary
movement. For both countries, I also monitored the media during the period
of my stay, and conducted an analysis of the two main newspapers at several
points in time. On the basis of these materials, the research compares the strategies and priorities of the Guatemalan and Nicaraguan women's movement.

Individual and Organizational Learning Theory

The theoretical framework inspiring both the selection and operationalization
of the puzzle – how has women's wartime activism influenced their current
activism for women's rights – derives from human learning theory (HLT).
Learning theories are used here to sensibly conceptualize the interaction
between material reality and ideas; and between psychosocial developments
and politico-contextual developments. As an open systems model it is thus *par
excellence* suitable for analyzing the link between the individual, the organization, their environment and the historical determinedness thereof, or, *in concreto*, of the way in which the war and the presence of external funding agencies
have influenced the identity and approach of both the individuals and the
organizations constituting the women's movement (Laufer 1989: 416). Learning
theories thereby introduce an element of agency in the analysis of the wom-
en's movements. They moreover allow for research which takes both an individual and a collective context-sensitive aspect into account, since the learning
processes of individuals active in organizations is by definition a process which
is transferred to the organization, and from there also feeds back to the individual (Maier 2003)

Next to considering the relation between the individual, the organization
and their environment, learning theories also invite for the consideration of
both conscious and unconscious processes and of both active and passive processes. They stress that both aspects are important, since untested and unconscious assumptions influence the learning process as much as explicit ones.
Kim (1993: 39) and Harris (1994: 317) even argue that the shared mental maps
which guide individual and collective action are usually not made explicit, and
have a big impact. Furthermore, human learning theory's notion of 'shared
mental maps' is comparable to the notion of frames, commonly used in social
movement literature. Whereas frames can be defined as the interpretive pack-
ages which activists develop to mobilize (Snow et al 1986, Tarrow 1998),

shared mental maps are the 'frameworks' which allow for organizational advancement and mutual understanding (Kim 1993). A critical discourse analysis can help to explain how these assumptions and mental maps can then be recognized.

Lastly, learning theories suggest that any analysis should take both rational and non-rational considerations and behaviors of actors into account. Emotions and affects are seen as equally important for organizational and individual learning as rational cognitive calculations (Levine 2010: 14; Vince 2002: 73; Scherer and Tran 2001). Combining learning theories with a critical discourse analysis thereby inspires a research which does not skirt the complexities of reality. Against the background of this theoretical framework the main topic of the book can thus be reformulated as a question about how the armed conflict has shaped beliefs, cognitive structures, identities and learning processes of those women working in the women's movement today. It is therefore important to flesh out the ways in which individual and organizational learning mechanisms influence the development of social movements and to present an elaborate analysis of those factors influencing the strategies of the women's movement until today.

Outline

The book is divided into two main parts. The first four chapters of the book shed light on the ways in which women's revolutionary mobilization influenced post-conflict women's activism and empowerment. The second part focuses on how several smaller women's organizations have tried to cope with this influence and negotiate a different position for themselves within the women's movement, vis-à-vis the political establishment, and vis-à-vis the donor community.

In the first chapter of the book, the stress lies on the modalities of women's revolutionary mobilization. On the one hand, this chapter traces the factors which can explain this type of mobilization, by, for example, looking at the dynamics of the conflict, the socio-economic position of women, the influence of leftist and feminist thinking on the revolutionary movement, and the presence of international actors. On the other hand, this chapter compares how these elements shaped the actual nature of women's revolutionary mobilization, and compares this for Guatemala and Nicaragua.

The second chapter of the book analyzes how women's organizations emerged from the revolutionary organizations and the organizations of women in exile. This chapter uses the concept of 'social movement spillover' to explain how dynamics spilled over from one type of social activism to another one, and in that way decisively shaped post-conflict women's activism. The notion of individual and organizational learning and adaptation is pivotal to understand the way in which this happened, without overlooking the agency of the women populating these organizations.

In the third chapter, the organizational effects of this spillover on the women's movement are highlighted. The chapter zooms in on the issue of fragmentation, asking whether the multiplicity of women's initiatives should be seen as a case of diversification and maturation of the movement, or rather as instances of duplication and inter-movement competition. Looking at these issues, raises questions about the actual existence of 'a women's movement' as one societal actor at all. These questions are addressed at the end of the chapter.

The last chapter of this part of the book also considers the effects of social movement spillover on the present-day women's movement, but looks at this in terms of strategies and priorities, rather than in terms of organizational dynamics. I posit that a rights-based approach has become the dominant strategy of the movement, and that this has entailed a politicization of women's issues. Several implications of this choice are assessed on the basis of women's testimonies.

Having discussed the roots, nature and effects of wartime mobilization on post-war mobilization in the first part of the book, the second part of the book focuses on how some women's organizations deal with this legacy. Throughout the first part of the book it becomes clear that women's organizations are increasingly relying on the politicization of women's interests and on a public approach. Initiatives which envision different strategies, such as a psychological approach, are losing ground in today's landscape. In Guatemala however, some indigenous women's organizations are calling into question the dominance of a rationalistic public approach, and use indigenous belief systems to formulate a new approach to women's empowerment. These organizations and their programs are the focus of the second part of the book.

In order to frame their criticism of current women's and feminist activism, it is important to have a clear idea about the notion of public vs. private in the work of these organizations. This is the focus of the fifth chapter of the book, which traces how feminist activists have traditionally positioned themselves on the public-private spectrum, and uses this to develop the notion of a 'private' approach of women's empowerment on the basis of local concepts and understandings.

The next two chapters consider how several organizations bring this approach into practice. These chapters compare organizations which combine several approaches to women's empowerment with organizations which rely uniquely on this 'private approach'. These chapters give an overview of the practical work of these organizations as well as a theoretical consideration of the implications of such a shifting paradigm. In the conclusion to the book, the relationship between revolutionary mobilization, ethnicity and empowerment is considered and complementary approaches to women's empowerment are explored.

PART ONE

The Influence of Conflict and Its Aftermath on the Women's Movement

∵

CHAPTER 1

A Social History of the Women's Movement in Guatemala and Nicaragua

With time, the Revolution's stance grew more and more rigid. Powerful economic groups and the extremist Left began to challenge the revolutionary reforms – the former because their own interests were being threatened, and the latter because their extremist demands were not being met. But their criticism was not met with an open mind. It was hard to forget previous Latin American experiences, like Chile in 1973, where leniency had ended in a bloody coup. Rather than working toward an all-inclusive social pact, we decreed a new order because we felt it was the only way to remain true to the impoverished masses. Lacking a democratic tradition of our own, we took advantage of the authority we wielded. We might have considered ourselves very benevolent, but the truth was we had inherited a long legacy of authoritarianism.

GIOCONDA BELLI, Nicaraguan Poet, Writer and Revolutionary, El País Bajo mi Piel,

2002

In Nicaragua women were mobilized by the thousands into guerrilla movements and revolutionary organizations the last quarter of the twentieth century (Kampwirth 2004: 14). Testimonies in Lupe (1983) illustrate the extent to which women mobilized in Guatemala: "There were women participating, women carrying arms, women equal to men" (1983: 107). This happened because of the confluence of several domestic and international factors, which opened up new spaces for women to participate in politics and society.

In this chapter, I explore the modalities of women's wartime mobilization in Nicaragua and Guatemala, and examine the factors explaining this type of mobilization which was different in both countries. The influence on contemporary women's activism of the armed conflicts and of women's revolutionary mobilization are a point of debate, with scholars often stressing the emancipating effect of women's involvement in revolutionary movements (for example Shayne 2004, Kampwirth 2004, Luciak 2001). Activists themselves on the contrary often argue that women's mobilization mainly consisted of women's participation in male-dominated structures and cultures and was not emancipatory in itself (Torres, president Colectivo 8 de Marzo 21 April 2010, Rivas, founder GRUFEPROMEFAM, 27 May 2010). Since the experience of armed conflict is of major importance to understand the development of the women's movements, and since the influence of these conflicts is contested, this chapter aims to provide a historical background to analyze how the experience of armed conflict influenced the discourses, praxis and priorities of the emerging women's movements in both countries. As the next chapter will show, this historical account throws light on the post-conflict development of the movement.

This chapter considers the period before the signing of the peace treaties, this means the pre-1996 period for Guatemala, and the pre-1991 period for Nicaragua. While it is debatable whether an actual women's movement is already in place in this period, I demonstrate that it is in this period that feminist consciousness and awareness of a shared gender identity and gender needs, are fostered. It is thus in this period that the foundations are laid for future feminist organizing. To provide a historical overview of this period which takes into account the complexity and diversity of multiple narratives and remains comprehensible at the same time, the chapter presents the dominant narratives on women's wartime mobilization and analyzes these from a historical point of view. I choose this approach of the interview findings as a solution to the problem of selection bias which is always present when working with multiple historical narratives (Lustick 1996).

I first consider the Nicaraguan case and then the Guatemalan one, and point out significant similarities and differences between both cases which can shed light on the development of the respective women's movements. The central factors for this chapter are women's economic role, their revolutionary mobilization, and the role of international actors.

Nicaragua

This section on Nicaragua explores both how women initially organized and mobilized and which factors can explain this. While it is difficult to pinpoint the precise start of the movement in time, there is a growth of women's activism in the period after the overthrow of the Somoza regime in 1979. This can be explained by the breakdown of the repressive political climate in which actual expressions of civil society were limited (Randal and Yanz, 1981: xi).

Modalities of Women's Mobilization
During the Nicaraguan conflict, women's activism did not only materialize as mobilization in formal – revolutionary – women's organizations, but also as women's increased economic activity, both elements are discussed in turn.

Women Joining and Establishing Women's Organizations

Despite a repressive political climate, there were some expressions of women's social activism already present before 1979. In 1964 for example, the Nicaraguan Organization of Democratic Women which opposed the Somoza dictatorship, was created. This was followed by the creation of the pro-Somoza Patriotic Women's Alliance in 1965. Both groups were, however, entirely linked to a political party (leftists and Somocistas respectively), and were in no way fighting for women's rights as such. Moreover, they counted with very limited membership (Montenegro 1997).

In the immediate run-up to the revolution, women's mobilization and participation in social organizations becomes more widespread. One of the most important examples of women's organizing in the pre-conflict period is AMPRONAC, or the Group of Women Confronting the National Crisis. AMPRONAC was established in 1977 as part of the FSLN's efforts to overthrow the Somoza regime, and was thus also a women's organization entirely linked to a political group (Chinchilla 1990). This popular mobilization of the late 1970s resulted in the overthrow of the Somoza regime by FSLN guerrilla-forces in 1979. This, in turn, led to the installation of a five-headed FSLN-junta. This marked the beginning of profound social, economic and political changes.

In this period, the new FSLN leadership faced the double task of creating a democratic state and a sustainable civil society (Serra Vázquez 2007: 39). This meant that Nicaraguan women were actively addressed, recruited and organized as a group by the Sandinistas. This mobilization, however, was in many respects a top-down process, structured by the discourse of the leaders. This was visible in several ways: in murals presenting the woman with a rifle in one hand and a baby in the other, in posters calling on women to get informed about their rights (Bujard and Wirper 2010), in the government programs declaring equal rights for men and women, land rights for women and the conviction of sexual crimes (Junta de Gobierno 1979), and in the creation of institutions and programs such as the Women's Legal Office and alternative job training programs for sex-workers. At the same time, in all these instances women were left with little room for their own initiatives, and were expected to follow the lines set out by the Junta.

AMNLAE (the former AMPRONAC) is a case in point of this dynamic. As Molyneux (1985: 283) demonstrates, AMNLAE's first priority was given as 'defense of the revolution' [...] AMNLAE became actively involved in recruiting women to the army and the militia. Under such circumstances it is hardly surprising to find that the efforts to promote women's emancipation were scaled down or redefined. Emancipation was to come about as a by-product of making and defending the revolution.

FIGURE 4   *FSLN poster for International Women's Day addressing different aspects of*
             democratization
             © BUJARD AND WIRPER 2010.

AMNLAE is exemplary of an organization which was 'to provide support for the
male-dominated FSLN without directly challenging sexual inequality'
(Kampwirth 2004: 28). Consequently, its demands were centered around political rights and social inequalities, and not specifically around women's issues.
This reflected the party's official line of thinking, which stated that women's
emancipation would be obtained if the overall goals of the revolution were
obtained. This meant that the priorities of AMNLAE were entirely determined
by the priorities of the FSLN. These priorities altered in 1983 when the Contra
war escalated. AMNLAE was left with virtually no autonomy to develop its own
goals, program or organizational model (Ellsberg et al 1997: 84). Its programs
fitted the FSLN's strategy of installing mass organizations to mobilize the people in support of the party and the revolution, and could – at best – stretch
women's traditional gender roles (Serra Vázquez 2007: 40). Also one of my
interviewees underlined how little attention there was for the issue of women's
rights, also amongst women mobilizing:

> For me it was never about women's rights in those days, but about our
> revolution. And 'our revolution', meant the revolution of the people. It
> was not about women's revolution or women's rights. That would have

FIGURE 5   *AMNLAE poster addressing the relationship between political and personal change*
© BUJARD AND WIRPER 2010.

divided us. More important things were at stake, it seemed. No one at that time would have dared to say that the revolution needed to be about women, that would have been considered extremely selfish and not done.

Interview with MUÑOZ, ex-guerrilera, 27 April 2010

Another interviewee indicated how strong the grip of AMNLAE over women's mobilization was, when she commented:

Now people sometimes want to make it seem as if the situation today is a direct consequence of the fact that the FSLN paid attention to women during conflict, but I can tell you, they didn't, not really. They never cared much for women's rights. They were excellent strategists, yes. They knew how to mobilize the largest possible amount of support, and knew that addressing different sectors of society was crucial for that. Therefore they established specific organizations for women, for children, for mothers of fallen soldiers. It was as if every social group you can think of had its own organization. So the fact that they had a women's organization, please, do not mistake, had nothing to do with a dedication to women's rights [...] Moreover, they knew very well how pivotal it was to organize this whole target sector – without any exceptions – in their respective organizations. It may seem that AMNLAE was an opportunity for women, and in certain respects it was, but do not forget that it also meant the closing down of several other opportunities. If, as a woman, you wanted to do something, socially speaking, your only way forward, was through AMNLAE. And, as everyone knows, AMNLAE was completely dependent on the FSLN.

Interview with JIMÉNEZ, member of the MAM, 13 April 2010

Both fragments are similar in how they assess the genuine importance of gender rights and women's autonomous activism for the revolutionary leaders: decidedly limited. It is important though to note the difference in tone used by these two interviewees. Whereas the first interviewee considers the absence of actual women's rights from the FSLN discourse as a potentially sensical strategy which could reinforce the revolutionary struggle, the second interviewee – who is currently an autonomous feminist activist – is much more critical about the motivations of the FSLN leaders. This is indicative of the different narratives surrounding the debate around women's mobilization. These different narratives show strong overlaps with the different political narratives which are dominant in Nicaragua today.

Both interviewees however concur in the interpretation that AMNLAE was the major women's organization throughout most of the 1980s, and that it was organically tied to the Sandinista party (Montenegro 1997: 379).

Despite the quasi-monopoly of AMNLAE on women's mobilization, and despite the fact that AMNLAE had a conservative view on women's issues and little room for independent actions, the FSLN's discursive strategy of addressing women as a group, triggered a growing consciousness of a shared gender identity, and shared rights and interests. This inspired the emergence of a number of dissident voices and smaller independent women's groups in the late 1980s, such as the Ecumenic Women's Movement and the National Women's Council. Some of these groups pressed for women's issues to be seen as issues in their own right, instead of being integrated into other struggles (Interview with Rivas, founder GRUFEPROMEFAM, 27 May 2010). Gradually these new organizations and critical individual activists developed a guiding frame which provided them with a coherent view of what they perceived as the major social problems, their causes and solutions. In this view, patriarchy became as important as class-based oppression for women's emancipation (Interview with Castro, member of the feminist Grupo Venancia, 2 March 2011).

The – dispersed and small – women's organizations which emerged in the second half of the 1980s usually had an ambiguous relationship with the FSLN. On the one hand, they criticized its tendency to centralize power and to control social organizations (Moberg 2005: 7). On the other hand, some of them initially (1980–1985) had a voice in the national legislative body, when they were still tied to an FSLN-affiliated organization. This voice meant that they could comment on law proposals, which made it difficult to renounce party-affiliations altogether. That this voice in the national legislative body was important, can be seen in the elaboration of the 1987 constitution, which foresaw the legal and judicial equality of men and women, and thereby set the tone for future changes (Montenegro 1997: 366; Bayard de Volo 2001). Women's organizations – tied to AMNLAE – were the main actor responsible for this provision in the 1987 constitution.

Progressive measures in the 1987 constitution and other legal provisions however, obliterate the fact that since the elections of 1984, it *de facto* became more difficult for women's organizations to influence national policy-making. This was due to a series of electoral and policy-decisions made by the FSLN, to which I return below. In this context, women's organizations which were not directly affiliated with the Sandinista party, or which were opposed to it, were relegated to the sidelines. As a consequence, several members of AMNLAE and unaffiliated women start to question the relationship with the FSLN, in which

AMNLAE came to be seen as the 'submissive wife' to the party concerns (Interview cited in Kampwirth 2004: 29).

What we see in Nicaragua is thus a rather tumultuous evolution of women's activism – from dispersed pro-Somoza initiatives to centralized mobilization in the FSLN-controlled AMNLAE to critical thinking on the position of women in the revolutionary movement. The vanguard role of the FSLN and its de facto monopoly on women's mobilization, resulted in markedly different assessments of women's revolutionary activism in the post-war years, whereby the narrative of the FSLN and AMNLAE is fundamentally opposed to that of autonomous feminists today.

Women's Increased Economic Activity

Post-conflict women's activism has not only been triggered by women's mobilization during the conflict, but also by the expanding economic activities of women in this period. Women already played an important role in the national economy before the conflict, but when men were abruptly removed from their homes to participate in the fighting, women became even more important in sustaining – cultural and – material structures of the community, i.e. care for the children and elderly, work the land, and keep the economy going. This meant that, from the late 1970s onwards women were actively drawn into the formal economy to go work in *maquilas* (sweatshops), which boomed in the second half of the 1980s (Bickham Mendez 2002b: 216, Berger 2006: 77, 79). While *maquilas* were no emancipating environments in themselves, the fact that women entered paid employment *en masse*, challenged traditional gender roles. Before, men had assumed the role of breadwinner and women had stayed at home. Now, women gained some economic independence, at least potentially.[1]

The emancipating effects of entering the formal economy should however neither be overestimated nor be interpreted as a direct cause of female emancipation. Interviewees from Huehuetenango who did not mobilize during the armed conflict but who did enter the formal economy, relate that in practice their families remained heavily male-dominated since both law and custom still prescribed that women hand over their wages to their husbands, or in the absence thereof, to male family members (Interview with Perez and Ruiz, noncombatants, 14 May 2010). Other women asserted how life became even more difficult due to their economic activities. As Anna Rivera, an ex-*guerrillera* from Puerto Sandino stated during an interview:

---

1 This is similar to what happened in Germany after World War II (Troger 1986) and Vietnam after the armed conflict there (Tetreault 2000).

> Times were difficult back then. Not for the reasons you would think of, not just because we had two dayjobs or because we received less pay, but because of the social changes [...] those men who stayed in the villages felt threatened by the idea of women also being able to provide for themselves, and saw their traditional roles challenged.
>
> 27 April 2010

These interviewees point out that the fact that women took on non-traditional gender roles made men nervous about having to rethink their traditional role. Another interviewee compared this resistance by the men who stay in the villages to the resistance of revolutionary leaders who, in their daily operations, resisted the emancipation of women which was implicit in their socio-political program (Interview with Martinez, ex-guerrillera, 27 April 2010).

Thus, despite the changing role of women in the economy, traditional gender constructs were still strong during the period of armed conflict. With hardly any attention being paid to how to transform these, and even less to how to prepare men to deal with these changes, men in some cases turned to more traditional notions of gender to deal with the new situation. Again, the interview with ex-guerrillera Martinez is illustrating. Martinez, herself an ex-activist from Puerto Sandino, remarked on the side that:

> It was almost funny, the more we argued that men in the family should also do something in the household, the more he [her father] would go against this and give us [his daughters] ever more things to do, and my brothers ever more liberties.

During this interview, also other ex-guerrilleras cited similar experiences with their partners or other male family members. Several of them also cited this experience as their reason for leaving and joining the guerrilla however. Yet, some pragmatic loosening of gender norms can be perceived, which – while not going as far as to encourage women to explore new gender norms – was needed to allow for women to participate in public life and enter paid labor (Blumberg 2001: 161).

A last critical note on the alleged emancipating effects of economic activities is that, when women entered paid labor – without joining any revolutionary organization – they were not often confronted with new ideas on gender or feminism. Several interviewees, who were non-combatants during the conflict and are not politically active today neither, indicate that they left their homes for paid labour, but mostly kept on interacting with the same women from their own villages and other people they already knew (Interview with Vargas et al, 20 May 2010; and Perez et al, 14 May 2010). At working places there were most often no unions until the early 1990s, and women working as market sellers had only rare – and superficial – contact with women from other social sectors. This type of contact did not allow for the discussion of gender norms. As Valdez, an indigenous non-combatant from Guatemala City, declared during an interview, '*Ai Seño*, going out for work was not much different from working at home. We did what we had to do [on the market] and then went back home. [...] Talking with other people? We just called out the names of our products and negotiated about the price' (Valdez, 20 May, 2010). However, despite difficulties in negotiating their new positions and roles, women acquired practical and technical skills, which were useful for women's mobilizing later on (Castillo 2007).

Factors Explaining This Type of Mobilization

The previous section threw light on the modalities of women's mobilization. In this section I assess the factors inspiring this type of mobilization. A first factor which facilitated both the mobilization of women and the actions of the FSLN, is the fall of the dictatorial Somoza-regime in 1979. This regime rendered the expression of any form of civil society activism virtually impossible. The social, economic and political changes fostered by its overthrow, were needed for any form of genuine social mobilization to be possible (Kallen 2009, Staten 2010).

To understand both why the FSLN paid attention to women and why women responded positively to this, it is crucial to take into account the socio-economic position of women before 1979. Women played an important – and prominent – role in the economic survival of the country. In the Somoza-era, more than 48 per cent of heads of household were women and more than 80 per cent of the employed women were heads of household (Valdivia 1991: 157). This meant that women constituted an important economic factor in Nicaraguan society. Yet, their contribution was not always acknowledged, meaning that the esteem for their socio-economic role was significantly lower than their actual contribution. As one older interviewee from Puerto Sandino, who only became an activist in the late 1980s stated:

> It was us. *We* bread the families. *We* fed the children. *We* worked the country. *We* sold maize and cilantro. *We* assured survival in *esos tiempos de mierda*. But nobody saw it, not even we ourselves thought of it as very exceptional. We just did what we needed to do to survive. Without our efforts [as women], the revolution would have erupted much earlier,

because people would have literally starved, and would have needed to revolt to survive.

Interview with RIVERA, 27 April 2010

As a popular movement which had strong grassroots initially, the FSLN was aware of this important economic role of women and of their low economic status and the potential frustrations this caused. Hence, when they came to power in 1979, a discourse of equality was installed which specifically addressed women by referring to the frustrations and the hardship which they incur in daily life (Randall 1981). On the reasons for this, there are different opinions today though. Autonomous feminists who participated in the popular struggle, almost invariable describe the FSLN's discourse on women as pragmatic and even utilitarian. When asked what explains the difficulties which women had in capitalizing the openings for progressive gender politics which were created by the FLSN in the revolutionary years, Sofia Montenegro, a journalist and prominent autonomous feminist, replied "There never was any opening. They never planned to give us any actual autonomy. Do you really believe they did?" (Interview, 2 May 2010). This interpretation of the FSLN's discourse is common amongst current autonomous feminists. Activists affiliated with the FLSN however are more moderate in their assessment of the FSLN's motivations for recruiting women, pointing out the fact that by engaging women, the FSLN was abiding with its own ideology of equality, and was aiming to bring this ideal into practice in its own daily operations (Interview with Alfaro, president AMNLAE, 30 April 2010).

So the combination of women's economic contribution and society's lack of appreciation was one of the reasons explaining why women were receptive to a mobilizing discourse, and why the FSLN employed such a discourse. The second reason which throws light on the emergence of initiatives like AMNLAE is the existence of smaller women's initiatives in the pre-conflict period. Even if these organizations were in many cases only relatively dispersed and isolated initially, they nourished the idea that women's issues were best dealt with at the societal level and spearheaded the introduction of women into the national political level (Valdivia 1991: 150–151). In other words, the existence of smaller women's organizations during the Somoza dictatorship held the germs of female consciousness and participation in public life later on.

Women's economic status and their experience with social mobilization thus explain why attention was paid to women by revolutionaries initially and why women decided to mobilize. These reasons are in themselves insufficient to explain the further modalities of women's mobilization during the decade of the 1980s however. To understand why some women increasingly took issue with the role of AMNLAE for example, AMNLAE's internal dynamics and several contextual factors need to be further explored. The reasons cited most often by interviewees in response to the question of why they broke away from AMN-LAE, is the increasingly top-down decision-making within AMNLAE and the nontransparent organizational structure, which did not allow for women's own initiatives and ideas to be taken into account. Kampwirth (2004: 29) – based on a series of interviews – uses the term 'the submissive wife' to illustrate the relationship between AMNLAE and the FSLN. AMNLAE's dependence on the FSLN and its neglect of women's specific gender interests, led several women to increasingly distance themselves from AMNLAE and the FSLN, and to organize independently in collectives which had a stronger focus on gender interests. What is interesting here are the different narratives surrounding the treatment of AMNLAE by the FSLN, on the side of the FSLN itself. While, during interviews, some FSLN-affiliates denied altogether that the FSLN imposed its themes and priorities, others argued that the FSLN did indeed to a certain extend impose its agenda onto AMNLAE, but that this was not a sign of patriarchal or machismo thinking, but a mere necessity in the context of war, which said nothing about the convictions of the leaders. As Espinoza stated, "To the extent the FSLN delegated tasks to us, they did this with the goal of the revolution in mind. A revolution which would benefit us all". (Interview, member AMNLAE, 30 April 2010).

Critical voices were growing stronger however. This was reinforced by – and in itself also reinforced – the strategy of the FSLN to gain a stronger control over civil society around the mid-1980s (Williams 1994). In 1984, the FSLN was democratically elected for the first time. Presented with an actual opposition from then on, the FSLN approved a series of measures to gain a stricter control over actors of civil society. One of those measures was the decree warranting that organizations of civil society in general and women's organizations in specific would no longer be given a voice in the National Assembly, which from then on consisted only of the representatives of political parties. This decree was indicative of a more general shift towards more closed forms of decision-making which further alienated grassroots activists (Miranda and Ratliff 1993).

Despite the absence of organizations of civil society from the National Assembly though, the FSLN proposes a series of constitutional amendments in 1987, including amongst others the legal and judicial equality of men and women and provisions like the freedom of organization. While being implemented without significant grassroots consultations, these provisions would set the stage for further legal changes and also facilitated the emergence of the women's movement as an independent societal actor, because there came more room for maneuver through the Freedom of Organization-act. Next to these legal changes, Kampwirth (2004: 36) points out the influence of social changes on the emergence of the women's movement. She argues that "[In 1988] while the war was far from over, the end was in sight, opening up more spaces for women's rights activists [...] women's movements began to sprout, and while it would not grow vigorously until after the Sandinistas' electoral defeat, the first hints were already notable in the late eighties".

One of the reasons why women did not yet structurally organize in opposition to the FSLN/AMNLAE in the 1980s is the fact that the ideology of Sandinismo still appealed to many of the organizations of civil society, which moreover owed their existence – directly or indirectly – to the FSLN. Furthermore, the political spaces for consultation and the perspective of social development which existed in the early 1980s, and potential for international funding through government of the late 1980s, allowed those organizations which did not challenge the control and dominance of the FSLN to extend their activities. Tensions and dissatisfactions were thus often not made explicit during the reign of the FSLN, and only really surfaced after the FSLN's electoral defeat of 1990.

It is relevant to remark that in this phase, international aid does not play a crucial role in putting gender on the agenda in Nicaragua. As one interviewee at Oxfam International stated "I'm not sure whether we contributed at all to the development of programs [on women/gender]. Maybe we mentioned it [gender] once or twice on the side, but I cannot remember any initiatives which we ourselves set up in that respect" (Declercq, 7 November 2012). The choice of women to mobilize and of the FSLN to mobilize women is thus a response to local sensitivities and necessities, much rather than being a reaction to demands of international donors at this stage. As the next chapter will show, the role of international donors changes in the period after the signing of the peace treaties.

In conclusion, what we see in Nicaragua is genuinely layered and complicated picture, which cannot be adequately explained by interpretations – like the following – which depict the FSLN's attention to women's rights as a purely utilitarian strategy and the mobilization of women as a purely top-down instructed process:

> In those days nobody cared about women's rights, not even the FSLN's women's organizations [...] it's only after we realized that they [the party directorate] were just using us once again, that we could start to really work for women's rights. It is our choice to break away

from them [the FSLN] which has allowed a women's movement to thrive, not their choice to organize women.

JIMÉNEZ, board member of the Nicaraguan Autonomous Women's Movement and ex-guerrilla, 13 April 2010

In the same vein, it would not be accurate to argue that leaders' attention for women and the fact that they committed significant resources to building an important women's organization was *per se* a sign of their genuine commitment to equality.

What we see in fact is a pendular movement from modest dispersed but critical grassroots activism by women to activism coordinated and controlled top-down by a vanguard party, and back to more critical and dispersed initiatives directed against AMNLAE. The smaller women's initiatives which existed before 1979 were an important factor in triggering attention to women's mobilization. The authoritarian way of organizing women's activism on the contrary was a factor triggering critical voices and new grassroots initiatives in the late 1980s. These new groups could more easily make themselves heard, because they could use the decentralized networks which the FSLN itself had set up, and to which they had belonged. There is thus a nuanced picture, in which we see a vanguard party explicitly aiming to structure the women's movement according to its own top-down discourse, in order to gain a monopoly over women's mobilization – in which it is relatively successful through AMNLAE. On the other hand it is precisely this top-down approach which triggers criticism. These critical voices will be the initiator of post-conflict autonomous feminist organizing, which no longer sees gendered oppression as subordinate to class-based oppression.

Guatemala

Modalities of Women's Participation

Also in Guatemala, the armed conflict nourished several forms of women's mobilization. The modalities of women's pre-conflict and wartime mobilization differed from those of Nicaraguan women however. Whereas Nicaragua had several all-women's organizations before the conflict already, which expanded during the period of armed conflict, the situation in Guatemala was different. While Guatemalan interviewees recall how women – usually referring to their mothers or older family members – became socially active in the pre-conflict period, there is no documentation on the existence of all-women's organizations – like the Nicaraguan Patriotic Women's Alliance – in Guatemala. The initial social activism of Guatemalan women thus happened within mixed-gender organizations, like the organized mobilization of the indigenous communities (*'mutuales'*) (Serra Vázquez 2007: 40).

Within the country, this situation – of women mobilizing within mixed-gender organizations – continued during most of the conflict when women joined the guerrilla forces rather than mobilizing in all-women's organizations like AMNLAE. In Guatemala, women's mobilization did however not only take place within the country. Also women in exile mobilized, and amongst these groups there were in fact attempts at all-women's organizations. I consider both types of women's mobilization in turn.

Women Joining the Guerrilla

In Guatemala, there is little documentary evidence of revolutionary leaders paying specific attention to women or their rights. Only limited effort was put into mobilizing women or developing propaganda specifically directed at women. Of all revolutionary pamphlets on social organizations in the Historic Archive of the National Police of Guatemala (AHPN)[2] which had been made available at the time of the research, only two explicitly address women as a group, illustrating the relative absence of women from the discourse and social imagery of social and popular movements at that time. As Carlos Jalón, researcher at the AHPN, added "This absence [of women from the leaders' discourse] is all the more striking if I compare it with my own research, which shows, over and over again, how important the role of women in the guerrilla units must have been, and how important government also found women's role, if you consider how many files of women are kept in their secret archive" (Interview, 15 May 2010). This shows that, women's activism was integrated in a struggle which had little or no gender dimension – except maybe in the negative sense: gendered killings formed an integral part of the government's strategies to counter insurgency (Esparza 2005, DNSA 2010).

The testimonies of two women fighting in the mountains in Guatemala illustrate how gender relations and the notion of patriarchy were not only left out of the formal discourse of the movement leaders, but were also non-issues in daily life, and how this complicated things for women who wished to challenge them. Both interviewees fought as *guerrilleras* in Huehuetenango

---

2   The AHPN are 8 kilometers of historical police and military files, discovered in 2005, documenting the 36 year long conflict. About 8 per cent of the documents had been classified and made public around the time of my fieldwork. A small section thereof concerned revolutionary publications. I consulted these archives on several occasions during my fieldwork, and analyzed a total of 256 revolutionary pamphlets.

Guatemala, and neither of them is still politically active today. The first interviewee asserted that:

> It was hard to be a woman up here. I was physically and emotionally pre-
> pared to join the guerrilla – to the extent one can be prepared at all. But
> the problem lay in what I felt was my duty. [...] On the one hand, I wanted
> to fight and help the cause of the revolution, on the other hand, we were
> assigned 'petty tasks' and I didn't know what to think of that. The truth is,
> I never really thought about it back then. I felt something was not right.
> Now I know what it was. We were copying the exact same structures [in
> terms of gender relations] in the guerrilla. It happened automatically,
> because nobody paid attention to it.
>
> GONZALÉS, 14 May 2010

This testimony illustrates the extent to which gender and gender relations
were absent from daily life and discourse, but also how they nevertheless influenced the dynamic and interactions in the guerrilla units. Another interviewee
from Huehuetenango affirms that, in her unit, there was somewhat more
awareness of this situation amongst women, but that this critical thinking was
not met with enthusiasm by – male – leaders:

> When we demanded other responsibilities [than care], the *compañeros*
> blamed us for not valuing domestic work, and of being comfort-seekers
> and *petite bourgeoisie*. Relations between men and women were not con-
> sidered as a source of oppression
>
> PENA, 2 June 2010

This statement shows that the roles which were assigned to women strongly
influenced how they experienced their revolutionary mobilization. The last
interviewee for example was explicitly critical about the extent to which the
guerrilla had lived up to its promises to its popular base, and cited the failure
to structurally improve the position of women on several occasions to illustrate this. The stories of most interviewees show that they were not usually
being treated as men's equals – while also not being treated as an independent
group with specific needs. In other words, women were almost completely
ignored by the revolutionary leaders – practically and discursively speaking –
despite their considerable participation in guerrilla efforts. The extremely
secretive nature of guerrilla organizations like the Guatemalan National
Revolutionary Union (Unidad Revolucionaria Nacional Guatemalteca, URNG)
makes it difficult to obtain accurate data with regard to the gender composition

of these organizations. Nevertheless, a European Union-sponsored study of the socio-economic background of the URNG membership gives a reasonably accurate picture of the URNG's gender composition. Women represented 410 (15 percent) of the 2,778 combatants surveyed and 356 (about 25 percent) of the 1,410 political cadres (Luciak, 2007). These data however leave out of the picture those women who mobilized in other functions than combatants or political cadres, which makes it plausible that the actual number of women in the guerrilla was significantly higher. Yet, as mentioned above, propaganda and campaigns by revolutionaries had a blind spot for women and women's issues, as is illustrated by the Declaration of Revolutionary Unity in Guatemala (Guatemalan National Revolutionary Unit 1982).

Most ex-combatants who are in non-aligned women's organizations, today or who are participating in the movement on an individual basis, say that the extent to which male revolutionaries accepted a more equal distribution of the tasks was most limited, and that when they did do so, this did not per se reflect a change in their concepts of gender roles, but merely entailed 'giving in to a growing pressure and abiding with the logic of their own egalitarian ideology' (Aguilar, ex-guerrillera, 17 May 2010). As I will demonstrate further, pressure from below to implement gender equality measures was limited though. This also meant that tensions between those adhering to traditional gender norms and roles on the one hand and those advocating a feminist interpretation of left-ist thinking on the other hand was more restricted than in the Nicaraguan case.

Moreover, it is only after 1986, when the military returns the government to civilian rule, that all-women's groups slowly also start to proliferate within the country (Berger 2006). Around this time, some women start to leave mixed-gender organizations and form groups which deal with specific women's issues, such as the psychosocial and economic issues faced by war-widows. Leading organizations of this time were the National Coordinator for Guatemalan Widows (CONAVIGUA), the Guatemalan Women's Group (GGM), the Women's Association 'Tierra Viva', the Women's Group for the betterment of family life (GRUFEPROMEFAM), and the Women's Union of Food and Workers (COMFUITAG) (Berger 2003, Aguilar 1997).

There are thus two sides to women's activism in the guerrilla. On the one hand, they are initially almost entirely incorporated into a general struggle and no attention is paid to them as a group by the revolutionary leaders. This raises questions about how emancipating this experience was for women. On the other hand, women gain useful skills through this mobilization, which allow them to set up all-women's organizations when the climate becomes less restrictive, and these organizations are moreover not confronted with the attempts at top-down influence of a vanguard party which Nicaraguan women's organizations have to deal with. Also women in exile are mobilizing during the conflict, and forming all-women's groups.

Women Organizing in Exile

The conflict thus influenced women who mobilized within the country, but also triggered the mobilization of women in exile. Whereas exile was only a minor phenomenon in Nicaragua – where it mainly affected dissidents from the FSLN-camp – a great number of Guatemalan women and men were forced into exile during the period of armed conflict. Their experiences with mobilization and social activism were different from those of women mobilizing within the country and also had a great impact upon the later women's movement.

The large number of people forced into exile meant that sometimes whole communities were re-established beyond the Guatemalan borders. In this setting women's organizations, like Mamá Maquín, emerged (Aguilar 1997).

Mamá Maquín emerged in 1990 from the Permanent Commission of the Representatives of the Refugees of Guatemala in Mexico (CCPP) (Mamá Maquín 1994). The CCPP was a refugee's interest organization, representing Guatemalan refugees during negotiations over group return (Castillo 2007). This organization was crucial, amongst others because it inspired those women joining it to also organize for themselves, as women, around their own needs. Indreiten interviewed one of the women who became active in the CCPP during this period. On this experience, the activist commented:

> First the Commissions were formed. Men and women entered the process of decision-making and learned to speak up for themselves in negotiations. It was there as well that women learned they could also decide and have opinions. In 1990 we started to think about how we could organize this, but this was difficult within the structures of the Commissions, where men still dominated the debate. Therefore we saw the need of having an organization where one [woman] could see her own needs, because most of the time, men paid no attention to this. At the first mass meeting we held, 700 women participated.
>
> Cited in INDREITEN 1994: 41

The former coordinator of the group of Santa Maria Tzejá – a village which was burnt during the conflict – however states that, like most women's organizations, Mamá Maquín had to overcome some hindrances to participation (Indreiten 1994: 94). First of all, the women in exile, like the *guerrilleras*, had to become aware of their own disadvantaged situation and their needs. After this, they had to break down the oppressive elements of traditional identities, like that of home-makers. This was not just a matter of changing norms, but also of organizing this change in practice. One of the most important practical issues was how women could join these groups and attend meetings when they were in practice the ones who had to take care of the children and the household and who already had a double dayjob. Illiteracy and language difficulties were two other constraints to women's participation in Mamá Maquín (Mamá Maquín 1999). The women who did in the end organize, testify that the very experience of setting up a *plan de campagne* and working towards it, fostered a sense of empowerment and a growing awareness of their situation (Garcia Hernandez, Mama Maquín, 26 January 2011).

However, the modalities of the mobilization of the women in exile were different from those of women who had remained inside the country. Firstly, women in exile were active in all-women's organizations which allowed them to work on gendered issues rather than on more general revolutionary issues. The existence of all-women's organizations moreover meant that there was scope for critical thinking on and the conceptualization of a shared gender identity. There was also more room to work on gendered issues because Guatemalan women in exile were not exposed to the same dynamic of all-out war as their compatriots who were active in the country. Moreover, women in exile, found themselves in more dynamic community structures, meaning that there was some scope to conceptualize their gender identities in a progressive way. There was still a community dynamic but norms became more flexible than they had been before because of the volatile context in which women found themselves (Indreiten 1994). Also upon returning to their home country, there were hindrances to be overcome, which shaped the modalities of women's mobilization. Not only had women in exile developed group structures which had not developed in their home country, they also encountered difficulties in keeping their own progressive social structures intact upon returning, due to the fact that in their home countries they sometimes lived too far from each other and that domestic chores multiplied (Pessar 2001). Below I assess how these dynamics come together around the time of the peace negotiations, which factors have been crucial in shaping this, and how this differed from the Nicaraguan context.

The fact that the vast majority of people who were forced into exile, were indigenous people, meant that there was an important degree of intersectionality in women's thinking on gender. Discussions on the conceptualization of a new gender identity were interwoven with discussions on how one's ethnicity influenced the formation of one's identity (Interview Carmen Álvarez, 21

February 2011). This intersectionality would strongly influence the dynamic of women's mobilization in the post-conflict period.

Due to the circumstances in which they mobilized, women in exile thus developed a specific narrative, a discourse which was explicitly mentioning women and their needs, and which laid the foundation for a growing awareness of women's oppression. This discourse was particularly important, especially when taking into account that amongst women mobilizing within the country, there was hardly a discourse on women or their emancipation at all, neither on the side of women themselves, nor on that of the leaders.

Several women in exile later stated that they had implicitly assumed that, upon returning, the situation in their home towns would have changed as well. They were surprised to find that 'those who stayed behind [in the villages] often did not know how to organize, and were not progressing, because they did not know their own needs' (cited in Indreiten 1994: 87). Because of the processes of critical thinking on gender which had started amongst these returnees from exile, a return to the old, more conservative state of affairs – in terms of gender norms – was not desired by most women. Upon returning to their home country, several hindrances had to be overcome however. In order to foster change in their home communities as well, several women's initiatives were set up by these women. The aim was to organize around the rights of women – namely rights to participation, education, health care and equality – and the awareness thereof. However, members of Mamá Maquín themselves also found it hard to keep their progressive social structures intact upon returning, (Pessar 2001).

Guerrilleras and Women in Exile Find Each Other during Peace Talks

Two dynamics are thus at play in Guatemala. On the one hand, there is the mobilization of women in the mixed-gender guerrilla organizations which pay no specific attention to women. On the other hand, we see the organization of women in exile, who specifically organize around women's needs and for whom their indigenous identity is an important factor in their mobilization. Both forms of mobilization provided women with new practical skills and new ideational frameworks. Both moreover met with resistance, the former from those with strict leftist views of egalitarianism, who argued that women should join forces with men to foster the goals of the revolution; the latter from more conservative sections of society.

Towards the end of the conflict in 1996, one can witness the occurrence of several women's initiatives and several efforts to coordinate the work of these various groups, such as the Coordinator of Guatemalan Women's

Groups (COAMUGUA). This is an important juncture in the development of the women's movement. Towards the end of the conflict and around the time of the peace negotiations, women activists from within and outside the country come together, and they do so under the auspices of international actors monitoring the peace negotiations. This last factor is of vital importance in explaining the occurrence of a Guatemalan women's movement.

Whereas women's mobilization seems to be an integral part of the local discourse in Nicaragua, this is not initially the case in Guatemala, and the requirement by international organizations that representatives of women's interests should be present during the peace negotiations, was an important impetus for women's future organizing. This does not mean that women's current activism has been entirely dependent on the incentives provided by international donors. There had been mobilization around women's rights by women in exile before the arrival of international donors as well. Moreover, there has been a dynamic interaction with the frames provided by international actors throughout. Nonetheless, the fact that women in exile met guerrilleras against a background of international actors demanding the participation of women, formed a strong incentive for the occurrence of a women's movement in the period following the peace talks.

Also in Nicaragua, women establishing organizations with a more feminist reading of the leftist ideology were often inspired by international thinkers whose ideas they adapted to the local context. In Guatemala the international influence was arguably stronger, however because international actors entered the scene *en masse* around the time of the peace negotiations, which is a markedly turbulent period in which new social norms and projects are defined (Reilly 2007: 158).

Feminist ideas which entered the country from abroad were actively adapted to the local context through a dynamic and complex interaction between foreign concepts and ideologies on the on hand and local realities on the other. This interaction has decisively shaped the identity, structure and priorities of the women's movement in the sense that the type of activism which emerged can be read as an integration of local and foreign sensitivities and ideas. The way in which these young organizations interacted with the discursive frames and the new ideas which they were presented with, displays a high degree of agency on the side of the 'host culture', and thereby challenges a cultural imperialist interpretation of how the globalization of ideas proceeds. The interaction between 'foreign' and 'local' discursive frames thus demonstrates the capacity of the local to produce new political, social and economic guiding frames. This has notably been the case amongst the indigenous women's organizations which constitute the focus of the second part of the book.

The fact that local dynamics are crucial in mediating the effect of international actors on the women's movement, means that the development of the women's movement is different for Nicaragua and Guatemala, despite a strong presence of international actors in both cases. In the conclusion to this chapter, I return to this interaction between the global and the local level.

Factors Explaining This Type of Mobilization

Several aspects of Guatemalan women's mobilization during the armed conflict and in exile require further explanation.

Firstly, there is the fact that Guatemalan women, unlike Nicaraguan women, mostly joined guerrilla units which only paid scant attention to their rights or their mobilization, and that they were, as a consequence, integrated into units and a struggle which ignored their rights in many respects. This can at least partially be explained by the nature of the Guatemalan conflict which was more brutal than the Nicaraguan one (DNSA 2010). From the late 1970s onwards, the state initiated a strategy of ferocious repression to destroy the leftist opposition movement and to restructure the economy and agricultural structure, thereby targeting indigenous people and their cultures (Berger 2006: 5, Doyle 2009). The ferocity and brutality of the armed conflict, especially in the period 1982–1983, required a strong focus on military and war effort. For this reason revolutionary leaders made little effort to explicitly mobilize women or to develop propaganda campaigns aimed at them. As a result, women's activism was integrated in a struggle which had little or no gender dimension (Esparza 2005). Of all revolutionary pamphlets on social organizations in the Historic Archive of the National Police of Guatemala (AHPN) which have been made available to date, only two explicitly address women as a group, showing the relative absence of women from the discourse and social imagery of social and popular movements at that time. The ferocity of the conflict thus nourished the idea that mainly male combatants were needed who could join the armed forces in militant actions. This situation is different from the Nicaraguan case, where propaganda addressing women was typically calling upon women to join the FSLN/AMNLAE as *brigadistas*[3], a function which was not prioritized in the fierce Guatemalan conflict.

At the same time, it can be remarked that – due to the ferocity of the conflict and the leaders' absence of attention to women as a group – there was also not

---

3   Brigadistas were for example sent to the villages to organize literacy campaigns and share knowledge on farming techniques among different populations to create synergy.

a strong voice from women themselves to demand attention to their rights. As Gutierrez (Interview, 17 May 2010) stated:

> The thing which I, we, cared about most at that time was our victory, and the question of how to arrive at it. You need good strategists at the top to win a war. And these strategists sometimes overlooked the detail, yes, but we (women) did not care about that too much. I can only speak for myself, but my dedication to the revolution was unconditional, and I would not have done anything that would have endangered our struggle [...] Why would we demand rights for women? We wanted rights for the people? What good is it to create division? Times were so difficult already, so that we needed all the unity and support we could rally.

This reluctance to demand – attention for – women's rights in order to maintain a high degree of unity was mentioned by several interviewees. The fact that women do not seem to see themselves as a legitimate social sector is decisively shaped by the fact that leaders leave any reference to women as a distinct social group out of their discourse. This also hints at how important the discourse and propaganda of Nicaraguan revolutionary leaders has been in triggering a sense of collective identity amongst women.

The impact of the fierce conflict on the leaders' interpretation of their priorities is also illustrated by the change of priorities and strategies as of 1986. When the military returned the government to civilian rule – after a period of severe economic deterioration, expansion of civil discontent and international pressure – a period with a less restrictive climate started. This proved to be a watershed moment for the women's movement, as women's activism increased and women's groups started to proliferate (Berger 2006). *In concreto* this means that as of 1986 there is some space for women's initiatives to develop, but there is still little attention for these initiatives from revolutionary leaders. As a consequence, the initiatives which start to emerge in this phase are not developing under the auspices of a revolutionary vanguard party – like the Nicaraguan AMNLAE – and thus to some extent have more room for independent action.

Below I assess how these dynamics come together around the time of the peace negotiations, and how this differed from the Nicaraguan context.

Comparing Women's Mobilization before and during the Conflict

'Before the conflict, women's participation in public life happened on an individual rather than a collective basis in both countries. Women remained largely excluded legally, economically and within the nation's social imagination' (Monzón, sociologist, interview 21 May 2010). Also from certain public spaces and activities women were excluded before the conflict (Berger 2006: 20). Even though there were exceptions, it was only after the profound restructuring of politics on the national level in 1979 and 1986 respectively, that the conditions for the emergence of a germinal women's movement, and for women to focus on women's issues, started to come into being. And it took another major political landslide – in 1991 and 1996 respectively – for these young women's organizations to become more active, and present themselves as an actual social movement.

The changing social and political context of the 1980s loosened social norms, created new tensions, activated new desires, stimulated new thinking on gender relations and increasingly allowed women to enter the public sphere (Valenzuela Sotomayor 2001: 24). Even if there was not yet an explicit concern with gender norms in the revolutionary movements at that time, this mobilization of the 1980s laid the foundations for the women's movement to emerge. These new experiences stimulated women's critical thinking and their awareness of their situation of double oppression.

In this section, I briefly revise the impact of the different factors influencing women's mobilization for Guatemala and Nicaragua, pointing out which factors have been most influential in both cases and in which way. I then turn to the effects these elements have had on future women's mobilization, to lay the foundations for the next chapter on the post-conflict development of the women's movement.

A first element which this chapter highlighted was the economic role of women. This element was more decisive in shaping the mobilization of Nicaraguan women than that of Guatemalan women, because the economic role of Nicaraguan women was so vital in the immediate pre-conflict period, and because FSLN leaders incorporated this important economic role of women in their discourse which promised women acknowledgement for their pivotal contribution to the country's economy. Moreover, through these economic roles, women participated in public life, which installed crucial skills for future mobilization. In Guatemala on the other hand, because the economic infrastructure inside the country was largely destroyed during conflict and because women in exile also did not have proper economic facilities, the element of women's economic participation was less significant for the Guatemalan women's movement than it was for the Nicaraguan one.

Secondly, the ferocity of the Guatemalan armed conflict meant that the priority of Guatemalan leaders lay with strategies centered on waging war, which de facto paid little attention to women. This means that the nature of women's post-conflict mobilization was also influenced by their wartime mobilization. This too differed significantly in Guatemala and Nicaragua. Whereas Nicaraguan women mobilized *en masse* during the armed conflict, especially in women's organizations like the AMNLAE or as *brigadistas*, Guatemalan women who mobilized did not have a specific organizational structure for women, nor a top-down discourse addressing them as a group or offering solutions to their specific problems. Guatemalan women who mobilized in exile on the other hand, set up several all-women's organizations, which they brought with them upon returning to their home countries around the time of the peace negotiations.

This situation may create the impression that Nicaraguan women had a comparative advantage because they had more experience with activism in all-women's organizations, and because they had been exposed to a discourse which fostered a sense of collective identity. Yet the flipside of this coin is that, because Guatemalan women were not organized in women's organizations from the top-down, they had the opportunity to develop their own all-women's organizations more independently from the bottom up, without the dominant voice of a vanguard party. Moreover, the eagerness of the Nicaraguan vanguard party to hold its strong grip over newly emerging social organizations – also when the socio-political context did not necessarily require this anymore – decisively influenced the attitude of new women's organizations *vis-à-vis* the FSLN specifically, and *vis-à-vis* government more generally. As the next chapter will show, this has led to strained relations and several explicit confrontations. While the mobilization of women in Guatemala was also not characterized by a great degree of autonomy, there was less of a *double morality game,* with on the one hand the formal promises of equality, and on the other, persisting inequalities in everyday life. This meant that the relationship between women activists and their leaders in the guerrilla, was less tense than was the case in many Nicaraguan guerrilla units.

A third factor influencing women's post-war mobilization is the influence of international actors. What we see in the Nicaraguan conflict is that international actors only play a limited role in nourishing the sense of the leaders that it is useful to address women as a group. Leaders themselves already saw the importance of addressing women due to the above-mentioned economic position of women, their pre-conflict organization in all-women's organizations, and the leaders' sense that they could build on these dynamics for pragmatic and ideological reasons. In Nicaragua, the influence of international actors on women's mobilization during the conflict consisted mainly of providing ideological inspiration to women who advocated a feminist reading of the leftist ideology. In Guatemala on the other hand, international actors also had a more direct influence on mobilization in the sense that they set women's participation in the peace-negotiations as a condition for international aid.

As mentioned above however, women's organizations have not been passive recipients of international aid and ideas. The *glocalization* paradigm (Giulianotti and Robertson 2007) can accurately explain how women's organizations have dealt with international influences, and how they adapted foreign ideas to the local context. This paradigm argues that universalizing and particularizing tendencies co-exist, meaning that there can be a substantial degree of ownership at the local level, even under conditions of globalization and international influence.

The way in which these emerging women's movements interacted with 'foreign' ideas thus actively contests the idea of a homogenizing global dynamic and illustrates the importance of local dynamics. The reinterpretations of feminism and of Marxist socialism, and their adaptations to the Latin American context, are examples thereof. In the first phase of the women's movement development, the guiding frames which were developed on the basis of Marxist socialism and feminism, stressed class issues rather than linguistics for example, and were aimed at reforming societal structures as well as ideology (Kampwirth 2004: 7). In sum, the interaction between 'foreign' ideological frames and the local dynamic of the 1980s, evidences how individual and collective actors have assimilated international leftist thought, while at the same time challenging it and critically engaging with it.

This was not only visible within the country, but also at an international and regional level, where women's organizations became increasingly active in the 1980s. The two years before the coming into force of the CEDAW (1979 – 1981) for example, saw the occurrence of many regional campaigns and think tanks in which women's organizations from different countries were active participants (Saint Germain 1993), meaning that in this context as well, there was a dynamic interaction between the local and the global level. Also towards the end of the armed conflicts, there were important interactions between the local, regional and global level, in the context of the Beijing summits in the late 1980s and the Meetings of Central American Women in Montelimar, Nicaragua, 1992 for example. I return to these below.

A critical note is important here though. Even though women's groups participated in the drafting of international tools such as the CEDAW, it is questionable how much the voice of these two small countries weighed on the overall debate, and as a consequence, how much influence they had on the final text. Moreover, the organizational context in which these meetings took place reflected a neoliberal globalizing tendency more than it reflected the

Leftist revolutionary frames of these young women's organizations. This raises the question of whether this context at all facilitated for the concerns of Latin American leftist feminists to be addressed and accommodated in the final text. The final text nevertheless was ratified and had to be lived up to. Furthermore, it is arguable whether women's organizations which were not part of the CEDAW process felt represented by the actors participating in their name.

Moreover, the influence of international actors in financial terms should be highlighted. The amount of potential aid which international organizations controlled, meant that the relation between international and local actors was not one of equals, and that the way in which the local women's organizations defined their position *vis-à-vis* their international counterparts did not only depend on their belief in their ideas, but also on financial incentives.

This issue soon became prominent, since international actors arrived *en masse* at a time when most women's organizations did not yet have solid organizational capacity, a well-defined identity, goals, or means to auto-finance. This means that the influence of these international actors on civil society was considerable (Babb 2001). The influence of international actors was thus not limited to providing new discursive frames, but also entailed actual agenda-setting potential because of the conditionality of aid (Booth 1998). Interviews show that virtually all women's organizations that have been able to survive until today have done so by securing international funding.

So, these international organizations played a crucial role in sowing the seeds for a civil society in the period of armed conflict and immediately after it. They provided the organizations of civil society with funding, logistical support and new ideas, and required governments which aspired to attract international funding to accept the presence of the local NGOs and engage in a dialogue with the non-governmental sector (Biekart 1999). The young women's organizations benefited from the fact that their governments wanted to uphold their democratic image in the eyes of possible international donors who were increasingly embracing gender concerns. In this way, the growing presence of international actors and money during the transition process to a neoliberal and democratic state, greatly benefited the young women's movement. Women's organizations were morally and organizationally supported by this presence and could proliferate because of it. All in all, the impact of international organizations on women's mobilization in both countries in this initial period was predominantly positive and it can even be seen as having been a necessary condition for women's organizations to consolidate themselves under difficult circumstances. In the long run however, the international aid would start to influence the movement in different ways as well. This is discussed in the next chapter.

Concluding Remarks

In conclusion, what we see in Nicaragua and Guatemala regarding the modalities and motivations for women's mobilization is genuinely layered and complicated picture, which cannot be understood without looking at the different narratives surrounding it.

In Nicaragua, the narrative of today's feminists runs counter to the interpretation of FSLN activists, especially regarding issues such as the facilitating role played by the FSLN, the existence of male chauvinism in the guerrilla units, and the effects and meaning of women's mobilization during conflict. In Guatemala, the most significant difference is the one between the narrative of women organizing in exile and women mobilizing within gender-blind guerrilla movements, whereby the former employ a more emancipating discourse on women's – and indigenous rights and in which the latter take recourse to a more general leftist discourse.

A constant factor for both cases and for the different narratives within them however is the fact that, in all these different circumstances and despite the different modalities, women's mobilization triggered a degree of awareness – of a shared group identity, as well as of the existence of collective interests and problems – and that their participation in social organizations nourished the idea that women's issues are best solved at the societal level, in the public domain. Both factors will have a decisive influence in shaping women's future activism, as the next chapter shows.

CHAPTER 2

Social Movement Spillover and Organizational Learning in the Post-Conflict Women's Movement

> They cannot forgive us that we triumphed where so many others fail...
> Courage is a virtue appreciated in a male but considered a defect in our
> gender. Bold women are a threat to a world that is out of balance, in favor
> of men. That is why they work so hard to mistreat and destroy us. But
> remember that bold women are like cockroaches: step on one and others
> come running from the corners.
>
> ISABEL ALLENDE, *Inés of my soul*, 2007

Women's revolutionary mobilization – and the friction this caused – encouraged women to problematize traditional gender constructs for the first time and 'to renegotiate their positions and relations within their private and public spheres' (Berger 2006: 1 and 37). As indicated in the previous chapter, this led to increased women's activism in the post-conflict period. Following the peace negotiations, there is a further expansion of the number of women's groups and organizations coming from different sectors of society.[1] This proliferation of different women's organizations meant that organizations became active in very different domains of society and on different levels, thus fostering a growing consciousness of gender inequalities in the 1990s.

When discussing the post-conflict period, I take the peace negotiations as a breaking point[2] and analyze how several socio-economic changes following this changing political constellation have influenced the development of the women's movement. For both Guatemala and Nicaragua, three elements are crucial in determining the post-conflict evolution of the women's movement. These are (a) the political changes, (b) the economic changes which are a by-product thereof, and (c) the organization of several regional women's events. In this introductory section, I discuss all three, to contextualize the emergence of the women's movement.

---

1   In Nicaragua, half of the women's organizations registered in 1995 emerged before 1990, while the other half were created in the short period 1990–1995 (Serra Vázquez 2007).

2   Note that I do not see the transition from 'war' to 'peace' as an absolute or immediate one, and that I acknowledge the persistence of high levels of societal violence in the 'post-conflict period'.

The most visible process indicating the beginning of the post-conflict period, were the respective peace talks in both countries. These indicated the start of profound social and political changes, which also triggered a process of diversification and specialization within the movement. Due to these political changes women's organizations had to rethink their position with regards to the political system and society more broadly, and had to reorganize their priorities to reflect changes in their environment. In Nicaragua, the anti-feminist election campaign and politics of Violeta Barrios de Chamorro were an additional incentive for women to organize and protest to demand their rights. This was rendered possible – formally speaking – thanks to a liberalization of the rules of mobilization in this same period (Biekart 1999). In the Guatemalan case, women found an additional incentive to mobilize by participating in the peace process, and creating a niche for themselves there.

A second element which accompanied the evolution from conflict to post-conflict societies, and which significantly influenced the women's movement, was the economic restructuring project which was an integral part of the program of the new political leaders. Metoyer (2000: 83) argues that Chamorro's structural adjustment program launched Nicaragua into a process of economic restructuring, which also had profound effects on women. This economic restructuring was also the heartland of the new civilian rule in Guatemala, where the economy had suffered severe blows during the armed conflict. This necessitated structural adjustments to the IMF and Worldbank requirements, which in practice meant the adoption of a decidedly neoliberal policy (Paris 2002). The economic liberalization in both countries had two important consequences for women's mobilization. Firstly, it reinforced the dynamic of women entering the public sphere – which was set in motion during the armed conflict – because it required women to work outside the house to generate a sufficient family income (Berger 2006: 77 and 79). Secondly, the neoliberal restructuring had important social consequences, such as the restructuring of the Nicaraguan Institute for Social Security and Well-being (INSSBI) in 1990 and 1995 and elimination of – the budget for – many social welfare activities.[3] This explains the occurrence of women's groups challenging these reforms, but moreover, the reforms meant that the state became more dependent on organizations of civil society to fill up gaps which it could no longer fill itself as a neo-liberal state, such as free healthcare, education in family planning and women's shelters (Berger 2006: 28). This meant that, on several occasions, organizations of civil society were actively turned to by the state to take on

---

3 In this period, unemployment rose to 23,5% and the number of people living in conditions of poverty to 75% in 1995 (UNDP, cited in Serra Vázquez, 2007: 46).

these functions. This explains the turn towards service provision of several women's organizations, an evolution which I elaborate upon in the next chapter.

A third element marking the transition to a new socio-political order and a new era for the women's movement, is the organization of several meetings of women and feminists at the regional Central American level. A crucial meeting in this respect is the 1992 Meeting of Central American Women 'History of Gender, a new woman, a new power' in Montelimar, Nicaragua. This meeting played a key role in the proliferation of feminist organizations and ideas in Central America, because this was the first time feminist activists from the whole region found each other and could exchange ideas. The fact that, on this occasion, women with such different backgrounds and motivations came together also meant that very different themes – such as autonomy, alliances, sexuality and identity – came together in a dynamic way (Babb 1997). At the national level, initiatives such as the Collective of the 8th of March (Nicaragua), the Women's Network against Violence (Nicaragua) and the Women's Network for Health (Nicaragua), the Coincidencia de Mujeres (Guatemala) were established. These platforms worked both within civil society and coordinated with the state. In 1993, 72 per cent of the Nicaraguan women who were active in mixed-gender spaces affirmed to be member of at least one of these coordinating bodies too (Montenegro 1997: 376). A consequence of women's organizations coordinating within these different networks is the process of diversification and identity formation, which in some cases led to ruptures and the establishment of new organizations and organizational spaces.

Thus, as of the early 1990s, it was no longer the political situation of armed conflict which prompted women to take on new non-traditional roles – and for men to accept these. Instead, neo-liberal restructuring and the opening of political spaces became a crucial factor for understanding the evolution of the women's movement (Ardón 1999, Babb 2001). These new opportunities triggered the occurrence of more women's organizations and – as a consequence – created a growing diversification and specialization within the movement, since new priorities, goals, and working methods arose. The fact that political, economic and legal changes created both the spaces and the perceived need for women to mobilize thus influenced the occurrence of more women's organizations.

This stress on windows of opportunity in explaining the exponential growth of women's initiatives fits a structural theory on social activism (McAdam et al. 1996). In this chapter, I complement this structural perspective with a theory on submerged networks in order to bring the actor back into the explanation of how women's groups proliferated. To assess how these individual experiences of women fed back into the organizational level, I use theories on individual and organizational learning and adaptation. Against this background I consider in turn the impact of women's revolutionary mobilization, women's interaction with foreign donors, and women's interaction with the political system.

The Women's Movement, a Spillover from the Revolutionary Movement?

Meyer and Whittier's framework (1994) on social movement spillover can throw light on the continuities between women's wartime mobilization and the post-conflict women's movement, because many of the *guerrilleras* of the 1970s and 1980s became the feminist activists of the 1990s and 2000s. Meyer and Whittier's idea is that social movements are not self-contained and narrowly focused unitary actors, but rather a collection of formal organizations, informal networks and individuals engaged in a more or less coherent struggle (Buechler 1990, McCarthy and Zald 1977, Staggenborg 1989). Because these social movement aspire to change both specific policies and broad socio-cultural structures, they also have effects beyond their articulated goals in the sense that changes which they advocate affect other social movements as well.

From Revolutionary Activists to Post-Conflict Women's Activists

According to Meyer and Whittier there is however also a more direct way in which social movements influence one another, namely when ideas, style, tactics and participants spill over from one movement to another. There is a whole strand of literature on how social movements have been mutually influential (see for example McAdam 1988, Evans 1979, DuBois 1978). Yet the framework of social movement spillover is particularly useful in this context because it incorporates an element of time, explaining how one movement can be seen as the outcome of another one, and how it builds on it through different types of organizational continuity. The four dynamics of social movement spillover which Meyer and Wittier describe – ideological borrowing, use of previously gained tactical skills, personnel continuity, and the recycling of organizational structures to avoid hierarchy – are all present in the Guatemalan and Nicaraguan cases (Meyer and Whittier 1994: 282). In this section, I discuss each of these aspects in turn, in the next section, I use learning theories to reveal the mechanisms behind this social movement spillover.

Frame Alignment

In the model of social movement spillover, the extent to which one organization builds on the frames of another organization to frame issues is seen as a decisive signal of movement influence. Like Staggenborg (1991) and Isserman (1987), Meyer and Whittier point out the persistency of ideology from one movement to another, and the way in which the emerging social movement draws on the ideological frames of the social movement from which it is emerging. They argue that new movements only adapt the ideology and frames of older movements in response to the organizational priorities and changing political opportunities (1994: 279).

This is something which we also see in the Guatemalan and Nicaraguan post-conflict feminist movements, where a traditional leftist guiding frame, revolving principally around equality continues to constitute the centerpiece of the mainstream discourse of autonomous feminist. With the exception of several indigenous feminist groups, the idea of equality between men and women is dominant in the discourse and praxis of most autonomous feminist organizations. As Asención, member of UNAMG (24 May 2010) argues, 'the women active in the movement unified the goals of class equality and social justice – promoted by the guerrilla – with the goal of sexual equality and reproductive rights promoted by feminists'.

However, while actively drawing on some elements of the Marxist-socialist frames of the revolutionary movement, there was also an antithetical influence of the revolutionary frames on the ideological and discursive frames of the post-conflict women's movement, whereby the women's movement explicitly rejected several elements of the classic revolutionary frames which had colored their former activism. So, for example, the classic Marxist-socialist idea was rejected that gender inequalities are a *Nebenwiderspruch*,[4] a matter which deserves no direct attention, but which will be solved automatically once the problem of class struggle has been dealt with.

This persistence of ideological frames should not be seen independently of women's concrete daily experiences within the revolutionary movements. Interviewees indicate that a belief in the ideology of equality constituted a strong incentive for joining the guerrilla, but several interviewees added that it was their daily experience which increased this belief in equality. Women who joined the guerrilla say that – while still experiencing significant gender-inequalities – this was a time when they were treated more equally by men

---

4   *Nebenwiderspruch* is a Marxist term indicating that some struggle for equalities are secondary to the more important class struggle.

than ever before. The discourse of egalitarianism combined with the reality of relative equality within the units was compelling, and greatly influenced the frames of these activists. As one former guerrillera stated during an interview 'even if there was no intention of improving women's rights [...] we learnt we had the same rights as men [...] only later we learnt how to defend these rights [...]. The equality between men and women, for us, has become the benchmark of a successful revolution' (Ferrín, member CODEFEM, 10 June 2010). It is around this strong belief in equality that the ideology of post-conflict feminist activists has developed.

Early feminists came from different sectors of society (academia, writing, journalism, etc.) and were present at several conjunctures (Babb 1997). Because of this, when round tables and conferences were being organized in the immediate post-conflict years, some feminists had an important voice therein, and had access to important media (Montenegro 1996: 43). During these events, these feminists advocated an approach which prioritized strategic gender concerns, and started to refer to feminism as a central part of their identity (Alvarez 1999: 182). An example of early feminist groups in Guatemala are GGM and Tierra Viva. In Nicaragua, MAM is a good example of autonomous feminist organizing. These groups defined themselves in opposition to other non-feminist organizations that only catered to women's practical gender needs, such as the Guatemalan Group of Women Workers and the Nicaraguan AMNLAE.

Next to the autonomous feminist organizations and the women's organizations focusing on practical gender needs, a strand of feminism developed in the early post-conflict years which refused to separate gender from class and ethnicity, and which 'embrace the integration of 'feminine' and 'feminist' movements' (Stephen 1997: 12). These feminists started from a gendered analysis to explain their socio-economic and political realities. This current mainly took on the form of indigenous feminism in Guatemala. CONAVIGUA is a good example of such an organization. The organization was formed in 1988 in the highlands of Quiché, and was one of the first women's organizations to link ethnic, class and gender rights. CONAVIGUA struggled 'to re-conceptualize the definition of citizenship based on gender and ethnic justice' (Berger 2006: 31). It is this strand of indigenous feminism which constitutes the focus of the second part of the book.

There is thus an evolution from women's activists involved in a general revolutionary struggle, to situation in which some of these women start to critically engage with the ideology of equality to also demand equal rights for women, to a situation – in the post-conflict period – in which these 'equality feminists' establish their own independent organizations for women's rights. There is, in other words a notable persistence of the framework of equality which runs from the revolutionary movement to the autonomous feminist movement today.

Tactical Skills and Methods

A second element – next to the persistence of ideological frames – which points in the direction of social movement spillover is the reliance of women's activists on the practical and strategic skills and methods which they learnt during the period of revolutionary mobilization. During the conflict, women activists established networks, gained practical, technical and organizational skills, and established a growing confidence in their ability to act, even in ways not traditional for women. Several of my interviewees indicate how participation in the revolutionary movement rendered them more aware of the social inequalities which existed in their communities, but also installed a sense of how to address these issues in practice (Asenció, member UNAMG, 24 May 2010; Delgado, member MRS, 13 April 2010). As Asencío stated 'Many women did not have a clear idea about the way forward, and had only ever been active in the URNG. [...] This was so helpful when the UNAMG was established, that we sort of already knew how to do things'.

On the one hand, these previous experiences and skills thus constituted a resource. Yet, on the other hand, they also created a biased preference for those methods with which women were familiar with. Many of these tactical strategies and methods were directly or indirectly derived from the revolutionary Marxist-socialist discourse of the leaders. For example the belief in massive and visible protest as a means to foster societal change can be discerned both in the revolutionary movements of Nicaragua in the 1980s and the current strategy of feminist organizations.

Asenció's quote above suggests that not only structural elements have been important in shaping the emerging women's movement, but that the individual experiences of and contacts between participants in the revolutionary movements have also been particularly influential, and that the learning process of activists has not only been shaped by the context in which they operated, but also by their daily experiences, informal communications and concrete actions.[5]

Organizational Structures Aimed at Avoiding Hierarchy

A third element which points in the direction of social movement spillover, according to the framework of Meyer and Whittier (1994), is the continuity of

---

5   On these type of relationships between participants of social movements, see Melucci (1996) on submerged networks.

organizational structures, and more specifically, the adoption of structures aimed at avoiding hierarchy. Caution is warranted when transposing this idea to the Guatemalan and Nicaraguan women's movement, because their starting situation differs significantly from that of the women's groups which Meyer and Whittier have analyzed. What Meyer and Whittier found is that the newly emerging women's movements which they studied, adopted the same non-hierarchical organizational structures as those of the civil rights movement from which they were considered a spillover.

What we see in the Nicaraguan and Guatemalan case however is that it would not have been possible for the post-conflict women's movement to build on the democratic and open decision-making structures of their predecessors, as these were non-existent. The predecessors of the post-conflict women's movement, i.e. the revolutionary movements in which women participated, cannot be said to have had open decision-making structures or decentralized organizational structures which were particularly democratic. On the contrary, revolutionary units in Guatemala for example often relied on closed and secretive decision-making and in Nicaragua the FSLN as a vanguard took on strong top-down structures (Destrooper 2012). One interviewee indicated that it was precisely a concern with avoiding these kinds of closed structures which inspired her organization in its initial phase.

> We met, *así*, just women amongst each other initially. We discussed our concerns, things which we faced every day. We discussed how we could help each other, how we could find solutions together. Just like that. Then more women came, and more, and we started to print leaflets, announcing that we were going to meet. And the meetings between friends became grand discussions. But we never felt as if it was us, the initiators, who owned the thing. It belonged to all of us women. I think we lost lots of time discussing everything. There were surely more practical ways to organize, more efficient ones. But this way, every one (woman) could have her say. We tried to continue doing this all the time, also when we were growing really fast. Every woman could make drawings or contributions for the leaflets, every one could speak during meetings, chairs rotated. It was truly a good experience, I think for all of us.
>
> RIVAS, founder GRUFEPROMFAM, interview 27 May 2010

Also the interview with Torres, president Colectivo 8 de Marzo (21 April 2010) was illustrative of a concern with open decision-making structure,

> I was always treated well by my comrades but I knew of many women who weren't. They were excluded from decision-making, were forced to

do menial tasks, and sometimes there was even violence within the units, which was then hushed up. [...] Here we need to avoid all these things [...] every woman can tell her story, every woman can participate in the organization, everyone has an equal voice [...] We are proving that we can do better [than them].

This shows the extent to which the newly emerging women's organizations used their revolutionary experience as a frame of reference to shape their own organizational decisions and priorities. From these quotes, the influence appears antithetical however, in the sense that interviewees use their experience as an indication of how they did not want to organize and as a factor demanding open and inclusive decision-making. Despite this strong concern however, it is increasingly rare to find organizations which succeed in bringing into practice this kind of open organizational culture. During the fieldwork, I did not find any organizations still working like this today. Even women's collectives in rural areas like Mozonte, Nicaragua for example, had some form of formal organization which entailed a degree of centralization. In most organizations in the capital, the participation of women was limited to the possibility of making suggestions in a dropbox. Large meetings with the target group were rare, and structural involvement of women – other than those on the payroll – were virtually non-existent. This hints at a tension within the women's movement concerning these formal organizational issues, whereby on the one hand the hierarchic structures are principally rejected because of women's experience with them in the guerrilla movements, but on the other hand, they are replicated because of dynamics of organizational learning (see infra).

Continuity in Personnel and Leaders

The former three indicators of social movement spillover all implicitly assume the last one, namely the continuity in movement personnel and leaders. My interviewees confirmed that nearly all of those activists who were old enough to have been active during the conflict period, indeed had a history in some popular movement. In more than eighty per cent of the organizations which I analyzed, there are one or more women with experiences in the revolutionary movements who still hold a leadership position today, fifteen to twenty-one years after the ending of the civil conflicts. Also Kampwirth (2004: 10) found, in the Nicaraguan case, that it was mainly the mid-ranking women from the revolutionary movements who became the leaders of the new women's organizations in the post-conflict period. She demonstrates that 'the later feminist leaders were drawn from the rank of would-be political elites within the context of revolutionary politics', i.e. female guerrilla commanders and mid-prestige guerrilleras.

The fact that these ex-guerrilleras became the leaders of the new social movements which were arising after conflict meant that they were significant in determining the organizational evolution, because their leadership position provided them with greater access to, and possible control over, relevant resources, and gave them a central place in the decision-making process (Brass 1984).

Because these activists' first experience with social mobilization came in a period of violent societal upheaval, it is plausible that his initial mobilization constituted a transformative experience for participants, which profoundly impacted on their personalities and ideas (Laufer 1985: 42). These ex-revolutionaries are the women who – as social movement leaders – influenced the evolution of the women's movement in the last two decades. It is therefore relevant to assess how their experiences have been shaped by the conflict in general, and more specifically by their participation in wartime popular movements. From the interviews, it indeed becomes clear that not only activists' ideas on mobilization and social change, but also decision-making and working methods in the movement have been decisively influenced by their personal experiences of wartime mobilization (e.g. Morales, member Tierra Viva, 1 June 2010). This will be important for the next section which explains the mechanism behind the process of social movement spillover in more detail by turning to learning theories.

Individual and Organizational Learning

As argued above, the paradigm of social movement spillover adequately explains how revolutionary mobilization has influenced the guiding frames and organizational choices of women's mobilization in the initial years of the women's movement because many of the current leaders of the women's movement have a history in the guerrilla movements. It is therefore important to lay bear the dynamics of how their revolutionary experiences fed back into their current activism to understand the process of social movement spillover.

For several of these women, joining the popular movements during the armed conflict was disappointing in terms of gender dynamics (Kampwirth 2004). Their male counterparts did not manage to live up to the promises of equality made in the pamphlets. Guatemalan interviewees mainly lamented the lack of attention for equal gender rights, whereas Nicaraguan interviewees denounced the fact that women's rights were supported officially but were entirely subordinate to the priorities of the vanguard party in practice. Two examples from interviews with ex-guerrilleras illustrate this.

> We were recruited to fight for the revolution. We fought with men, and
> we carried arms. Often I heard that people talked behind my back, that

> I was someone 'who likes to be around men' [...] I believed in our cause. Their cause. [...] In the end we [women] had little to gain from the efforts we made. We didn't even really consider we had different interests initially. [...] There was no attention for this, other things were more important.
>
> GONZALES, Guatemala, 14 May 2010

> It was always 'patience', 'First comes the revolution, then come your rights [as women]', 'Just do as we say for now, and you'll be better off when we win', It was always 'We will fight for your rights, but not now, a little more patience' always more patience, always there was something more important for them [the men].
>
> MARTINEZ, Nicaragua, 27 April 2010

Moreover, women were allegedly empowered by their exposure to a leftist ideology which implied gender equality, only to feel disappointed and disempowered when acting upon these newly-learned ideas and demanding them from their superiors. Many interviewees, looking back in hindsight, indicate how they now perceive their initial mobilization as a farce which had nothing to do with emancipation (e.g. Interview with Mendez, Actoras de Cambio, 18 February 2011, and with Pena, ex-guerrillera, 2 June 2010). In retrospect, many consider that they were lured into a struggle which in the end did not serve their gender interests but only the interests of the revolution. As Jiménez, member of the Nicaraguan Autonomous Women's Organization and ex-guerrillera bitterly remarked,

> To hear people talk about how we did not manage to act upon the openings which were made during conflict [sighs...] There were no openings. We were never expected to have a mind of our own, let alone to think as independent creatures. Our mobilization, by no means, was meant for our benefit. *Era una broma.* But we couldn't laugh about it.
>
> JIMÉNEZ, 13 April 2010

So while the armed conflict indeed triggered women's mobilization, the concrete experiences of women also meant that women were critical about this mobilization. Their experience with popular mobilization influenced women's decision-making strategies and methods when they created new women's organizations in the post-conflict period. As Hirschman (2002: 9) argues, women's disappointment with one form of public involvement – revolutionary mobilization – can explain their organizational choices in the post-conflict period. To explain how this happened, I turn to theories of organizational behavior which explain the psycho-social dynamics in organizations and emphasize the relation between the individual and the organization.

I subscribe to a classic interpretation of organizational behavior as developed in the Carnegie School, which I complement with insights from anthropological organizational behavior theory (Gavetti et al. 2007). To explain the process of social movement spillover specifically, classic insights on routines, learning and decision-making are complemented with anthropology's qualitative methods and the concept of organizational culture (Weick 1974). The basic assumption is that the individuals making up the organization influence the organization's norms, culture and functioning and are in turn influenced by it (Rothman and Friedman 2003: 398). The process of social movement spillover can be framed in the open-systems model of organizational behavior. The open-systems model holds that organizational strategies are influenced by both the external and internal culture and by the behavior of the individuals in these organizations (Duncan 1978 and Polletta 2008: 84). The idea that the social influence on organizations emanates amongst others from the individual (Barnard 1938, Brass 1984 and Cartwright 1965), justifies the consideration of individual wartime experiences when analyzing the development of the women's movement.

How have these wartime experiences entered the future women's organizations? To explain this, I use the notion of learning. According to Lewin, learning in individuals is experiential.[6] This means that individuals have concrete sensory experiences, which they observe and on the basis of which abstract concepts and generalizations are formed, which are tested in new situations. This leads to new concrete experiences. On the basis thereof, the individual forms mental models. These are deeply held internal images of how the world works, which represent the person's view of the world and have a deep impact on what one does, because they provide the context in which to view and interpret new materials (Senge 1990: 192). These mental models are dynamic cognitive knowledge structures which enable individuals to orient themselves within their experiential terrain (Louis 1983, Markus 1977). Note that I do not see mental models as structures automatically determining behavior in a way which does not allow for conscious thought, but rather, as roadmaps or frames for action. They are important though, because they contain much of the tacit knowledge underlying individual and organizational

---

6 Lewinian experiential learning model, for more information, see Kim (1993: 38) and Kolb (1984: 38).

behavior. Mental models are thus a mixture of what is learned explicitly and what is absorbed implicitly (Kim 1993). It is therefore important to consider the skills and ideas women acquired during their mobilization as well as the role of women's disillusionment with the wartime popular movements. Both can have an influence on their mental models concerning social organizations.

The empirical part of this section is important because it attempts to make explicit the implicit mental models of those women who were active in the guerrilla movement, and who, as shown above, became the leaders of the newly arising women's organizations. By invoking the notion of *shared mental models,* I give an account of how organizations react to these individual mental models without anthropomorphizing the entity. I explore these shared mental models on the basis of Kim's reading (1993) of March and Olsen's cycles of organizational choice (1975: 149).

March and Olsen posit that cognitions and preferences held by individuals affect their behavior, and through this, their organizational choices. Kim (1993: 44) argues that not only cognitions and preferences, but also individual habits and affects, will influence the organizational level because habits and preferences are also part of the individual mental model, and will thus become part of the organizational shared mental models or the organizational *Weltanschauung*. The organizational shared mental models define 'what an organization pays attention to, how it chooses to act and what it chooses to remember from its experience' (Kim 1993: 44). Through this process, individual habits and preferences are thus eventually reflected in the organizational behavior and routines. The implication of this view on organizational adaptation is that several biases emanating from the individual level have to be taken into consideration when analyzing the strategic decisions of organizations.

Traditionally, cognitive and evaluative limits are pointed out as the crucial factors in determining the potential for organizational adaptation (March and Olsen 1975: 147). However, Kim shows that the role of emotions and beliefs, which are not per se rational or explicit, is not to be overlooked either, especially when analyzing organizational behavior which is largely discretionary (also see Levine 2010, Pouliot 2008, Vince 2002, and Scherer and Tran 2003). This is so because discretionary behavior and actions follow belief and attitudes, which are not strictly rational processes (March and Olsen 1975). This means that the negative affects of women *vis-à-vis* their militancy in the popular movements require consideration when analyzing their strategic choices today, because these affects may direct the organizational focus – potentially in a biased manner (Scherer and Tran 2003: 386).

These emotions and affects, based on generalizations of experiences in the past, may prevent further development of the organization and may inhibit individual as well as organizational learning. Women's revolutionary mobilization does thus not guarantee learning per se. It is possible that precisely this experience hampers the possibility to increase the potential for individual and organizational capacity and lead to suboptimal organizational adaptations. As the above quotes by Martinez (ex-guerrillera) and Torres (Colectivo 8 de Marzo) show, many of the ideas about how to organize the newly emerging women's organizations had their immediate roots in a rejection of the *modus operandus* of the revolutionary movement. This was visible in inter-organizational choices as well as in the relations between different organizations of civil society. These relations were on many occasions fraught with tensions which had their roots in the armed conflict, as I will show below. This shows that preferences and affects do not only influence the choice of the individual organizations, but can also hamper or damage normal organizational relations and interactions, and 'prevent the development of synergy' (Scherer and Tran 2003: 387).

Yet, despite the importance of individual affects and preferences for organizations, the role of emotions has often been seen as 'uncomfortable knowledge' in organization theory (Vince 2002: 73). Also on the ground, emotions are often not mentioned by activists as an influence on the development of the movement. In specific, when talking about their experiences in the popular movements, interviewees would often frame the story of their lived experiences and emotions as a logical cognitive argument. They would refer to studies and common understandings about how their revolutionary activism had shaped their mobilization or to the measurable added value of their approach, without paying much attention to their personal experiences – even when I told them that I was interested in their own personal life histories. This was particularly prominent in the interview with Alfaro and Espinoza (30 April 2010). These members of AMNLAE – the FSLN-affiliated women's organization – structured their responses to the question about how their revolutionary mobilization had influenced their current activism for women's rights, along the lines of a particularly rational and logical discourse. As Alfaro replied to the question about how she looks back on her experience within the revolutionary units:

> It was thanks to the FSLN and the sincere dedication of our leaders and in particular of comrade Ortega, that I had my first chance to start working on women's rights. I learned a lot there. And we know that we can still turn to the bigger structures when we need advice. [...] I have no doubt

that our country would not be where it is today without the FSLN's revolution. We have all learnt a lot and we know what we stand for.

Interview 30 April 2010

In response to this reply, I asked several follow-up questions probing for an answer which would shed light on the personal experiences and motivations of these two women, but personal stories or motivations did not enter the discourse at any point. Yet, their opinions on their role in the popular movements and on how these were organized often seemed to have rational as well as emotional roots. This was also the case when Jiménez (member of MAM, interview 13 April 2010) for example, argued that her dissatisfaction with the work of *feminine* organizations was one which was based on objective parameters, such as studies which indicate that structural inequalities need to be addressed before women's situation can change. However, in personal communications, Jiménez mentioned how her personal experience of mobilization had also shaped her belief in feminist organizing. Here she told how a personal conflict with one of her superiors in the guerrilla unit, nourished the idea that a genuinely new approach to women's issues was needed, and how she still thinks of this to remind herself of 'how I don't want to become'. These kind of personal motivations however never entered the narrative during formal interviews, even if they informally seemed to have an important impact on organizational choices.

I discuss the psychodynamic processes at the individual level to explain the evolution of the women's movement and the dynamic of social movement spillover because I see the cognitive and affective experiences of its members in the popular movements as an important determinant of organizational choices. This is especially true for the formation period of these organizations, immediately after the conflicts, in the mid-1990s. In this period, the beliefs and affects of the ex-*guerrilleras* were all the more important, since this phase was characterized by what March and Olsen (1975: 161) call 'conditions of ambiguity'. In this state of uncertainty, the significance of pre-existing beliefs becomes more apparent because other frames of reference appear volatile. This means that the implicit beliefs which individual activists held about how an organization ought to function, have crucially fed back into the blueprint of these newly-emerging women's organizations which had few other frames of reference than the individual opinions of their future leaders. As one interviewee enthusiastically told,

It was a very interesting and exciting period. The regime was new, everything was new. Nobody knew what was going to happen. Being able to start off in such a period is unique. There was a *tabula rasa* for us to write all our plans on.

GALVEZ, head of a small NGO, 12 February 2011

For the initial conceptualization and materialization, the newly emerging women's organizations were thus almost entirely dependent on the experiences of their leaders, who were often former revolutionary activists, and who shaped these new organizations on the basis of their personal experiences. Starbuck and Hedberg (2003: 339) argue that organizations then integrate the initial knowledge and structures into more rigid and coherent organizational frameworks which are meant to resist the pressure of environmental and internal change, that could challenge their chosen approach. In this way, the personal experiences and affects of the future leaders, became institutionalized at the organizational level.

In conclusion, a significant way in which revolutionary mobilization has influenced women's organizations is by shaping activists' mental models. This was crucial in the initial years of movement formation, but also influences the organizational choices of the women's movement today because the individual mental models became institutionalized and translated into the organizational *Weltanschauung*. My interviews indicated that the vast majority of former activists were skeptical about the way in which popular movements were organized, but at the same time relied on their experience in popular movements when organizing for themselves. The quote of Valenzuela, member of CICAM, is illustrative in this context. To the question about what inspired the choice for the rather complex organizational structure of the CICAM she replied,

> On the one hand, we reckon that this is the most efficient way to organize. Every unit has its own independence and the possibility to decide on its own program, without having to pass through the whole system for every decision. But what also matters is the fact that we wanted several smaller divisions in order to avoid centralization of authority. [...] We have had our share of centrally-organized secretive decision-making [...] Most of us had no longing for that anymore.
>
> 3 June 2010

This statement suggests the dominance of a mental model which is largely hostile towards central organization, collectivization or vanguard parties (also see Aguilar 1997: 112). Also an ex-*guerrillera* who was member of a post-conflict women's organization, commented,

[w]e had the advantage of having been active before. We had learnt how to organize, and, more importantly, we had learnt how we did not want to organize.

RAMIREZ, 22 May 2010

Linking this back to the elaboration in the previous chapter, on Guatemalan and Nicaraguan activists' respective experiences, and how these differed cross-nationally. It could also be assumed that Guatemalan and Nicaraguan activists – on average – have developed different mental models, which can help to explain differences in the evolution of the women's movement. In specific the rejection of the FSLN by Nicaraguan feminist activists has significantly shaped the individual mental models and the evolution of the Nicaraguan women's movement. In Guatemala, it is the importance of ethnicity which has significantly influenced the development of the women's movement by influencing the mental models of former activists. I return to both evolutions in the next chapter.

However, women's – shared – mental models and learning processes have not only been influenced by their revolutionary experience, some aspects of these mental models have also been mediated the presence of international organizations which entered the country *en masse* during and after the civil conflict, bringing along new ideologies and creating new conditions for mobilization. This is the focus of the next section, where I first discuss the role of international actors and then the process of learning through interactions with these international actors.

Glocalization[7] or the Impact of International Actors[8]

In both countries, the international organizations and donors – and their discourse and praxis – was crucial for the development of the women's movement initially, and allowed the movement to make substantial advances over time, mainly in the sense of forging legal breakthroughs (Aasen 2009, Piron 2005). These advances were not only related to the initial financial

---

7 *Glocalization* refers to the simultaneity, the co-presence, of both universalizing and particularizing tendencies and the tempering effects of local conditions on global pressures (Robertson 1994).

8 This section discusses the imposition of discourses and praxis which come with conditional aid and financial dependence rather than the influence of international treaties – as national actors have arguably contributed to the creation of these treaties and ratified them.

assistance and confidence-boosting provided by international actors, but also to the fact that the members of the different organizations have become more competent in negotiating and managing their relations with their donors over time, meaning that they have also become more apt in selecting those donors whose goals best overlap with their own ones (Interview with Álvarez, 2 June 2010, and Asenció 24 May 2010, also see Berger 2006: 32).

Nevertheless, the influence of external funding agencies in the long run is controversial. The continuing presence of international organizations and their funding, risks creating a sense of dependence, passivity and underestimation of their own potential for action amongst women's organizations, and created an organizational model 'formed on the back of readily available donor funds, with weak social roots and no independent supporter base' (Hulme and Edwards 1997: 277). Dependency here, I argue, does not only refer to the financial and logistical reliance on other actors, but also to the more subtle process by which international donors are turned to, in order to set goals and to justify actions. This hampered the movement's formation of an independent identity in the 1990s and challenged its legitimacy and accountability to its audience (Edwards and Hulme 1996: 966–967). In the post-conflict period, the notion of foreign-imposition is increasingly important due to the vast amounts of – conditional – international aid.

One organization that illustrates the issues of economic dependence in the second period is the Guatemalan Centre for Research, Training and Support of Women (CICAM). CICAM was established as a centre with legal personality in 1999 and worked in three domains: legislation and investigation, education and formation, and direct assistance. Initially there was also a fourth branch of activities, namely auto-sustainability. The idea of generating money to sustain the other three branches by means of organizing informative workshops and competence training for companies was abandoned in 2005 because it was not profitable. The project raised 5000 quetzales (about 500 euro), which was just enough to pay for the electricity bills. The reason why this project was not sustainable was not what the local team had foreseen might be the problem, i.e. the fact that there would not be much demand for such workshops. On the contrary, Valenzuela, head of the legal unit at CICAM, pointed out in an interview that the demand was so high that CICAM could not organize accordingly, because the workshops consumed too much of their time, meaning that the staff was no longer able to focus on their core activities. She explains that in the initial funding which they received from their principal donor, no budget was scheduled for the financing of auto-sustainability activities, meaning that there was no budget for specialized staff and that the existing staff had to manage this task of auto-sustainability on top of their other duties, which meant the project soon had to be abandoned because it created too much workload (Valenzuela, 3 June 2010). Hence in order to be able to meet the requests that were mentioned in the conditions by the donors, the CICAM had to abandon its auto-financing program and focus on the other three domains which were mentioned in the program. As Valenzuela testified,

> A considerable first investment is needed before you can make this work. We would have needed two teams really, but who was going to pay us for a fund-raising team, which made no direct contribution to the goals they set us? They gave us money to rent an office, but not for a project like this one.
> VALENZUELA, 3 June 2010

This case is illustrative of how low economic viability has been on the priority list of international benefactors, and how much dependency this created. According to the glocalization paradigm however, this economic dependency does not automatically lead local actors to adopt the ideological frames of their benefactors. Women still negotiated the imported ideological concepts and priorities and incorporated them in their own frames in a critical way.

In organizational terms, the effect of economic dependency was more outspoken. The type of aid provided by international donors favored the creation of small women's organizations which often took on the structure of NGOs. This triggered the multiplication of small initiatives all over the country (Ewig 1999: 82). The occurrence of smaller local organizations can as such be indicative of a locally embedded, growing and maturing women's movement. However, as Ewig argues, the fact that these small initiatives all take on the legal status of an NGO suggests a limited legitimacy at the grassroots level. Ewig uses the term *NGOization* to refer to a women's movement model which is characterized by 'the presence of many women's groups which have taken on the legal status of an NGO, and – at the same time – the relative absence of informal grassroots forms of female mobilization'.[9] This means that the growing attention for women and gender of the last few years, which is shown by statistics, is not per se indicative of a growing societal awareness of women's issues. It can rather be seen as an expression of the tendency towards NGOization present throughout the region, and of the ideologically inspired multiplication of organizations.[10] These uncoordinated projects and small organizations run

---

9   Also my interviewees often use the term *'oengeización'* to describe the current structure of the women's movement in their country.

10   In 2007 60,9 percent of all civil society organizations mentioned women and gender as one of their priorities and 139 of the organizations registered with the MIGOB in 2005

the risk of not creating synergy or potential for replication, and not being sustainable in themselves. The viability of these small civil society organizations is further challenged by the fact that international agents are starting to leave both countries because of an overall shift of attention of development aid away from Latin America in favor of African countries (Kwon 2010, Interview with Neirynck, fieldworker, 28 April 2010). Moreover, interviewees highlighted the conditionality of the aid as a factor which hampered efficient programming, and which furthered ideological divisions. As the founder of GRUFEPROMEFAM stated,

> Unfortunately, in some cases it's the financial organizations which impose the themes, and in some other cases, our organization cannot find funding for a certain project, because it's not on the agenda of the international co-operation.
>
> RIVAS, 27 May 2010

Or more strongly as a feminist activist in Nicaragua, asserted during an interview,

> There exist several international interventions which do not even coordinate with local actors and programs, they impose themselves. These actors bring their plans and money and come here for a restricted period of time to conduct this specific project, and they will do it, come hell or high water. This creates big tensions because the plans they have set up, do not apply to our reality. But I think some organizations just have to accept them.
>
> ARÓSTEGUI, 29 April 2010

What is contradictory about this is that, while acknowledging that this type of interventions exist, nearly all interviewees state that they have never accepted this sort of conditional financial aid. This however should not be taken at face value, since they affirm that many international donors only offer conditional funding, and that many organizations by force of circumstance accept this. Only one interviewee, from the Collective for the Defence of Women's Rights in Guatemala (CODEFEM), asserted that while there is a general tendency

---

defined themselves as women's organizations. These organizations had a budget of 170 million dollar in 2004, mainly coming from international co-operation. In that year they employed 6963 full time equivalents, and provided services to 2 million women (Serra Vázquez 2007: 89).

amongst organizations to reject or question conditions of the international co-operation, 'they [external aid agencies, to some degree] always impose themes, concepts and rhythms, which are not favorable for us' (Ferrin, 19 June 2010). It appears from the interviews that the degree to which international actors explicitly condition programs is indeed limited, but that to the extent there is conditioning, local actors are not always aware of this.

In conclusion, given the movement's continuing high dependency on foreign funding and logistical support, international donors have a big influence on the actions of the movement (Pearce 1998). This does not mean that local organizations blindly adopt the ideology of donors, quite the contrary. But it does mean that their praxis is strongly shaped by the preferences of donors. Conditional funding, limited coordination and inter-institutional friction, foster potential competition between organizations. Pearce (1998: 610) also points out the extent to which local dynamics are often overlooked as the factor which reinforces a situation whereby organizations increasingly overlap with one another, and at the same time render the movement more divided. Yet, it should also be noted, that the influence of – conditional – funding is mainly that it limits the options available, and that this is not as such a case of ideas, ideologies or guiding frames being entirely imposed from elsewhere. Local actors have the potential to actively engage and interact with ideas and guiding frames which come from elsewhere. How this happens is the focus of the next section.

Organizational Learning through Interactions with International Organizations

In this section I analyze how activists fitted new ideas in their existing individual and shared mental models, because this influenced the organizational development of the movement.

I argue that the way in which new ideas were adapted to the local context can be seen as an instance of *hybridization* as described by Giulianotti and Robertson (2007: 135 and 2006: 173), whereby the social actors, who are presented with new influences, which have to be made sense of, 'synthesize local and other cultural phenomena to produce distinctive hybrid cultural practices, institutions and meanings'. As one interviewee, who started a women's organization in her municipality during the armed conflict, illustrated,

> We had clear ideas about what we wanted, but no clear roadmap about how to achieve it. So the help of donors on how to set up an efficient plan for action was initially quite welcome actually.
>
> RIVAS, head of GRUFEPROMEFAM, 27 May 2010

Another example of how local women's organizations synthesized local and foreign practices and ideas is the fact that many women's groups formally took on the status of an NGO in reaction to the expectations of external funding agencies, but informally preserved their own ways of proceeding. This was most notable in the process of Actoras de Cambio, a nationwide initiative aimed at collective healing from war-inflicted trauma in Guatemala. This initiative – which is discussed in detail in the second part of the book – took on the formal structure which was required to optimize the channeling of foreign funding and assistance, but at the same time worked with indigenous healing practices to address their target group. Actoras is thus an example of an initiative in which the combination of local and foreign elements was possible, and even encouraged by the external actors in order to create synergy. However, several – anonymous – interviewees also testified how it is sometimes necessary to omit the use of locally embedded methods from their reports to donors, if these methods do not fit the paradigm of the donor. This means that the reports of these organizations do not always reflect their reality – or that of their target audience.

Moreover, several women's organizations based in the capitals increasingly seem to favor the practices and institutions of the donors. This is for example visible in these organizations' increasing reliance on a rights-based approach. Their choice to adopt the methods and frames of the donors, can be seen as an instance of *transformation*. This is described by Giulianotti as a process whereby local actors come to favor the practices, institutions or meanings associated with other cultures (Giulianotti and Robertson 2007: 135). Transformation may procure fresh cultural forms or, more extremely, the abandonment of the local culture in favor of alternative and/or hegemonic cultural forms. The effect of the increasing reliance on transformation is the focus of the next chapter.

Opposed to these NGO's in the capital, are several – indigenous – organizations in the municipalities, which have an inclination towards *accommodation* and *relativization*, i.e. only pragmatically absorbing foreign practices in order to be able to maintain the key elements of their own culture, or not absorbing these practices at all, and instead committing themselves to stressing the difference with the international organizations which are offering funding and logistical support. As Consuelo, head of the Nicaraguan Council for Indigenous people in Mozonte, argued,

> We are deliberately refraining from becoming an NGO, of course we are. Yes, it costs us money, money which we are not receiving because we don't have the organizational structure required for receiving this money.

> But at least, we can do what we want to do, instead of abiding by some-
> one else's rule. Here, many congratulate us for that. They say that we are
> setting an example. [...] We are respecting our own customs, because
> they [donors] won't. [...] There is a world of difference [between local
> organizations and international donors].
>
> 26 April 2010

These diverging ways of dealing with foreign influence imply that the difference between women's organizations in the capital and those in the municipalities is still growing in the early 2010s.

The mechanism through which interactions with international donors have
influenced women's organizations, is different from the mechanism through
which participation in revolutionary popular movements has influenced them.
I argue that interaction with external funding agencies are triggering a process
of organizational learning – even if this is often pragmatic and situational –
whereas the effect of revolutionary mobilization has in essence been a case of
organizational adaptation.

The reason why the interaction with international organizations led to a
pragmatic kind of organizational learning, whereas the legacy of participation
in the popular movements mainly led to organizational adaptation, is related
to the role of motivation. There is at present no direct incentive for members
of the women's movement to actually revisit their position vis-à-vis the armed
conflict or the former movements which they were part of. On the contrary,
there is a strong – financial – incentive for careful consideration and constant
revisiting of their position towards international donors: the presence of an
explicit financial incentive promotes the modification of behavior and incites
these organizations to act as a learning entity.

The nature of the incentive – practical and financial – means that the sort
of individual and organizational learning which is likely to occur will also be
characterized by pragmatism and rational calculation, and will be aimed at
maximizing possibilities rather than at aligning frames and ideas (March and
Olsen 1975: 148). As one interviewee from a Guatemalan feminist organization
in the capital claimed,

> We have learned how to communicate with them [the donor agency]
> more efficiently. At first we reported on everything we did. When we
> could no longer do so for practical reasons, we neglected our reporting
> duties too much apparently. This led to a warning from their side, which
> we took very seriously. Now I think we found a good balance in what we
> do, and what we do not report on, and in which way we do this; a balance

which allows us sufficient freedom, and still keeps them informed
accurately.

MORALES, Member Tierra Viva, 1 June 2010

This statement clearly illustrates the extent to which learning is inspired by
rational calculation and experience in the case of interactions with donors.
The statement also hints at the professionalization of women's organizations
however. This has been another consequence of the modalities of the interactions with donors. As other interviews suggest, professionalization and institutionalization were deemed the best strategy to secure good contacts with
the international organizations whose funds were needed to be economically
viable.[11] As Aguilar, head of Q'anil, commented,

> It is becoming increasingly hard for rural women's groups to survive.
> They have always been part of the community, but after the communities
> were reshuffled during and after the civil war, their position was compro-
> mised. This was even further aggravated by the influx of foreign capital.
> All of a sudden, they needed to start behaving as competitors for funds in
> an open market. They needed different skills, a different mindset, and
> most of all, they needed to dedicate a substantial part of their time to
> activities which were not their core tasks and which they were often
> not trained for. By contrast, organizations in the capital, are doing much
> better. Even though they often have no real societal roots and are much
> less embedded, they can attract highly-educated staff because they can
> offer competitive salaries and exciting jobs. This means that they can
> interact with donors in an efficient and professional way. It's a vicious
> circle. You see, they can pay attention to all these things, because they
> don't have the same kind of backbench [as rural women's organizations]
> which needs them, which suffers when they spend one or two days per
> week working purely on administrative issues instead of being with their
> people in the field.
>
> Interview 26 May 2010

---

11   Only some organizations have programs to become self-sustaining, but usually this only
      considers parts of their work, and is not sufficient to allow for complete independence
      from foreign donors. One example is Ixchen Nicaragua, the largest health-service pro-
      vider, which is making a concerted effort to become self-sustaining, but which can only
      do so because of its large size and the significant number of middle-class participants
      (Ewig 1999: 95).

Not only the effects of this kind of pragmatic learning are potentially problematic, also the nature of the learning process itself is ambiguous. While learning refers to the capacity of an organization to improve its potential for efficient action, it has not always led to optimal performance in the long-run in the case of how Guatemalan and Nicaraguan women's organizations interact with their donors. This has to do with contextual factors, such as the socio-political context in which women's organizations act, but also with the nature of the learning. What we see in both countries, is that new skills are being learned, but that these are mainly the skills that are needed to obtain short-term benefits. The learning process is rather fragmented and opportunistic, and does not necessarily create conditions for long-term change.

Another factor nourishing the fragmented nature of the learning processes, which is the reluctance towards revealing much about their practices, implicit in the mental model of several activists. Several interviewees – influenced by their experience with revolutionary mobilization – expressed this reluctance and one interviewee in particular claimed that,

> Of course we didn't report on everything. Doing so would have been too much of an administrative burden, but moreover, it would have made us more vulnerable [...]. If there is one thing which I have learnt [from revolutionary mobilization], it is that you have more leeway, as long as nobody knows what you are doing.
> RAMIREZ, ex-guerrillera, 22 May 2010

This predisposition towards secrecy on the side of this interviewee, was to some extent present in many of the interviews I conducted with members of the current women's movement (e.g. Pedrosa, member of GAM, 3 June 2010; Tuyuk, member of CONAVIGUA, 7 June 2010). This is an important tendency to flag out, since it challenges the potential for structural organizational learning.

In conclusion, interactions with international donors are a crucial factor influencing the women's movement today, since the acceptance of increasing volumes of foreign aid involves entering into agreements about which activities and approaches to prioritize. This influences both priorities and working methods (Hulme and Edwards 1997: 8). The mechanism through which these interactions with international donors affect women's organizations, is distinct from the way in which women were influenced by their own participation in revolutionary movements. Whereas revolutionary mobilization mainly triggered several types of organizational adaptation based on affective grounds, interactions with international donors and their financial incentives mainly prompted a type of pragmatic organizational learning based on rational calculations. This increased the capacity of organizations to take – certain kinds of – effective action. Also the period in which both factors influenced the women's movement was different. Revolutionary mobilization has had the biggest impact in the constitutive years of the movement, by influencing the memory, mental models, beliefs and actions of participants. Today it is much more latent and not always explicitly referred to. The influence of interactions with international actors on the other hand, has been present since the emergence of the women's movement, but has had a growing importance, as more donors entered both countries. What the effects of this type of organizational learning have been, is the focus of the next chapter. Before turning to this issue however, I discuss how a third factor has influenced the evolution of the post-conflict women's movement.

Relations with Government and the Political Establishment

Above I discussed those aspects of the evolution of the women's movement which were comparable in both cases. There are however also important differences between both countries which are mainly related to the movement's relations with government. I discuss both countries in turn.

Nicaragua: Reacting to a Polarized Political Landscape
In Nicaragua, the FSLN lost power to Violeta Barrios de Chamorro in 1990. Her anti-feminist program pushed family relations toward an older, more hierarchical model (Kampwirth 2004: 47).[12] Even though this was the first time a woman was elected president in Nicaragua, the election of Chamorro did not foster a favorable climate for the women's movement. On the contrary, Chamorro adopted a conservative and explicitly anti-feminist program in an attempt to restore societal order. By claiming, 'I am not a feminist. Nor do I wish to be one. I am a loyal wife and a woman dedicated to my home, like Pedro [her assassinated husband and newspaper publisher] taught me' (La Cuadra 1990: 2), Chamorro explicitly propagated traditional gender roles which had been absent from public discourse for over a decade. Kampwirth (1998) argues that she adopted this discourse because its symbolism resonated with that of large sections of society which supported a traditional hierarchical model of the family.

---

12   Antifeminist organizing rhetorically responds to and attacks feminism, whereas a feminine organizing merely reinforces the status quo of power differences between men and women.

Her election also entailed changing state-civil society relations. In the 1990s, FSLN-allied organizations of civil society lost ground. They felt the FSLN's electoral loss both economically (loss of state funds) and psychologically (loss of prestige). Therefore, relationships with the party were revised and more autonomy from the party was requested by some organizations who wished to act in accordance with what the membership expected rather than with the party lines. This brought about the opportunity for several fractions to break free from the vanguard party and start to work on their own topics (Criquillon 1995, Bickham Mendez 2002a). Feminist organizations were the first ones to break free from this vanguard party and to explicitly reject its dominance because they believed that a lack of organizational and ideological independence hampered the fight for personal independence, autonomy and the rights of women (Interview with Montenegro, autonomous feminist, 2 May 2010).

The conservative backlash and anti-feminist politics of Chamorro thus triggered a growth and diversification – but also a growing degree of polarization – of the women's movement in Nicaragua. In 1997, Ellsberg et al. write that 'Despite the conservative backlash, or perhaps in response to it, the women's movement has grown tremendously in recent years, emerging as one of the most dynamic and diverse social movements in Nicaragua' (1997: 83).

The Network of Women against Violence, Women Worker's Organization Maria Elena Cuadra, the Federation of Female Manufacturers and the Committee of Rural Women are all organizations which emerged after their founders left mixed-gender FSLN-affiliated popular organizations after they came into conflict over the formulation of the strategic needs of women. At the national level, there were often tense relations between government and these women's and feminist organizations, and interactions mainly concerned some coordination in the fields of health and childcare or lobbying work with relation to the penalization of violence against women and the ratification of the 1979 convention of the Committee on the Elimination of the Discrimination Against Women (CEDAW). Yet throughout their history, organizations of civil society in Nicaragua have, at least formally speaking, always been on the demanding side to establish spaces for coordination with government, especially so for the follow-up and implementation of policies related to women (Bickham Mendez 2002).

The approach of the women's movement to focus on service provision and of the feminist movement to adopt a rights-based approach, combined with Chamorro's respect for the liberty of organization, meant that several institutional and legislative advances could be made in the domain of gendered policy (such as the ratification of the CEDAW-convention and the penalization

of violence against women) despite the return to more conservative and patriarchal values which the Chamorro-government promoted.

This changed under the Alemán-government in 1997. The first major blow to
the women's movement in this respect was the reform of law 147 (general law
on not-for-profit legal entities, *ley general sobre personas jurídicas sin fines de
lucro*), which brought about the departure of many international funding
agencies and curbed the international aid to civil society organizations (Kwon
2011). The reforms to law 147 were a clear attempt to control the NGOs and their
resources, as they required civil society groups to answer to the government
and installed financial control mechanisms in the form of a tax over the income
acquired through foreign development agencies (CINCO 2009). Moreover, civil
society organizations had to work in a context of increased polarization since
the electoral process of 1996. The election results of 20 October 1996 reflected
how deeply polarized society had become.[13] This was reinforced on the one
hand by the electoral campaigns which had become more confrontational and
which influenced the daily discourse of people identifying with this confrontational rhetoric (Delli Carpini 2004). This electoral process also meant that the
political centre parties came to play a marginal role or disappeared altogether
when Alemán's conservative government came to power (Dore 2006).

This situation made the actions of the women's movement more arduous,
and protest actions became more common, especially since Alemán's Liberal
Alliance did not subscribe to the Minimal Agenda, i.e. the core demands of the
women's movement (Kampwirth 2004: 69). In this period those mechanisms
of interlocution between the movement and government which were not pro-
tected by law, were scaled back. Furthermore, large parts of the responsibilities
of the – independent and controlling – Nicaraguan Institute for Women (INIM)
were transferred to the government controlled Ministry of the Family (Franzoni
and Voorend 2011).

This contingency curtailed the room for maneuver of the women's movement, but did not abrogate the movement as a whole. Despite these difficulties, the movement found itself reinforced in certain respects. For one,
grassroots organization and mobilization were boosted in the wake of hurri-
cane Mitch in 1998. The local committees for reconstruction which were created in the wake of the natural disaster helped the women's movement to
regain some of the strength it had lost in other domains by bringing the grassroots level back in (Kampwirth 2003). Another factor is that, when president
Bolaños (Constitutionalist Liberal Party, PLC) came to power in 2002, the

---

13   50,99% of the vote went to Alemán from the Liberal Alliance. Ortega (FSLN) obtained
        37,83% of the vote (Nohlen 2005: 503)

movement's relations with the state improved substantially and organizations of civil society were notably free from state interference. The willingness on the side of government to enter into negotiations with women's organizations in the early 2000s was however not per se inspired by idealism or conviction, but rather by the insecure position of Bolaños which necessitated the adoption of a policy which was aimed at gaining support from civil society (Metoyer 2000). Thus, tensions with government continued – epitomizing in the increased harassment of some national and foreign NGO's from the tax authorities and the Public Ministry in 2007 – and curbed the initial optimism on the side of women's organizations (Freedom House 2010: 5).

The above suggests that the dynamics within the Nicaraguan women's movement have been significantly shaped by the political situation in which it operates, and most notably so, by the governing party. In this respect, the 2006 Nicaraguan presidential elections can be seen as a particularly significant point in the development of the Nicaraguan women's movement. In the run up to these elections, therapeutic abortion – which had been legal for the past 105 years – was rendered illegal. This was partially due to lobbying from conservative sections of the Catholic church, and was seen by the women's movement as an indication of the persisting strength of patriarchy and conservative catholicism. It triggered heavy protests and virulent reactions from some parts of the women's movement, while not provoking much reaction from other organizations. These mixed reactions were indicative of how several parts of the women's movement had evolved in distinct directions. This can as such be seen as a sign of maturing and of different organizations developing their own identity, priorities and framework. On this occasion, however, the rupture between feminists and non-feminists and between pro-FSLN and anti-FSLN women's organizations became an almost absolute one. Since then, the divide between organizations which rely on protest politics, awareness-raising and media campaigns on the one hand, and those which engage in service provision on the other hand, is growing.

This dynamic was reinforced when FSLN candidate Ortega was elected president in 2007 – and re-elected in 2011. While the FSLN's new discourse was pinned on the promise of civilian participation and equality, legal changes to the contrary have provoked the outrage of several actors within civil society who see their freedom of expression threatened through several reforms. The establishment of a Council for Communication and Citizenship (CCC)[14] in 2007 for example increasingly hampers the work of women's organizations

---

14　This is an inter-ministerial body controlling actors of civil society, without representation of non-governmental agents and violates their right of free organization. Also at the local level, several – allegedly unconstitutional – governmental actions hamper the work of women's organizations (Interview with Montenegro, CINCO, 2 May 2010 and with Jiménez, MAM, 13 April 2010).

How women's organizations react to these changes, reflects the divisions within the women's movement. Some women chose to collaborate with the FSLN and Ortega, whereas other sections of the movement vehemently opposed government attempts to curb the power of civil society. This is unlike Guatemalan women's organizations' reaction to government actions, as the next section will show.

Guatemala: Women's Engagement in the Peace Process

In the run-up to, and the aftermath of, the peace process of 1996, different types of women's organizations with different focuses which were formed inside and outside of the country increasingly found and strengthened each other. The peace process was the first time in Guatemalan history when women were participating in high-level political negotiations as a group. Initially women's participation in the peace negotiations – like their participation in popular movements – was mainly in the context of non-gender specific organizations, and their decision to 'go alone' ('*ir solas*') was often not well received by the different sectors of civil society from which they came, because this could potentially divide civil society (Gomáriz Moraga and Jovel 2007: 64). As Erazo (member ECAP, 25 January 2011) put it,

> There was still the old idea which also reigned the URNG, that we were stronger united. Some even suggested that the insistence [by certain foreign actors] that women for example would organize for themselves, was an attempt to internally divide us and make us weaker. Suspicion was rooted very deep in those days.

Nevertheless, several organizations were formed to defend women's interests during the peace negotiations, such as the *Sector de Mujeres*.

By organizing as a group, women managed to introduce new themes onto the political agenda and to propose their own vision on the solution of the national problem. The *Sector* was effective initially in uniting most of the women's organizations and in putting gender politics on the agenda for a wide audience for the first time, especially regarding the national process of healing from war inflicted trauma. This way, they managed to include women's needs – albeit in a vague and fragmented way, and without specific implementation procedures – in the peace accords of 1996. Of the twenty-eight specific demands of the Sector, two were followed up by the new government: the creation of specific institutions for the promotion of women's rights and the installation of the Plan for the Full Participation of Women (Morales and Morán 2006: 3). Also, several projects which the Sector initiated were picked up by government. One example is the Project for Women and Judicial Reforms. This project evaluated the points where the judicial system discriminated against women and proposed specific actions to overcome this situation. It was in the framework of this project that the law which defines female adultery as a penal crime, was abolished in 1996.

The relations between the women's movement and the first post-conflict government are thus from the start different in Guatemala than in Nicaragua. In the Guatemalan case, there were no principled attacks on the women's movement from the side of government, as was the case in Nicaragua under Chamorro, and women's organizations were a respected interlocutor. Moreover, because the Guatemalan peace negotiations were considered a pivotal turning point, many international actors were present to support the organizations of civil society in raising their voice in these negotiations. Thus, the existence of a forum for women's voices during the peace negotiations and the benefits which were to be expected from working together, proved to be strong motivations for collaborating – both with one another and with government agents.

However, while this collaboration during the peace negotiations resulted in the government's adoption of certain demands made by the women's movement and incited women's organizations to work together, the role of the peace negotiations in the development of the women's movement was not unequivocally positive. The creation of specific government organs for the advancement of women – such as the Foro de la Mujer (Forum for women), the Secretaría Presidencial de la Mujer (presidential secretary for women, SEPREM) and the Defensoría de la Mujer Indígena (agency for indigenous women, DEMI) – obscured the fact that the new conservative right-wing government of Alvaro Arzú in 1996 started to use delay tactics, bureaucratic politics and intimidation to restrict the advancements of these bodies (Berger 2006: 36). The Forum for Women, for one, was often outmaneuvered by government policy-makers and lacked adequate funding. Moreover, it was gradually replaced by the SEPREM which took on an ambiguous gender discourse and policy focus (see for example SEPREM 2001). Several leaders of the women's movement today, such as Luz Mendez, see the SEPREM as a mere facade, which creates subdivisions within the movement, amongst others over the issue of ethnicity (Mendez and Morán 2006: 11).

Over time, also the Guatemalan women's movement came to face an increasingly hostile political regime. This influenced its priorities and

structure. Aguilar, a prominent member of the Guatemalan women's movement, argues that 'the conflict installed a climate of generalized distrust at the
political level', i.e. between the powerholders themselves, and between these
powerholders and civil society. She claims that this distrust was also present
between actors of civil society and in personal relations, and that it still plays a
role today (1997: 112). Under these conditions, also the Guatemalan political
context became more polarized.

This challenged diverse impetuses to organize from the bottom-up. While
the 1990s show a growth of women's organizations in Guatemala, their relationship with the state has been an ambiguous one throughout (Berger 2006).
Some women – called institutionalists – joined the state in SEPREM, individually or collectively, to work on common objectives in the late 1990s. Others
maintained cordial relations with the state and sometimes established formal
or ad hoc associations of different kinds with state bureaucrats in order to have
their goals implemented through a strategy of double militancy. A third group
organized in protest against conservative state policies, and adheres to a strategy of public protest. All these strands of activists adopted different narratives
on what the causes and solutions to women's issues were, as the next chapter
will show.

SEPREM, for example, was charged with the task of coordinating public
politics for the development of women and maintaining a permanent dialogue with civil society (Berger 2006: 55). Women's groups played almost no
role in the creation of the SEPREM. Yet despite this, and despite the influence
of certain political actions on its functioning, SEPREM plays an important role
in the relations between the state and civil society in Guatemala. While relations are tense, antagonisms – both between feminist organizations and the
state and between different sections of the women's movement – are on average less explicit than in the Nicaraguan case. The institutional infrastructure
allows for more co-operative relationships between different parts of the
women's movement, and many organizations today have relatively good
working relations with the state. Nonetheless, these relations between the
women's movement and the state are highly volatile, and are strongly influenced by changes in government (Cabrera Perez-Armiñan 2009). The one
constant in how the Guatemalan government reacts to the organizations of
civil society since 1996 is its pragmatism. Government actions have, on the
one hand, been inspired by pressure from the international level, which in
some cases made aid dependent on the existence of coordinating bodies for
civil society, and on the other hand, by the domestic pressure that necessitated the collaboration with extra-governmental agencies, for service provision for example.

Concluding Remarks

Polletta (2008: 81) argues that 'along with political opportunities and mobilizing structures, a third component for movement emergence was [...] cognitive liberation'.[15] In Nicaragua and Guatemala, the armed conflict and subsequent political changes created these three conditions.

Both in Guatemala and Nicaragua the end of the armed conflict brought about profound political and economic changes which significantly shaped the evolution of the women's movement. Whereas the political change – the end of conflict and the installation for democratic regimes – created the conditions of freedom for women to organize, the economic changes had more complex effects on women's mobilization and can partially explain the modalities thereof. The foremost economic measure in the transition to neoliberal democracies in both countries was the elimination of several elements of social security. Some women's organizations reacted to this by engaging in service provision to fill the gap which was created by the withdrawal of the state. These are the organizations which still have cooperative relations with the state today in most cases. Other – feminist – groups reacted to this elimination of social security by engaging in protest politics. Especially in the Nicaraguan case, there is an explicit divide between these two types of women's initiatives.

Both groups have their origins in women's wartime mobilization, as well as having been triggered by the presence of international actors. This chapter explained how the different groups draw on these organizational roots by means of individual and organizational learning and adaptation, and how this has influenced the different narratives and priorities which occur.

In conclusion, in Nicaragua, the post-conflict women's movement emerged from a strong organizational base led by the Sandinista revolutionaries, which provided them with initial experiences. It is however breaking free of these initial forms of organization which shaped the women's movement in the post-conflict period. This period was characterized by difficult relations with the political establishment, as well as difficulties in creating and maintaining good working relations amongst the women's organizations themselves. In Guatemala, the revolutionary roots of the women's movement are more dispersed and less explicit than in the Nicaraguan case. This has allowed women's

---

15 The term cognitive liberation was first used by McAdam (1982: 34), who used it to refer to the fact that 'objective' opportunities for action only lead to action when potential protesters recognize these opportunities as such. He thereby brings a cognitive component and the importance of perception back into a framework of political opportunities.

initiatives to develop free from a vanguard party, and, in combination with international actors' broad attention to women's issues during the peace negotiations, this has allowed the Guatemalan women's movement to develop in a less polarized way. In the next chapters, I explore how this is manifested in the priorities and programs of the movements.

CHAPTER 3

Is There a Real Women's Movement? Cooperation, Fragmentation and Divisions in the Movement

As the previous chapters established, the Guatemalan and Nicaraguan women's movements are characterized by a substantial degree of fragmentation. This chapter explores the nature of this fragmentation and its effects on the potential for cooperation, for creating synergy and for establishing a collective identity. The second section of the chapter considers the dynamics which nourished this fragmentation.

Fragmentation: Diversification or Duplication?

In the constitutive phase of the women's movement, several factors – such as a high degree of dedication amongst the participants, newly opened political spaces, massive international aid, and growing awareness of women's issues – benefited the expansion of the women's movement. In parallel with this expansion, a process of differentiation took place. This section analyze how the process of differentiation affected the goals, identity and structure of the women's movement.

In both countries, what I call the women's movement is comprised of many individual organizations, each with their own specific goals and ideas. The organizations are often united by little more than the overall aim of improving women's situation. In the early 2010s, there is little clarity – also amongst women's organizations themselves – on the nature and extent of relations between these different organizations, and most deal with the issue of alliances on a day-to-day basis. The fact that there is little structural collaboration amongst actors of the movement means that alliances within the women's movement and between the women's movement and other social actors are unstable and hard to map. Moreover the mere existence of differences between organizations is invoked by some interviewees as a reason which impedes the formation of coalitions. Differentiation is thus impeding collaboration in some cases. As a member of a think tank for the decriminalization of therapeutic abortion expressed:

> It is very hard to coordinate between actors which see things differently, even if, in essence, they have the same goal. Organizations work

differently, have different priorities, different responsibilities towards
their followers and partners...Sometimes it's just easier to *go solo*.

BLANDÓN, 26 January 2011

In both Guatemala and Nicaragua, the way in which actors of the movement
are dealing with the process of differentiation is thus leading to divisions.
There are many overlapping dividing lines within the women's movement. My
interviews showed that, in the movement as a whole, women from many different layers of society and different backgrounds are represented, but that
within one organization, women often have similar socio-economic characteristics, and that the extent to which these women actually interact with one
another or join the same organizations is relatively limited. Feminist organizations active in the urban area for example mainly consist of educated middle-
class *ladina* women[1] with social networks and professional skills, often having
a leftist orientation. Women working in organizations in rural areas and those
fighting for practical gender needs on the other hand, oftentimes lack formal
education, yet have an impressive level of expertise and competence in their
field. Between both types of organizations, there is often little communication
or collaboration.

This lack of collaboration and interaction was for example illustrated by the
round table on femicide organized by the Latin American Faculty for Social
Sciences (FLACSO) in Guatemala City in the Spring of 2010. The topic of this
event, which concerns the lives of many women from all sectors of society,
only attracted five representatives of indigenous women's organizations, on a
total of one hundred to one hundred and fifty participants. Talks with both the
organizers and one of the participants from an indigenous women's organization afterwards showed two different realities. A member of the organizing
panel suggested that over time they have experienced many difficulties in
reaching indigenous women, because 'there is a tendency amongst these
women to withdraw to their own structures and facilities'. On the contrary, the
representative of an indigenous women's NGO confirmed that there is indeed
little participation of indigenous women in the mainstream structures of the
women's movement, but she attributed this lack of participation to the latent
'persistent discrimination' which still characterizes the interactions between
indigenous and non-indigenous women's groups. In this case, divisions on the

---

1   The word Ladino – not Latino – in Guatemala officially refers to a distinct ethnic group (MIN-
    EDUC 2008) However, in popular use, it refers to the non-indigenous population, and espe-
    cially mestizo people (mixed – European and native american – origin) from the middle class
    whose primary language is Spanish.

basis of class, geography, employment, ethnicity and education in practice overlap, and these divisions influence which women's organizations do, and do not, collaborate and interact with one another.

Acknowledging divisions, however, should not lead one to overlook the fact that there have also been numerous efforts to coordinate actions. Three examples deserve specific attention here. One group that was particularly pertinent in both countries in bringing together different actors, was the 'Beijing committee'. This group arose in 1994 as a platform to support the participation and action of women's groups in the IV World Conference of Women. It managed to create a strong negotiating position precisely because it was specifically created for developing dialogue within the movement and between the movement on the one hand and the state, international actors and other sectors of society on the other hand. Herewith, the committee was the first group which had the installation of dialogue between these actors as a priority.

A second successful initiative at coordination was the institutionalized dialogue between the leaders of the movement and the leaders of the main political parties in Nicaragua since October 1995. This dialogue led to the formation of the National Women's Coalition, which established the framework for an 'Agenda Minima' between party leaders from the left, right and centre, and the women's movement. The priorities of the Agenda were the guarantee of women's human rights as political, economic, civilian, cultural and social rights, exercised both individually and collectively (Coalición Nacional de Mujeres 1996, Metoyer 2000: 103).

A third successful attempt at cooperation is the "Red de la No Violencia" in Guatemala. This is a platform with a permanent character which is aimed at coordination of actors and actions in the domain of gender-based violence. In addition, the Guatemalan 'Sector de Mujeres' is a platform in which many actors from civil society find each other, and which managed to maintain good contacts with state institutions, despite its explicitly feminist position. In this way, the Sector was able to press for legislative changes, such as the adoption of the Law on the Granting of Dignity to and Integral Advancement of Women, the Law on the Prevention, Sanctioning and Eradication of Domestic Violence, the Law on Social Development, the National Policy for the Advancement and Development of Women and the Plan for Equal Opportunities (PNPDMG and PEO), as well as the establishment of several institutions for the advancement of women at the state level, such as the Advocacy of the Indigenous Woman (DEMI), the President's Office for Women (SEPREM), the National Commission for the Prevention of Domestic Violence (CONAPREVI), and the Women's Office of the Legal Office for Human Rights. The Sector was weakened though due to internal struggles, over the issue of official delegates (anonymous interviewee, June 2010).

These instances of coordination are rather exceptional however. Overall, structural coordination and collaboration is limited, and the general tendency is for coordination to happen on a more *ad hoc* basis, if at all. On the one hand, this has the advantage that meetings are organized only when this is required, which is potentially more efficient. On the other hand, this does not create the climate for stable long-term working relationships.

Effects of Fragmentation and Divisions within the Movement

Today the women's movement in both countries is characterized by its multiplicity of organizations which have shown strong overlaps in terms of organizational format and demands. As such, fragmentation is not problematic and might even be constructive. However, when looking at how this plays out in practice, we see that the nature of the fragmentation, and the way this is dealt with has had many negative effects in Guatemala and Nicaragua. This section pays special attention to the effects in terms of alliance politics, duplication of efforts, downward accountability and identity formation.

Politics of Alliance
Divisions within a movement can hamper the building of alliances and good working relations, both within the movement, as with policy-makers and external audiences (Bernstein 2008, Della Porta 2006). In these cases, this kept the movements from efficiently lobbying the national political system or international organizations as one force. This was exemplified in Nicaragua, in the run-up to the law on the recognition and penalization of domestic violence. The fragmentation hampered coordinated action and limited the potential of the movement to make a strong political statement and influence politics in a structural way. The level of disunity and infighting that emerged in a highly inclusive attempt at writing recommendations, meant that the movement was unable to agree on a common document until six days before the vote on the law. At this point, there was no time to get the main political parties on board, and the movement did not have a strong voice in the eventual formulation of the law (Peetz 2008: 17). Examples like these also exist for the Guatemalan case, where, many round tables are organized, but as one interviewee from a smaller NGO indicated "in the end it's only the SEPREM and the organizations which have direct affiliations with the government which are listened to. This is something which we overlook all too often".

(Galvez, legal unit GGM, 12 February 2011). This suggests that divisions even allow governmental actors to pit the interests of one organization against another.

The absence of structural alliances also poses a problem when aiming to alter societal values surrounding the position of women. Participatory observation suggests that the credibility and potential for action of women's organizations is challenged by the fact that they are *de facto* divided amongst themselves and fail to speak with one voice. As a local community leader in Mozonte, Nicaragua, commented on the existence of gender-related workshops:

> There are so many of them. They come, they talk, and they leave. They always leave as soon as the workshop is finished. They get a nice grant for the travel here, but the ladies in Managua, they don't know anything about how life is here. They do know it's different, but they talk to us as if that weren't the case. They ignore work which we, or other women's organizations, have been doing here.
>
> CONSUELO, Council of Indigenous People, 26 April 2010

Whether or not the criticism of the interviewee is justified, is secondary to the fact that it expresses a general sentiment, heard in different regions away from the capital. The criticism is that the feminist section of the women's movement is only a small section of women who are there to self-sustain, and who are out of touch with the majority of women and women's organizations. These proposals for change are not per se widely shared. Yet, to embark on this process of societal transformation, an actor would be needed who can press for these changes with one voice and a broad basis of support (see Pizzorno 1986: 362).

Duplication of Efforts and Lack of Synergy

Divisions and fragmentation also restricted the movement in the sense of there being no effort to map and systematize projects which could serve as a basis for inter-organizational learning and replication. This in turn fostered the emergence of groups and organizations doing the same work. As a consequence, organizations with similar objectives sometimes find themselves competing for the same resources, rather than collaborating. An example of this type of duplication is the Guatemalan law on the prevention, sanctioning and eradication of domestic violence (*Ley para prevenir, sancionar y erradicar la violencia intrafamiliar*). I found seven different – high gloss paper – folders explaining this law, issued by seven different women's organizations. All printed their logo in a most visible place on the first page (in four cases the logo was in a bigger font than the name of the law). This was illustrative of the urge of these organizations to affirm and make visible their own accomplishments towards donors, rather than working together in a systematic way in order to set up more encompassing campaigns. Another example of the lack of collaboration is the document 'Mapeo de las Organizaciones de la Sociedad Civil en el Tema Violencia Contra les Mujeres en Guatemala' (Cabrera 2009). This is a listing of all organizations in the field of violence against women, which could serve as a resource and a tool to find women's organizations working on similar issues. When asking interviewees if they knew this document or worked with it however, nobody answered affirmatively. This hints at how little potential there is in establishing alliances within the movement. This lack of interest in collaborating, also means that actions proposed during round tables often receive little follow-up. During a high-key conference of the National Coordinating Agency for the Prevention of Domestic Violence and Violence against Women (CONAPREVI, 27 May 2010), several actions in the field of violence prevention were proposed and agreed upon. In February 2011, I asked several interviewees which elements of this conference had influenced their strategy and priorities in the past eight months. Only one interviewee from the legal unit of GGM affirmed that there had been a direct link between this conference and the current approach of GGM to femicide:

> We [the two women of GGM who participated in the conference] have organized a small workshop in the office to share what we had learnt. And we have also used the documents and advice given during the conference when determining our own strategy for 2011, especially with regards to our actions on the prevention of femicide .
>
> SAY, GGM, 8 February 2011

This was the only organization working with the conclusions of this critical event. In general, when I asked questions about how the movement functioned as a whole and how much collaboration there was between the different actors, answers suggested substantial degrees of collaboration and coordination, but to concrete questions like the ones about the incorporation of the CONAPREVI conclusions, interviewees would often mention a set of factors – outside of their own realm of responsibility – which explained the lack of coordination in the movement. That the actual amount of cooperation was lower than remarks about this would suggest at face value, also showed when asking about this indirectly. When questions about external donors and political parties came up, – and interviewees were no longer explicitly asked about the internal dynamics of the movement – they would, for example, indicate that the policies of donors had a deeply dividing influence. Norma Cruz, founder of Sobrevivientes, for example, replied to the question about divisions in the movement that "there are of course differences between different organizations, but we are building bridges, and most women's organizations today have good working relations with one another". Later in the interview, when asked about the impact of donors on the programs of women's organizations, she argued, "It is hard to collaborate with organizations who advocate abortion if your main donor is a US-based pro-life organization. It is hard to lobby for the right for women to divorce, if your donor is a conservative catholic organization. [...] So we turn to organizations which have the same vision as we do". (7 June 2010). This illustrates the inconsistence between how activists describe their engagement with other organizations, and that this actually looks in daily life.

This is also illustrated by the case of AMNLAE, a heavily funded Nicaraguan women's organization supported by the FSLN. Because of its size and influence, it could very well facilitate capacity flows. What we see instead though, is that AMNLAE entirely withdraws to its own structures and is very reluctant to enter into debates or information exchanges with any non-FSLN-affiliated agents. This is also the case with other FSLN-related women's institutions, such as the *Comisaria para la mujer y la niñez*, which has vast statistical resources, but does not share these with non-FSLN-affiliated organizations. The same logic holds for anti-FSLN women's organizations. These organizations have adopted defensives strategies and also shield off their own information from organizations affiliated with the FSLN, thereby also *de facto* blocking any information exchange. This is the case with the Autonomous Women's Movement MAM for example, which only shares information with a limited number of partners since its offices have been invaded by the national police in 2010. So in this case as well, synergy is not being created.

Downward Accountability

The fragmentation of the movement also negatively affects its accountability. As Killby (2006: 951) argues, "the accountability of NGOs, particularly their 'downward' accountability to their beneficiaries, affects NGO effectiveness in the process of empowerment". The fragmentation challenges this downward accountability because it challenges the consistency and coherence of different programs and renders the movement unsurveyable for its audience and for society at large.

This does not mean that the movement lacks agency overall, but it suggests that the relationships between the women's movement, its audience and international actors continues to be strained in the early 2010s. In the words of Olga, a Nicaraguan activist in Rivas, today the movement finds itself in a dynamic of "responding to the needs of the international donors, not to the needs of local women; of professionalizing and developing legal personality instead of focusing on its target audience" (García, 19 April 2010). Already in 2002, members of the Nicaraguan women workers' organization MEC lamented that "no one wants to do grassroots work anymore" (cited in Bickham-Mendez 2002: 208). This move away from the target group and towards the donors, is also visible in geographical terms, with the vast majority of women's organizations having their main office in the capital rather than in the municipalities they serve (Aguilar 1997: 112). This is surprising because, as Aguilar showed in 1997, most of their target group – as well as most of the women who are organized (as widows, agricultural workers, *maquila* workers, etc) – is based in the rural areas. However, the organizations that have been most successful in obtaining funding are precisely those which are located in the capital and prioritize work at the policy level (Lemus, member GGM, 5 May 2010; Meneses, member RMCV, 19 April 2010; Aguilar, founder Q'anil, 4 February 2011)

As Montenegro (1997) underlines, systems aimed at increasing involvement and accountability should start from the bottom-up, namely with efforts to include women in the decision-making process of the organization itself. However, very few of the organizations which I analyzed have formal structures to encourage participation in their own proceedings. Those organizations which do, would usually give women – both staff and target group – the possibility to leave a written suggestion in a box. These suggestions were then discussed during staff meetings. Even this system was not widespread and had limitations, since it excludes illiterate women, and leaves women without agency after they posted their suggestion.

Another strategy to increase women's participation and thus to stimulate downward accountability is the implementation of training and workshops to prepare women for a position within formal political decision-making structures at the national and local level. Several of these programs were also permeated with contradictions however. One program organized by the National Union of Guatemalan Women (UNAMG) in 1995 for example – in which women were trained for participation in local and national politics – found itself in a difficult position when one of the women who had participated in it, eventually decided to join a different party than the one which the UNAMG supported. This resulted in the dismissal of this person from further participation in the program (Desgranges, member UNAMG, 12 May 2010).

A more successful example of increasing women's involvement and strengthening downward accountability is the program which Ixchen, a Nicaraguan centre for the promotion of women's health and development, launched in 2008. This program envisioned open decision-making systems and the participation of women in their own organizational functioning (Cubillo Rivas, IXCHEN, 24 April 2010). This program is still in place, and is set up as a series of workshops to train women to become community leaders themselves, and to act as advocates for their own rights and for change. In this program, women decide on the direction and the content of the workshops. The argument is that this is empowering for these women themselves, but also serves the overall aims of the organization because these women are more credible when they go to the communities to lead workshops, because they come from the grassroots themselves.

This approach is gaining popularity, and falls under what Snow et al (1986) call the 'processes of frame alignment'.[2] Frame alignment refers to "the linkage of individual and SMO [social movement organizations] interpretive orientations, such that some set of individual interests, values and beliefs and SMO activities, goals, and ideology become congruent and complementary" (Snow et al 1986: 464). Attempts to link individual, organizational and societal frames are a key component of social transformation (Snow and Benford, 1988). Aligning frames, according to this theory, is therefore a precondition for participation of women, no matter the nature or intensity of the alignment. This approach can thus be said to have a democratizing influence, both on women's daily lives as on the structure of the women's movement.

Frame alignment is hindered by the fact that the women served by the organizations are increasingly poor, whereas the movement itself is largely made up of middle class women. Divisions present in society are thus being replicated in the movement. According to one interviewee:

> This growing division [between the movement and its target group] is more important than any other internal division within the movement. The tensions amongst organizations will never affect their work as much as the growing tension between the organization and its audience; because, whereas the former merely affects what an organization does, the latter affects whether it can at all reach its audience.
>
> LEMUS, legal officer GGM, 2 June 2010

Accountability is also challenged by the fact that leadership was often governed by personality politics. With three exceptions, none of my interviewees

---

2 The term 'frame' refers here to the schemata of interpretation that enable an individual to locate, perceive, identify and label occurrences in their life space and the world at large. They thus organize the experiences of the individual and guide action (Goffman 1974: 21).

indicated that they were aware of a formal regulation on how the leader of their organization could be impeached or challenged.[3] These issues were dealt with on a day-to-day basis according to the interviewees. As Say, junior legal officer at GGM mentioned, "I never had a problem with [name superior]. If I were to, I think I'd ask others in the office what to do. I don't know. It'd be awkward" (8 February 2011). The fact that the staff of several organizations are unaware of how to hold their leaders responsible opens the door to the concentration of executive power in the hands of some.

In the next section, I show how the historical, social and political context of the women's movement in Guatemala and Nicaragua, has rendered autonomy and professionalization two of the most salient values. This in turn challenged openness and transparency at an organizational level for most organizations. In almost all the interviews with women working in women's organizations, questions about accountability were interpreted by the interviewee as accountability towards the donors, only few answered questions about accountability with reference to their target group when not specifically asked about this.[4]

The Formation of a Collective Identity

Divisions within the movement have challenged an overall feeling of commonality and a sense of a shared identity. I do not wish to use the concept of collective identity in a post-modernist way requiring 'deep identification' (Munkres 2008: 190), but rather in a more utilitarian way to refer to a resource which social movements can use to recruit and sustain members and to maintain the movement in difficult times (Rupp and Taylor 1999: 381, Della Porta and Diani 2006, Laraña et al 1994, Polletta and Jasper 2001, Reger et al 2008). In this view, the lack of a collective identity can be interpreted as the absence of a resource for collective action. Therefore, the step of carving out a niche for oneself, establishing well-defined and coherent objectives and a clearly marked identity, are crucial steps for any social organization to ensure efficiency and avoid protracted disagreements over strategies and goals (Escobar and Alvarez 1992: 147, Laraña et al 1994: 20).[5] Diverse socio-economic issues which women's

---

3 Note that this does not mean that such a policy did not exist. My question was about whether my interviewees knew about such a procedure.

4 Exceptions are Aguilar, founder of Q'anil (4 February 2011) and Álvarez, member of Kaqla (14 February 2011).

5 It should be noted though that developing such a base of commonness is not the same as installing a common ideological commitment, which would preclude diverse opinions from being expressed (Polletta and Jasper 2001: 296). For a more critical view on the role of collective identity in social movements, see Hercus 1999, McDonald 2002 and Lichterman 1996: 17,

organizations faced in their initial years however, meant that the search for a collective identity and other elements of commonality was not high on the priority list of many women's organizations in the early 1990. Soon however, feminist organizations came to see the necessity of speaking with one voice. They organized round tables, conferences and communiqués in an attempt to formulate a collective identity and present themselves as a cohesive entity, especially *vis-à-vis* society. This tendency can however not be witnessed for the women's movement as a whole, where there is often a degree of reluctance towards the concept of a shared identity, because there is often very little which unites the different actors of the movement.

The fact that the movement has not constructed a collective identity for itself is thus related to the fact that there is little clarity amongst the different women's organizations as to whether or not this would at all be desirable, and what the characteristics of that identity should then be. This means that the concept which I refer to as 'the women's movement' is in fact a place for the confluence of multiple identities, organizations and programs.

In theory, such a confluence can advance the formulation of diverse strategies and goals to address women's interests, protect them from incorporation in mainstream politics and avoid the colonizing effects which a collective identity can potentially have (Holland 2008, McDonald 2002, Hercus 1999). It is thus not the issue of diversification, or even fragmentation, as such which is potentially problematic. A lack of fragmentation can even be problematic for dissident voices within the movement. Many – and maybe most – social movements show a certain degree of fragmentation. In various contexts, there are also examples of feminist movements adopting a strategy of ideological and organizational fragmentation precisely to manage dissidence and become more effective (see for example Armstrong 2002: 64). In these cases however, social movement structures tend to be identified by *fluidarity* or hybrid identities, i.e. the capacity of an organization to work without a rigidly defined identity to pursue its organizational goals and the possibility to shape-shift to adapt to the context and maintain oneself in different environments (McDonald 2002: 119). What we find in Guatemala and Nicaragua on the contrary is not a case of deliberate *fluidarity* or *structurelessness*[6] as advocated for example by early North American anti-organizational feminists but rather a situation of polarization and division. In the next section, I explore which factors explain this development.

---

who see collective identity as a mode of social control and a paradigm of social relationships which limits the choices of social movements and curbs dissident voices.

6 For a discussion, see Freeman 1972.

Causes of Fragmentation

Four dynamics – all related to the aftermath of the armed conflict – are particularly relevant to explain the growing divisions within the women's movement: autonomy-seeking behavior, the deepening of political and religious cleavages, the role of feminism, and the NGOization of the movement.

Autonomy-Seeking: Sensible Calculation or a Divisive Strategy?
The struggle for autonomy has defined the movement since its emergence, and is becoming more important since the mid-2000s, especially in Nicaragua. It is a multi-faceted struggle, waged on several fronts. Activists emphasize the importance of autonomy of each organization within the movement as well as the importance of autonomy of the movement from the political system (For example Morales, member Tierra Viva, 1 June 2010, Torres, president Colectivo 8 de Marzo, 21 April 2010). This autonomy from the political system refers to the potential of women's organizations to define their own programs, have control over their own budgets, and minimize political interference in their proceedings. This is one of the most salient, and at the same time most problematic, postulates of the women's movement, because the dynamic of this relation is unpredictable and partially out of their own control.

The debate of autonomy can be framed in the 'autonomy vs. integration' debate. This debate asks whether the best strategy for women's organizations is to challenge and denounce the current socio-political system, or to try to change things from the inside, by participating in governmental bodies in the field of women's rights. The debate has become increasingly divisive, especially in Nicaragua, where many female activists have chosen a strategy of *double militancy*. These activists have decided to be active in the women's movement, as well as being active in political parties or the state institutions in order to protect themselves from collisions with the state. Yet others joined oppositional political parties next to their membership of women's organizations. As Cubillo Rivas, legal officer at IXCHEN (24 April 2010), stated:

> The incorporation of women's activists into the state machinery was one of the factors feeding the perception of others that our autonomy had to be protected from state interference. [...] Yet, also amongst feminist leaders, there are divergent opinions, with some leaders being radical anti-party and anti-government, and others joining parties like the MRS or advocating an all-women's party to press politics.

In Nicaragua the issue of autonomy from the state is particularly pertinent due to reasons related to the armed conflict. The position of AMNLAE – the first mass women's organization – is illustrative here. Progressive voices in the women's movement claim that AMNLAE did not adequately reflect the needs of women because it did not have much autonomy to create an identity for itself independently from the FSLN. Women opposing this situation established new women's organizations (such as IXCHEN, Maria Elena Cuadra and the Autonomous Women's Movement) in the early 1990s, which explicitly declared their ideological, financial, political and organizational autonomy from the centralized organizations of the FSLN. They created new organizational spaces for women which were not embedded in, or linked to, the party structures, and which saw autonomy as one of the highest values of their mobilization (Aguilar 1997).

The apprehension of these new women's organizations at being controlled once again by a vanguard organization, combined with the fact that autonomy tends to be defined as the absence of central coordination, meant that attempts at coordination often met with great resistance. This was reinforced by the fact that members of these newly emerging organizations believed autonomy to be more vital for women's organizations than for other organizations of civil society, given the history of female mobilization and the context of hegemonic masculinity (García, feminist activist, 19 April 2010). Yet, at the same time, concerns about efficiency did inspire the installation of some forms of coordination in the mid-1990s. Most of these networks for cooperation had been disbanded by the early 2010s however. In Nicaragua, only the networks on violence and on health are still active. This has arguably left the women's movement as a whole in a weakened position. In 1998, for example, meetings between diverse women's organizations were arranged to discuss the creation of the National Institute for Women (INIM). During these meetings several agreements were reached on coordinated action regarding the Congress. However, these agreements were not respected and everyone of the organizations in the end went their own way, meaning that no strong unified voice from the side of the women's movement was heard in Congress (Castro, member of the feminist Grupo Venancia, 2 March 2011).

Efforts to avoid central coordination have however not always served the goal of bringing about operational and organizational autonomy. Many interviewees indicate that they still experience a deficit of autonomy, in the sense that "Most women's organizations are dependent on external actors, not just for funding, but often also for logistical reasons" (Desgranges, coordinator at UNAMG, 12 May 2010).

The Guatemalan case shows parallels with the Nicaraguan case, with the first women's organizations also being created at the grace of groups whose political project had little affinity with women's issues or feminism. Facing a repressive and authoritarian political regime, the importance of establishing one's autonomy was maybe even more primordial to Guatemalan women's organizations than it was to Nicaraguan ones. As one interviewee who fought in the URNG guerrilla army in the 1980s stated, "we were used to do things on our own, with as little interference and publicity as possible. Being independent, being invisible, in those days was a way to survive" (Ramirez, 22 May 2010). The learning theories in the previous chapter help to explain how this experience of operating in a clandestine way impacted on the Guatemalan women's organizations and affected their attitude towards authority and coordination, both within the movement and towards government.

Autonomy-seeking behavior thus has its roots in the armed conflict, but also relations with the international donor community have played a role. The financial prominence of external funding agencies created a sensation of unequal relations, which triggered coping mechanisms. Interviewees in Guatemala and Nicaragua indicated that communication with donors is often limited, and mainly takes place by means of exchanging formal reports and requests (e.g. Espinoza, legal officer Ixchen, 3 May 2010; Valenzuela, director CICAM, 3 June 2010; Meneses, coordinator RMCV, 19 April 2010). Four interviewees acknowledged that they omitted from these reports those actions which they knew the donors would not support, or areas in which they had not reached their objectives. One Guatemalan activist at CODEFEM noted:

> Why talk about donors so much? They are important in financial terms, but they're not here in the field. They don't know what we do day-to-day really. What they have is the report, and, well...What I mean is that they sometimes ask us to do this or that, which we find irrelevant, but which we have to accept to get the funds, you see, and it's not as if we can just tell them they are wrong...Don't bite the hand that feeds you.
>
> FERRÍN, 10 June 2010

This shows how eager women's organizations are to preserve their autonomy, also towards donors, even if this means engaging in biased communication and partial interactions. In summary, the armed conflict, the consequent presence of international donors and current political developments, installed a desire for autonomy. This desire is divisive in these two countries because, as interviews suggest, today, autonomy is often declared rather than negotiated in relation with others, and it used as a synonym of organizational individualism, in which every organization pursues its own goals.

The Influence of Political Ideology and Religion

Autonomy-maximizing behavior is not the only cause of fragmentation. Incompatible ideological stances of the different women's organizations also constitute an obstacle for coordination between different organizations. By ideology, I mean a system of abstract ideas about how the politics in a society should be conducted (Duncker 2006). These ideologies provide a justification for social change, can motivate people for action, and can establish a framework to connect people who envision the same changes (Ferree and Miller 1985). Ideology thus provides the rationale for how people act and is a crucial element of social mobilization (Ryan 1992: 60).

In Guatemala and Nicaragua, ideology, religion and party politics played a particularly important role in structuring the women's movement. This means that also the polarization of the political landscape was reflected in the structure of the women's movement. Also religion strongly influenced the development of the women's movement, as it joined forces with political parties. This is true for both cases, but most prominent – and divisive – in Nicaragua since the late 2000s.

Most Nicaraguan activists whom I interviewed would express a positive or negative opinion on a certain project or organization based on the ideological position of that organization, rather than referring to the actual content the program in their argumentation. In practice, this meant a pro-FSLN or contra-FSLN position. Very few interviewees had an intermediate position. As one staff member of a Nicaraguan feminist organization commented on the functioning of another – pro-FSLN – rural women's organization, which engaged in essentially the same activities:

> It's just no good how they do it. I wouldn't know how to explain you in words, but if you're here, you feel it. There is us, and how we do things, and there is them and how they do things. And it's not compatible.
> ANONYMOUS, 2010

Interviewees of women's organizations affiliated with the governing party FSLN, such as AMNLAE, would generally not explicitly express a negative opinion on organizations which were known to be anti-FSLN. During interviews, they never explicitly named groups which they did not collaborate with, and refrained from expressing a negative opinion about them when explicitly asked about their relationship with these groups. As Alfaro, first secretary of AMNLAE, commented, "We are willing to collaborate with any organization which envisions the betterment of women's daily lives" (30 April 2010). At the same time, this should not be taken at face value as an indication that AMNLAE is indeed willing to collaborate with all women's organizations. On the contrary, in the current political regime, marked by an increasingly conservative and anti-feminist atmosphere, FSLN-affiliated organizations are pressured to follow the party line. This prevents collaboration with social organizations of a different ideology.

In the run-up to the 2011 elections, political polarization peaked. This was also reflected in the women's movement. During interviews conducted in this period, women's organizations would often deny the achievements of their counterparts with a different ideology, to the extent of even denying their existence. When asking my interviewee from the pro-FSLN Casa de la Mujer in Granada about the organizations they collaborated with, the reply was, "we have no organizations with whom we collaborate in Granada, since we are the only women's organization in town providing practical assistance to women, but we do have several partners in the capital". (Astorga, 22 March 2011). This statement ignores and denies the existence of three anti-FSLN women's organizations with similar goals located in the same part of the town.

The bulk of Nicaraguan civil society organizations however are anti-FSLN, and contrary to the pro-FSLN organizations, most interviewees of these organizations indicated explicitly that they do not work together with FSLN-affiliated organizations, mainly because they disapprove of the FSLN's authoritarian governing style and anti-feminist program. As Jiménez, member of the Autonomous Women's Movement MAM expressed "In which way – and more importantly, why? – would we collaborate with them? We have been boycotted, threatened and even attacked. I, for one, cannot imagine how this climate of fear which they installed could ever be undone". (13 April 2010). Because they make this position explicit, there is no confusion over their politics of alliances.

The divisive influence of political ideology in Nicaragua is increasingly bound up with the role of religion as a divisive factor. Conservative sectors of the catholic church strongly supported and influenced the electoral campaign of the FSLN in 2006 and 2011 (Kampwirth 2011, Destrooper 2012). The recent alliance between the FSLN and conservative catholicism means that the political establishment is becoming increasingly unaccommodating towards progressive feminist demands which are not in line with conservative catholicism. This helps to explain the widening rift between feminists and the government in general, but also between feminist organizations and FSLN-affiliated women's organizations. Moreover, the growing importance of conservative catholicism, shapes the cultural frames of ordinary women. The castigation of certain topics – such as sexuality, the body or intimate relations – means that the public debate on these topics is becoming increasingly difficult, and that these topics become or remain taboo. This implies that there is a growing incoherence between the frames used by progressive feminists and those frames determining the lives of ordinary women. As one feminist activist from Nicaragua asserted, "Whereas we used to just fight against traditions [in terms of gender roles and relations], now we also have to fight against people who are trying really hard to actively bolster up these traditions, and to get an ever firmer grip on the lives of women" (Montenegro, MAM/CINCO, 2 May 2010).

Political and religious divisions are present in both cases in the early 2010s, but are more pertinent in Nicaragua, where conservative catholicism has actively established alliances with the FSLN, thereby complementing existing political divisions with a religious dimension. In Nicaragua, very few organizations do not take a position pro or contra-FSLN, and those who do, find themselves in a deadlock when it comes to cooperating across the divide on practical projects. This is related to the fact that Nicaraguan women's organizations have, from the 1980s onward, been intimately bound up with the vanguard party. Relations between organizations with different ideological positions remain tense and heavily susceptible to party political dynamics due to this history of origin.

In Guatemala, ideological polarization is not as pertinent on the political level, and is thus not as prominent in the women's movement. In fact, political restructuring has influenced the women's movement 'to turn from protest politics to policy work' around the turn of the century. This meant formulating more conciliatory proposals, which do not seek confrontation *per se* (Berger 2006:2). In this sense political ideologies are less divisive within the Guatemalan movement in the last decade. Furthermore, also religious divisions are of another nature, and are not so much related to the role of conservative catholicism, but rather to the existence of indigenous belief systems. This is the focus of the second part of the book.

Feminism: A Basis for Progressive Action or Deepening Divides?

The ideological divides discussed in the previous section, are not limited to party politics and religion. Feminism, as an ideological frame, also constitutes a particularly divisive issue in both countries. All the activists whom I interviewed saw themselves as members of a women's movement,[7] but not all these women saw themselves as feminists, or as belonging to a feminist movement.[8] This means that not all women's organizations support a project of political and societal transformation to tackle the roots of gender-based oppression. In Guatemala and Nicaragua feminism as a system of thought, thus draws a line, and often creates rancor, between those organizations interested in alleviating practical gender needs and those which work in the domain of strategic gender needs. Aguilar (1997: 14) argues that the main tensions between these two groups are based on prejudices about one another and on the myth of what feminism is: a current which "only seeks confrontation with men and existing political structures, without offering a solution for the daily problems of women" (Alfaro, AMNLAE, 30 April 2010). This denial and neglect of the actual contributions of feminism casts a negative light on feminism and discourages some women from self-identifying as feminists while in fact their discourse and praxis are feminist, Aguilar (1997: 14) argues. This is illustrated by the fact that during the interviews, women who answered negatively to the question whether they saw themselves and their organization as feminist, often explained this by saying that they did not want to call themselves feminist because "the movement ought to pursue a strategy of collaboration instead" (Espinoza, legal officer IXCHEN, 3 May 2010).

Also, amongst indigenous women's groups there is a reluctance to subscribe to the idea of feminism, because the subordination of indigenous women is assessed as something at the crossroads of different societal dynamics. As one interviewee from the Guatemalan Council of Mayan Women (CMMG) indicated:

> Feminists have contributed in an important way to the development of the women's movement. However we cannot call ourselves feminists because we differ in one crucial aspect, namely that we seek the roots of our oppression elsewhere: as being imposed by the colonists onto us as indigenous people.
>
> CASAGRANDE, 23 May 2010

---

7 The conceptualization of what the women's movement is, differed greatly amongst interviewees however.

8 Also amongst those self-identifying as feminists, there are different opinions on the causes, consequences and solutions to the subordination of women, depending on the strand of feminism which is adhered to. I do not go into detail about this, since these differences are subordinate to the opposition between those self-identifying as feminists and those not doing so, and since women themselves do not often make this explicit.

Despite the controversial and divisive position of feminism in both countries, initiatives which promote a better understanding of feminism are gaining ground since the early 2000s. In Guatemala, two organizations have made a significant contribution to the promotion of feminist theory as a guide for practical action: the Coincidencia de Mujeres, which actively aims to break prejudices, and Tierra Viva, which aims to translate the theoretical premises of feminism to women's daily lives. From the beginning in 1989, the goal of Tierra Viva was "to promote a form of feminism which was useful for the popular sections of the movement and to install a debate on the usefulness of feminism for the local context" (Morales, 1 June 2010). The idea was thus to adapt feminist premises to the necessities of Guatemalan society, with all its complexities, and to avoid feminism from becoming a divisive issue. Yet, as Morales, president of Tierra Viva, explains:

> If we would have only pursued the conceptualization of a feminist position which appealed to the intellectual elite, we wouldn't have encountered major problems with the traditional women's organizations. It's because we aimed to translate the feminist premises to the lives of women here, that we have this confrontation which we have now, not just on an institutional level, but also on a personal level, with other women who do not support this view of which causes underlie the oppression of every woman. They take issue with our message because we are bringing a coherent story about how to change women's situation [...] We are seen as competitors in a small market.
>
> MORALES, 1 June 2010

The interview with Evelyn Morales illustrates the extent to which feminism is a divisive issue and what the practical consequences are of such a situation. Specifically, she mentioned the organization of two different protest marches on the issue of women's rights on the same day in spring 2010, one by feminist organizations, one by non-feminist women's organizations. "Women were demonstrating in different parts of town for the same issue, hardly greeting each other on busses. Quite sad". A second example she mentioned were the lobbying activities and awareness-raising campaigns going in different directions:

> In February [2011] we visited one of the *basureros*[9] near the capital. The plan was to see if we could find support for a project which would

---

9 A *basurero* is a garbage dump, on – and around – which people established small communities.

guarantee that a woman who is abused by her husband and asks for a divorce, can stay in her house, the abusive husband leaving. However, we heard that a couple of months earlier, another [Christian] organization had come in with a project envisioning that the couple would stay in the house together and that a reconciliation program would be set up for them. That's where we ended our intervention, but all too often communities experience a see-saw effect between one extreme and the other. In this case for example, many organizations would chose to implement their program anyway, even if it contradicted the support structures which another women's organization had just set up months before.

MORALES, 1 June 2010

These were two of the most significant instances in which the division between feminist organizations and non-feminist/anti-feminist organizations created duplication rather than synergy.

These divisions play out similarly in Nicaragua. In Nicaragua, Women Worker's Organization Maria Elena Cuadra (MEC) and the Autonomous Women's Movement (MAM) are the two organizations which have heavily influenced the debate over feminism since the mid-1990s. MEC was formed as an autonomous and feminist organization in 1994. Unlike the MAM, and despite its feminist program, MEC managed to maintain good working relations with several state agencies, which were becoming increasingly patriarchal. This is mainly thanks to the nature of the work of MEC, which has a strong focus on improving the labour force, and thus supports the national economic development. This focus makes it an important partner for government. In this way MEC has been able to secure a platform in parliament at times when legal changes to the labour code which would affect women, were discussed. MEC has been a partner in consultation processes with women of different sectors, meaning they could identify voids in the labour code and provide feedback about this in their negotiations with state bodies (Dalton 2007: 34). In this manner, they have managed to maintain a position between government and citizens. One example in which MEC managed to use this advantage to promote feminist thinking, in an environment which on average was rather hostile to feminist ideas, was during their involvement in the National Commission for Salaries, under the Ministry of Employment. In these negotiations they participated as a partner with a voice, albeit no formal vote (Dalton 2007: 14).

In both countries, the influence of the 'mujeres intelectuales' on the feminist debate should also be acknowledged. These women, such as Irmalicia Velazquez (Guatemala) and Sofia Montenegro (Nicaragua), participate on an individual basis, or through their work in academia, international organizations, state bodies (such as the Attorney's Office for Human Rights in Nicaragua and the National Women's Office in Guatemala) and NGOs. They have a decisive voice in the debate since they are the driving force behind many conferences and round tables, have media access and, on average, have good relationships with the international donor community. However, these women often share certain social characteristics, such as having enjoyed a formal education, coming from the middle class and having a paid professional occupation, which means that they are not per se representative of the women whom they claim to defend. Hence, the fact that it is precisely these women who steer the debate on feminism, rather than those feminists who are active in rural areas, means that the dominant conceptualization of feminism often meets with much resistance from large sections of the women's movement and even from feminists in rural areas. It also means that there is a growing inconsistency between the feminist programs advocated by progressive and influential members of the movement and the daily realities and beliefs of many people. This daily reality in many cases is heavily colored by the influence of conservative parts of the Catholic church which rejects progressive feminist ideas, for example about divorce in case of domestic violence. In a reaction to this trend towards conservatism, feminists have started to defend their position even more fiercely, meaning that compromises are increasingly difficult to find. Most feminist activists, refer to this situation to explain why a constructive debate with non-feminists is not possible.

Feminism, as an ideological position, has thus further nourished existing divisions in the movement. It has however also been an incentive for some structural attempts at coordination among the feminist current of the movement itself. In both countries, feminist organizations are increasingly finding each other and organizing themselves in feminist spaces for coordination, meaning that they have come to form a sub-movement of the larger women's movement, which is more coherent in terms of ideas and praxis. However, the feminist current as well is dealing with issues of identity, autonomy and fragmentation within its own ranks, as well as facing tenuous relationships with other parts of the women's movement and with government. Disputes over key convictions between the feminist current and the other organizations are increasingly overriding common practical concerns. While this is seen in many social and women's movements (Ryan 1992: 61), the way in which this division is dealt with in these two cases is becoming increasingly problematic, since ideological differences are being used as a factor by which to judge other actors in the field, rather than as a means to construct one's own identity. This is potentially immobilizing and polarizing.

"NGOization": Professionalization and Projectization

The tendency towards professionalization and institutionalization is both a cause and a consequence of divisions within the women's movement. Like the previous three factors, this factor too is related to the legacy of armed conflict, the presence of international organizations and the political-economic crisis of the 1990s. The previous chapter laid out how entering into relations and negotiations with international benefactors – indirectly – triggered certain organizational choices (Hulme and Edwards 1997: 8). For example, while Nicaraguan 'feminist organizations are diverse in their objectives, size and operating style, the movement is composed largely of NGOs run by paid professionals, and offering services and advocacy, as opposed to membership-based organizations, grassroots communities or neighborhood organizations' (Ewig 1999: 78, also see Cabrera 2009). The long-term effects of this pragmatic learning have been substantial in organizational terms. As Franceschet (2003: 9) argues, the institutionalization of the movement provided it with important resources and legitimacy and helped it to attract new international funds, circulate strategies beyond the national borders and shape state policies. However, the institutionalization and professionalization also had considerable negative effects. For one, it favors women with certain social characteristics and 'leaders are drawn into the institutional arena, thereby depriving grassroots groups of leaders' (Franceschet 2003: 16). This progression altered the power balance within the movement, pushing women with a different background, and organizations without a formal structure, out of the picture. This created a widening gap between the professional organizations of the women's movement and their target group.

This process of *"oengeización"* (NGOisation) whereby externally funded NGOs slowly came to replace individual activists, grassroots mobilization and *ad hoc* initiatives is to a large extent inspired by the assumption of donors that NGOs are an efficient means to develop democratizing countries economically and socially (Edwards and Hulme 1996). Because of this assumption, much attention and money is spent on the process of strengthening the internal organization and administration of these organizations, meaning that female activists are increasingly becoming *femocrats*, service-providers, NGO-members and professionals, working within institutionalized organizational cultures (Ewig 1999: 97). This creates a situation in which NGOs are consulted as experts, rather than being seen as social actors. As Mendoza, member of Kaqla, formulated it "There are very few women in the offices who ever organized a group of women in the communities, who ever set up a meeting in the villages. They are no doubt very good at what they do. But we have to ask, what is it that we want the women's movement to do?" (interview 31 January 2011).

This statement expresses how little experience these formal organizations have with mobilizing from the bottom up. The professionalization of the movement thus affects its mobilizing potential (Alvarez 1999: 192). Schild (2000: 25) warns for the extent to which "the advancement of women's rights – a political goal – is being transformed into a technical task".

Contrary to the high degree of institutionalization which marks the movement as a whole, we can however discern a more organic form of organizing within each individual organization. The *'tendencia a la no-estructura'* at the managerial level for example, co-exists with the inclination towards institutionalization at other organizational levels. Whereas the tendency to avoid structure can be ascribed to a desire for autonomy – best explained in terms of the history of the movement and the tenuous relations with government – the tendency to adopt formal institutional structures can be traced back to a pragmatic necessity to channel funds. As Monzón, a sociologist and renowned Guatemalan feminist, argued:

> Before external funding agencies decide to invest in an organization, they want to be sure about where their money is going and that it is a good investment. There are talks, audits, and follow-ups, to assure that the [receiving] organization is organized in the most efficient way, according to them [the donors] and that it can live up to the goals which were set.
>
> MONZÓN, 21 May 2010

This necessity to channel funds was one of the most important reasons justifying the professionalization of the movement, which my interviewees mentioned. A second reason was the political climate in which the organizations operate. 'Inefficiency' and 'hostility' on the side of the government bodies which administer laws and policies regarding women and civil organizations were cited as an important trigger to organize in this way, because "formal organizations are harder to render invisible than grassroots initiatives" (Morales, member Tierra Viva, 1 June 2010, Montenegro, president MAM/CINCO 2 May 2010).

Next to external funding agencies and political constellation, the revolutionary mobilization also helps to explain the professionalization of the movement. Mid-ranking revolutionary activists – who later populated the women's movement – developed a degree of organizational and professional skills when participating in wartime popular organizations. This made them preferred potential employees and interlocutors of the international organizations entering the country after the armed conflict (Blumberg 2001: 161). However, as was discussed above, those former guerrilla activists who took on formal positions in the women's organizations were likely to have certain social characteristics prior to their activism (Kampwirth 2004: 10).

In conclusion, political changes, combined with international dynamics offered women a chance to participate in restructuring the political system in Nicaragua and Guatemala. Yet, at the same time, the political spaces for women's struggle were constricted because women's demands were funneled into delineated institutional spaces and treated as technical issues. This put women in a difficult position. Not participating in these spaces given to them, entailed the risk of being excluded. Conversely, working within them, entailed the risk that the state and international organizations would reshape and co-opt their agenda. Thus, revolutionary mobilization and international recovery programs in the post-conflict period did not per se have their acclaimed democratizing effect. Instead, the fact that they were laden with tension bolstered the evolution towards a highly institutionalized civil society consisting mostly of NGOs, which are not per se the optimal format for facilitating grassroots activism, even if they are a potentially powerful base from which women can organize around gender-based interests to impact on state policies and social values (Ewig 1999: 98). In these two cases, the NGO-structure has notably had positive effects in terms of policy changes. This however also means that the ability of such an NGO-dominated movement depends on the shape of the state institutions – which at best decides to accommodate the demands of the NGOs, and at worst, may use the existence of these NGOs as an excuse not to take on its own responsibility towards its citizens. The largest setback, however, is that the uneven distribution of power and resources which the NGOization of the movement fosters, does not favor democratic practices within the movement itself, meaning that the movement has not fully managed to live up to its own ideal of democratic change and equality.

Concluding Remarks: Women's Organizations, a Social Non-Movement?

Since the end of the armed conflict, Guatemalan and Nicaraguan women's organizations have been amongst the most visible organizations of civil society, with growing organizational capacity and spaces for interlocution. Yet, at the same time, they are increasingly facing issues of autonomy, both from national political institutions and from external funding agencies who entered the country during and after the civil conflict.

The women's movement in both countries made big advances in the 1990s. In terms of its internal functioning, this was visible in the sense that it was consolidating itself and growing in numbers. In terms of output, legal changes improving women's position can be cited. Nevertheless, these changes have not always taken root in society at large, and the women's movement today does not always stand as one block to defend the legal changes which it brought about. While there has never been a broad and genuine commitment from the side of society or the political establishment to transform gender norms and improve the position of women, both Nicaragua and Guatemala have, at certain points in time, known a discourse in which changes in gender relations were proposed. In Guatemala, this was especially so during the peace negotiations, in Nicaragua during the guerrilla fighting. This could have created a dynamic of rhetorical entrapment.[10] However, since actors of civil society who had an interest in consolidating these proposed normative changes lacked a shared agenda and voice at that time, they were unable to pressure those actors who were proposing change, to live up to their promises.

This can be explained in terms of unresolved strategic, ideologic and identity issues. While the movement's capacity for political incidence has grown in the last decade, this growth has remained limited because of the absence of a coherent program and shared goals amongst the different organizations. In both Nicaragua and Guatemala, the identity formation process of the women's movement is dragging. Neither the movement as a whole, nor the different networks within it – except maybe for feminists – have succeeded in creating a coherent identity for themselves, nor in defining the central objectives which all participants share and press for in unison. Identities are still mainly defined in opposition to the other, i.e. in opposition to government, to other organizations of civil society or to other women's organizations. This means that the movement as a whole remains disarticulated, but also that the different networks often miss a clear stance on key issues, and in many respects remain inchoate despite being around for over two decades.

The organizations making up the movement are in many ways indeed still inchoate, in the sense that they were created relatively recently, and are still establishing their organizational identities and priorities. Yet, I argue that precisely this process of conceptualizing their identity and strategies needs to receive explicit and conscious attention in order to develop a strategy which is tailored to their local context and that of their target audience. This process of aligning frames is a crucial step to gain more legitimacy and negotiating potential (see for example Snow et al. 1986). Today however, the lack of

---

10   The proposition of an idea can create a situation in which those parties involved no longer have an opportunity to opt-out because of the expectations which were created by airing the idea. (Schimmelfennig 2001).

economic viability, render the movement even more dependent on international benefactors, whose presence impacts upon the situation of autonomy-seeking, ideological battles, *"oengeizacion"* and fragmentation. This, in turn, impacts upon identity-formation processes, both at the level of the individual organizations and at the level of the movement as a whole. Hence, most organizations are still struggling with their own identity at the moment when they engage in coordinating efforts and networks aimed at creating an identity as a movement and at arriving at greater coherence at the collective level.

I argue that this fact, that organizations missed this step of constituting themselves as coherent entities first, is crucial to understand why the women's movement as a whole has not managed to create a collective identity and goal. The absence of a clear and established identity at the level of the individual organization means that organizations are afraid of losing themselves in processes aimed at collective identity formation, which explains why they resist these attempts in practice, while supporting them rhetorically. This situation makes it problematic to speak of a-singular-women's movement as such, and creates the impression that the idea of a women's movement needs to be revisited in order to adequately account for female mobilizing in Guatemala and Nicaragua. I engage in this effort in the second part of the book.

CHAPTER 4

Shifting Paradigms
Womanhood as a Political Strategy

The development of the women's movement in Nicaragua and Guatemala illustrates that there is nothing inevitable or straightforward about the impact of armed conflict on the development of women's organizations. Actors in the field have adopted different organizational forms and strategies in response to the history and context in which they developed. This chapter complements the analysis of the previous chapters by looking at how revolutionary mobilization, international actors and national political changes influenced the substantive approach and priorities of these organizations.

A prominent Guatemalan feminist initially defined the mission of the movement as a multi-faceted one, revolving around breaking the silence and taboos on violence against women, transforming oppressive structures, contributing to a higher life quality and fighting for women's human rights (Aguilar 1997). Over time, and under the influence of international donors, the element of women's human rights has gained importance. Hence when Chejter reassessed the priorities of the movement in 2007, she found that there were six priorities which the movement set itself: sexual and reproductive rights, labour rights, promotion of equal opportunities and human rights, promotion of citizen participation, political lobbying and access to justice, and combating impunity. While the substantive content of these programs was not per se very different from the one cited by Aguilar in 1997, we are witnessing a marked paradigm shift here, towards a rights-based approach.[1] In this discourse, gender issues are all framed as issues of human rights.

The attention to women's rights is not only taking place on a discursive level. Also the actual programs of women's organizations increasingly reflect a concern with women's rights. Lobbying for legal change and strategies of political impact are becoming increasingly important amongst women's organizations like the National Women's Coalition (Coalición Nacional de Mujeres) and the Autonomous Women's Movement (MAM) in Nicaragua, and the Guatemalan Women's Group (GGM) and the National Commission for the Prevention of Violence Against Women (CONAPREVI) in Guatemala. According to Montenegro (1997) seventy-eight per cent of all women's organizations mentioned political

---

1   See Corrêa (1997) for an in-depth analysis of how the rights-based approach replaced the health paradigm in other contexts.

incidence (*acción política*) as one of their organizing axes in their programs. The types of action which fall under this heading are varied – ranging from lobbying to protest marches and awareness-raising programs for policy makers – but all have in common that they envision changes at the political level, and more specifically, the promotion of women's human rights in the legal domain.

The praxis of the women's movement is thus increasingly shaped by a rights-based approach. In this chapter, I fist consider the nature of this approach and how its dominance is visible in the work of the women's movement. Then I assess its causes and implications as well as the existence of alternative and complementary approaches. Here, I consider how these approaches too have been shaped by the rights-based approach which has become the dominant paradigm in the women's movement. Following this, I explore in more detail what the impact of this approach is on women's lives and on the potential for action of the feminist movement. Lastly, I explore whether other strands of feminism could complement the rights-based approach in order to optimize output.

Tracing the Rights-Based Approach

The question of what constitutes a rights-based approach has become the topic of major analytical debate (Piron 2005). My definition is that a rights-based approach sets the achievement of human rights as an objective for development (ODI 1999: 1). This interpretation can also be applied to the study of the feminist movement and women's rights, which stress women's human rights not only as a precondition for development, but also as a precondition for changing gender relations.[2] In this section I consider the factors inspiring this approach in Guatemala and Nicaragua, the main mobilizing issues, potential shortcoming and the alternatives and complementary strategies which the movement uses at present.

The Origins of a Rights-Based Approach

The growing influence of a rights-based approach triggers the question about what explains this increased influence of this paradigm. In this section, I examine how this paradigm shift, can be traced back to the three factors discussed above: revolutionary popular mobilization, national political changes, and preferences of international donors. I argue that a combination of these

---

2   The contribution of gender to the rights-based approach has been that of foregrounding the issue of power and unequal relations, suggesting that power has to be explicitly addressed, thereby combining a concern with rights with a concern with power relations (Uvin 2007).

factors can adequately explain the choice of the women's movements in both countries to increasingly organize their struggle around women's rights.

To explain the focus the public domain in a general sense, the armed conflict needs to be considered. Initially the women's movement in Guatemala and Nicaragua was heavily influenced by its legacy of popular mobilization, in the sense of relying heavily on protest politics (Berger 2006: 2). As one interviewee stated:

> In the 1980s mass demonstrations were a cornerstone of the FSLN's strategy to involve the people and create a sense of togetherness against a common enemy. Today, they still rely heavily on this strategy. But we [in the women's movement] also know how to do this [...] I have colleagues who are actively involved in organizing these protests [...] so we are able to gather a lot of support when we try to push through certain changes.
>
> RIVERA, ex-guerrillera, 27 April 2010

Also the idea of former revolutionary groups – like the FSLN and the URNG – that a transformation of policies at the state level will automatically have consequences for women's daily lives, is still discernible in the feminist movement today. As one representative of the MAM put it "[w]e need a democratic state first. You cannot fight for women's rights within an authoritarian regime. If this is not overthrown first, no struggle will ever succeed." (Jiménez, 6 April 2010). This quote illustrates why approaches which are aimed at legal changes and changes at the policy level resonate well with the preferences of women activists.

Also political changes of the 1990s in Guatemala and Nicaragua help to explain the choice of women's organizations to politicize women's issues, and the blind spot for women's personal lives which sometime follows from this. The post-war political and neoliberal restructuring and the creation of new political spaces meant that there was much scope for policy change, and that mobilizing for change became pivotal. This triggered more co-operative relations with government, especially in Guatemala, where women's organizations had an official voice during the peace talks. Not taking this chance to participate in political negotiations entailed the risk that reforms would take place without them, so political incidence became the *raison d'être* of many young women's organizations. More importantly, the willingness of women's organizations to collaborate with government and to look beyond their own program meant that they became more credible social agents in the Guatemalan case (Berger 2006, Craske 1999, Stephen 1997). Cooperation was especially beneficial on economic issues for example, which were crucial in the immediate post-conflict period. In Nicaragua, many feminist organizations however, relied on protest politics rather than cooperation. What unites those actors adopting a strategy of cooperation with government and those engaging in protest politics is the strategy of politicizing gender issues.

Also, the combination of national political dynamics and factors related to the armed conflict reinforced the politicization of gender issues and the focus on the public aspects of women's lives. Mobilization around property rights for women in Guatemala, for example, is closely linked to the post-conflict debates on property and ownership rights for women who had lost their husbands and their land during the conflict. The women's movement joined this debated by lobbying for the formal attribution of property rights to women and by orga-nizing campaigns to raise awareness of these rights amongst women. Thereby, they too focused on rights of women, which could be claimed in the public domain. Also employment – without discrimination – and access to credit were particularly important for the women's movement in a post-conflict set-ting, since the absence thereof had the potential to generate civil unrest and because women often acquired new skills during the conflict period which they wanted to continue using (Kampwirth 2004: 49). Hence women's organi-zations mobilized for the right of women to take up paid employment. The attention for women's public economic role was further inspired by the priori-ties of the UN Decade for Women (1976–1985) which focused its programs on understanding the complexities of women's employment rather than on wom-en's role in the family (Moser 1989: 1799). In other words the UN's 'Women in Development Approach' which was advocated in this decade addressed women in their productive rather than reproductive and maternal role, thereby again reinforcing the attention to women's public roles and to those aspects of their lives which could be framed in a rights-based approach.

Due to their own historical preferences outlined above, the Guatemalan and Nicaraguan women's movement were particularly receptive to this change in the international development agenda of the 1990s. The evolution towards a rights-based approach at the international level was moreover particularly attractive to local feminists because this way, women's demands could be framed as rational and legitimate claims (Wölte 2002: 181, Friedman 1995: 15).[3] Next to this, there is the element of financial and logistical dependence on donors, which also made women's organizations more susceptible to adopt those approaches which were in concordance with the preferences of their international benefactors.

---

3   Some of the most effective organizing of the global women's movement has indeed been around
     rights-related claims, such as social welfare policy related to child-rearing, the penalization of
     domestic violence and sexual exploitation, and the issue of access to justice (Antrobus 2004).

As Bradshaw (2006: 1339) notes on the Nicaraguan case, while some local feminist actors explicitly rejected the rights-discourse because they felt it had been co-opted by agents such as the World Bank, others employed it in order to secure funding. She gives two examples of NGOs which brought in a 'consultant' to assist the organization with funding proposals. The consultant suggested they rename their training and consciousness-raising activities as their 'rights package' in the first case. In the second case, the consultant proposed to use 'the language of rights more explicitly in their work' (Bradshaw 2006: 1335). One of her interviewees says how "this had arisen from participation in a European Union-funded project on rights. She noted how in general they 'learnt' from the people themselves how best to present ideas but that participating in the program had led them to reflect on the fact that the work they had been doing did have a rights focus, and on the importance of naming it as such, at least in terms of ensuring finance". Also in Guatemala, several organizations have followed this strategy, because they became aware that the rights discourse was a more acceptable one to international donors than a gendered discourse about patriarchy or than women-only projects. As Evelyn Flores, head of the training department of a Nicaraguan women's organization, argued, "reframing our projects like this, allowed us to adopt the more balanced approach which [our donors] expected from us" (20 April 2010). The shift towards a rights-based approach can thus also be explained in reference to the evolution of the international development agenda towards programs focused on rights, participation and citizenship.

The Materialization of a Rights-Based Approach

This section considers how the women's movements in both countries applied a rights-based approach in their existing programs. What this shows is that the paradigm shift has not per se implied a change of priorities, but mainly meant that existing priorities were addressed in a new manner. Violence against women, for example, has been framed as an issue of societal and economic concern, a health issue, a matter of women's human rights and currently as an issue which is best addressed through awareness-raising. The same holds for economic issues and health matters.

Economic Assistance, Economic Rights and Economic Development

Immediately after the armed conflict and due to major economic upheaval, anti-poverty and employment equity programs were petitioned, mostly by the female part of the population (Aguilar 1997). In this context, many women's organizations emerged which had economic assistance and the alleviation of women's practical gender needs, as their first goal. Examples are the Nicaraguan Women's Association Luisa Amanda Espinoza (AMNLAE), Unemployed Women (Mujeres Desempleadas), the Union of Food and Allied Workers' Associations of Guatemala (COMFUITAG) and Women in Action (Mujeres en Acción) in Guatemala. These organizations operated within the existing patriarchal socio-political structures and started from the daily economic realities of women, without explicitly challenging gender roles or norms governing gender relations. They sought, for example, the establishment of a sufficient household income, rather than a fair income for women themselves. As West, a missionary involved in community projects in the North of Nicaragua, explained:

> The first goal is to keep the family together. [By letting women work in these workshops] we give them a chance to contribute their part to the family income. [...]. This way women's role in the family becomes more important.
>
> WEST, 22 April 2010

These types of initiatives are becoming more infrequent however, as most women's organizations are now incorporating economic topics in an approach which targets strategic gender needs. This means that economic issues are still an important mobilizing theme for women's organizations in Guatemala and Nicaragua, but that they are increasingly being framed in the rights discourse, rather than being addressed as practical issues. In specific, gender-aware land-tenure, inheritance rights for women or micro-financing are mentioned in many program brochures which were analyzed. This discursive acknowledgment does however not always mean that there are actually funds for these type of programs. Instead, these organizations set up lobbying programs and programs for political incidence to foster a climate in which women can exercise their economic rights. Direct economic assistance is thus making way for programs aimed at structural change. According to interviewees this is because economic betterment is seen as a crucial aspect for the improvement of women's everyday situation, but at the same time as an element on which strategic action is needed in order to allow for genuine change (Jiménez, member of MAM, 13 April 2010). The choice to address these issues discursively and through a rights-based approach is however not always only inspired by a belief in the need for strategic long-term action, but also by the pragmatic fact that there are not always resources to set up actual aid programs, and that a rights-based approach is more manageable in these cases.

Many of the organizations which incorporate economic issues into their programs today thus do not have the economic advancement of women as their first goal, but discursively address several economic problems of women in the language of economic rights in their overall rights discourse. These organizations do not address economic issues as a matter of meeting women's practical gender needs, but build their discourse around the existing economic injustices, stress the structural nature thereof and conceptualize economic problems as strategic gender needs, i.e. those long-term issues related to structural change in the domain of women's subordination and gender inequities. These organizations do not so much advocate an improvement in women's economic situation as a means to assure economic survival, but as a first step towards overcoming structural inequalities and changing gender relations. As Neirynck, fieldworker for UNAM, stated:

> We're not just setting up these projects [producing local candy] for women to be able to make some money without being dependent on foreign resources or imported products. It's also a way to make them more viable, and independent in the long tun [...] Moreover, we try to talk about their rights while we have them gathered here to prepare the candy.
> NEIRYNCK, 28 April 2010

This statement is illustrative of how a rights-based approach is becoming increasingly influential and increasingly interwoven in all aspects of women's programs. It also shows how economic issues have moved from being seen as practical gender needs to being addressed as a strategic gender need through a rights-based approach.

Health, a New Feminist Mobilizing Theme?

Health is a second important mobilizing axis of the women's movement in both countries. In 1997, Montenegro found that fifty per cent of all Nicaraguan NGOs defined health as one of their priorities. The issue of health gained importance because the neoliberal restructuring entailed a cutback in the state's health expenditure and brought the provision of health services in danger. As one midwife remarked, "CODECOT is fighting this injustice [insufficient health care for women] by training midwives to serve women throughout the department of Quetzaltenango. But one can only wonder who provides healthcare to women in the rest of the country?" (Pena, 2 June 2010). In order to meet the needs of their target group, women's organizations thus had to organize around the issue of health.

Like with women's economic needs however, the number of organizations which is actively providing health services as a means to alleviate women's practical gender needs is declining since the late 2000s (Franzoni 2011: 43). The growing strength of feminism within the movement as a whole meant that the idea gained ground that health service provision is not the core task of the women's movement. Because of this, a growing number of women's organizations, formerly dealing with practical health matters, are now organizing around strategic interests in the domain of health, and practical assistance has become the province of women's organizations organizing only around practical gender needs.[4] This suggests a hierarchization of strategic over practical gender needs, while work on practical gender needs can also improve women's strategic gender needs (See Franceschet 2004).[5]

The growing importance of feminism as a current within the movement thus means that there is a growing attention for the strategic side of women's health issues and that health issues are increasingly being framed as matters of public concern. This means that it is mainly those health issues which have an obvious socio-political component, such as abortion and violence against women, which receive attention (Yamin 2009, Pizarro 2000). This attention happens along the lines of a rights-based discourse. The choice to proceed in this way, which most feminist organizations and other women's organizations adopted, has yielded many positive results in both countries, mainly in the sense that the women's movement has been able to press more forcefully for legal changes in the domain of health, resulting in the adoption of ministerial decree 67–96 of the Nicaraguan Ministry of Health (1996), amongst others. This decree was enacted as a response to pressure brought to bear by the Autonomous Women's Movement (MAM). The decree was an important step towards the recognition of violence against women as a public health issue (CEDAW 2005: 13). Partially because of this decree, the issue of violence against women gained more legitimacy and entered the public debate in a more prominent way. In combination with a changing discourse at the international level, this also led to the issue of violence against women increasingly being formulated within a rights-based approach rather than as a health issue. The rights-based approach to health thus fostered important legal changes and added a degree of legitimacy to issues formerly deemed irrelevant in the public realm.

---

4   This raises the question of who caters to women's practical health needs in a neoliberal regime where the state is unable to provide for women's health needs, and where women's organizations are increasingly focusing on the strategic side of the issue (Franzoni 2011).

5   Franceschet established how Chilean women who organized for practical gender needs built on this experience in other domains of their life as well, and felt more empowered through their social work.

Also in Guatemala, large sections of the women's movement adopted the strategy of framing violence against women as an issue of public policy and legal rights rather than as a health issue. This resulted in several forms of violence against women being recognized in the penal code, and to the creation of government bodies specializing in gendered violence (IAHCR 2007). Yet, despite this merit of a rights-based approach to health in terms of fostering legal breakthroughs, one should not overestimate the extent to which these legal provisions have actually been brought into practice, and the extent to which women's health needs are actually being catered to because of these legal changes. The next section offers a critical assessment of the shortcomings of a rights-based approach which are often obscured in many formal evaluations.

Benefits and Shortcomings of a Rights-Based Approach

Next to meeting with approval from the side of donors, the rights discourse thus had the advantage of allowing for a reframing of issues which were formerly discussed within the health framework for example – such as abortion and violence – thereby shifting the attention from biological determinants to power relations. This allowed for more debate and facilitated mobilization (Yamin 2009: 6). Moreover, the fact that the rights-based approach gave more legitimacy to issues, meant that it became increasingly difficult for the state to oppose women's demands. More specifically, a responsibility was placed on the shoulders of the state as the main guarantor of women's rights. This was convenient for feminists operating in a highly polarized context, because it allowed for a strategy of blame-shifting in which the adversarial state, which was unwilling to guarantee women's rights, was pointed out as the root of all problems. Yet, at the same time, this meant that women became dependent on this – often unwilling – state to guarantee their rights. The strategy of addressing and criticizing the state through a rights discourse was thus mainly instrumental for the feminist movement itself, and not per se for women in general. The creation of 'a common enemy' in the state and the formulation of universal demands, created a sense of commonness amongst women's organizations. The universal nature of the rights-based discourse thus served as a common ground amongst feminist organizations and thereby allowed the feminist movement to consolidate itself to some degree (Ruppert 2002: 156). The rights-based approach thus created more legitimacy for the women's movement itself, facilitated efficient lobbying activities and created more public appreciation and awareness of women's interests and gender relations because these were framed in the universalizing discourse of human rights. It has also been particularly important in denouncing socio-political injustices and creating a legal framework to guarantee women's rights.

Most importantly however, the rights-based approach has strengthened the movement's struggle for rights and democracy, by fostering the creation of a legal framework. Since the rights-based approach was adopted in Guatemala and Nicaragua – partially in reaction to changing priorities at the international level, partially due to political calculation – it has triggered numerous changes in the legal domain. In Nicaragua alone, 179 laws have been created or modified since 1979 to meet gender needs of women (Destrooper 2012). Also in Guatemala, women have been successful in shaping the laws surrounding gender issues. Women's organizations influenced the Guatemalan peace accords in 1996 and lobbied the national political system to push through significant legislation in favor of women, such as the law of 9 April 2008 against femicide (Guatemalan Human Rights Commission 2009). Some of these laws are far-reaching and open up the private sphere for public interference by regulating for example paternal and maternal responsibility within the family (law 623 of 2007, Nicaragua) or by rendering domestic violence punishable (decree 97 of 1996, Guatemala). The positive results of this approach have often been very visible, in the sense that they led to formal agreements and laws which received considerable media attention, both at the national and at the international level.

As a consequence of the rights-based approach, both countries have a relatively advanced legal apparatus for dealing with gender violence (Klugman 2009: 181 and NAM 2009a and 2009b). Yet convictions for gendered crimes lag behind according to activists within the women's movement (e.g. Norma Cruz, founder of Sobrevivientes, 20 May 2011).

Today, programs are increasingly aimed at bridging this gap between *de jure* and *de facto* protection of women's rights. Many women's organizations dedicate substantial resources to assuring the follow-up of the legal change which are implemented for example through workshops to familiarize judges with legislation on women's rights, lobbying at the policy level, and policy research on the levels of impunity. Several of these initiatives produced tangible results, such as the adoption of a gendered focus by the Guatemalan Commission for Historical Clarification,[6] or an augmentation of the staff in the Nicaraguan Magistrates Court working on the issue of violence against women (Green, Nicaraguan Institute for Women 29 April 2010). Yet, the gap between the legal reality on women's rights and daily practice remains significant.

This can also be witnessed in other Central American countries where women's movements have relied heavily on political activism and a politicized discourse to address gender issues. Lamas (1997) for example describes how

---

6   See for example the CEH's analysis of the massacres of Xaman and the Plan Sanchez (1999).

the feminist contribution to the defense of women's sexual and reproductive rights in Mexico has mainly been based on activist campaigns and a rights discourse. Lamas critically analyses whether this type of activism is sufficient to change the daily lives of women, and argues in favor of other types of campaigns to support these efforts, such as further discursive and awareness-raising work which addresses women in their personal lives. These efforts are existing but premature in Guatemala and Nicaragua. As one activist illustrated:

> It's a matter of priorities really, we can't be involved in everything. There are workshops, but you need different staff with different skills for that, and we feel that the first thing we need now are legal changes, so that we can at least work in a healthy climate
>
> TUYUK, member CONAVIGUA, 7 June 2010

Next to ambiguous results in terms of changing the daily lives of women, the rights-based approach – or at least the way in which it has been adopted by Guatemalan and especially Nicaraguan feminists – had several other arguably negative consequences. Firstly, it further strained the movement's relations with government, which became more confrontational due to a strategy of finger-pointing. Also, relations with the movement's own audience came under strain however, because the division widened between the movement's audience and the staff working on these rights-based programs, who often had a Ladina middle-class background and a higher education. The approach thus also catalyzed the institutionalization and professionalization of the movement discussed in the previous chapter (Dzodzi 2004). As Piron (2005) claims, this means that inherent characteristics limit the potential of the rights-based approach to directly question the existing structures and power relations and to empower marginalized groups, as it reproduced existing divisions by favoring women who have certain socio-economic characteristics in its own organizational structures. Yamin (2009: 12) goes so far as to argue that the approach reinforces existing power relations by rhetorically shifting the agency away from women themselves and into the lap of power holders. As Alsop (1993) also affirms, this approach is explicitly politicized and thus liable to the actions of politicians who may be sensitive to the interpretation that men will lose out in the process of empowering women. Discursively granting the state the role of critical guarantor of the human rights of women, in this view is problematic since the state itself is seen as patriarchal (Peterson 1977). The rights-based approach thereby reinforces the idea of masculine and masculinist protectors and leaders vs. passive women, and ascribes a protector role to the state, thereby subscribing to masculinist logic and constructs of power (Young 2003).

Complementary Approaches: Awareness-Raising

As was pointed out however, women's organizations are not solely engaging in activities aimed at changing the legal framework. In both countries, a growing amount of resources is invested in workshops and awareness-raising programs in both countries. Yet, these initiatives too are colored by the dominance of the rights-based approach in the women's movement.

The focus on education and awareness-raising to some extent counterbalances the centrality of initiatives aimed at fostering change at the policy level. Awareness-raising initiatives envision a transformation of women's situation from the bottom-up, rather than starting at the state level. In practice however, awareness-raising programs are often used as a complement to the rights-based approach, rather than being seen as a tool in their own right. The aim of many of these awareness-raising programs is to raise awareness amongst women of their rights and how to press for these. They are thus often used as a tool supporting the rights-based approach. Awareness-raising activities outside the realm of legal rights are rare in Guatemala and Nicaragua, and the discourse used during workshops is usually laced with references to women's legal rights rather than relying on a vocabulary which builds on women's everyday experience for example.

The history of the movements show that this has not always been the case. Initially workshops organized by women's organizations had an entirely different focus and function. Workshops offered by the women's movements can broadly be grouped under two general headings: life skills training and *capacitación* on the one hand, and emancipation and empowerment programs on the other hand. Initially, workshops revolved mainly around *capacitación* and life skills training. FSLN-affiliated Nicaraguan *brigadistas* for example were sent off to the villages to organize literacy campaigns and share knowledge on farming techniques among different populations (Randall et al 1981). In the immediate after-war too, life skills trainings were dominant because the armed conflict had led to interrupted schooling and a shortage of material and human resources for education. This disproportionately affected women (Zuckerman and Greenberg 2004: 76).

According to Montenegro (1997), in the mid-1990s fifty per cent of the Nicaraguan women's organizations defined education as one of their priorities. My research shows that the number of organizations engaging in trainings and workshops has augmented since then. Only two of my interviewees at women's NGOs in Nicaragua and Guatemala indicated that they did not have some sort of training program for women, when asked about this.[7] Yet at the same time, the proportion of organizations focusing on actual education and life skills training has diminished and has been replaced by organizations prioritizing emancipation, empowerment and awareness of rights. This happened under the influence of shifting priorities at the international level (Neirynck, fieldworker, 28 April 2010).

These awareness-raising workshops can be divided into three categories. A first type of program is aimed at raising-awareness amongst women themselves. This type of program exists in several forms, but tends to rely on a rights-based discourse to foster women's emancipation. Organizations working in this way often link women's awareness of their rights to other forms of emancipation. Blumberg's research (1998 and 2001) on El Salvador however suggest that no formal link can be established between different forms of empowerment and emancipation if there is no conscious coordination of several strategies. Since this is not always the case in Guatemala and Nicaragua, due to the fragmentation of the women's movement, initiatives aimed at raising awareness about women's formal rights are not always embedded in larger efforts aimed at empowering women and thus not per se fostering a growing awareness of their oppression. One interviewee illustrated how dominant the rights discourse is in these workshop when giving an overview of their activities. Virtually all workshops envisioned an increased awareness of their rights amongst women:

> We have many programs. I think we are maybe the organization which has the most comprehensive approach to women's issues. There is currently a program on violence against women, where we teach women about the legal and judicial tools which they have at their disposition in case of domestic violence, because local police officers are often not sufficiently aware of this legal framework. There is a program for the economic betterment of women, where we stress that they are entitled to pursue jobs and get equal pay for them, that they have rights as mothers when they take up work, that they are entitled to holidays and pregnancy leave, etc. [...] We have programs on health, where we teach women where to go to claim their right to basic healthcare [...]. We have programs on reproductive rights, and these are maybe the most important ones today, because of the recent developments [...]
> GRANDISON, Procuradora de las Mujeres PDDH, 21 April 2010

---

7   Casa de la Mujer in Granada, Nicaragua and Mama Maquín in Guatemala.

As the interviewee stated later however, there was no real strategy regarding which women they reached. In other words, there was no link between the programs on economic rights, health rights, reproductive rights or the right to a life free of violence. She stated that, in practice, they even aimed not to provide different workshops to the same group, as their aim was to reach as many women as possible. This means that the workshops which women attend, are isolated events without structural follow-up, which are not part of a program which envisions the spill-over of emancipation in one domain to another. This lack of structural efforts is potentially problematic. Underlying these workshops is the – untested – assumption that an awareness of their rights will foster a more general awareness of their situation of oppression amongst women. However, for this more general awareness to occur, individual workshops may be insufficient.

A second type of awareness-raising activities are those directed towards society as a whole. These awareness-raising activities usually take on the form of larger media- or poster-campaigns, rather than being organized as workshops. The goal is increasing societal awareness of gender issues. Examples of organizations engaging in this type of activity are the different women's networks (*Redes de Mujeres*) in Nicaragua, and the Civico-Political Women's League (Convergencia Civico-Politica de Mujeres) and the Guatemalan Women's Group (GGM) in Guatemala. These organizations engage in mobilizing activities, protest marches, public information and apprise and strategic publications. All of these activities are aimed explicitly at the transformation of oppressive structures, by fostering a more general societal awareness of the structural nature of women's oppression. These organizations are thus working on the structural causes of women's oppression, and can as such be called feminist. However, not all these organizations self-define as feminist.

A last type of awareness-raising activities under the rights-based approach, which is offered by many women's organizations, is the one aimed at educating and informing judges, civil servants and lawyers about women's rights and legal changes in this domain. These efforts have the goal of overcoming the gap between the progressive legal climate and the often more conservative interpretation of new gender laws amongst policy-officers and regulators. Initiatives in this domain are not ubiquitous however. An interviewee at the Colectivo 8 de Marzo – which organizes this type of workshops itself – cited two important reasons when asked about the modest number of initiatives like these:

> I wish I could state otherwise, but the truth is that it is very hard for any women's organization not affiliated to the party [FSLN], or for any organizations of civil society really, to work with government officials. Many

women's organizations, and especially feminist organizations are treated as the enemy, and in such conditions, obviously, we are not invited to share our knowledge. [...] Then on the other hand, there is also a factor inherent to the movement. At least, I can't speak for all organizations, but I think, as a women's movement, we are to work with women first. There are limited resources, and I think our core task is to spend these resources on women themselves first. So it's an understandable choice if an organization choses to organize workshops for women rather than for policy makers, and this is something which is happening increasingly [...]. It's a difficult decision though.

TORRES, 21 April 2010

This apparent belief in the use of awareness-raising workshops should however not only be attributed to a concern with establishing a link between formal legal changes and women's daily lives. There may also be a more pragmatic argument for this choice of methods. As one interviewee argued:

It is increasingly difficult to meet all the demands which are placed upon us by the donors. Many feminist organizations are running into trouble when they cannot present any measurable advances they made. Donors always want to have the numbers on how many women you have reached, how many vaccines were placed, how many micro-enterprises were set up,...and this is something incredibly difficult to accommodate if your goal is long-term structural change.

MORALES, staff Tierra Viva, 20 April 2010

This hints at a manifest contradiction in the demands of the donors, who on the one hand demand structural programs for long-term change to the situation of women's oppression, and, on the other hand, require immediate and measurable output. This suggests that the choice to rely more heavily on awareness-raising programs and workshops can – partially – be seen as a pragmatic solution of women's organizations. Neither feminist nor non-feminist organizations can easily achieve this dual demand by donors. Feminists who adopt a public approach have difficulties in presenting immediate results since their goal is to structurally change power relations. Non-feminist organizations working on practical gender needs can only indirectly challenge power relations, and thus cannot easily prove their merits in this domain (Bayard de Volo 2003). By organizing workshops and awareness-raising campaigns in the framework of a rights-based approach, women's organizations can still make the argument that their activities are aimed at structural change and empowerment, while at the same time being able to present donors with real figures on the number of women they reached in this way. Evidently, this brings about new problems, such as the fact that many organizations prefer to organize one workshop for a several groups of women, rather than installing a long-term program aimed a triggering more profound changes with one group, because the former strategy boosts the figures about how many women have been reached. This issues is discussed in more detail in the second part of the book.

Politicizing the Struggle, Politicizing Women's Lives

At present there is a climate in which all organizations, including those working on practical gender needs and on personal issues, experience a pressure to use strategies which increase their visibility, in order to secure their financing and legitimacy. Pressing for legal change is often a cornerstone of this approach. That this choice is not always inspired by a belief in the effectiveness of such a strategy is illustrated by the remark of Van Vuuren, a representative of Rotary International in the North of Nicaragua:

> At the *comedores* we need all the human and financial means we can get. However, sometimes I incite one of the volunteers to go to the capital to participate in protest marches for women's rights and take pictures. If I can present these during the meetings [with the donors], I know that this will gather more goodwill.
> VAN VUUREN, 22 April 2010

This means that both feminist and feminine organizations are increasingly turning to this type of strategies in the public realm. Because of this, some programs are becoming increasingly hard to sustain as members have to combine their work for women's practical gender needs with activities which fall outside of this realm, and in which they are not per se experts. These activities are costly in terms of human and financial resources, and draw crucial resources away from their core activities. Moreover, the evolution towards public and rights-based approaches, in practice entailed a predisposition for top-down mechanism, aimed at influencing the policy level. Especially feminist organizations are advocates of this rights-based approach, because these organizations see equal rights and the rule of law as a '*cultura de vida*', necessary for the advancement of women's rights and for the improvement of their daily lives (MAM 2009: 34). For this reason, the transformation of existing social and legal regulations, and the full participation of women in public life is at the heart of the feminist struggle. This top-down struggle which mainly takes place in the public domain has had several implications, which are discussed below.

Implications of a Public Focus on Women's Lives

In Guatemala and Nicaragua, the strong reliance on a rights-based approach allowed issues which formerly pertained to the private lives of women to enter the public debate. An important example here is the introduction of sexual and reproductive rights onto the agenda of the women's movement, and thereby onto the political agenda. This was illustrative of an increasing concern with how policies and societal dynamics touched upon the daily lives of women. The choice of politicizing these elements of women's daily lives, turned women's practical and daily needs into strategic gender needs (Aguilar 1997: 23). Kirkwood (1986) argues that this means that the women's movement created new ways of 'doing politics' and that they made women participate in greater numbers and on a greater diversity of issues than before. For the first time, gender issues entered the public realm on a significant scale, meaning that public debate about them was possible. There are however also potential negative consequences to this approach, notably so in terms of how this approach has affected the lives of women. I discuss four issues here, the problem with translating rights-based work and awareness-raising to women's daily lives, the fact that only those elements of women's lives which fit into a rights-based approach are picked up by the women's movement, the fact that those elements of women's personal lives which do enter the priority list of organizations are only addressed through a discourse which is relevant in the public domain, and the fact that the rights-based approach favors the development of a certain gender-identity which does not necessarily reflect the daily lives of many women.

Firstly, as Alsop (1993: 373) argues, dealing with private issues through public top-down strategies can also have negative effects if awareness-raising efforts and public campaigns are not adequately translated to women's daily lives. I argue that the recent development of complementing a public strategy with awareness-raising activities, which is described above, is a positive one, because it opens up the issue of gender violence and gender inequality to a broader audience and allegedly creates more awareness amongst women themselves of their situation. These awareness-raising activities constitute a bridge between public methods and the private lives of women, and thereby illustrate the flexibility of a public approach, and its potential to matter in women's private lives. Specifically, awareness-raising activities – in accordance with Freire's theory of critical pedagogy (1972) – are aimed at exploring the bases which are commonly invoked to justify oppression and at providing ideas on how to overcome this:

> We are explaining to women that there is nothing inevitable about this
> situation, that this is not a fact which we cannot change. We try to show
> this by means of very practical examples. For example, the fact that they
> are even coming to these workshops usually means that they have to find
> someone to look after their children. We see that many women either
> bring their children or leave them with a sister or a neighbor rather than
> with their husband. We praise them for coming here, but at the same
> time, we tell them that 'equal rights' starts with very small tangible things,
> such as a having equal responsibility to take care of the children and
> equal opportunities to go out. Doing so, I have heard a million reasons
> about why they could not ask their husbands to look after the children,
> and a million excuses made by these husbands. But step by step, we try to
> show that these are sophisms, arguments which are only used to perpetu-
> ate the situation of women's subordination to men. Through discussions,
> we try to present arguments for countering these reasonings, but it's not
> at all easy, not at all evident to succeed.
>
> VALENZUELA, director CICAM, 3 June 2010

This way, top-down methods and discourses are being extended, so as to
make them more relevant in women's personal and daily lives, and to give
women an insight into how public dynamics impact upon their everyday
lives.

At the same time though, the awareness-raising activities in which the feminist movement engaged have often been to some extent detached from the
everyday lives of women, in the sense that they lacked an experience-based
component and sometimes did not offer women the tools to translate ideas
about oppression to their own lives in a way which was immediately useful for
them (Alvarez 1998). In the example mentioned above, it is valuable that
women are presented with a discourse on how they should in theory be able to
ask their husband to care for the children, because this illustrates how theoretical concepts apply to their daily lives. Yet, at the same time, the fact that
there is usually no follow-up to these workshops means that women are left on
their own as to how to bring this into practice. The daily reality of many participants to these workshops is not a priori conducive for a discussion between
equals about equal rights and equal care responsibilities. This is ignored all too
often. This can partially be explained by the institutionalization and the professionalization of the women's movement, which means that the movement
is populated with women who often have different socio-political characteristics than their target group. This often results in a blind spot for the daily realities of ordinary women, and creates a mismatch between the discourse and

concepts used at the level of the movement and the daily realities of its audience. In practice, this is discernible in the overrepresentation of projects which stress gender as a political issue, and the underrepresentation of structural projects which translate these political projects to the lives of ordinary women without formal education and with a different frame of reference (Berger 2006: 57). The process of 'frame alignment' (Snow 1986) between the guiding frames of the movement and those of its audience, has thus not always taken place with regards to the issue of women's rights, despite the existence of workshops set up to this end, because efforts structurally lacked an experience-based component or are too isolated to have a long-term effect. The quote by Doña Consuelo cited in chapter three is evincive here: "There are so many of them. They come, they talk, and they leave. They always leave as soon as the workshop is done. They get a nice grant for the travel here, but the ladies in Managua, they don't know anything about how life is here".

Also in theoretical literature on this topic, there is no consensus on the possibility of translating public actions to the private lives of individuals, or on the potential of public action to change values and norms in everyday life (see for example Blumberg 2001 and Zimmerman and Rappaport 1988). Zimmerman and Rappaport describe three studies on the relationship between empowerment and citizen participation.[8] The programs under consideration were aimed at increasing citizen participation, because this was seen as a means to increase individual emancipation. They conclude however that this higher rate of public participation did not always have the envisioned effect of increasing a feeling of personal empowerment. Equally so, Blumberg (1998), demonstrated that there is only limited evidence that programs for women's economic emancipation in El Salvador have had an obvious effect beyond the public sphere, and did not usually translate to women's family lives for example.

The fact that the Nicaraguan presidential election campaigns of Chamorro (1990) and Ortega (2006 and 2011) could still use particularly conservative and explicitly anti-feminist rhetoric- imbued with women-unfriendly gendered images (Kampwirth 1998, 2006 and 2008, Mann 2005) -without this being challenged from the grassroots, shows that there has been a problem with translating the values which are promoted in the public discourse of women's organizations into values which women identify with in everyday life and will stand up for. This was also illustrated when discussing the 2006 Nicaraguan presidential election campaign with some of my feminist interviewees. These

---

8　Their studies involved laboratory settings as well as groups actually involved in community activities.

activists continuously stressed how this campaign was a setback for the women's movement and for society as a whole. Yet, none of the interviewees linked the effects of such a conservative campaign to their own personal lives, by mentioning ways in which it affected them personally or how they dealt with this for example. Delgado, a feminist member of the Reformist Sandinista Party (MRS), replied to the question about how this campaign had influenced her daily life that "this is not about my daily life, it's not about me as a person. This is about the situation of all women being becoming worse, and about women being forced to retreat to traditional roles and accept the dominance of men". When asked, then, about how she had seen the lives of women around her change in response to the campaign, she insisted "again, it is not just about the life of so and so, this is a societal problem which cannot be solved by looking only at individuals" (13 April 2010).

That public discourses have not always been translated to women's private lives is also visible in the fact that there is still a lot of silence and acceptance of injustices in women's personal and family lives (Ellsberg et al 2000). The survey which Ellsberg et al carried out among women from León, Nicaragua, showed that the meaning which is ascribed to violence shifted over time, and that women were increasingly condoning of certain forms of partner violence.

This problem with translating issues to women's everyday lives is directly related to a second ambiguous consequence of a public and rights-based focus, namely that women's personal experiences are often overlooked.

Under the adage that "the personal is political", demands related to women's personal lives have been formulated as if they were public issues. This has been beneficial in the sense that it remedied the idea that politics is a public issue with no relationship to the private lives of individuals, and helped the movement to question the public-private divide (Kampwirth 2004: 15, Berger 2004: 83). Questioning this divide was important, because not doing so, would mean that the private realm would continue to be seen as a domain in which the state could not interfere, and this would, consequently, result in the absence of legislation on domestic violence for example. However the almost exclusive reliance on a public and rights-based approach also meant that only those elements of women's lives which could be formulated as public issues and around which a rights-based approach could be developed, entered the debate. This meant that issues such as socio-political transformation and political citizenship were easily picked up by the movement, whereas healing from trauma and psychological issues were soon abandoned. The latter initially was an important mobilizing theme for Guatemalan women's organizations whose target group had experienced severe violence during conflict. However, the psychological needs of women soon disappeared from the priority list of women's organizations as these did not easily fit a rights-based approach because of their emotional and psychological component.

This is particularly obvious when analyzing programs of organizations such as the Nicaraguan Autonomous Women's Movement (MAM 2009). This organization defines four goals in its mission statement which explicitly relate to the public domain and four which relate to the private domain. Those goals relating to the private domain – economic rights, respect for reproductive rights, sexual education and right to a life free of violence – however also only mention aspects of women's lives which can easily be framed in a rights discourse. The item "respect for reproductive rights" for example, clearly indicates an interest on the side of the organization in developing activities relating to women's sexuality and intimate relations, and envisioning their empowerment in these domains. Because of this framing however, they limit themselves to a very narrow aspect of women's sexuality – their reproductive rights and sexual education – and skirt the possibility of more holistic programs in this domain. Also the fact that women's rights in their private lives are narrowed down to economic and reproductive/sexual rights and a life free of violence, hints at a very narrow interpretation of women's private lives. Further in the statement, the text reads 'Proposals in the private and personal realm' (MAM 2009: 37), the first demand under this heading is 'The right to personal integrity and a life free of gender violence in the economic, social, cultural, political, private and public sphere'. Again, while labeling this demand as one relating to women's private lives, the interpretation is an obviously public-inspired one. Of the six domains which are mentioned in which women should be able to live lives free of violence, only one is actually personal, the others aim to protect women in their public roles. Also the description of what MAM sees as sexual rights only focuses on those elements of sexuality which are easily framed in a public discourse, and around which a rights-based approach can be developed. It demands '...the exercise of our sexual rights, expressed in [...] scientific sexual education, the dignity of women as social and political subjects and not their portrayal as sexual objects'. Equally so, the section on economic rights – which are earlier on in the statement referred to as a 'proposal in the private and personal realm' – demands 'the full exercise of our economic and juridical rights [...] to have access to goods, means for production and reproduction: right to property [...], equal access to work and equal pay, and equal access to credit, technical assistance and the market'. Again the public component is stressed more heavily than the way in which these issues actually touch upon women's private lives, and only those elements around which politicized activism or a rights-based approach are possible are mentioned. This means that certain aspects of women's lives are excluded from a rights-based approach, but also that those which do enter the debate are only addressed in a specific way, which dismisses experience-based work. This relates to a third ambiguous effect of a rights-based approach on women's daily lives.

The politicization of the struggle meant that formerly private issues are drawn into the public domain and addressed through politicized discourses and strategies which are most appropriate in the public domain, such as public debate and mobilization, political pressure, or protest marches for legal change, but which do not per se fit activism on those gender issues which do not have an obvious public dimension (Jaquette and Wolchik 1998: 89). For non-feminist organizations and organizations organizing for practical gender needs, the stress on public and visible action contrasts with their goal of providing elementary health care, economic assistance, literacy training, etc. These organizations do not benefit from a public or rights-based approach, because their working topics are best addressed by 'local-level planning, to achieve a more integrative approach which takes account of women's particular requirements' (Moser 1989: 1802). Yet, organizations which only work on practical gender needs and organize only on a grassroots level – without explicitly challenging power relations in their program and discourse – face increasing difficulties in attracting funding for their programs. In the history of virtually all social organizations, activists have translated the specific issues they face into a broader aggregated form to facilitate public action. This is not problematic as such, and is necessary to allow for social mobilization, awareness and public pressure. What is problematic in these two cases however is that in these two countries the decision to focus on public activities is not always a conscious or free choice, but that it is often inspired by pressures from the side of donors, on whom social – women's – organizations are almost entirely dependent. If these donors only facilitate programs which have a public or rights-based approach, this entails the risk of eliminating the activities of organizations which fall outside of this realm and which are also needed by the poorer sections of the population.

Moreover, in the present climate, under the growing influence of feminism and international donors, programs with a public focus are becoming increasingly influential and usurping not only many initiatives with a different focus, but also colonizing women's private lives. Methods which are appropriate in the public realm are increasingly used for activism on private issues and thereby invade private life. While private issues are drawn out of this realm and are made into part of the public realm. For example, at the protest march organized by Tierra Viva for the occasion of women's day in 2010 one of the speakers declared "...It is for this reason that today we take our struggle out on the streets, to affirm once more that it is us, women, who are the ones who are to take the decisions over our bodies, our lives and our future" (Protest March Guatemala City, 8 March 2010). This statement shows that even intimate issues such as taking decisions over one's own body are petitioned and declared by means of public action Also awareness-raising workshops on the topic, tend to revolve around issues such as rights, rather than incorporating experience-based elements, which women can connect with directly.

Lastly, not only were some aspects of women's lives a priori excluded because they did not fit the reigning paradigm of the women's movement, also certain parts of their identity were hard to fit in the dominant feminist approach. The strongly politicized methods inspire the promotion of a specific gender identity. The choice of feminist organizations to organize around a shared liberated feminist identity and to distance themselves from other traditional women's identities like *campesinas*, *sandinistas*, etc, was deemed necessary as a 'source of cohesion', and as a means of 'distancing ourselves from patriarchal structures of government' (Santamaria 2004: 22).[9] This means that a new gender identity was conceived on which the feminist movement had a major impact. Under their influence, women's public role became the core of this new identity. As one interviewee illustrated "women were locked up in their houses long enough, now it's time to come out of the house and focus on our role in public life" (Cabrera, member UNAMG, 27 May 2010). 'Softer' roles are thereby being overlooked and excluded from this new emancipated identity.

A root cause of these problems lies in the assumption that women's organizations focusing on practical gender needs or personal needs of women are not part of the women's movement because they do not explicitly envision structural change in the situation of women. These women's organizations are often seen as aid and relief organizations rather than as social actors. Bayard de Volo (2004 and 2006) demonstrated the fallacy of this claim when she showed that women's organizations focusing on practical gender needs also contributed significantly to women's empowerment in the case of a Nicaraguan mother's organization. This means that women's organizations which have no immediate goal of changing social structures may be more relevant in terms of structural long term change than what is commonly believed. Not only have these non-feminist organizations showed their merit in terms of women's empowerment, in addition they have the advantage of addressing women in their daily needs with practice and discourses which reflect, and are

---

9 See Polletta and Jasper (2001) and Della Porta and Diani (2006) for an elaboration in the relationship between identity and social mobilisation.

complementary with, women's daily reality – something which is not always the case with feminist organizations located in the capital. Yet, while these non-feminist organizations address women in their daily needs and work from the bottom-up, they risk being winged by donors' current focus on public and rights-based approaches.

A New Type of Feminism?

In the current Guatemalan and Nicaraguan context, activists' belief in public strategies often translates into a range of programs revolving around those aspects of women's lives which can easily be framed in a public rights-based discourse. Both feminist organizations and organizations which initially had no aim to change societal structures are increasingly relying on such an approach. There is however a small number of women's organizations which is not relying only on a rights-based discourse and which is not only working with practical or strategic gender needs. These organizations transcend the dichotomy of feminist vs. feminine/non-feminist. Their aim is to foster long-term structural changes, without necessarily proceeding through a public or rights-based approach. These organizations self-define as social actors and aim to facilitate long-term change by working with elements from women's personal lives in an experience-based manner.

One interviewee from a prominent Guatemalan women's organization illustrated how easily actions in the personal domain are overlooked as a source for empowerment by mainstream feminist organizations, when she stated, "we must fight for empowerment on multiple fronts: legislative, material, institutional and cultural" (Asenció, coordinator at UNAMG, 24 May 2010). She did not mention women's personal lives as a sphere in which to fight for empowerment. This can be considered particularly problematic in the Guatemalan case, where women have experienced high levels of violence during the armed conflict which caused personal and collective trauma (CEH 1999). Several programs focused on individual healing processes once the immediate post-conflict relief ended. Yet most of them had an explicitly public agenda, namely of helping society as a whole "move beyond the traumatic experience of war", without there being much attention for personal needs (Berger 2004: 79). Some groups emerged from this process, however, which addressed gender issues in a genuinely new way, and whose programs revolved around women's personal experiences and their psychological needs. These organizations set the stage for a new more inclusive approach to women's issues.

Thus, to capture and value the whole range of actions of the women's movement, a new category is needed to complement the categories of 'feminist' and 'feminine' activism. This category would refer to those organizations which work directly with women's – personal and psychological – needs while also envisioning long-term structural change. They combine work on practical and strategic gender needs in a manner which does not require the validation of actions in the public domain. These organizations work with women in a direct experience-based manner in order to empower them in their personal lives, and by extension, in the public realm. Their goals are similar to those of the autonomous feminists who adhere to a rights-based approach. These organizations deliberately and consciously choose to focus on the private side of women's lives and also choose not to engage in a public struggle about this in the first place, because of the conviction that "change starts in the individual's psyche and spreads from there", rather than the other way around (Aguilar, founder Q'anil, 26 May 2010). They do not accept power differences between men and women as natural but aim to break the *status quo* by explicitly acting within the private domain, starting from the most intimate relationships in which women engage rather than fighting inequalities from the top-down. This section proposes the introduction of the term *experience-based feminism* to describe this type of women's activism.

This type of activism requires the patient translation of old feminist principles into new concepts, and the integration thereof in the actions of the organization. Yet, it has been overlooked and often marginalized in literature and in the field alike (for a discussion, see Reynolds 2010). The second part of the book is dedicated to a critical analysis of the work of women's organizations which work in this way by deliberately working with women in the personal domain in an experience-based manner to bring about long-term changes, rather than proceeding through a politicized top-down approach.

Concluding Remarks

This chapter argued that factors – indirectly – related to the armed conflict influenced the movement's substantive approach of gender issues. On the one hand, the rights-based approach took root because it fitted the preference for political goals which women's organizations inherited from their revolutionary predecessors and strengthened the women's movement *vis-à-vis* the political establishment. On the other hand, it reflected a paradigm shift at the international level, as well as a shifting balance between feminists and non-feminist in the movement.

However, the rights-based approach does not cover the entire scope of women's gendered needs. Needs which are not easily framed in a public or rights-based discourse are often overlooked. This also meant that only certain parts of women's identity entered the public discourse. Analyzing which aspects of women's lives are structurally overlooked in the public domain and assessing what happens to these issues which do not make it to the public discourse is an important step to gauge the impact of the current approach and discourse of the feminist movement on women's lives.

In both Guatemala and Nicaragua the growing importance of the feminist subsection of the women's movement, combined with changes in the political climate and the need to secure international funding, has boosted the women's movements' reliance on rationalistic public approaches (Franceschet 2004). The feminist section of the movement gained strength in parallel with the rights-based approach, because its goals were compatible with the premises of a rights-based approach. Because of this, feminist organizations strongly advocated the rights-based approach, thereby strengthening it in turn. This renders it increasingly difficult for organizations engaging in service provision and assistance to attract funding, which creates an imbalance in the movement in favor of organizations adopting a rights-based approach.

The fieldwork pointed out some ambiguous effects of such an approach however. As one feminist interviewee suggested, rights ought to be seen as "The lowest rung on the empowerment ladder [...]. Seeing rights as the end goal rather than part of a process would mean we progress no higher" (Aguilar, founder of Q'anil and co-founder of Actoras de Cambio, 26 May 2010).

A rights-based approach has thus been crucial for the women's movement at a time when it was facing a hostile political regime and was in need of more legitimacy. It also showed its merits in creating the legal framework for guaranteeing women's rights. However, while legal provisions for women's rights and for readdressing gender relation are ample, they do not always take root in the existing societal climate, and their influence has not always spread to women's daily lives accordingly (NAM 2009a and 2009b, INE 2002 and 2009 and OECD 2008). In reaction to this, the women's movements started to engage in awareness-raising campaigns. The effect of the latter has however also been ambiguous, in the sense that many interviewees could declaim those insights which had been passed on to them through workshops, without always being able to explain how these were practically useful for them in their daily lives. This can be explained by the fact that workshops were not organized around women's concrete personal experience, were too isolated and were mainly seen as a tool for strengthening the rights-based approach.

Thus, women did gain some of the advantages that normally flow from an approach focusing on their rights and their public empowerment, such as a progressive legal framework, increased economic opportunities, more avenues for societal participation and slowly changing gender relations in the public sphere. Yet, advances in other domains, and in particular in the private domain, are more ambiguous.

In addition to this, the nature of the rights-based approach, has reinforced the movement's predilection for focusing on women's emancipation in the public domain. The assumption that public empowerment will automatically entail other forms of empowerment is still strong amongst interviewees. As one interviewee from a UN-program for economic empowerment of women, asserted, "in order for a battered wife to leave her husband, what she needs is sufficient economic means to survive on her own, a police force which will apply the law to support her, and a state which guarantees the respect for her rights in the future" (Cassisi, coordinator at MyDEL, 21 May 2010). This clearly illustrates the absence of any references to women's psyches from mainstream empowerment programs.

In summary, the colonization and negligence of private life by a politicized discourse and approach meant that attention for the actual dynamics of women's personal lives was further curtailed, and dynamics which could not be pulled into the public discourse – but which required, for example, psychological assistance – became 'no go' areas for the women's movement. This shows not only how the values of public life have been introduced into women's personal lives, but also how the opposite is much less the case. The extent to which personal values and rhetoric are introduced into the public debate is much more limited.

The next part of the book explores possibilities for alternative and complementary strategies to the one which feminists are using at present. In doing so, it acknowledges the important contributions of public and economic empowerment, of rights-based approaches, and of programs focusing on practical gender needs. However, it also argues that there are more than just cultural, strategic and practical gender needs (Moser 1993), and that there is a category of personal-psychological gender needs, which falls outside of these categories, but which can be addressed in a structural way by women's organizations. Acknowledging these personal-psychological gender needs suggests the need to rethink common-sense ideas about feminism, mobilization and empowerment.

PART TWO

Complementary Approaches to Women's Empowerment

∴

In the first part of the book, I analyzed the effect of armed conflict on the current priorities and working methods of the women's movement in Nicaragua and Guatemala. This analysis showed a strong predominance of programs envisioning women's emancipation in the public domain. These programs are influenced by women's experiences during the armed conflict and by international donors who entered both countries *en masse* after the armed conflict.

In this second part of the book, I explore in more depth how the movement's priorities and working methods can be located across the public-private dichotomy (e.g. Pateman 1983). This alleged opposition between a public and a private sphere is an idea which local feminists challenge, but at the same time implicitly subscribe to. The reason for problematizing this issue is fourfold. First, it is related to my fieldwork, which showed a significant preference on the side of actors envisioning women's empowerment – mainly feminist organizations – to prioritize topics and working methods which are situated in the public domain, such as women's rights, protests marches and advocacy strategies. By contrast, the personal experiences of women are often neglected – both their experience of oppression and other personal experiences. While this is not inherent to approaches that revolve around public mobilization – and while public mobilization is a pivotal aspect of the feminist movement's focus on structural change – Guatemalan and Nicaraguan feminist organizations often do not link activities in the public domain to women's personal everyday realities. When I refer to the "personal experiences" of women in this part of the book, I refer to those experiences which women have themselves in their daily lives, but also to the meaning they ascribe to these experiences on the basis of their particular personal background. This means personal experiences are subjective and might not follow the logic of rationality which reigns the public realm. The logic of these experiences is in contrast with the rights-based approach of Guatemalan and Nicaraguan feminist organizations.

In the empowerment programs of mainstream feminist organizations, relatively little attention is paid to the role of subjectivity and emotion compared to other contexts. Research has shown that in other countries (Hercus 1999 and Reger 2004) and with other types of women's organisations (Taylor 2000), as well as amongst smaller women's organizations in Guatemala and Nicaragua (Bercian 2004), feminists paid explicit attention to women's emotions and employed emotion in a non-politicised way as a means for women's empowerment. In North America and Europe, for example, the importance of subjectivity is increasingly acknowledged. Research by Reger (2004) on the NYC NOW feminists and by Hercus (1999) on Australian feminist organizations have demonstrated the positive consequences of this strategy, as much for the organizations themselves as for their target group. Women were offered tools to link their public mobilization and demands to their personal everyday lives, and felt they could do more with the information which they were presented with this way. Also, the case studies in the next chapter demonstrate the potential of complementing a rationalistic rights-based approach with an experience-based approach.

Overall though, feminist discourses and action often pay relatively little attention to subjectivity (Chejter 2007). Amongst mainstream feminist organizations in Guatemala and Nicaragua, there is also little discursive acknowledgment of the role of personal everyday experiences and emotions in women's lives, meaning that there are only a few programs working with this sphere of women's lives. The reason why I delve into the significance of personal experiences of oppression here is the fact that the oppression of women does not only have societal causes and effects, but also directly affects the individual's subjective experiences. There is consequently a complex and intriguing mechanism of feedback and feeding-forward between the effects of oppression on society at large and on women's individual's lives (See for example Heyzer 1998: 17, DeKeseredy et al 2011: 6, Murthy et al 2010: 20 and Basile and Black 2011: 111). While this interaction is theoretically acknowledged, it is often not reflected in practical action. Acknowledging this dynamic implies recognition of the importance of personal experiences. Both from a theoretical point of view and for programs aimed at the eradication of gender-based violence, recognizing the importance of the individual and personal experiences means that the existing focus on the public domain should be complemented with an expanded attention to the individual's personal life. This is also important for activists, since balancing the current approach holds the promise of becoming more effective, because programs which incorporate personal experiences address women in all domains of their lives, resulting in a more holistic approach (Sardenbergh 2008: 19). Yet, overall, feminists' lack of interest in women's subjective personal experiences is so striking that it triggers questions about the relationship between feminist activism and personal experiences, and the possibility and desirability of combining the two.

A second reason for problematizing the relationship between public and experience-based approaches to women's empowerment is the fact that the current strategy of public mobilization around a particular ideal of liberated womanhood entails a degree of normalization. In particular, the ideal sets a standard which appears culturally normal and hence, desirable. Thus, if women's personal experiences are neglected in the strategies of the women's movement, the danger exists that personal experiences will also be excluded from the norm of liberated womanhood, and that the ideal of liberated womanhood will only concern the public position of women and their access to rights. This dynamic of normalization is analyzed by Hercus (1999: 37), who argues that the feminist strategy of justifying certain behaviors which normally pertain to the taboo sphere, at the same time creates the boundaries for the expression of these behaviors. Franceschet (2003: 16) is particularly straightforward about this when arguing that the movements that exist today in Latin America are particularly normalizing in themselves because the strategy they have adopted has pushed women of different class, race ethnic and regional positions to forge some common goals, and strategies for achieving them. She points out that, while this has made the movement stronger in some respects, it has also imposed a common organizing theme, which can hold women captive, and fails to take account of the diversity of women's experiences (Also see Veraeli Swai 2006, Pontes 2008, Ellsworth 1989: 320). This diversity can only be appreciated through an empowerment strategy which also considers personal experiences of women (Heyes 2007). It is thus crucial to find a strategy that allows for collective mobilization on the basis of shared values, and at the same time to value women's personal experiences as a basis for their empowerment.

A third reason for exploring the importance of personal experiences and an experience-based approach for Guatemalan and Nicaragua feminists is the fact that theoretical literature on women's oppression and emancipation increasingly stresses the importance of the private realm and personal experiences, as well as the importance of a balance between the private and the public to bring about long-term sustainable change (See for example Prokhovnik 1998, Ryan 2001, Simões et al 2009). The argument in this literature is that promoting the full citizenship of women should not be reduced to a question of political or socio-economic citizenship, but should instead be broadened to a gendered and ethical non-instrumental understanding of what unites us as citizens. It is crucial then to take into account the specific activities which people carry out in both the private and the public realms. Prokhovnik (1998) further argues that a radical redefinition of the public-private distinction is crucial to this effort, in order to involve the dynamics of the private realm in emancipation efforts, without creating the idea that women need to be liberated *from* the private realm. Also Simões et al (2009: 232) argue that on the basis of their case study findings, the private realm should be turned to as a sphere which enables public action, rather than as something which is to be shunned altogether. Also, the case studies in the next part of the book offer the possibility to link these theoretical propositions to the concrete situation of women in Guatemala and Nicaragua.

A final motivation to explore the potential of experience-based empowerment programs which incorporate personal experiences, is that several interviewees, who were long-time activists in mainstream women's organizations, implicitly suggested that they themselves were not fully satisfied with the long-term results of their current approach – but ascribed this to contextual factors, such as political hostility and frequent personnel changes. As Alvarez, member of REDNOVI, commented, "We have been working on this topic [curbing violence against women] for years now, and, in all honesty, it's true that the situation is not getting better. Or at least not to the extent we hoped for. This is frustrating, but there is little else we can do. Taking into account the organizational inconveniences and the context in which we are operating, I see no way how we could have obtained better results" (2 June 2010). Statements like these, justify research on complementary strategies to the current approach which would be less susceptible to intervening contextual obstacles.

At this point, it is important to emphasize that the inspiration for exploring potential complementary strategies does not stem from a drive to export existing Western individualistic models to a different cultural context in which they might not be appropriate. Instead, the research builds on the subtle but growing discontent on the side of feminist organizations, their donors and their target group regarding precisely those elements which other theories and organizations in different contexts have used successfully, and which might be compatible with the work of the movement in these two cases.

It is also relevant to remark that in this part of the book, the question of the influence of armed conflict is not central. The first part of the book showed that one of the important consequences of wartime mobilization on present day women's movements is the reliance on public methods which it generated. This part of the book mainly analyzes the role of these public methods in women's emancipation process and considers complimentary strategies.

For this reason, this part of the book is also focused on feminist organizations rather than women's organizations in general, because feminist organizations are the ones most active in terms of women's emancipation and empowerment. For feminist organizations, their position on the public-private divide is furthermore particularly pertinent because they envision long-term structural changes to the position of women. It is precisely because of this ambitious goal that their methods should be assessed even more critically than those of other women's organizations. Failing to do so and not rethinking their basic assumptions and their approach to bring about such a long-term change – which goes beyond the mere modification of laws – gives rise to the risk that feminist organizations would become paralyzed and that improvements to the situation regarding the oppression of women would stall.

I therefore focus on feminist organizations and emphasize the need for a complementary strategy that focuses on the subjective, everyday experiences of women. Feminist actors have traditionally neglected this, as they were almost by definition predisposed to situate their actions in the public domain, since their goal is the establishment and defense of equal political, economic and social rights and equal opportunities for women – a task which has an important public component. Also their strategy of collective action and mobilization reinforces this focus on the public domain. However, it is precisely this focus and this strategy which I wish to call into question because, despite their significant influence on the legal domain, feminists in both countries seem to have been unable to influence women's everyday lives in an equally significant way. This is visible when looking at the growing number of cases of violence against women for example (García Santiago 2007, INE 2002, 2009). These statistics show that reinforcing the legal position of women has not been able to deal with this.

At the same time, there is a general tendency in the region – both at the societal level, and from the side of women's organization – to pay only limited attention to the dynamics which rule one's personal life, such as emotion, experience and intimacy (Jenkins and Karno 1992). It is for this reason that the book explores whether there may be opportunities for the women's movement in this domain.

This part of the book consists of three chapters. In the first chapter I problematize the way in which public and private life are commonly conceptualized, both by conservative social forces and by feminist thinkers. I argue that this dichotomy is still relevant when analysing the work of Guatemalan and Nicaraguan feminists, and that it influences the strategies of these actors. In both countries, social actors are discussing this topic and organizing around it (MAM 2010, Aguilar 1997, Kaqla 2007). The chapter introduces a new frame along the lines of which the actions of the women's movement can be analyzed. I do not aim to develop an elaborate unrivaled theory or blueprint for action on the basis thereof, but merely to offer a more balanced approach to the public-private issue. The last two chapters analyze of the work of three women's organizations which deviate from the norm in terms of how they assess the value of women's personal experience, and how they incorporate these in their empowerment program. Their approach may be complementary to the mainstream feminist in Guatemala and Nicaragua in the early 2010s. On the basis of these chapters, I consider the need for a reconceptualization of the very concepts which underlie Guatemalan and Nicaragua feminists' assumptions about women's oppression and empowerment.

CHAPTER 5

Revisiting Mainstream Feminist Approaches
A New Framework for Feminist Activism

Life has shown me that not every commitment requires payment in blood, or the heroism of dying in the line of fire. There is a heroism inherent to peace and stability, an accessible, everyday heroism that may not challenge us with the threat of death, but which challenges us to squeeze every last possibility out of life, and to live not one, but several lives all at the same time.

GIOCONDA BELLI, El Pais Bajo mi Piél, 2002

The first part of the book showed that the feminist movement in Nicaragua and Guatemala in the early 2010s mainly focuses on those elements of women's empowerment which can be addressed through a rights-based approach or a public strategy of collective action. This chapter raises several questions concerning the relationship between this strategy and the dominance of the public realm. What does it mean to focus on the public aspects of women's empowerment? Are there any alternatives to this for feminist organizations? Would focusing on women's private lives and personal experiences depoliticize the movement and even challenge its status as a social movement? What explains the current preference for working in the public domain?

To answer these questions, I first consider what is commonly seen as public and private, and assess how this alleged dichotomy inspires the approach of the women's movement in Guatemala and Nicaragua. In the first section of this chapter, I analyze how the public-private dichotomy is relevant for this research, and how it can be a framework to categorize choices of the women's movement. I thereby consider both theoretical literature on the topic, and the stance of actors on the ground. I conclude the section by arguing that the public-private binary does not only refer to two realms of life, but also to the dynamics and values which characterize these realms. Therefore, I also distinguish between approaches that build on the dynamics which characterize the public realm of life, and approaches which draw on the dynamics which characterize the private realm. I explore what these dynamics are and how they feed back into the working methods of the women's movement. I argue that Guatemalan and Nicaraguan autonomous feminists also use a 'public approach' to address issues which pertain to the private realm, for example when they organize a protest march on the issue of women's sexual rights. This triggers the question about whether the opposite – i.e. using an approach with roots in the private realm to address public issues – would also be possible.

After having examined what constitutes a 'public' and a 'private' approach, the chapter turns to the potential relevance of a 'private approach' for women's empowerment, exploring whether such an approach could be an added value to existing feminist programs. Consequently, I operationalize this approach, so as to render the notion relevant for actors in the field. On the basis of my field-work, I single out four elements traditionally related to the private realm – emotions, bodily experiences, enjoyment and spirituality – which can underlie a complementary approach to women's empowerment. Lastly, I examine whether and how these different approaches can be combined in practice, touching upon theoretical as well as practical and organizational hurdles.

Linking the Public-Private Binary to Feminist Action

Several socio-economic developments of the last decades have stimulated the disintegration of the public-private dichotomy in different parts of the world (Reynolds 2010, Hirschman 2002). Moreover, feminists have heavily criticized this alleged dichotomy because it presented the private realm as one in which no targeted public action was possible (for example Pateman 1983). Rather than doing away with this dichotomy as obsolete however, I contend that an accurate exploration of these categories is particularly compelling because it can shed light on the nature of several choices made by local feminists. This section therefore answers two critical question. How should the public-private binary be interpreted in the Guatemalan and Nicaraguan context? And how does this binary – implicitly – influence the approach of the feminist movement?

Defining the Public and the Private Realm
This section defines the public-private dichotomy in a manner that is relevant to the Guatemalan and Nicaraguan context. The public realm consists of three analytically distinct elements: the state, the formal economy and the arenas of public discourse (Fraser 1990: 57).[1] It includes political and economic activities that take place or have an impact beyond the personal life of a particular person, and it is therefore universalistic rather than particularistic in its nature

---

1   Feminists are particularly active in these three domains, respectively by means of lobbying and rights-based approaches and through workshops and awareness-raising campaigns and collective mobilizations.

(Sanday 1974: 190). This means that the public realm is more concerned with formal and universal norms and publicly recognizable practices than with the informal and personal knowledge, emotions and experiences of individuals (Parsons and Shils 1951: 82). It also implies that rationality, measurability, equality, inclusivity and objectivity can be seen as key components of the public realm (Habermas 1989: 55). As Benkler (1999: 355) suggests, when something is seen as belonging to the public domain, it is accessible to anyone. This makes approaches rooted in the public domain particularly interesting for feminist organizations, which use its logic as a means to publicly discuss issues previously deemed private. By pulling the issue of sexuality for example out of the private realm and into the public realm, feminists have been able to construct a broadly acceptable and recognizable discourse on the sexual rights of women which was pinned on the values of inclusivity, objectivity and equality, and around which public action became possible.

The private realm then is the complement to the public realm. It is often characterized as an opaque and feminized space, which revolves around subjectivity, particularism, non-rationality and sentiment (Fordham 1998: 130, Koelsch et al 2008: 253, Sapiro 1983: 31). As a consequence of socio-economic developments in Latin America – and elsewhere – the public realm has increasingly penetrated the private realm (Safa 1990: 368). This happened in several ways. One of the most tangible examples is the extent to which legal provisions in the public realm have increasingly come to influence the private realm, thereby also regulating how people can behave in the private realm. An example thereof is how relationships are influenced by laws on gay marriage, age of sexual consent, etc (Plummer 2003). Because of this, the private realm became more intimately entangled with the public realm (Rudder 2008: 900). This is also caused by the fact that feminist organizations in both countries have relied heavily on approaches which are pinned on the values that are dominant in the public domain, also when addressing issues pertaining to women's private lives. The public-private binary thus does not only refer to certain realms of life, but also to certain values commonly ascribed to these realms, i.e. inclusivity, objectivity, rationality vs. subjectivity, particularism and sentiment. The next section assesses how these values can also inspire certain actions or approaches.

'Public' and 'Private' Approaches to Empowerment?

This section argues that certain approaches can be coined public or private, depending on whether they are pinned on the dynamics and values which dominate the public or the private realm. While the boundary between the private and the public is permeable, considering that different dynamics may

govern both realms is analytically useful because this allows for the establishment of a new framework, against the background of which different approach
can be analyzed in a novel way. Specifically, this section analyses the approaches
to women's empowerment of Guatemalan and Nicaraguan feminists against
the background of the public-private dichotomy, and thereby highlights and
explores an avenue for empowerment which has been left largely unexplored,
namely the one based on the dynamics of the private realm.

The distinction between a public and a private approach is related to
Pouliot's distinction between systems of knowing. As Pouliot (2007: 267)
argues, there are two modes of knowing which co-exist and complement each
other. The difference between these two is that the rational system of knowing
is analytical, logical and controlled. It considers what is sensible, encodes reality in abstract symbols and is oriented toward delayed action. Because this way
of knowing is generalizable, it is accessible to all, and thus particularly appropriate in the public domain. Moreover, the rational system of knowing requires
justification via logic and evidence. This rational system of knowing also
impacts on the praxis of those subscribing to it, in the sense of resulting in
practices which are developed along the same lines which govern the rational
system of knowing, i.e. predictability, logic and control. An experiential, or
tacit, way of knowing on the other hand is more holistic, associative and con-
text-specific. It is based on what feels just and is oriented toward immediate
action. The experiential way of knowing is also self-evidently valid since it cannot be tested through rational means, but rather builds on an innate understanding (Pouliot 2007: 268).

This characterization of the rational and experiential system of knowing,
shows strong parallels with the distinction between the dynamics of public
and private life described above. I will therefore refer to a public approach, i.e.
an approach following the above-mentioned logic of the public domain, as a
rationalistic approach. This approach builds on a rational system of knowing.
This means that a public or rational approach is characterized by objectivity
and rationality, inclusivity and universality, and equality (Habermas 1989: 55).
These values are particularly influential in the feminist movement in
Guatemala and Nicaragua in the early 2010s. Establishing the equality of men
and women, finding rational arguments to counter women's oppression, and
appealing to the inclusivity of citizenship to demand women's human rights
are all strategies which have been fruitfully tried by the feminist movement,
and which are therefore highly valued and prioritized when developing
strategies.

I use the term experience-based approach to refer to an approach in accord
with the above mentioned characteristics of the private realm and which

builds on the experiential system of knowing. This approach incorporates elements of subjectivity, non-rationality, exclusivity, particularism and sentiment (Koelsch et al 2008: 253, Sapiro 1983: 31). It builds on a gendered subjectivity, tacit knowledge and the person's immediate sensory and emotional experience (Plummer 2003, Reynolds 2010). It revolves around the psyche, the body, as well as identity and the interpretation thereof, rather than being premised on public validation (Inness 1992: 75). In this approach, moral inwardness and authenticity are more important than outward events and external endorsement. These values are relevant because they form a substantial part of the everyday lives of many women – and men. Yet, at the same time, they are difficult to integrate in approaches which are developed in the public domain because of their specificity and volatility. The virtual rejection of these values by feminist organizations – in favor of an approach which exclusively builds on the values of the public realm – thus leaves untouched an important part of women's lives, a part of life in which they may feel comfortable. Moreover, turning to a private experience-based approach holds the promise of tapping into the unconscious and intuitive systems of knowing which operate differently from those of a rational or rights-based approach (Epstein 1994: 710). Also Ogrodnick (1999), referring to Rousseau's autobiographical work, argues that the private and the personal cannot be fully expressed through a public or rational approach, and that a different approach is needed to tap into the full array of dynamics which exist in private life.

I therefore argue in favor of building a framework which theoretically distinguishes between these approaches, in order to be able to assess the nature, strengths and pitfalls of both, and to assess where they can be used in a complementary way. In specific, a framework which underlines that there are alternatives to the current approach is useful. I distinguish between approaches which assume that private life is reigned by the same dynamics of the public domain and address private issues accordingly, and approaches which build on the individual's own psyche and sensory experiences to foster empowerment.

In this vision, the critical distinction between these approaches does not lie in the topics addressed, but in the fact that a 'private approach' is experience-based and acknowledges the dynamics of the private domain and the importance of psychological processes, whereas a 'public approach' relies on the dynamics and characteristics traditionally ascribed to the public realm. An awareness-raising workshop which discusses sexuality in terms of sexual and reproductive rights for example is thus not seen as a private approach merely because it a addresses a topic form women's private lives. This is important to remark, because it explains why I argue that organizations adopting a private approach were largely absent at the time of research in Nicaragua and

Guatemala. While there were many organizations offering awareness-raising campaigns – on how oppression plays out in women's private lives for example – in both cases, the discourse during these workshops was pinned on a rational system of knowing, aimed at inclusivity, equality, generalizability, rather than acknowledging particular experiences and subjectivity.

Creating these two categories to analyze the work of the women's movement is not a mere lexical undertaking, but draws the attention to the fact that feminist organizations in Guatemala and Nicaragua have so far relied almost exclusively on an approach which has its roots in a rational system of knowing. It also allows for the analytical distinction between different types of action. Failing to distinguish between different approaches to women's empowerment would mean that all issues in the private domain were liable to public and political definition and direction (Elshtain 1979: 497).

Rationalistic and Experience-Based Approaches in the Work of Local Feminists

In Guatemala and Nicaragua, much of the feminist discussion on women's empowerment and on more equal gender relations, has taken place against the background of an unsatisfactory classification of 'public' and 'private', in which the public realm is commonly seen as the realm of citizenship and of exercising freedom through participation in the political and socio-economic realm, and the private as the 'dark' realm of natural rhythms which is to be avoided (also see Prokhovnik 1998: 85). Therefore, the feminist movement has traditionally focused its activities and goals on the public realm. Those adopting a public approach to empowerment argue that women need to be liberated from the private realm in order to be able to take part in the public realm as equal citizens, either through political participation or through socio-economic activities. In this view, women's empowerment depends upon their access to the public realm. This idea of empowerment is not *per se* liberating, because it is pinned on an implicit hierarchy which devalues experience-based approaches and implies that women must transcend the – allegedly inferior – private realm and enter the public realm in order to exercise their freedom (Sardenbergh 2008, Jaggar 1983: 127). This is also the case for most empowerment programs where most organizations adopt a public approach to empowerment, thereby often ignoring the changes of women's private lives which are needed.

This approach can be questioned for three reasons. Firstly, it reinforces the legitimacy and dominance of the male-defined public realm. Secondly, it implies that women must leave behind their gendered subjectivity upon entering the public realm dominated by the rational system of knowing (Meyers

1994: 91, Prokhovnik 1998: 91). Thirdly, the approach denies the possibility of working with the private realm in its own right to empower women, and builds on a narrow conception of empowerment.

Moreover, amongst interviewees from the feminist movement, there was an understanding that their approach already takes into account the private domain, because they mobilize around issues commonly understood as private. However, these private issues are only addressed through approaches rooted in the public domain, such as the rights-based approach. The Autonomous Women's Movement (MAM) in Nicaragua and La Cuerda in Guatemala are examples of organizations with such an approach. These organizations have turned to personal experience, intimate relations and the individual lives of women, or in in other words, to topics from the private realm, and framed them as issues deserving policy attention. They thereby uplifted the public sphere conception of politics in favor of a focus on the link between personal problems and political problems. In doing this, they took a first step to questioning the categories of the public and the private. In accordance with the first new leftist women activists of the U.S. in 1962, they pressed for participatory democracy because they see politics as a means to finding a meaning for the self (Port Huron Statement in Miller 1987: 332). Issues from the private life are thus drawn into the public domain as a means to emancipate women and public changes are seen as a means to foster personal changes.

This approach, however, also had important setbacks, because it approaches topics from the private realm in a utilitarian way, as a tool for change the public realm, rather than seeing the private realm as a domain with inherent value. The approach thus only introduced the rational systems of knowing from the public sphere into the personal realm, without considering how the dynamics of the personal realm could be introduced into the public realm. This is due to the underlying assumption that the private realm should be politicized before action in it is possible (Dietz 1985). The approach thereby denies the possibility that the private realm is ruled by a different dynamic and foregoes the possibility to tap into this dynamic to foster women's empowerment. What Guatemalan and Nicaraguan feminists see as a private approach should therefore rather be seen as a variant of a public approach which addresses topics from women's private lives in a public manner.

It should also be acknowledged that the private realm and its experiential and tacit system of knowing, cannot and do not have to be escaped from, and that approaches which build on this system of knowing may also be useful at a societal level where another system of knowing is dominant today (Rowbotham 1993). As Lorde (1984: 112) stated, "the master's tools will never dismantle the master's house", or, applied to this context, relying solely on the logic of the public realm will not create the conditions for genuinely changing this realm. This is not to argue that feminists should aim to rely exclusively on experience-based approaches, but rather to acknowledge the potential of working with unconventional approaches in a complementary way. As Lister (1995: 12) argues, 'women have to participate politically as citizens if they are to transform the conditions under which caring work is performed', but this exercise of power is not, in itself, a necessary part of women's empowerment. While it is thus valuable for women to enter the public realm and challenge the reigning idea that this is an area belonging to men, it could be equally valuable to explore resources which lie in the private domain which women can introduce into the public realm upon entering it.

In the next section I examine additional – theoretical and practical – reasons for complementing the current approach to empowerment with an experience-based element in the Guatemalan and Nicaraguan case.

Experience-Based Approaches as a Complementary Strategy to Empowerment

I argued above that empowerment through a private or experience-based approach refers to forms of empowerment which goes beyond the mainstream feminist conceptions of empowerment which see confidence, self-awareness and empowerment as semi-automatic consequences of other factors such as having a job. Experience-based approaches to empowerment are centered around women's personal experiences and believe these to be crucial in their empowerment process. This vision is valuable for several reasons.

Firstly, an experience-based approach acknowledges that there are different systems of knowing and acting than the one which reigns the public domain. This establishes a space in which the individual can act in a way which is not directly impinged upon by the dynamic of the public realm. Moreover, acknowledging these different dynamics protects the private realm from commodification and objectification (Inness 1992). This is a precondition for women to be able to live out their personal realities, which in turn can be seen as a crucial aspect of their empowerment, because women's oppression is internalized and experienced in the first place in the private realm, i.e. in their psyche (Reynolds 2010: 34, Flores-Ortiz 2003: 354).

Secondly, approaching the private domain and women's personal experiences in their own right and through an approach which does not require public validation, can also be useful for social actors envisioning public change, since psychological transformation can support the realization of public and political ideals (Simões et al 2009, Levine 2010). Turning to the potential of the private realm moreover avoids a situation in which the – patriarchal – state alone would become the guarantor of women's emancipation and in which women can only proceed by participating in the public realm on the reigning conditions (McKinnon 2005, Pateman 1988). It also provides organizations with a better understanding of the needs of their target group because it gives an insight into how women judge themselves and how they experience and interpret their own achievements, personal hurdles, and material situations. On the basis of this, organizations can judge where action and attention is most needed and which resources women have at their disposal in their specific situation (Bayard de Volo 2006b).

Furthermore, the nature of the changes which feminists envision makes it crucial to engage with the private realm and with women's personal experiences in a genuinely new way. The feminist ideal of structurally altering social structures, assumes a changed relation between the individual and these social structures, which in turn assumes a change in identity. The supposition of a fundamental change in women's identities and private lives thus already underlies the struggle of Guatemalan and Nicaraguan feminists. Such a change, however, requires an experience-based approach which takes into account the personal lives of women, since these are crucial in shaping the identity-formation process (Devos 2003, Adams 1989). James (1950: 297) asserts that 'the central part of the self is *felt* and rooted in emotion' (stress in original, also see Mead 1964, Ward and Throop 1992: 80). In his legacy, Goffman (1963: 105) defines this self as the 'felt identity'. An approach and language adequate to describe these feelings and subjective realities is thus needed (Das 1996: 67, Butler 2005, Erickson 1995: 126). Such an experience-based approach allows women to move toward experiencing their aspirations for themselves and developing an internal system of reflection and judgement (Havens 1985: 376). This is needed for the development of an individual consciousness in which one can experience a state of 'being for oneself' – as opposed to the state of 'being for others' (Fulchiron 2004 and Plummer 2003: 60). According to Erickson (1995) this development of an individual consciousness should be the centre of every empowerment strategy. An experience-based approach facilitates this process of self-observation and self-exploration, which can provide women with a better understanding of their self-worth, and how they have internalized oppressive patterns (Reger 2008). This is important for the formation of an identity which is based on self-awareness, rather than being derived from oppressive schemes (Taylor 1989). As the cases in the next chapter show, feminist organizations can play an important role in this process, by organizing workshops for example.

Lastly, exploring the potential of an experience-based approach is relevant in this context, given the interest on the side of certain actors from the feminist movement – especially in Guatemala – to work in this way. However, issues of time, expertise or resources often mean that such an approach is abandoned in favor of an approach which is more conventional, generalizable, easier to measure, and supported by the donors.

In conclusion, both the public and the private realm, and thus both rational and experience-based approaches, are important for women's empowerment. Approaching women in their private lives in a way which is distinct from political participation or economic independence, and which does not conceive of their maternal role as an absolute value neither, takes account of the diverse ways in which women engage in activities on the basis of gender, ethnic, cultural and other differences (Prokhovnik 1998: 98). Forms of action which acknowledge the existence of dynamics other than those of the public domain can thus complement the current public focus (Weismantel 2004).

A broader scope of action on the side of the women's movement holds the promise of acknowledging what people actually do, and of being able to tap into the full array of experiences in these two spheres. This is important in order to respect each realm in its own right, and not turn one into an attribute of the other. An experience-based approach acknowledges the existence of empowering practices in the private realm. To arrive at such a non-rejectionist, non-oppositional, non-hierarchical interconnection between the public and the private, or between rational and tacit/experience-based, new conceptions of politics amongst feminists are needed, which acknowledge that the cause of women's oppression is not their private life or gendered subjectivity, and which aims to overcome the suppression of women's gendered subjectivity in the public realm. Yet while the private realm has come to play an important role in the work of Guatemalan and Nicaraguan feminist organizations, conscious reflection on how to approach this domain in a way which draws on its inherent dynamics and values lags behind, because the current public approach of feminist organizations does not easily accommodate for the volatile and subjective experiences of the private realm. In order to help close this gap, the next section operationalizes what constitutes an experience-based approach of empowerment. It thereby turns the theoretical exploration above into a useful tool for the feminist movement.

Operationalizing What Constitutes an Experience-Based Approach

Having established the conceptual difference between rationalistic and experience-based approaches, and the potential merits of the latter, this section explores on which basis an experience-based approach can be developed in practice. This is an important step because the subjectivity and volatile nature of such an approach contributes to a marked reluctance on the side of the feminist movement toward such an approach which is not easily generalizable and not as easy to replicate. This section demonstrates that there are different ways for feminist organizations to engage in a dialogue with women's private lives, which are not defined by the dynamics of the public domain. This facilitates a more complete acknowledgment of the private realm, as well as recognition of its potential to contribute to women's empowerment.

In this section I explore four elements which can be used as building blocks for an experience-based approach: emotions, bodily experiences, enjoyment, and spirituality. While all four also have a substantial public component, I am interested here in the extent to which they can underly an experience-based approach. The choice for these four factors is based on the fieldwork and most specifically on the work by organizations which are discussed in the next two chapters.

Emotions

Emotions refer to the psychological arousal, expressive behavior and the conscious subjective experience of individuals (Meyers 2004: 500). They provide the – positive or negative – affective component to motivation to direct and energize behavior (Gaulin and McBurney 2003: 121). Turning to emotions in a study on women's empowerment does not mean that I embrace the sex-stereotype that women are emotional and men rational (Stillion and Noviello 2001, Martin and Doka 2000). Such a view has colonizing effects on a person's life options, and says little about the emotions themselves (Fischer 1993: 303). Emotions are discussed here as a crucial aspect of the private realm, for both men and women. The choice of many Guatemalan and Nicaraguan feminists to contest gender stereotypes by turning to a rationalistic public strategy deprived of any emotional content, fails to address emotions or the private realm in its own right.

How Working with Emotions Can Inspire an Experience-Based Approach

Emotions are present in both the public and the private realm (e.g. public expressions of anger during demonstrations, populist discourse which appeal to primal feelings, etc). Berlant (2000: 33) illustrates how emotions are not just resources employed in the private sphere, but used and felt within the often very public reproduction of social categories. Her research on the cultural politics of pain in the u.s. for example, showed that expressing suffering through testimony was often a political act, an attempt to demonstrate who had been most excluded from 'happiness' and was, as a consequence of this, most enti-tled to compensation. Emotions thus have a social value and even a subversive potential in the public domain. However, emotions first arise in the individu-al's psyche, and are also first experienced there. As Barrett (2005: 261) argues, the experience of emotions is a perceptual act, based on immediate experi-ence, which first causes sensory, perceptual, motor and physiological changes. Because of this direct experience-based nature, which is not accessible by a narrative discourse, working with emotions requires a specific approach.

Furthermore, emotional issues have a different dynamic in the private domain than they do in the public domain (Barrett 2005). Addressing emo-tions by adopting the same methods and logic that characterize the public domain, *de facto* downgrades the role of subjectivity, relationality and affectiv-ity therein. Therefore emotions are not always served by an approach based on objectivity and rationality (Fordham 1998: 128). An experience-based approach of emotions is thus potentially more subversive than the commodification of emotions in an otherwise rational public discourse (Mumby et al 1992: 472, Arendt 1958: 50–3).

Moreover, revaluing the role of emotions can provide women with an alter-native, experience-based approach to their personal process of healing and emancipation from oppressive situations, which goes beyond the societal and legal side of their oppression or abuse. This means that women can gain a more comprehensive view on their subordination and that they can start incorporating the experience in their psyche to make sense of this in a felt way (Rosenwasser 2000). Holmes (2010) presents a convincing illustration of the emotionality and *relationality* of this type of reflexive processes, concluding that processes of social and self-reproduction benefit from the attention to emotions.

Emotionality is thus not simply an imposed role-pattern which necessarily debilitates women and makes them dependent on the rationality of men. It is also a socially significant experience in the private realm, which deserves attention in its own right. Working with emotions in an experience-based approach provides women with an alternative scheme and tips the balance away from a rationalistic and analytical approach drawn from the public domain, to a more emotion-centered and experience-based approach with roots in the private domain (Hercus 1999). While this is a personal process, a credible social actor – such as the women's movement – can facilitate this, and present women with the tools to embark on such a personal process.

When operationalizing an experience-based approach it is thus key to addresses emotions in a direct and experiential way, without making them subject to a public validation – which is an inevitable consequence of a public approach. This is important because these experiential, interpretive and emotional elements cannot adequately be addressed through a rationalistic approach (Jaggar 1989).

An experience-based approach which takes emotions into account can thus lead to more balanced approaches of empowerment. Several smaller Guatemalan feminist organizations show that this is possible (see following chapters). Also amongst several other women's organizations, methods are gaining ground which take women's emotions as a point of departure to develop a more experience-based approach. They do so by approaching women's emotions as a resource rather than as a hurdle to their empowerment, or as an issue which is best addressed in a rationalistic discourse. Their approach acknowledges the importance of working with emotions – not only cognition – to empower women. They promote an integrated understanding in which thinking and feeling are considered equally important. Yet, the number of social actors experimenting with emotion-based or experience-based approaches in their empowerment work is limited. These organizations are the focus of the next chapter.

Bodily Experiences

Working with bodily experiences can also be a building block of an experience-based approach. When I refer to bodily experiences here I mean the subjective conscious experiences that directly impact upon the body, i.e. they are bodily sensations and perceptual experiences which no amount of physical information includes (Jackson 1982: 273). In theory, all experiences are bodily, since they are registered through the senses and processed in the brain. However, I limit myself here to those experiences which specifically revolve around the body, such as movement therapy, intimacy and sports, but also physical abuse.

When operationalizing an experience-based approach, it is relevant to take into account bodily experiences for four reasons. Firstly, body and mind cannot be separated. The body plays an essential role in the human psyche (Aldama 2003). Acknowledging this avoids dichotomizing body and mind, which would hamper a more holistic understanding of women's psychology and obscure the complex ways in which experiences of violence and oppression affect the entire sense of self for women (Lara 2008). Oppression and abuse are internalized and embodied. This can lead to the alienation of women from their bodies and psyches, since both of these come to express the dominant discourse of oppression, rather than women's own identity (Flores-Ortiz 2003). DiCarrie (2007: 10) argues that designated sensory stimulation opens up a field of reflexivity in which the subject becomes more self-aware and gains a self-understanding by feeling through the body. Approaching bodily experiences in such a way has an empowering effect because experiencing their own bodies again can be a means for women to gain a better understanding of the effect of their psyche on their body. Bodily experience is thus relevant in an experience-based approach because it raises awareness about the mechanisms through which the internalization of discourses happens and plays out, by increasing women's bodily awareness. This also facilitates a growing awareness of other aspects of their own situation and of the effect of the societal discourses they are exposed to (Lagarde 2001: 302, de Cicco 2009, Actoras de Cambio 2006).

Next to fostering awareness of the impact of oppressive discourses, working with bodily experiences through an experience-based approach can help to recover traumatic memory for women who have been victim of violence. Flores Ortiz' (2003: 350) researched the recovery process of abused Latin-American women in the United States. In these community projects, the process of becoming aware of their own bodily experiences played a central role in women's empowerment process. One of her interviewees illustrated how working with the body can foster awareness of psychological processes as well, when she testified, "It's like my body remembers certain things, even though I don't want to remember". Working with the body can thus be a direct way to explore how women's situation of oppression or abuse has affected them, and to become aware of their own situation. An experience-based approach which works with the body can thus facilitate the act of bearing witness to oneself and one's own life circumstances (Laub 2009), but also avoids the colonizing assumption that bearing witness is necessarily a narrative act (Caruth 1996, McKinney 2007). This facilitates the reintegration of experiences in a non-rhetorical way, which leaves more space for the uniqueness of the experience. Working with the body thus provides the possibility to live through the memory and the experience, in a way which a purely rational narrative method does not per se facilitate, because of its limiting imperative of presenting a coherent story (Lambek and Antze 1996: xix, Caruth 1995). It thereby goes beyond the limited understanding of self which narrative strategies can convey (Baehr 2009: 108). Working with the body thus offers a solution to Das' (1996: 167) demand for "new ways of talking and listening, which involves the whole human experience and not only the mental part".

An experience-based approach can thus use the body as an entry point to start processes of *re-feeling*, remembering and bearing witness, thereby raising awareness. This is complementary to rationalistic narrative methods of bearing witness and can even be a precondition to them. Because the effects of trauma, violence and oppression are often difficult to express in words, other forms of remembering and sense-making may be needed, which address that which has been internalized (Herman 1997, Olff et al 2007). Therefore, exploring avenues to render this awareness-raising more comprehensive is crucial, and fit the priority list of Guatemalan and Nicaraguan feminists. In practice this means that an experience-based approach revolving around the body can also be useful for goals in the public realm. This could be an alternative to always overlying the private realm with a public approach. In the next chapter, I explore how some Guatemalan women's organizations have used this approach in practice. Their programs facilitate awareness about how violence and oppression are inscribed in the body, thereby raising awareness of their own situation amongst women.

Secondly, empowering women through an experience-based approach revolving around the body does not only facilitate a growing awareness, but can also be a means to regain ownership and agency (Bermúdez 2001:140). Alienation of the body causes a loss of ownership and control (deVignemont 2007). Bringing women back in touch with their bodies can help to regain a sense of agency and to create narratives which make sense in their own lives (Anazaldúa 2002). The empowering effects of such an approach are also illustrated by the work of Flores-Ortiz (2003). One of her interviewees (2003) testified:

> I finally inhabit my body, I feel the beating of my heart, I know what I am thinking at the moment, I can translate my emotions and I have conquered fear. I can say that I am no longer afraid to live, to love, to make love, to be touched.
>
> 2003: 357

This illustrates the extent to which working with the body can facilitate awareness and a sense of ownership and potency.

Lastly, it is useful to work with bodily experience when operationalizing an experience-based approach because this has transgressive potential. The very fact of paying attention to the body is transgressive in a society where self-care and bodily experiences are controversial and are usually – if at all – addressed through a rational discursive approach, rather than an experience-based one (Hernández 2009). Challenging this controversial status in a culturally relevant way can have an empowering value. Culturally relevant, as Álvarez (14 February 2011) argues, means that such a strategy needs to appear fairly uncontroversial on the surface so as not to shock people too much, but introduce little infringements on taboo-laden issues gradually. Organizing workshops to teach women to care for themselves and convey the message that they are allowed to do so, for example, is not *per se* a rupture of the dominant cultural scripts, and is something which a feminist movement can play a role in (CLADEM 2000: 68). Taking care of and talking about the body is accepted in most indigenous communities, to the extent it concerns hygienic or aesthetic aspects (Palencia Prado 1999). This can be used as a point of entry on which the movement can build an empowerment strategy with transgressive potential. This transgressive potential also lies in how corporal performance challenges culture. Variations in corporal performance – such as cutting one's hair short, walking with a straight back, etc. – can be instances of resistance and can accumulate and cascade into forms of resistance that have profound effects on conscious decision-making and social practice (DiCarrie 2007: 3). Women's organizations can encourage such experiments and modifications which can lead to the questioning of norms and help the subject make conscious decisions. For women to be able to consciously use this transgressive potential however, they need to have sufficient bodily awareness.

The body can thus be seen as the site where structures of oppression are reinforced, as well as a site for empowerment and resisting oppression. It is the space where social constructions and interpretations of oppression can be addressed in a direct way, and this can lead to new or increased awareness (Aldama 2003: 5). While focusing on the internalization of oppression can obscure the political roots of this oppression, reconnecting women with their bodies represents a more direct way of exposing the impact of societal injustice and therefore facilitates a bottom-up approach. Moreover, strategies which only focus on societal dynamics are unlikely to be able to deal with the effects of oppression and violence which women experience in their private lives – such as feelings of personal guilt – or to teach them how to renegotiate cultural scripts on the basis of their own meaning system (Hernández Avila 2002).

That the body is a relevant site to explore was also illustrated by the fact that several interviewees referred to their own body despite strong taboos. Statements such as "I felt it [situation of oppression] as a heavy pain in my stomach" (Delmorales, participant to a workshop of Kaqla, 31 January 2011), "I felt as if my hands had been untied and my body could move again" (Arellano, participant Actoras de Cambio, 17 February 2011), and "Being able to look at my own body again in a mirror, was something which I had never expected" (Valderrama, participant Kaqla, 26 February 2010), all indicate that the body constitutes an important site to work with when deconstructing oppressive structures oppression.

To date however, women's nascent desire to work with their intimate and bodily experience is usually not picked up by local women's organizations. And where the body does enter the discourse, it is often presented as a site of problems and danger, for example in relation to abortion or sexual violence (deCicco 2009, SI Mujer 2006, Pizarro 2000). A discourse which emphasizes the positive and joyful potential of the body can help overcome the idea that the body is a site surrounded with dangers and inconveniences. This links back to a third potential building block of an experience-based approach.

The Role of Enjoyment: The Politics of Fun

For a depressed and austere society cannot have a solid civil foundation
AFTAB-E-YAZD, 9 January 2001, cited in Bayat 2010: 144

This section discusses enjoyment as a third crucial building block of an experience-based approach. Enjoyment refers to the full array of ad hoc, non-routine, and joyful pursuits ranging from playing games, joking and dancing, to involvement in playful ways of art, music, sex, sport, laughing, speaking and carrying oneself, where the individual temporarily breaks free from the disciplined constraints of everyday life, normative obligations and organized power (Bayat 2010: 138). It can thus be seen as a metaphor for the expression of individuality, spontaneity and lightness. This is why enjoyment – more than other basic human sentiments – deserves special attention when operationalizing an experience-based approach to empowerment. Next to this empowering and transgressive potential, enjoyment is important as a basic human feeling which has an effect on the psyche and the body, and which is expressed and invoked through the body (Izard 2007). It is thereby at the intersection of emotions and the body, both of which are key aspects of an experience-based approach. Enjoyment originates in the individual's psyche, and also plays out there in the first instance. Because of its immediate and subjective sensory and emotional experience which makes it an intrinsically and universal human experience, enjoyment cannot be labelled a Western cultural import and cannot easily be co-opted (Barrett 2005, Fredrickson and Losada 2005 and Ekman 2003).

The Relevance of Enjoyment for an Experience-Based Approach
Since enjoyment can be present in most human activities, it can be incorporated into almost every empowerment program (Bayat 2010). The reason why enjoyment – as a direct and particular experience – is relevant for an experience-based approach, is twofold.

Firstly, showing women – through workshops – to enjoy themselves in general, and their own bodies in particular, can provide a sense of well-being (Fredrickson 1998 and 2000). These immediate instances of enjoyment create a niche in which a more pleasurable life can be lived in anticipation of structural changes. Incorporating enjoyment in an experience-based empowerment

strategy is interesting for the feminist movement itself, because it can introduce a more immediate satisfying and gratifying dynamic in the work of feminists, which is often burdensome. This is important in practice because many
feminist activists indicated during interviews that they find their work challenging and often de-motivating because there are so few visible or tangible
results. Introducing an element of enjoyment in their own approach can thus
create a niche for feminist activists to conduct work in a more inspiring way.

The acknowledgment by participants that joy is not a sin, but a deeply
human emotion, is moreover transgressive because it can challenge the idea
that one only has responsibilities towards others, and instead install the idea
that one is also entitled to a joyful life of one's own (Bayat 2007, Valdez Medina
1999, Poal Marcet 1995). Thereby, focusing on enjoyment exposes the taboo
which surrounds women enjoying themselves (Portocarrero 2008). The dominant social script in Guatemala and Nicaragua sees women as care-takers, who
are not supposed to enjoy themselves (Franzoni and Voorend 2011). Women
who go against this, often meet with social disapproval. Doing so, however,
they indirectly challenge the existing norms and set the stage for change, also
in the public realm (Stephen 1997, Wieschiolek 2003). For this reason it is all
the more remarkable that so few feminist organizations have incorporated this
element into their programs.

Secondly, empowering women by bringing them back in touch with feelings
of joy brings back a sense of agency, related to the fact that women can decide
to enjoy what they are doing. This is especially useful in a context where the
political situation leaves little scope for public agency. Improvised, spontane-
ous, free-form, changeable and thus unpredictable expressions and practices
of people can lead to unpredictable and motivating forms of protest, in the
face of which governments often find themselves powerless. Several case studies on social movement strategies have illustrated the powerlessness and fear
of political leaders and other social figures before simple displays of spontaneity and joy and the pursuit of everyday pleasures which are harder to control
and discipline than organized forms of social action (Ehrenreich 2007 and
Makar 2011). This shows that introducing fun and enjoyment in an empowerment strategy, can also have immediate social effects, which go beyond wom-
en's empowerment in the private realm.

Examples of the Social Value of an Experience-Based Approach
Centered Around Enjoyment

A case in point of the subversive and social power of enjoyment is the research
on Green activists in the United States by Lichterman (1996: 36–48). He
describes how in this case, many activists saw enjoyment as an integral part of

their strategy during their protest marches for environmental causes, in the sense that it motivated them and inspired them to continue their struggle in a passionate way. For these activists, fun was a crucial element in influencing the group dynamics. This shows how a volatile and non-rational element can convincingly be introduced in an otherwise rationalistic public strategy. Lichterman (1996) argues that the contrast between these forms of social protest and the rank-and-file marchers representing established and well-defined organizations with a clear social goal could not be clearer, since these forms of protest expressed much more than solidarity or the belief in one cause. They gave expression to a lifestyle and were therefore much more difficult to contain.

In Latin America, the example of the Familia Galan in Bolivia shows how this element from an experience-based approach can be introduced in a public approach. This is an even more explicit example of how fun can be incorporated into the program of a social movement. Paulson's research (2002) on this group pointed out that the main idea behind the marches of this LGBT-group is to combine two goals: social protest on the one hand, and, on the other hand, introducing enjoyment into lives which are usually characterized by a high degree of discrimination and strain. Galan's marches are colorful expressions of participants' identities, accompanied with music, dancing, singing and other artistic expressions. The main aim of the Familia Galan is thus not only to change the political structure which contributes to the perpetuation of their oppressed condition, but also to create a niche for enjoyment in their daily lives. It thereby combines the private and the public, both in its methods and in its goals.

In Nicaragua and Guatemala, the theme of sexuality is illustrative of how elements from the private lives of women, and specifically enjoyment, (can not) enter the public discourse. The topic of sexuality is often used by the feminist movement, but it is mainly presented as a rights issue, deprived of its private content related to the body, emotions or enjoyment. An example is the 2000 campaign by the Nicaraguan Network of Women Against Violence (Red de Mujeres Contra la Violencia 2000). This campaign proposed that women were entitled to sexual rights, but the argument was immediately linked to the debate on abortion. Due to the highly polarized and politicized nature of the abortion debate which soon became all-encompassing, sexual issues not fitting this politicized discourse were left unexplored. Another example is that of the Nicaraguan Autonomous women's movement MAM (2009: 8), which argues that the expression of one's sexual freedoms can be used in the struggle against patriarchy because sexual freedom challenges the taken-for-granted roles women tend to adopt. Sexuality is thereby only addressed in a functionalist and utilitarian way however, which disregards women's experiences. A dis-course of enjoyment oriented at women's experience can complement these functionalist interpretations of sexuality; both the dominant conservative interpretation which only links sexuality to reproduction, as well as the femi-nist interpretation which pragmatically sees sexuality as the political founda-tion for women's liberation (Gagnon 2004). Conveying the message that women are allowed to enjoy their sexuality thus gives them a sense of agency and well-being, while at the same time being transgressive (Mosby 2011, Pereira 2009, Hamel 2008). It also connects long-term goals and the immediate needs of social movement actors and can as such be a valuable strategy for social movements.

Yet, due to practical difficulties, few feminist organizations incorporate an element of enjoyment in their programs. Firstly, because strategies based on enjoyment are often non-rational and non-quantifiable by definition, they can be hard to incorporate in an organizational planning – especially in those pro-grams which have to be approved by third parties in order to obtain funding. Moreover, because the politics of fun challenge existing approaches (such as lobbying or traditional forms of protest) and the dominant script that femi-nism is a serious political struggle, they are often confronted with skepticism from within the social movement's ranks. Several interviewees saw enjoyment as being incompatible with what they saw as more 'serious' matters needed for women's emancipation, such as political pressure. As Castro, member of Grupo Venancia replied when asked about this, "Of course it would be nicer if we could derive more enjoyment from doing this, but the truth is that this is hard work. It simply isn't something enjoyable. We need to pressure government [...] For women to enjoy themselves, they first need a context in which this is possible" (2 March 2011).

The idea that an approach which incorporates fun or enjoyment would challenge their credibility, meant that the complementarity of this focus was usually not considered by feminists. While this consideration is valid in a society where a turn to emotion and enjoyment might encounter resis-tance, adopting a two-track strategy could overcome this and allow femi-nist organisations to engage more fully with the dynamics of private life. A last difficulty of incorporating a focus on enjoyment in their empower-ment programs is that effective politics of fun are not so easily developed because they require a great deal of creativity and originality, and these cannot easily be produced artificially. Several organizations in the field have, however, tapped into this domain by adopting a more flexible and organic structure themselves. How this occurred is the focus of the next chapter.

Spritiuality

Spirituality is defined here in opposition to religion. I use the term spirituality rather than religion, because religion is defined as the institutionalized system of beliefs, whereas spirituality here refers to the personal experience and sense-making of individuals in this domain (Hill 2003: 64, Hill et al 2000: 52, Zinnbauer et al 1997).

While spirituality – like emotions, bodily experiences and enjoyment – manifests itself in both the public and the private realm, the above definition emphasizes the personal experience and interpretation of spirituality. Spirituality can therefore be seen as a building block of an experience-based approach. In specific, I discuss it here because it was a crucial element of the programs of – indigenous – organizations working through an experience-based approach.

The Relevance of Spirituality for an Experience-Based Approach

That spirituality can inspire an experience-based approach is illustrated by several indigenous Guatemalan women's organizations which rely on indigenous belief systems as a means to empower women. In their case, elements of Mayan *cosmovision* were incorporated into their work in an experience-based manner, i.e. according to a logic which is not drawn from the public realm but which focuses on women's personal experiences and interpretations in this domain. Their approach is thereby progressive because it does not shy a controversial interpretation of spiritual elements in order to foster women's empowerment, within a culturally relevant framework and on the basis of their own experiences. An example of how this happens is that, instead of equality, the activists of Kaqla, an indigenous women's organization from Guatemala City, advocate the complementary nature of men and women in their empowerment programs. This strategy is based on the idea of complementarity, which runs through the whole Mayan belief system, and which is explored with reference to women's personal experiences and understanding (DePuy 2006, McLeod 2010, Marcos 2009). This suggests that the values of particularity and complementarity, which are pivotal in the Mayan *cosmovision*, color women's frames of reference more than the values of universality and equality which normally underly a feminist approach to empowerment. These values are therefore important to take into account in this specific conceptualization of an experience-based approach.

Also, literature on this topic increasingly focuses on the relation between spirituality, social activism and identity (Avila and Parker 1999, Fukuyama and Sevig 1999, Keating 2005). This research points out the potential relevance of spirituality both for women's psychological well-being and for their role as activists. This underlines the relevance of considering how spirituality can be incorporated in a feminist empowerment strategy in an emancipatory and progressive way. In the section below, a basis for this is set out.

Combining Strategies: Avoiding the Pitfalls of Rationalism and Relativism

The previous section built on findings from the fieldwork to operationalize what an experience-based approach can look like, how it can contribute to the revaluation of – non-rational – experiences, and how it can influence the public realm. But is an experience-based approach compatible with the current approaches of feminist organizations in both countries? I analyze this question by assessing the theoretical compatibility, as well as practical objections leveled by interviewees. I first briefly discuss how the current feminist approach based on rational systems of knowing influences the everyday lives of women. Consequently, I consider whether this approach can be combined with an experience-based approach, and if so, what difficulties this might entail. To conclude, I consider the organizational challenges of combining both approaches.

Consequences of Feminist's Public Approach of the Private Realm
The predisposition of the Guatemalan and Nicaraguan feminist movement for a rationalistic public approach, also when addressing issues which directly relate to women's personal experiences, can be explained by the movements' historical development. The rhetorical and militant strategies of feminists were adopted in a historical period when social mobilization and activism were crucial because of the vast societal changes which were occurring in the aftermath of civil conflict, and because activists wanted to shape these changes to the favor of women (Moberg 2005, Kampwirth 2004 and Nakaya 2003). Both in Guatemala and in Nicaragua, feminism developed into a persistent social force, in part because of this strategy which presented women with new points of view which allowed them to re-evaluate taken-for-granted patterns (Castillo 2007). The social changes which feminists envisioned are still far from complete however, and still meet with much resistance on religious, moral and political grounds (Mendez 2006, Kampwirth 2006). This means that the current priority of fostering change at the societal level, remains important, but that complementary avenues for proceeding may have to be explored in order to arrive at more profound change.

While feminists have already turned to the private realm as a domain which could foster women's empowerment, they have mainly addressed private issues in the same way as they addressed public issues, i.e. by organizing social protest, lobbying for legal changes etc. Their aim of denouncing the social dynamic of oppression in practice turned all attention to the public domain and thereby closed some doors for the feminist movement. There has been a neglect of those elements of women's lives which cannot be captured in a rationalistic discourse – such as emotions, the body, enjoyment and spirituality – but which can be empowering for women. This makes it difficult to incorporate these elements as a resource for women's empowerment (see MAM 2009, CINCO 2006, Montenegro 1996). Elshtain (1981: 216) argues that this depreciation of an experience-based approach is related to an implicit value hierarchy which feminists borrow from the dominant discourse of the public realm which revolves around rationality. In this discourse elements such as emotions, care, intimacy and affection are often seen as feminine, and therefore undervalued (Prentice 2002). Elshtain argues that the inability of feminist activists to incorporate certain traditionally "feminine" traits is what causes their repudiation of these qualities and of the identities and roles linked to them. The feminist ideal of a strong and assertive emancipated woman does not allow for such 'soft' characteristics, which are seen as disempowering. The discourse of mainstream autonomous feminist organizations is therefore implicitly condemning the maternal identity, suggesting that this is the part of female identity that *de facto* keeps women repressed and keeps them from becoming fully empowered (for example Chejter 2007).

This was illustrated by the remark of one interviewee from a Nicaraguan feminist organization, who argued that:

> To empower women, we have to show them that they are not *just* the mother of someone, or not *just* the wife of someone, but that it is important for them to also become active in other domains of life which are open to them
> CASTRO, Grupo Venancia, 2 March 2011

Even though subtle, the word 'just' in this sentence suggests that a maternal identity cannot be a fulfilling one in itself, and the assumption that women by definition ought to explore new roles in the public realm is normative. Similar assumptions underlay many statements by Nicaraguan and Guatemalan feminists who envisioned women's empowerment. These assumptions turn the role of caretaker, for example, into an unresolved and problematic part of women's identity. Women who chose to organize their life around these alleged feminine identities, are thus *de facto* ignored by these sorts of empowerment strategies.

In order to integrate this part of women's identity in feminist programs as well, an approach is needed which accepts that the meaning of these characteristics is different for each woman personally because every woman has different experiences. An experience-based approach can serve this goal. Complementing the current approach with an experience-based approach can help to make women's individual experiences, needs and emotions more central in social movement work, thus revaluing these as a resource for empowerment. There are several aspects of an experience-based approach that are compatible with the work of the feminist movement and can further strengthen its cause.

The Complementarity of a Rationalistic and an Experience-Based Approach

This section considers the possibility of complementing the current rationalistic and rights-based approach with elements from an experience-based approach. At first sight, an experience-based approach which revolves around emotion, bodily experiences, enjoyment and spirituality seems to be in conflict with the current approach of the feminist movement in Nicaragua and Guatemala. Yet, I argue that such an approach can be relevant for the feminist movement for several reasons.

Firstly, an experience-based approach is compatible with the current goals of the feminist movement in Nicaragua and Guatemala because it helps women to become more aware of their emotions, body and personal situation and of how oppression impacts upon these. Moreover, it can help women to discover their own emotions and bodies, and thereby become more aware of these and experience more ownership. This can help, for example, to resist the pressure for *autosacrificio* and *autonegación* which women experience every day (Valdez Medina 1999). This can affect women's behavior in the public realm: discovering one's identity is intricately related to the position one takes in the public realm and one's connection with others (Heidegger 1962).

Moreover, traditional gender-stereotypes are often criticized by feminists as being inherently limiting and normative, but Fromm (2005) argues that behavior which is wholly in accord with the social mores or gender norms can still be authentic, if it results from a personal understanding and approval of its drives and origins.

This means that it is more important for feminist organizations to facilitate personal understanding and self-knowledge, than to simply reject specific identities, roles and values which are deemed submissive. The goal should thus not only be to provide abstract information on emancipation, but to provide women with strategies to critically assess this information on the basis of their own experiences (Broughton 1978). In other words, to facilitate authentic decision-making, women do not only need information but also tools to assess the relationship between this information and their personal life. These tools can be provided through an experience-based approach, which brings them back in touch with an otherwise unresolved part of their identity. On the basis of this work, women can formulate their own goals and desires, which potentially reflect their authentic desires better than the pre-given goals of feminist organizations. An experience-based approach to empowerment can be useful in triggering reflexive processes on this topic (DiCarrie2007). Mobilizing on the basis of these goals which women set themselves then, is more motivating for them than rallying behind goals imposed from above (Colker 1989). However, herein lies one problem of this new approach, namely that it challenges the central position which many feminist organizations currently hold, and may therefore cause a degree of resistance and unease amongst activists. Gross (1981b: 78) argues that such an approach is usually turned down because 'such a focus may make feminists uncomfortable by forcing them to abandon some of their unexamined premises'.

The argument most commonly invoked by interviewees to resist a focus on the personal life of women in an experience-based manner, however, is that such a focus would entail a depoliticization of women's oppression (also see Franco 1998). As one interviewee from a leading Nicaraguan feminist organization stated:

> To address this issue [of women's oppression] as if women could just straighten their back and say 'no'; as if they were the one's who ought to take action, is like punishing them again, and placing an even bigger burden, and even more feelings of guilt upon them. It's saying "Hey, it's your responsibility you are in this situation, so it's your responsibility to find a way out of it" instead of acknowledging the responsibility society [...] has
> JIMÉNEZ, MAM, 13 April 2010

Several interviewees argued along the same line, claiming that an experience-based approach would make it seem as if women's oppression were an individual issue, "as if it were a personal rather than a social problem" (e.g. Morales, Tierra Viva, 1 June 2010; Ferrín, CODEFEM, 10 June 2010). This concern is shared by scholars and practitioners in other contexts (Bayard de Volo 2006, Chejter 2007). Pupavac (2004) for example argues on the therapeutic peace and justice program in the Bosnian case, that these therapeutic programs risk being pathologizing and lowering the goal of self-governance to the aim of healing.

At the same time, other researchers point out the merits of an approach revolving around women's personal experiences. Johnson (1989: 13), for example, presents working with women's emotions as a valid approach because oppressive relations are related to people's individual attitudes. She argues that as soon as we manage to change our internal world, our external world will respond to this. However, such a view opens the door to far-going relativist positions which deny the existence of a material reality of oppression. This can explain why feminist organizations in Guatemala and Nicaragua today have a negative attitude towards the idea of adopting an experience-based approach.

A more balanced version of this argument is possible however. It is crucial not to equate an experience-based approach with the idea that every problem is an exclusively psychological problem for which there is a psychological solution (Hora 1996). This can be achieved by using rationalistic and experience-based approaches in a complementary way. Such a strategy acknowledges both the importance of a material and social reality of oppression as well as the importance of intrapersonal dynamics related to this. It thereby avoids denying the responsibility of society, which would erode the very basis for feminist activism, while at the same time avoiding a situation in which both public and private issues of empowerment are only addressed at the public level through a rationalistic rhetorical and rights-based strategy. There is thus need for a balance between programs which confront the social and political structures 'out there', and programs which confront oppression through an experience-based approach. Such a mixed approach has the advantage of not only helping women to break their silence and discover their own needs, but also facilitates changes at the societal level.

Organizational Issues

When considering whether an experience-based approach can be integrated into the current programs of feminist organizations, two factors should be considered. Firstly, because the feminist movement is a social movement, it is inclined to focus on the collective level and have a public approach (Klandermans 2007). Demanding of it to also adopt experience-based strategies to empowerment might entail a loss of capacity and resources in terms of their public work and rights-based, and may initially challenge the role they play in this domain. Yet, at the same time, as was argued above, experience-based approaches can also influence the public realm, and more importantly so, they have the potential to do this in such a way which does not make them dependent on the goodwill of policy-makers. This is important to consider in a society where there is little or no willingness from the side on the government to guarantee women's rights, and where the traditional methods of feminist organizations have proved to be insufficient to foster an actual changes in gender norms (Kampwirth 2006, 2008, Morales 2006). Yet proceeding through a rationalistic public approach and proceeding through an experience-based approach require genuinely different skills. There may thus be a need for new organizational forms in which more systematic work with an experience-based approach is conducted, and which allows the current feminist organizations to continue focusing on, and specializing in, their work in the public domain, while at the same time, a different type of women's organization shapes its empowerment programs around an experience-based approach. In other words, it may be more feasible and desirable for both types of empowerment programs to exist in parallel, rather than being incorporated into one program.

Yet, thirdly, since the feminist movement is one of the most potent social actors in both countries (Sternbach 1992), it can be argued that it should also consider its responsibility in facilitating a different kind of awareness of the private domain, than the one which currently prevails. It could for example engage in a two-track approach by pressing for the funding and institutionalization of programs for individual therapy or a new type of organization which specializes in an experience-based approach of public and private issues. In this case, the role and priorities of international donors are central once again.

In conclusion, a more systematic use of an experience-based approach can offer individuals the possibility to explore and experience their needs and desires on a personal level. Such an approach recognizes that the societal organization is indeed a cause of suffering and that therefore action in the public domain is needed. However, at the same time, it also acknowledges the importance of the dynamics of the private realm. I argue that, apart from being more helpful for women in their private lives, an approach which brings women back in touch with themselves will also pay off at the social level. Feminist organizations, moreover, can play a role in supporting women in this personal process, since it is a crucial part of women's empowerment, which is one of the main goals of the feminist movement. Since genuinely different skills are required for a rights-based and a experience-based approach however, I argue that new resources to complement the work of current feminist organizations in the public domain.

It is controversial whether those women's organizations which proceed through an experience-based approach can still be seen as part of a social movement or as feminist, because an experience-based approach is often seen as individualistic and depoliticizing. This is not per se the case however. The goals of the organizations discussed in the next two chapters are fully in accord with those of classic feminist organizations, and their methods are complementary to them. Women's organizations adopting an experience-based approach can therefore still be seen as social actors and as feminist, even though they are not involved in formally changing the societal structures. This invites for a rethinking of what constitutes a social movement – an effort in which I engage in the next chapters.

Concluding Remarks

This chapter argued that the public-private binary can shed light on the work of Guatemalan and Nicaraguan feminists. I showed how the approach most commonly used by feminists in both countries is pinned on the dynamics of the public realm, i.e. a rational system of knowing, and that this approach is also used when working with issues from women's private lives. Treating issues from the private realm only through such a rationalistic public approach, as if they were public issues ignores the specificities of both realms. I therefore argue that it is vital to acknowledge the existence and inherent value of both realms, as well as the fact that both are characterized by a different logic. Only this way can approaches be valued which revolve around the non-rational, experience-based and subjective nature of the private realm. Operationalizing this approach in the third section of the chapter rendered the notion practically relevant for actors in the field. Three issues are highlighted in conclusion.

1)   *The Experience-Based Approach in Feminist Thinking and in the Nicaraguan and Guatemalan Practice*

Feminist research traditionally presents the private realm as a legitimate object of study and field of action. However, only certain parts of private life seem to be considered, namely those which can be addressed through public action or a rationalistic discourse (see Hanish 1964). More specifically, topics such as emotions, intimacy and enjoyment are often left out of the feminist discourse, or are only addressed in a rationalistic and universalistic public discourse rather than in an experience-based approach. Moreover, feminists' attention to the private realm combined with a uniquely public approach has, in practice, often meant that the instrumental logic of public life invaded the private realm and that women have been required to adopt the logic of ratio-nality that reigns in the public domain (Hochschild and Ehrenreich 2003). Virtually no attention was paid to emotionality and relationally, while these two elements are crucial for reflexive processes and for understanding social and self-reproduction (Holmes 2010: 146, Havens 1985: 376). This can be observed, for example, in the functionalist and universalizing discourse on sexuality, or in the way in which emotions are used as a resource for mobilization in the public domain rather than being addressed in their own right as a resource for empowerment. Feminists' acknowledgment of the importance of the private realm has thus *de facto* meant that those aspects of women's personal lives which were deemed relevant by feminists were moved into the public realm, where they were addressed accordingly through strategies of public mobilization and lobbying, for example. At the same time, this public logic also increasingly invaded women's private lives.

In the early 2010s, Nicaraguan and Guatemalan feminist organizations continue to act through public and rationalistic strategies without offering programs which directly address women's personal experiences, thus denying the possibility that different parts of life are governed by different dynamics. In so doing, these programs often adopt a gender-neutral position which conceals the differences between women's personal and public lives and which takes men's experiences in the public domain as universally representative.

2) *The Advantages of Combining a Rights-Based and an Experience-Based Approach*

Combining a rationalistic with an experience-based approach by also addressing women in their private lives through inward-looking processes serves many feminist goals (Field Belenky et al 1997). It empowers women from the bottom up because it brings them back in touch with their own experiences, and creates a greater sense of agency in their private lives. This sense of empowerment in their personal lives, can foster a sense of responsibility and potency in the public domain, and is thus more likely to mobilize for social change (Simões et al 2009). Moreover, it envisions immediate results as well as structural long-term changes (Reynolds 2010: 36, Inness 1992). Lastly, there is no intrinsic incompatibility between a rationalistic and an experience-based approach, in the sense that they can be seen as each other's complements in the same struggle for empowerment.

Complementing both strategies can be enriching for women, by showing them that features such as affection, enjoyment and bodily experiences can also be empowering (Weintraub 1997). Revaluing the characteristics of the private realm – emotionality, relationality, particularity, etc. – does not reinforce gender stereotypes, but instead acknowledges the daily experience of the target group, and shows them a more empowering take on issues and dynamics which they are familiar with. This way, complex experiences in this domain can be accounted for and the empowering potential of an important part of their lives – which is often overlooked – can be explored (Fordham 1998).

3)   *In conclusion*, the feminist movement in Nicaragua and Guatemala has been instrumental in making women more visible in society and fostering significant legal change to protect women. In so doing, they focused on the question of how material conditions and power relations shaped women's oppression. This remains important. However, to move beyond this, feminists in both countries need to broaden their scope to also account more explicitly and structurally for women's everyday experiences. To this end their rationalistic public approach needs to be complemented with new approaches which are more apt for this end. This change, however, would involve no less than a paradigm shift and a change of values (Ariès and Dubuy 1990: 1). Bringing such a change about requires structural and co-ordinated efforts by those actors involved, and in specific by feminist organizations and international donors. These efforts are important because they hold the promise of changing value systems at the micro-level. Not engaging in such efforts, is likely to alienate women further from their personal experiences. Therefore a combination of both approaches is needed to tap into the full potential of both the feminist movement and the individual woman (Walker 1983: 239). Because of this potential of an experience-based approach, the next two chapters are dedicated to an exploration of the work of three organizations which have embraced such a two-track approach successfully. On the basis of these findings, I analyze whether their logic is useful for other Guatemalan and Nicaraguan women's organizations.

CHAPTER 6

Indigenous Feminism and Its Experience-Based Approach to Women's Empowerment

> This world is not going to change unless we are willing to change ourselves.
> RIGOBERTA MENCHU TUM, 1994

This chapter explores the work of two Guatemalan women's organizations, *Actoras de Cambio* and *Kaqla*, which have structural change to the situation of women's oppression as their long-term goal, but which incorporate elements from an experience-based approach into their efforts to bring these changes about.[1] These organizations use conventional awareness-raising efforts in the public domain and experience-based personal counseling of groups of women in a complementary way.

Both Actoras and Kaqla were created in response to the violence perpetrated against indigenous women during the armed conflict. The organizations emerged at a time when indigenous organizations and communities all over Latin America started to revalue and revitalize their own systems of meaning (Sieder and MacLeod 2009: 1). In this context of growing ethnic awareness, both Actoras and Kaqla linked women's rights and healing processes to the rights and recovery processes of indigenous communities, and reflected on the relation between gendered and ethnic identities. They addressed women's empowerment on the basis of indigenous belief systems, in an attempt to advance both. This entailed the adoption of an approach to women's empowerment which was pinned on indigenous traditions, rather than being rights-based.[2] This approach pays considerable attention to women's own experiences and frames these in a culturally relevant way. While several initiatives in the immediate post-war period operated in this way, today the feminist preference for a rights-based approach replaced most of these programs with programs revolving around public awareness raising and women's rights.

---

1   I use the term structural change in opposition to micro-scale or short-term change. Structural change refers to long-term and fundamental changes to social structures.
2   This can also be observed in Mexico where indigenous Zapatista women claimed their right to autonomy as a group and as individuals within their family and community on the basis of indigenous principles (Millán 2006). The absence of large indigenous groups in Nicaragua meant that in Nicaragua this was not happening to the same extent. This explains why both case studies in this chapter are Guatemalan.

Because of the fundamentally different nature of experience-based and rights-based approaches, absolute claims about their comparative efficiency are hard to sustain. This problem of comparison is exacerbated by the fact that the skills and values which Actoras and Kaqla emphasize – such as self-esteem and self-awareness – are not easily expressed or measured in a quantitative way (Palencia 2010: 55). This chapter therefore relies on testimonies of participants in both types of workshops – mainstream feminist awareness-raising programs on the one hand, and experience-based indigenous empowerment programs on the other hand – and compares their assessments of their participation in these programs, especially in terms of whether they have been able to apply emancipatory concepts to their own lives. Interviewees at Actoras and Kaqla indicated more often than others that they could link the message about empowerment back to different domains of their life because of the experience-based approach. As Galindez, a former participant to a workshop of Kaqla commented:

> I had been at other workshops before, but here they taught me to listen to my body, to get to know my emotions [...] When I went home, I could take these things with me [...] While preparing breakfast, at work, when I couldn't sleep, I could use this. The problem with other workshops was that they were often centered on the goal of that specific workshop. I didn't know how to move beyond that or what to do with it when I left the room. I felt empowered by the idea that I knew about my rights as a woman, a K'iche woman, but well, then came the question, 'so now what?' [...] Sure, it's important to know that my oppression as a woman is a general problem, not my own. But here, I was offered coping mechanisms which were relevant in my own life, not just in a general sense.
>
> GALINDEZ, 31 January 2011

Actoras and Kaqla thus frame the content of a rights-based approach in a more holistic and culturally relevant way which links this message back to women's own experiences. This way they address women in a direct manner and focus on how they internalized their oppression (Asdeco 2005). The premise of these actors is that personal processes of reflection and awareness-raising have an immediate effect on the collective level since both are inextricably linked. Therefore they proceed through an approach which allows women to reconnect their bodies and minds, and to become more aware of their situation, more self-confident and more assertive. These are crucial elements to render women capable of holding accountable those who are responsible for this situation (Sieder and MacLeod 2009).

The chapter examines the origins of these premises, the way in which these organizations put them into practice, and the relevance thereof for other feminist organizations. I present a descriptive analysis which pays special attention to how both organizations balance goals in the private and public realm and to how the dimension of ethnicity influences their action. The chapter first analyzes this for both organizations in turn, and then concludes on the relevance of these findings for the work of other feminist organizations in Guatemala and Nicaragua.

Actoras de Cambio, from Victims of Sexual Violence to Actors for Change

Actoras de Cambio will enable women to move beyond heroic confrontation with adversity to something more positively creative: designing alternatives for peace

YOLANDA AGUILAR, founding member Actoras de Cambio, 4 February 2011

After the armed conflict, the agenda of most Guatemalan NGOs was dominated by the issues of national and individual recovery from violence and seeking justice for wartime violence (CEH 1999, Pearce 1998, Ardón 1999). Both topics were related to personal experiences as well as to the wider structures of class, ethnic and gendered oppression (Pessar 2001: 475, Hooks 1993). Actoras de Cambio also mobilized around these issues, and interpreted them in a way which reflected the realities and needs of the people they were working with as accurately as possible (Castañeda, advisor to Actoras, 12 February 2012).

While they agreed that societal changes were needed, Actoras did not see the issue of recovery from violence as being exclusively related to a functional judicial apparatus or changing socio-political processes. Actoras assumed that women's self-perception was often one of the most important barriers to seeking justice for crimes perpetrated against them, and that this issue needed to be given equal consideration as the issue of changing social structures (Erazo, director of ECAP, 25 January 2011). Acknowledging women's emotions and interpretations of oppression and violence was therefore crucial in Actoras' work. They stressed the process of becoming an autonomous subject who is the protagonist of one's own life. This went beyond the idea of becoming an autonomous subject in the judicial or public domain, and addressed the beliefs of guilt, fear and dependency, around which these women's gender identity had historically been constructed (Pisano 1996: 43, Erickson 1995). In this section, I examine Actoras' approach, by analyzing its history and vision, its practical work and the relevance of this approach for its goals in the public domain.

History and Vision

The Actoras de Cambio project emerged in 2003 in the framework of the National Program for Reparation (Programa Nacional de Resarcimiento), with the aim of facilitating the recovery of memory of indigenous women who had experienced violence during the armed-conflict. A nucleus of feminists around Yolanda Aguilar, Luz Mendez and Amandine Fulchiron convened important social organizations to set up an organization which emphasized the importance of women speaking out about the violence they had experienced, as a step towards both personal healing and societal justice. Actoras de Cambio was an attempt to address both the psychological and structural aspects of women's oppression. Two important partners to the project were the Group for Community Studies and Psychosocial Assistance (ECAP) and the National Union of Guatemalan Women (UNAMG). The ECAP is an organization with roots in the exhumations of war crimes of the 1990s during which it offered psychosocial assistance to those involved. Also in the Actoras project, they brought in the expertise in psychology and psychotherapy to facilitate women's personal empowerment process. The UNAMG on the other hand is an autonomous feminist organization created in 1980 to contest political repression. They provided the feminist analysis and activism in the Actoras project (IIARS 2009). Both UNAMG and ECAP are amongst the most important actors of civil society and have a lot of expertise in their respective fields, i.e. psychosocial assistance to victims of torture and relatives of war victims, and political action for women's rights respectively.

Actoras had three aims. First, to reveal the truth about the extreme sexualized violence against women during the thirty-six years of war in Guatemala in a more explicit way than the REMHI, CEH or UN reports had done, on the basis of women's own experiences. To this end, beginning in 2003, they conducted extensive research across Guatemala to find women who had survived rape and other kinds of sexual brutality and encouraged them to give their testimonies. National meetings on this topic have taken place in many local languages, to raise awareness. A second goal of Actoras was to promote healing in women survivors by enabling them to come together in small local groups to tell their stories and hear those of others. At each meeting, both a feminist from the UNAMG and a psychologist from ECAP were present so as to promote an integrated understanding of both the psychological and social aspects of women's oppression and the violence perpetrated against them. Actoras' third goal was achieving justice for wartime violence. To this end, the group started several court cases in the Guatemalan courts and in the Inter-American Court of

Human Rights in Costa Rica, as well as a "Tribunal of Conscience" in 2008. In 2006 Actoras also published a volume on legal strategies regarding impunity for violence against women. Actoras threefold mission – societal awareness, personal healing, and justice – thus envisioned the public denunciation of violence as well as a personal awareness amongst women (Fulchiron 2009: 369).

Because of the reputation of the social organizations and actors involved, donors gave the Actoras project much leeway on how to administer its daily operations (Meoño Magarin, member ECAP, 3 June 2010; Asenció, member UNAMG, 24 May 2010). Several donors, such as the city council of Barcelona, the Association of Cooperation in the South (ACSUR-Las Segovias), and Education without Borders (Educación sin Fronteras) moreover shared Actoras' goal of linking psychosocial healing processes to processes for socio-political change. Because of this endorsement by donors, Actoras could set up exhaustive programs which allowed women to turn to their own personal experiences and healing process in order to feel more empowered, and to do this in a way which revealed the societal component of this process. This had transgressive potential, because it emphasized the agency of indigenous women and conferred ownership of their own histories and processes upon women (Lopez, member of Actoras de Cambio, 16 February 2011). The assumption was that women needed to feel ownership over their own experiences, before organizing around them in public. While practical factors sometimes challenged this chronology in reality, Actoras kept systemically emphasizing women's personal process throughout (Méndez, coordinator at Actoras, 18 February 2011)

Next to the fact that Actoras was innovative in its bottom-up linkage of personal and societal processes, the project was an exponent of the tendency to revalue indigenous principles and values (Sieder and MacLeod 2009: 4). Actoras explored the empowering potential of certain indigenous rituals and beliefs. This allowed them to work with rituals and concepts which women were familiar with and could relate to, while at the same time presenting a new and empowering interpretation of these concepts. The indigenous belief in complementarity, for example, became an important organizing principle to promote women's empowerment (Jocón 2005). The next section explores how this was put into practice.

A Phased Approach to Women's Recovery and Empowerment
Actoras started to work in June 2003 by identifying women who had experienced violence during the armed conflict. Group discussions were set up with these women. These discussions were facilitated by a psychologist and a feminist activist. During the discussion women discussed the convictions they held about the violence perpetrated against them, the influence of social conditions on their personal lives, and their priorities for change. Also the resources

which women actually had at their disposal were discussed. This was accompanied by a reflection process on gender and ethnic identities, and on how these manifested themselves in women's daily lives. During these discussions, women indicated that issues which are often overlooked in other feminist programs, such as the empowering potential of the mother role, were central in their daily lives. Actoras built on these discussion to develop an experience-based approach which revolved around women's personal and daily experiences and frameworks, and which combined the goal of women's empowerment with that of ethnic empowerment. The goal was the acknowledgment and incorporation of women's daily realities in their empowerment program. Because their ethnicity played an important role in women's daily lives, it was also incorporated in Actoras' practical work.

On the basis of consultations with women, a specific working program based on the Nawal-tradition was implemented from July 2005 until May 2007.[3] The goal was to allow women to connect to their emotions and experiences, and to make sense of them in a way which was direct, tangible, and which was recognizable. This increased self-awareness was seen as a means to also facilitate a growing awareness of their social position and of social structures (Diez, psychologist of Actoras, 16 February 2011). The Nawal-program consisted of six phases, referred to as circles. The first three phases were set up as a personal healing and empowerment process. In these phases, ownership over their own bodies and emotions, allowing women to enjoy themselves and breaking the cycle of guilt, were central. In the last three phases the social dimension of transformation was foregrounded. Here, demanding rights, organizing at the societal level and creating the societal conditions for change in their own communities were discussed (Fulchirone 2009). There were fortnightly meetings in each region. In total, three regions and 54 women directly participated. Funding proposals mentioned 840 beneficiaries however, referring to families and community members who were involved (Cooperaccio 2009). The project was concluded with the publication of a comprehensive volume *Tejidos que lleva el alma* (Fulchirone 2009). This is a systematization of the working method as well as being a document with policy recommendations.

Below, I discuss the first three phases of the Nawal-program, which envisioned a personal process of awareness and the occurrence of an empowered

---

3   The concept of Nawal or Nahual occurs in the Popol Vuh, a standard corpus underlying much of Guatemalan Mayan worldview. Nawal is considered that part of the individual which is in connection with the sacred, and is therefore sacred in itself. Key to the notion of Nawal is the idea of self-transformation.

identity on the basis thereof. The last three phases show strong overlaps with the work of mainstream autonomous feminists discussed in the first part of the book. For this reason, I do not offer a detailed analysis of them here. However, I conclude the chapter with an assessment of how the organization's work in the public domain benefits from attention to women's personal processes, as well as exploring of the potential for mutual learning between both types of action.

The Circle of Noj. Acknowledging the Effect of Violence and Oppression

"Noj", the first phase of the program, prioritized psychotherapeutic and psychosocial counseling (Méndez 2006-2008). This circle was in the first place about women themselves, and not so much about their communities yet. As *Tejidos* reads, 'In this phase, women start to walk the path of getting to know themselves, of feeling and understanding that they have gone through something horrible [...]. This phase is about re-establishing women's free will and dignity [...] about acknowledging their angers and anxiety. In a later stage, we step-by-step address and help to articulate the actual trauma experience and incorporate that' (Fulchirone 2009: 371-372, own translation). This circle thus envisioned a process of healing from trauma and inviting women to explore the conflicting feelings which repeated instances of direct and indirect violence had installed in them. This was seen as a pre-condition for women's empowerment. As a facilitator argued:

> How could you change someone's self image, if she hasn't even explored what image she really has of herself? Any program which fails to ask women about what they are experiencing and what they want, is by definition taking away their agency and is, thus, by definition, oppressive.
>
> BARRIOS KLEE, academic and member of Actoras, 26 January 2011

The core assumption of the program is that, primarily, awareness and acknowledgement is needed of the fact that one has been a victim of violence and of what this means in one's own life. Only through such a process of acknowledging and re-integrating one's own past and by assessing it on the basis of one's own feelings and truths can the process of healing and empowerment start. Ignoring this step in the empowerment process, is considered to impede the possibility of any other form of empowerment (Aguilar 2006). Re-interpreting violence and oppression on the basis of their own feelings, redefining it in their own words, and assessing the impact thereof on their own lives can be seen as a personal process. Yet Actoras shows that feminist organizations can play a role in this process, by complementing the psychological analysis with a feminist analysis of the problem. As Schwarz (2002: 2) also noted, "we often suppress, ignore, misinterpret and/or lack confidence in our own interpretations of our emotional responses [...] other people are needed to help focus our attention on these responses." The techniques which Actoras used to this end in practice were manifold and were adapted to each group of participants, because trauma was seen as a deeply individual and unique experience, so methods had to reflect this diversity. As Cabrera, former head of the psychosocial program of Actoras, argued:

> Since every individual who experienced trauma has a different interpretation thereof, a different life history, different desires, values and capacities, we could not but adapt our own methods to this. We were dealing with very profound processes of personal and collective transformation, which unravel in very distinct manners for each of the women whom we were accompanying, depending on their possibilities, their social networks, their personal history and the social pressure they felt. We had to respect the rhythms of the women, and the decisions they made about how much they wanted to change in their lives and to which extent they wanted to be involved [...]. That being said, it was difficult sometimes, or actually most of the time, to find a way to address the issues women were dealing with in a way which did right to every person's experience and provided the best chance for every individual person to heal, and which was at the same time manageable. But we had a very dedicated team, working long hours, and there were women who needed us, and whose needs inspired us to keep probing for more appropriate approaches.
>
> CABRERA, facilitator at Actoras, 15 February 2011

Cabrera also explained that Actoras began working with a clear blueprint for action, partially inspired by the donor's desires, but that this was soon replaced by a process of trial-and-error, which was aimed at incorporating the actual needs of women. One goal underpinned all efforts though, namely bringing women back in touch with their own bodies, feelings and their interpretations of the violence perpetrated against them.

Women were first offered an individual intake interview, during which it was explained to them that the approach was pinned on a process of personal healing and transformation as well as on an engagement with societal goals. After these intake interviews, groups were created which made use, inter alia, of creative art therapy, socio-psychological tools and indigenous rituals.[4] Actoras assumed that access to violent memories could not be established on the basis of narrative techniques alone, because these do not adequately reflect the complex emotions which women experienced in relation to the violence (McKinney 2007). Examples of methods which were used are drawing their story (rather than only narrating it), psychotherapy in women's own language, traditional cleansing rituals with fire and herbs, group reflections, movement therapy, etc. While it is unlikely that all techniques aimed at releasing emotions were equally pertinent – as some interviewees suggested (e.g. Durán, participant Actoras de Cambio, 17 February 2011; Lopez, member Actoras de Cambio and Kaqla, 16 February 2011) – facilitators had a lot of expertise in their domain and came from within the communities, meaning that they were more likely to be more in touch with what lived amongst these women, what they needed and how to facilitate this.

The circle of *Noj* was thus about accessing those feelings which influenced women, and which shaped their process of healing and empowerment. In specific, anxiety, guilt, powerlessness and contained anger were topics which surged in many sessions. These issues were explored on the basis of Mayan *cosmovision*, because this constituted an important frame of reference for participants. An example thereof is the way in which the issue of fright was dealt with.[5] Fright refers to the sudden feelings of intense fear which these women reported to feel sometimes, without a clear cause. Instead of adopting a medical or rights-based discourse to deal with these feelings, fright was interpreted in a traditional culturally-specific way. Actoras explored how this fright manifested itself in women's bodies, whereby women commonly described fright as a tense feeling around the celiac plexus. Actoras linked this back to traditional Mayan medicine, which locates emotions and feelings in this region just above the belly button (Palencia Prado 1999). In traditional culture, also the spirit (*Jaleb*) is believed to be located in this area (Médicos Descalzos 2005). Fright was therefore treated as something directly related to women's emotions, corporeal experiences and indigenous systems of meaning. With this in mind, Actoras set up a program aimed at reintegrating these spheres of women's lives. As one of the participants stated in the program reports on the issue of fright, "It feels as if my spirit has left my

---

4   For an elaboration of the therapeutic component of each technique, see for example Susan and Hertica Deaton (2002) and Walker (1994), who both explain the importance of changing belief systems before social systems.

5   I use fright as the translation of '*susto*', which is stronger than fear.

body, and that, thereby, I have lost my *self* and am disintegrating" (Fulchirone 2009: 292).

A culturally relevant experience-based approach which would help women to recover and integrate these experiences was seen as primordial by Actoras. Following the circle of *Noj*, which was aimed at accessing emotions and interpretations, followed the circle of *Q'anil*, aimed at expressing these.

The Circle of Q'anil. *Expressing Chaotic Feelings*

After becoming more aware of how violence and oppression influenced their daily realities, women entered a phase which focused on expressing these conflicting feelings in a way which was relevant for themselves. The aim was to return a degree of agency to women by exploring relevant ways to make them heard and expressing their needs. The first task of *Q'anil* was therefore the creation of a non-normative environment in which women could talk and act freely, on the basis of their own feelings and truths, without fear of being judged or victimized again (Beristain, n.d., Fulchirone 2009: 375). The approach which emerged in this context was unique, in the sense that it complemented narrative techniques with body-based and emotional work in a culturally relevant way. They thereby strove for a non-linear and non-rational interpretation of *testimonio*, or bearing witness, which did justice to women's complex experiences and integrated the different domain of their lives. The mode of expression which emerged was thus one which drew heavily on women's emotions and bodily experiences and which encouraged them to conceptualize their own desires and strategies in an experience-based manner, rather than by relying on the existing narrative structures which reign the public domain. This new form of rationality challenges the existing normativity and dominance of the public realm and was experienced as genuinely empowering by participants as they found new ways to express themselves, which were actually theirs. As one former leader of Mamá Maquín remarked on organizations failing to incorporate this aim into their programs:

> Throughout the whole process of assistance to returning refugee women in which they learnt to speak up for themselves, the claims which they made were linked to their condition of exile, to their role as mothers and home-makers, but never to the most personal of all spheres, never to what happened with their own bodies or how they felt for example. That was taboo.
>
> GARCIA HERNÁNDEZ, 26 January 2011

This suggests that most programs aimed at empowering women by offering them tools to speak up for themselves still subscribe to the normativity implicit in rationalistic discourses which reign the public domain, and from which certain elements (such as emotions or intimacy) are excluded or under-valued. Women are not taught to give voice to their own feelings in these programs. Actoras on the other hand, aimed to incorporate these elements in their empowerment strategy, rather than ignoring them. As one of the first methods employed, '*Q'anil*' worked with these intimate aspects of women's lives through a strategy which arose from constant feedback from the women themselves. This way, women explored new ways of expressing themselves which best reflected their realities, needs and resources. Throughout, both a psychological and a feminist interpretation of the process were offered, whereby the facilitator from ECAP would stress how normative narratives influenced women and held them down, and whereby the facilitator from UNAMG would complement this insight with a debate on the social roots of this normative discourse.

After naming their needs, desires and resources, the women of Actoras entered the third phase of the empowerment program, aimed at coping with the emotions and interpretations of violence and giving these a place in their lives.

The Circle of Ajmaq'. Breaking the Cycle of Guilt and Changing Women's Self-Image

In this last phase of their personal empowerment process, women were offered tools to channel and integrate the feelings surrounding the violence. These tools were based on traditional Mayan belief and on body-based work.

Indigenous frames of reference were particularly important in this phase because of the existence of numerous cleansing rituals in Mayan cultures. These cleansing rituals were used by facilitators in various workshops because women believed these rituals to provide emotional and energetic solace (Diez, facilitator at Actoras, 16 February 2011). Traditional cleansing rituals were introduced in several forms. Most common were those rituals based on the cleansing powers of fire and water, whereby the facilitators combined the traditional form of these rituals with a dynamic interpretation of their meaning, in order to apply them to women's personal process of healing. The reliance on these rituals was proposed as a means to balance the emotional, spiritual, physical and mental state of women, and to facilitate more general insights on the basis of their own culture, which could serve as a foundation for women's further empowerment (Also see Rybak 2004).

Ajmaq also linked women's personal empowerment process back to traditional cultures by exploring how traditional beliefs impacted on women's self-image, and re-victimized them. Women embarked on a long process of

FIGURE 6   *Use of traditional rituals and symbolism in the third cycle of the healing program*
            © KAQLA 2003.

unlearning traditional beliefs which had been internalized by generations of
women. One of the ways in which this was done was by facilitating that women
get to know and respect their own bodies and feel at ease with them, without
feelings of guilt.

In this context, also body-based work was deemed vital for women's healing process. Initially, many women saw their bodies as synonyms of fear, shame, guilt and danger, which had triggered acts of violence against them. Women often had learnt that the fact of having a female constitution by definition gave men power over them (Fulchirone 2009: 380). They thus considered their bodies to be taboo and a source of problems. This also explains the guilt women often felt about what had happened to them, and the fact that they did not allow themselves to enjoy their bodies anymore. Theoretical literature on the topic demonstrates that the alteration of lived bodily experience can enhance autonomy, and that this autonomy is related to the ability to engage in self-discovery and self-definition (see for example Schwarz 2004; Meyers 1989). Re-appropriating their own bodies and replacing existing feelings of guilt with a new self-image was therefore a crucial step in returning agency to these women (Lopez, consultant of Actoras project, 16 February 2011). Moreover, many participants indicated that feelings linked to the violence, manifested themselves in the first place in their bodies as physical maladies (Castañeda, advisor to Actoras project, 12 February 2011).

Ajmaq's multi-faceted approach therefore relied heavily on corporal techniques – such as cleansing exercises, movement therapy, therapeutic massage or respiration exercises – which envisioned breaking the feelings of sin and distrust towards their own bodies, and demystifying the body, thereby allowing women to move closer to it (Fulchirone, 2009: 383). As Berlanga, organizing member of Actoras emphasized:

> To untie the knot of feelings of guilt and shame, implied a long and slow process of unlearning the beliefs which women held most of their lives, and which had been passed on from generation to generation. This entailed the need to be aware of one's body, to get to know it, to respect it and to have a good relationship to it, without guilt, fear or shame.
>
> BERLANGA, 24 February 2011

The body was thus not only addressed in relation to the reported pain and feelings of guilt, but also as the site to begin to deconstruct long-held and internalized beliefs about sexuality, guilt and oppression (Cabrera, facilitator at Actoras, 15 February 2011). Deconstructing beliefs in this way was seen as an alternative to programs which only facilitated an intellectual and rationalistic understanding of how beliefs were internalized (Fulchirone 2009: 382). There was, however, no clear blueprint for action and no rigid design about which techniques to use. Methods had to be appropriate for working with a group of approximately twenty people, and had to facilitate respect and positive feelings in relation to women's own bodies, and to reduce the distrust which women had *vis-à-vis* their own bodies. The usefulness of an approach aimed at exploring their bodies and feelings and to express them in a direct way, is illustrated by the statements of two former participants:

> I felt more at home in my own body and felt the need to care for it, and to have people respect it
>
> ARELLANO, 17 February 2011

> To embark on this process is to learn that these powers lay within me all the time. That they were just waiting for me to discover them. They were my eternal fire, which ran through my body like a river which I discovered piece by piece in my own body, my vagina, my womb, my breasts, my head, my hands, my legs, my feet, my eyes, my hair, my heart. Now my body can tell the story of my journey and I can pass it on.
>
> DÚRAN, 17 February 2011

These statements suggest a link between recuperating one's own body and improving self-awareness and self-appreciation. They hint at how a body-based approach contributes to women's personal process of healing. By coming to terms with their pain and fear – but also with their joy – step-by-step, women felt more in charge of their own body. This fostered a feeling of ownership and empowerment for which women were not depending on external factors (Méndez, facilitator at Actoras, 18 February 2011). This way, regaining their own bodies was a way to create both awareness about the beliefs which culture had installed, and to foster a sense of ownership.

Since *Ajmaq* was the last step before engaging more explicitly with the societal component of women's oppression and the violence perpetrated against them, this phase also had a bridging function. Sessions organized in *Ajmaq* also involved the communities at certain points (Fulchirone 2009: 372). Firstly, the feminist analysis accompanying their personal recovery process, meant that the group reflected on the link between personal feelings and experiences an the societal dynamics shaping these (Fulchirone 2009: 385). This way a gradual transition was made from insights about personal life to insights about public life, and from the feeling that one can be an agent of change in one's personal life to the idea that one can be an agent of change for society. Secondly, women's social context was incorporated in the sense that women were offered tools to apply the things which they learnt during the workshops in their family or professional situation. Learning how they could carry out similar exercises with their children to help them to heal from violent experiences they might have had, for example, was something which women valued highly. Thirdly, the community was directly involved by means of societal debates, or, more commonly in this phase, when facilitators visited women in their homes. *Ajmaq* thereby went well beyond the goal of healing from trauma or recovering memory, and approached women in a more holistic way, considering both their social context and their personal experiences. This underlines the need for an experience-based approach to also work with men. It is thereby an explicit attempt to bridge goals in the personal domain and goals in the public domain.

Feedback between Personal Processes and Work in the Public Domain
This section considers how the first three phases of the program fed into the last three phases which had a focus on change in the public domain. The section thereby also analyzes the potential usefulness of the first three phases of the Actoras program for other feminist organizations which only mobilize around goals in the public domain.

By offering both psychological and feminist analysis throughout, *Actoras* linked personal experiences back to public ones. The assumption that emancipation, access to justice and changing gender-norms require far-reaching change – both at the collective and at the individual level – meant that Actoras included women's personal processes and experiences as an integral part of its strategy. The personal process of deconstructing internalized and embodied beliefs was perceived as an indispensable stepping-stone to bring about changes in different domains of women's lives, also in the public realm. The last phases of the program for example linked insight about their personal processes back to their professional roles.

In practice this meant that women explored the potential and strategies for public change on the basis of their own personal experiences. Participants would, for example, conclude a psychotherapeutic session with a group reflection on how women's own experience during that session were related to those of other women, and by extension, to their place in society. This reflection was experience-based in the sense that the topic was systematically linked back to women's own experiences during the workshop. Yet, at the same time, the analysis was facilitated by a feminist activist who emphasized the role of societal structures influencing these experiences (Berlanga, 24 February 2011; Castañeda: 12 February 2011, facilitators at Actoras). Thus, in the last three circles of the program – women set out to take action with regard to their historical and social condition of oppression on the basis of these insights about themselves and about their context. These three phases were set up along the same line as the first three phases, albeit with a focus on society instead of a focus on their personal process. This means that women first engaged in acknowledging the existence and effects of uneven social structures, then participated in workshops where they learnt to name these injustices and express their own desires for change, and lastly, they engaged in efforts to bring about those changes which they themselves deemed necessary. As several participants testified afterwards, the attention paid to their personal processes, helped them to apply the things which they learnt about social dynamics to their own lives and to feel more empowered when acting upon this (Arellano and Durán, 17 February 2011).

The linkage of topics and insights from the public and the private realm is interesting in the Actoras program. While the six phases are organized around the idea that the personal process should be tackled before turning to public issues, in practice women already started to engage with societal dynamics in the first three phases, on the basis of their own experience and through reflections on how their personal experiences related to social dynamics. This makes the Actoras-project particularly relevant for other feminist organizations. Experience-based approaches may require more resources and do not have the immediate advantage of scale which work in the public domain offers. What this project shows however, is that introducing some elements of an experience-based approach in a public strategy, can render it more relevant for women. This suggests that elements from an experience-based approach can usefully complement a rationalistic approach and even optimize its impact, without requiring a major overhaul or complete paradigm shift. In the case of Actoras for example, 48 of the 52 women involved in the project indicated in 2009 that they were still active as community leaders (which they were not before 2005) and all of them indicated that they still felt the benefits of their participation in the program in their personal lives and daily routines (Fulchirone 2009). Also Asdeco's research of 2009 showed that the foregrounding of indigenous frameworks and personal processes of empowerment has eventually resulted in more women taking on public roles in their communities because they felt more agency.[6] Asdeco states that, "It is not yet common that women become community authorities, but there is a growing tendency in many Guatemalan regions. Networks of indigenous social women's organizations have played an important role by valorizing the specific contributions women make at this level" (2009: 8).

Providing a quantitative comparison between Actoras and other programs is difficult because of inherent differences between both approaches. Moreover,

---

6   Asdeco is a Guatemalan community organization working in a similar way, and has reached over 3000 people directly in its workshops. It is not specifically working with women though, and is therefore not discussed in detail here.

since most feminist organizations which organize empowerment workshops do not organize follow-up meetings, there are no reliable figures on what happens with participants afterwards, and there is thus no material to compare the results of Actoras with. While it is true that only 54 women participated directly in the Actoras program, it is important to also consider the community effects of these programs. Mainstream empowerment workshops may be able to reach more women initially, but they often do not offer follow-up, meaning that it is not possible to confirm the positive results which are presented to donors or to consolidate changes. The 54 women of Actoras on the other hand indicate that they felt a high degree of ownership, even years after the formal program had ended, and not only over their personal process but also over the entire process, which they felt was *theirs*. Precaution is therefore advised when analyzing these programs in quantitative terms.

Participants stress the positive effects of these programs however. Next to the positive results in terms of long-term sustained empowerment, Actoras also avoided another pitfall of many empowerment programs by actively engaging men and the community. The choice to do this, was inspired by group discussions with women, who often explained violence perpetrated against them by saying that men felt that they had more power than women (Fulchirone 2009: 379). Also the way in which men and the communities as a whole were involved was inspired by the needs which women expressed during group discussions. By tailoring this process to what women themselves proposed, a degree of ownership over the program was created, and it was assured that women could continue these initiatives after the formal program would be concluded. Thus facilitators directly engaged with the communities through meetings and home visits, and indirectly worked with the communities by providing women with resources and tools to raise awareness amongst members of their family and community. This means that also their interpretation of changes in the public domain diverges from that of many feminist organizations. Rather than focusing on change in the legal domain and at the national level, Actoras de Cambio envisions societal change from the bottom up, and offered women tools to work within their communities in a more direct way. This way, women mobilized for change at a level which they were familiar with and which was more tangible. For example, tools to pass insights about their personal processes on to their children were highly valued amongst participants (e.g. Díez, 16 February 2011). This way, Actoras aimed to apply insights from the first three Nawal circles to women's daily lives in their families and communities. There is thus a compatibility between individual-level change and social change in this view, but Actoras attempts at social change within this Nawal-program take on a form which differs greatly from that of other feminist organizations.

In other components of the Actoras program, the concept of social change and social justice overlaps more with that of mainstream feminist organizations. For example, the axis of raising societal awareness about the violence through publications and the working axis on impunity for violence against women, overlap with the priorities of other feminist organizations. Here as well, interviewees expressed that they have benefited from their participation in the Nawal-program, because they felt more self-confident. However, linking the Nawal-program with its other working axes was not a clear focus of the Actoras project.

Also on a conceptual level the approach set out by Actoras can make a contribution to the debate on empowerment. Developing a strategy around the ethnic and gender identities commonly attributed to women, allowed the organization to work with certain characteristics regularly ascribed to these identities, such as corporeality, emotionality and complementarity. Rather than opposing these characteristics as normative or oppressive, Actoras explored how these elements which were an important part of women's daily lives can be interpreted in an empowering way. The importance of Mayan *cosmovision* and ethnicity in this project means that this approach cannot be applied in the work with non-indigenous women in the same way. In the next chapter though, I analyze an organization which adopts a similar approach in its work with non-indigenous women, to assess whether ethnicity should be seen as a precondition for an experience-based approach.

The facilitating role of ethnicity is this process was one of the arguments why other non-indigenous feminist organizations refrained from adopting a similar approach. Next to this, three problems were commonly cited by interviewees from other organizations. Firstly, the perceived incongruence between personal work with a fairly small group of women on the one hand, and the need to address much broader audiences as rapidly as possible on the other hand, created the impression that there was a problem of scale entailed in an experience-based approach. What this project shows, however, is that for those women involved in the Actoras program, an experience-based approach also affected the way in which women carry out their work in the public domain and their willingness to take on public roles in which they can facilitate societal change. The long-term effect of introducing elements from this approach into empowerment programs is thus likely to be positive, even if immediate results at the societal level may seem to take more time. Also Actoras' engagement with communities and with the media, challenges this argument about scale (see, for example, Escobar Sarti 2011).

A second argument of mainstream feminist organizations against this kind of approach concerned the duration of the empowerment process. If women need to go through a personal process before their social issues can be addressed, this would in theory mean that no social action would be possible until every woman has fulfilled this precondition. The approach of Actoras de Cambio shows, however, that there is constant feedback between personal and public processes and action, and that they are not delineated activities which have no interaction with one another. Actoras inscribed its attention to personal processes in its public program in order to render their public program more efficient, meaning that attention to women's personal processes need not hamper public action.

Lastly, some mainstream feminists argue that this approach, by definition, requires more resources to reach the same number of people, and that it is therefore not relevant for feminist organizations that engage in large-scale awareness-raising activities. In practice however, it can be observed that most feminist organizations in Guatemala and Nicaragua are already organizing some sort of empowerment workshops, meaning that they are already working with women in relatively small groups, and that it is thus a matter of fine-tuning the strategies which they use during these meetings, rather than setting up a whole new program for which extra resources would have to be made available or which would slow their efforts down. Moreover, in the case of Actoras, 48 of the 52 participants have gone on to take up public roles afterwards, meaning that they are working with this approach themselves, and that Actoras has not only reached 52 women, but also affected their communities through them, making the argument of a high investment per capita harder to sustain. This also shows that the perceived gap between both approaches – those focusing on the personal or the public domain – is smaller than what is commonly assumed because both can feed back into one another.

One of the organizations still active today which shares Actoras' idea that women need to go through a personal process of empowerment before they can effectively mobilize for social change, is Kaqla. Also Kaqla works in a way which is atypical for most feminist organizations in Guatemala, in the sense that it is amongst the few feminist organizations which aim to achieve their goals in the public domain through an experience-based approach.

Kaqla, *Senti-Pensar* and *Sanación* as Avenues to Empowerment

> For women to change their reality. They first have to know their reality
> This doesn't only require the will to do so, but also a genuine process
> of personal reflection
> Because doing politics, is connecting politics with one's personal project

> It is as much about changing things in one's own life as it is about societal changes.
>
> CHIRIX GARCÍA, Alas y Raices 2003: 209

At first sight, Kaqla does not seem to differ significantly from other indigenous feminist organizations. Their mission statement reads that their goal is to strengthen the autonomy of Mayan women and indigenous people by constructing individual, corporal, economic, social and cultural independence for Mayan women through the deconstruction of the internalized oppression (Kaqla 2010: 1). The references to the internalization of oppression and to individual and corporal autonomy in the mission statement are, however, illustrative of a vision which genuinely differs from that of most feminist organizations. Namely by placing a stress on personal experiences. Moreover, Kaqla is one of the organizations which were created to denounce both gender-based oppression and oppression on the basis of ethnicity. To this end, they prioritized the process of exploring and dealing with the impact of this oppression on women's personal life. They combine elements from alternative psychotherapeutic approaches with elements from their indigenous traditions to accompany women in an integrated process in which they deal with emotional, corporeal, spiritual and social issues. Moreover, Kaqla only works with leaders of indigenous communities. This is a significant choice to which I return below.

Members of Kaqla did not only mobilize to resist their oppression, but also to propose new strategies to this end; strategies based on their own history and needs as oppressed indigenous women. Kaqla is relevant here because its experiences as a feminist indigenous women's organization present us with new ways of looking at women's oppression and empowerment, and new methods and priorities to deal with these issues. This also inspires a new conceptualization of empowerment, which goes beyond the discourse of women's rights. In Kaqla, like in Actoras, ethnicity and indigenous culture are important in facilitating an experience-based approach. The facilitating role which ethnicity plays for these organizations is explored in the conclusion to this chapter and in the next chapter, which compares the approach of Actoras de Cambio and Kaqla with that of a non-indigenous organization working in a similar way. This section first examines the history and practical work of Kaqla, and then turns to the relevance of its approach for other feminist organizations.

History and Vision

Kaqla started working in 1996 as an informal gathering of seven women who met in the context of the peace negotiations, during an academic process of reflection and analysis on the social roots of the oppression of indigenous women. Initially they met to reflect on the meaning of their experiences during the armed conflict and on society's response to this. They found that recovery programs which were set up in the framework of the peace accords were inadequate to deal with these experiences because these programs omitted the realities of indigenous women and tended to rationalize the issue of violence and only express it in a technical and linear narrative which could not adequately express the traumatizing experiences of some women (Álvarez, founding member of Kaqla, 14 February 2011, also see Caruth 1995). In order to generate a social debate on this topic, these women organized several public forums which were only open to indigenous women, so as to create a space where indigenous women could discuss their experiences in a way which was not customary in the Ladina-culture, but which was relevant for them. When the women of Kaqla set up an independent organization in 1998, their main aim was to facilitate the appropriation of their identity and their rights as indigenous women on the basis of their own experiences and histories (Gomáriz Moraga and Jovel 2007: 67). It was thus not so much their priorities which set Kaqla apart from other indigenous women's and feminist organizations, but the way in which they set out to achieve these goals.

Kaqla's vision and approach was developed on the basis of participatory forums with members. The baseline is that, as a social actor,[7] it has to provide women with an insight into themselves and facilitate an integrated change in both self and society (Kaqla 2008). This means that attention to women's psyche, body and spirituality are an integral part of Kaqla's program for social transformation. This is seen as a means to acknowledge and reclaim aspects of women's daily lives which have been de-valorised throughout their history. Even though these issues did not easily fit the existing priorities of donors, Kaqla refrained from abandoning this approach because it reckoned that this held the key to women's empowerment. Sara Álvarez, founding member of Kaqla, explains that this belief is not only based on group discussions with women, but also on core members' personal experiences. Despite a formal education, technical skills and good social networks, they were not always able to make the best use of these resources because of unresolved psychological issues – such as feelings of inferiority – which they were dealing with

---

7   Despite working with a small nucleus of people, placing an important stress on the individual lives of women and being dependent on the financial assistance of foreign donors, members of Kaqla themselves define the organization as a social organization, and not a mere NGO or group of therapists, because of their stress on social change and the way in which they reach out to large segments of society (Kaqla 2007).

(Álvarez, 14 February 2011). The main aim of Kaqla thus became the creation of a space for affirmative action for indigenous women, which would allow for the reflection on different forms of oppression and where personal barriers which impeded women from using their legal rights and technical skills, would be addressed. The goal was the formation of female leaders and the construction of a mode of thinking which takes into account the history, practices and culture of Mayan women (Méndez 2010: 9). In these spaces, women could talk about their history and their feelings, and define the sort of society they envisioned. An emphasis was placed on finding a language to deconstruct the oppression that went from the social level to the personal level, and to critically assess the role of society, community and the family on the basis thereof (Bercian 2004: 41). Kaqla thereby did not only address women in their personal experience but also engaged in a dialogue with the societal level. Firstly, they did this by working with community leaders and by offering participants tools to apply that which they learnt in the workshops in their own communities. Secondly, personal change and societal change are seen as inextricably related and during workshops the link between both levels is continually stressed because self-acknowledgment seen as a precondition for both individual and community empowerment. And thirdly, Kaqla has programs which explicitly target the public domain.

This concern with the social level is also expressed in Kaqla's working axes, which are defined as 1) political and theoretical reflection and analysis on the topics of gender, class and ethnicity, 2) *sanación*, i.e. group therapy, exercises to open up the corporal memory, and reflection upon, and collective analysis of, emotions and feelings, and 3) systematization and social projects, i.e. institutional capacity building, formation of therapists, awareness-raising, community projects, etc. (based on Chirix 2003). These intersecting working axes envision the integration of different spheres of life and different forms of action. In specific, they are a combination of goals in the public realm (such as raising awareness and fostering legal change) and goals in the private realm, (such as opening up women's corporal memory and facilitating personal change). They are also a combination of techniques from the public domain, such as lobbying and distributing pamphlets, and techniques with roots in the private domain, such as collective therapy.

Therapy groups are a crucial element of Kaqla's programs. On the one hand, this is because of the direct violence which many members experienced during the armed conflict. On the other hand, the oppressive conditions under which – indigenous – women live are considered equally problematic, in the sense that both direct violence and and indirect forms of violence, such as continued oppression, give rise to a profound feeling of distrust and challenge the woman's dignity, and thus need to be addressed (Lopez Mejía, facilitator at Kaqla, 8 February 2011). Because of this encompassing interpretation of violence, therapeutic workshops – or the *"sanación"* program – are conceptualized in a broad way which acknowledges the effects of indirect violence on women's lives and the need to deal with this. The next section explores the logic behind this program in practice. This is followed by a presentation of how Kaqla proceeds in practice.

'Senti-Pensar', a New Rationality to Address Women's Empowerment
This section sets out the logic behind one of Kaqla's priorities, namely the creation of a new language and rationality to address women's empowerment and to deal with certain aspects of their personal lives which are not easily captured in a linear discourse.

The logic behind this goals is that only through a direct and encompassing understanding of their oppression will women be able to understand the process and effects of oppression. To facilitate this understanding, the organization prioritizes women's personal processes by working with women's emotions, bodies and spirituality. It does this in a multifaceted and multidisciplinary way which considers both women's personal experiences and processes at the societal level. The approach is based on consultations with participants, who indicated that topics such as the internalization of the oppressor, the re-valorisation of their own body and learning to give affection to themselves, were the topics that were most pertinent in their life and in their work with women and indigenous communities (C. Álvarez, 21 February 2011, also see Kaqla 2007). The organization underlines the importance of a new language – and by extension, a new type of rationality – which better expresses the experiences of these women. Moreover Kaqla states that:

> Our own approach as well can be authoritarian and [...] our activism can be irresponsible if we act with the language and the symbols which have been passed on to us by the oppressor. For that reason it is crucial to go back to our own deepest selves to discover a new vocabulary and an approach to the issue of oppression which is more suitable.
>
> KAQLA 2007

It explores both this process of personal awareness-raising and the invocation of a new type of rationality by focusing its workshops on women's emotions, bodily experiences and or Mayan spirituality. Below I explore each of these three aspects.

Emotions

Emotions are actively addressed in the empowerment process of the Kaqla community leaders, because Kaqla sees the re-appropriation of emotions as a crucial step towards women's autonomy (Kaqla 2008). Moreover participants themselves indicated that they were interested in strategies to deal with conflicting emotions which they could not express elsewhere. In the empowerment process, negative feelings are acknowledged and reintegrated in women's lives. The focus is however not only on these negative or conflicting feelings but also on the value and potential of positive emotions. Creative art projects, such as theatre workshops for example, incorporate fun and enjoyment by providing a non-normative environment for experimenting with new roles and for exploring feelings which women do not have access to in their 'traditional roles' (S. Álvarez, 21 February 2011). Kaqla assumes that integrating an element of enjoyment and exploration in their empowerment strategy can bring women back in touch with the joyful and playful side of themselves which is often absent in daily life. It also allows women to enjoy their own bodies again and deal with feelings of guilt and stress which are often linked to this. The organization states that "women have been taught to give, to be at the service of others who depend on them and for whom she is taught to suppress her own feelings and needs. Introducing an element of careless playfulness can then be a window of opportunity through which women can experience the positive feelings which come with choosing for themselves" (Chirix 2003: 35). Becoming aware of, and dealing with negative feelings, is thus seen as a first step towards greater self-awareness, whereas work with positive emotions is valued for its empowering potential. Women are encouraged to explore both types of feelings and create meaning on the basis thereof. To facilitate a greater awareness of these emotions and the effect thereof, Kaqla focused heavily on bodily experiences.

Bodily Experiences

Participants often mentioned their body as a site of violence and grief and saw it as an important factor in their oppression because thirty-six years of armed conflict and 500 years of oppression and discrimination left their marks on women's bodies (Álvarez 2006: 20, interview with García Hernandez, member of Mamá Maquín, 26 January 2011). As one of Kaqla's manuals reads:

> Our whole body stores the memory of all the beatings we received, of the humiliations, of the impotence, of the suffering. Our conscious memory forgets, so that we can move on, but our body remembers and its memories shape our behavior
>
> PALENCIA 2010: 85

For this reason, Kaqla works with the body and women's perception thereof, both as a means to raise awareness of the effects of this oppression and as a point of entry to start working with emotions and facilitate self-understanding (Chirix 2003: 169). As Sarah Álvarez, a facilitator at Kaqla, expressed, "we carry the signs of oppression in our body. They are visible in our postures and in the way we move. You cannot be a convincing leader if your whole body expresses submission [...] This is the first thing we want to have women reflect about" (Álvarez, 21 February 2011). Several interviewees testified how they found it important to observe themselves first, to understand how complex and internalized oppression is. Moreover, several of them testified how it was important to get a sense of the possibilities which their bodies gave them and to explore the positive experiences which their bodies could provide them with. Acknowledging the presence of imperfections and the pain of their own bodies, is seen as an important first step towards a more general self-acceptance and self-awareness. As one interviewee who was a participant to a 2011 workshop of Kaqla, stated:

> I don't know how else to explain, but to say that I felt a pressure on my chest. It's like this way my body was telling me something which I have tried to forget for a long time, but when I thought about it, or when I saw something similar happening to someone else, this pressure was always there. This way my body tells me things I have no access to in any other way. I can't control it, neither can I explain it in words, but it's here, it's a part of me that needs acknowledgement.
>
> GALINDEZ, 31 January 2011

Another participant also illustrated how important bodily experience had become for her in her process of dealing with, and recovering from, the violence and oppression in her past, when she stated that:

> For me it's as if I wasn't really present when I went to these meetings [of a local organization for victims of domestic violence]. I was sitting in the room physically, but I didn't really hear what anyone said. They were just words to me. Words which did not touch me or did not concern me. I didn't even know how I felt about my own situation, how could the story of someone else really touch me? Through exercises which have taught me to feel my own body and emotions again, I am coming to terms with my own history. Only now can I really capture the full extent of what happened to me, and only now can I gauge the full impact thereof; for myself, but also for others.
>
> DELMORALES, 31 January 2011

This disconnection from the experience and from their own bodies often kept women from identifying with other women in the same situation, or from acknowledging the effects of violence on their own bodies and in their own lives. Both testimonies also hint at the shortcomings of a narrative strategy to assess and express these feelings. Both interviewees repeated on several occasions that it was through exercises focused on their bodily experiences that they gained access to their trauma story, and that the *narrative imperative*,[8] which exists in many contexts was genuinely distorting their experience (also see McKinney 2007, LaCapra2001, Caruth 1996, and Edkins 2003). This illustrates the importance of Kaqla's objective of finding a new language and a new rationality to frame these experiences.

Focusing on the body thus facilitated more self-awareness on the one hand and the creation of a new form of knowledge based on their own bodily experiences and emotions on the other hand. Moreover, working with bodily experiences has a subversive potential in itself, in the sense that Kaqla contested the interpretation of the body only being a site of danger and oppression, and instead explored those transgressive experiences and interpretations which felt empowering to women. Facilitating new insights about their bodies in this way also facilitated the occurrence of new insights about themselves more broadly and helped women to create a new self-image which is not entirely determined by their situation of oppression. Also ethnicity and Mayan belief systems play an important part in the construction of this new self image.

Spirituality

Kaqla incorporates Mayan spirituality in its program aimed at developing a new type of rationality, because its participants are all Mayan women. This is amongst others visible in the use of altars and traditional ceremonies. Kaqla uses these forms which are known to women, but explores alternative meanings thereof which support women's empowerment process. Traditional cleansing rituals for example were used as a means to 'cleanse oneself of the effects of oppression', rather than as something which women do after their period to cleanse themselves and become 'pure' again (Chirix 2003: 80).

---

8   I.e. the expectation that all experiences can be expressed in a linear rationalistic discourse. Some scholars argue that the ineffability of bodily experiences, and in specific of trauma, means that they cannot be communicated or comprehended by any other means than direct experience. Bodily experiences are thus not communicable through a generalized discourse (de Vignemont 2007: 427).

Framing their personal processes along the lines of Mayan *cosmovision*, makes this process more concrete and recognizable for participants, and stresses the existence of other systems of thinking than the one which reigns the public realm at the national level. Moreover, the fact that spirituality has historically been a factor in the submission of indigenous people also meant that revalorizing the indigenous system of beliefs is considered empowering in itself. The underlying assumption is that re-appropriating their own spirituality can decolonize women's thinking and re-install a sense of pride in their own culture (Bercian 2004: 10). In practice, facilitators take the culture in which these women grew up – and which traditionally gave them little guidance on how to break free from oppressive restrictions – as a point of reference, and create new meanings on the basis thereof. As one of the facilitators explained:

> We don't just work with spirituality because we see this as a means to create a state of well-being for each individual separately. The way in which we incorporate spirituality, gives the women a chance to link their personal change and insights to the values which exist in their family, their community and their culture.
>
> MENDOZA, 31 January 2011

Kaqla thus explores the potential of indigenous belief systems to create a new framework to think about women's oppression, which is relevant and culturally acceptable to these women.

In conclusion, Kaqla pursues its goal of exploring a new rationality and a new discourse to think about women's empowerment through an approach which revolves around women's personal and bodily experiences and around their indigenous belief systems. This work in the different domains of women's lives has lead Kaqla to develop what they call *senti-pensar* (Méndez 2010: 11), or a form of reasoning on the basis of feelings. The aim of developing this new framework is not only to offer women a tool to assess their own experiences in a more relevant way, but also to provide an alternative to the existing rationalistic discourse which is currently dominant in the public domain. In the next section I explore the practical content of the workshops which are offered in this context, whereafter I turn to the meaning of this *senti-pensar* for other programs.

'Sanación', Reintegrating Different Spheres of Women's Lives
Kaqla foregrounds the development of a new system of knowledge and a new discourse on women's empowerment, because its approach differs genuinely from that of other empowerment programs. Their central assumption is that

listening to one's body and acknowledging the pain there is a central step to heal and become full members of society, but that a new discourse is needed to facilitate this process (Bercian 2004, also see Das 1996). On the basis of this new discourse, Kaqla set up an empowerment program emphasizing the reintegration of different spheres of women's lives. Two cycles of workshops are particularly important in Kaqla's work, namely the one focusing on the internalization of the oppressor and the one focusing on affection and self-acceptance. In this section, I examine where this focus comes from, how workshops are organized in practice and what participants' overall assessment of this approach is.

Kaqla's reason for focusing on these two topics is that the history of indigenous people – and women in particular – is characterized by oppressive discourses, which also heavily impact upon women's personal lives. Kaqla considers that, "If we want to eradicate this oppression, we can, and have to eradicate the oppressor in every one of us. We cannot change our environment without changing ourselves. [It is about] bringing to an end the transmission and repetition of learnt patterns, in ourselves and our families' (Bercian 2004: 13). A second motivation for focusing on the internalization of the oppressor and issues of affection is that during group reflections, women themselves indicated that both topics heavily affected them in their daily lives (Chirix 2003). Yet, very few feminist organizations pay attention to these issues in their working programs (Cabrera 2009). Especially the topic of self-acceptance and affection was brought up in several group discussions, with many women indicating that they had never learnt to appreciate themselves or pay attention to their own needs, and that they felt that this heavily affected them in their daily lives (Álvarez, founding member Kaqla, 21 February 2011).

The reason for addressing these topics on the basis of women's emotions, bodily experiences and indigenous spirituality is that such an approach, according to the organizers, allows one to gauge the effect of oppression in relation to mind, behavior and body.[9] Moreover, the fact that bodily experiences are intrinsic, i.e. non-relational properties, implies that they do not change or depend on the relation to other things and are thus inherently personal, and cannot easily be co-opted. This also means that they can be genuinely empowering because individuals have absolute ownership over these experiences. Working with these bodily experiences and emotions, which are personal, sheds a light on how this internalization of the oppressor influences

---

9   See Clinton's work on advanced integrative therapy for the therapeutical underpinnings of Kaqla's work and Mendoza 2007 for a practical example.

how women see themselves. A facilitator argued that women are often unaware of how deeply ingrained the oppressive structures are and how much they have affected their own emotions, bodies and minds (C. Álvarez, 21 February 2011). This leads women to reproduce the same oppressive patterns to which they have been exposed themselves. Only by becoming aware of these embodied patterns and the marks they have left, can women acknowledge, deconstruct and change them. This also facilitates an exploration of what one's capacities and necessities are (Mendoza, facilitator at Kaqla, 31 January 2011). Taking their own capacities and desires as the starting point, rather than finding an external criterion for change, means that the empowerment process becomes more recognizable for women, and becomes more adapted to their own personal realities.

In practice, work on the issue of embodied patterns and external structures happens in group therapy sessions which explore the effect of the internalization of oppressive discourses on their everyday lives. Workshops are therefore organized around experiences from women's daily lives and use methods which they can apply in daily life (Chirix 2003: 56). Groups meet four to six times per year, for three days, and consist of approximately twenty to twenty-five women and one facilitator. The facilitator rotates because every woman is believed to have her own strengths and to influence the empowerment process in a specific way (Palencia 2010: 72). Kaqla uses a phased approach, which is pinned on the idea that certain aspects of women's personal lives have to be resolved before they can deal with other issues.

The first phase of the workshops is aimed at enabling women to listen to their bodies and bringing them back in touch with their own experiences and needs. By facilitating more awareness of their bodies, a growing awareness of their own situation is envisioned. Women also state their position on the topic of oppression or self-acceptance in this phase, as well as what their goals for this workshop are.

In this phase, a rhetorical strategy and applied exercises are used in a complementary way to assess the deeply ingrained beliefs women hold, about the functionality and purpose of their body, about their self-esteem, their place in society, etc. The rhetorical component – which is grounded in Kaqla's *senti-pensar* – consists of two elements. On the one hand, there are group reflections on women's personal interpretation of their situation, whereby a facilitator asks guiding questions to push women to reconsider their own taken-for-granted principles and apply general statements about their oppression to their own lives *in concreto*. This way, women were invited to consider their oppression in a very tangible way. Why did they not value themselves highly? Which specific instances in daily life had re-enforced this belief? Had they undertaken anything to change this? Which practical hurdles kept them from doing so? (Álvarez, 21 February 2011).

Next to these group reflections, women also receive a small notebook with guiding questions in the first phase of the process. On the basis of guiding questions, women are invited to continue their process of reflection on their own oppression and empowerment in between workshops (Mendoza 2007). The guiding questions in the notebook have a strong focus on women's bodies, because this is something that they always have at their disposal and that they may use as a measure of their emotions and mental state. This way, working with the body is used to unveil existing attitudes and to deconstruct embodied beliefs. It also offers strategies to replace these beliefs with acceptance and awareness. In this way, the notebook assures that women's personal process obtains a more permanent character and is not limited to the meetings. Because of this advantage and because of its low cost, tools like a notebook constitute an accessible and affordable tool to give a more permanent character to women's empowerment process. It is thereby also a tool which other feminist organizations can easily incorporate to relate the content of their workshops to women's daily lives in a more structural manner.

Next to these two rhetorical approaches, the first phase relies heavily on experience-based work. Techniques range from respiration exercises, to drawing their own bodies the way they see them, to exercises with mirrors in which women learn to look at themselves again (Mendoza 2007: 6-8, Kaqla 2007). These exercises are aimed at facilitating a concrete awareness of their bodies and emotions, which is seen as a precondition for a more general understanding of their own position and needs, also at a societal level. The first phase thus revolves around facilitating an awareness amongst participants.

The second phase builds on this growing awareness and revolves around deconstructing the oppressive discourse and stimulating women's self-respect. Whereas the first phase aimed to open the corporal memory and to give violent and oppressive experiences a place in women's lives, the second phase is more specifically aimed at breaking the cycle of shame and guilt in which many women are caught (Álvarez, 14 February 2011). Women explored how oppressive discourses prevented them from growing, but also how this affected their self-image and self-respect. Whereas exercises in the first phase mainly deal with negative and conflicting feelings, exercises in the second phase encourage women to explore the opposite, namely how they could bring a sense of well-being, affection and joy back into their own lives. According to facilitators, this step gives women an opportunity to experience themselves and their bodies in a genuinely new way, different from how they normally behave in their everyday interactions, to acknowledge ingrained patterns of oppression and to develop healthy coping mechanisms (Chirix 2003). Becoming more aware of their own bodies through exercises, thus entails an awareness of the restrictions which they hold in their bodies as well as the joy (Kaqla 2008).

In this phase, tangible and known frames of reference are used to make exercises as concrete as possible for women. This means that traditional Mayan rituals and bodily experiences are important tools in this stage. Exercises based on Mayan rituals are set up along the lines of traditional rituals. They, for example, take place around an altar which represents the cosmos, or refer to other symbolism based on the Nawal tradition. The three-day workshops start with a traditional ritual to indicate that women have entered a place where they can freely express themselves. Participants indicated that this act of creating a symbolic rupture in time and space, made it feel safer for them to be themselves without being judged (Alvarez, facilitator at Kaqla, 14 February 2011, Galindez, participant at Kaqla, 31 January 2011). The workshop also closes with a traditional ritual, aimed at inspiring women to apply insights from the workshop to their daily lives, and to give roots to the changes which had taken place (Kaqla 2008, also see Mendoza 2007). These practices are held in participants' mother tongue, and are not only aimed at stimulating women's empowerment, but also at stimulating an ethnic awareness and pride (Palencia 2010: 75).

Next to the indigenous frames of reference, the body is used as a basis for women's empowerment. Also these exercises are made as concrete as possible, for example by making use of mirrors to reflect women's image. As one of the facilitators explained:

> To know their bodies is to know themselves. If a woman can manage to learn to accept her own body, this is a first step to accept herself, and thus a first step to love herself and give herself the affection which she often does not obtain from elsewhere. This however is a clear case of breaking with deeply ingrained patterns. Only just looking at their bodies was something which was nearly impossible for many women.
>
> MENDOZA, 31 January 2011

This does not only hint at the importance of working with the body for women's own personal process, but also at the transgressive potential thereof.

In practice, the corporeal techniques most used in this stage can be grouped in three categories: massage, movement and breathing exercises. The goal of all three is bringing women back in touch with their bodies and emotions, and more specifically creating positive experiences in this domain in a way which gives agency to women themselves. The exercises are set up in such a way that women can incorporate them in their daily lives, so that their process of *sanación* gets a permanent character. A method commonly used by Kaqla is a specific massage technique, based on Mayan ancestral traditions, which is aimed at releasing emotions. Women practice this technique in the groups, but are also offered means to do this exercise on their own after the workshop (Palencia 2010: 75). As a manual reads: "with this technique, we awaken the memory of our bodies and obtain valuable information to understand our personal history, and our history of oppression" (Palencia 2010: 75). Movement exercises then are seen as a medium to stress women's own responsibility to give to themselves what others cannot give them, to feel more balanced physically and mentally, to express what lives inside them, to recognize those parts of their body which are sore and which ones are powerful, and to come to know themselves through this (Palencia 2010: 90). Respiration exercises are framed as cleansing and calming. Techniques to breath more deeply for example are offered to calm the mind. Breathing out is also framed as a means to release negative feelings about one's self. All these exercises revolve around integrating and transforming emotions related to women's oppression.

Several interviewees who participated in the workshops indicated that they had started to look at themselves in a different way and to appreciate their bodies as *theirs*. Several remarks implied a growing self-acceptance and self-appreciation, which Kaqla sees as a precondition for genuine empowerment. As one participant stated:

> Throughout my life, I have never heard the message that my body is worth appreciating and is valuable. It had always been a source of trouble more than anything else. I had to teach myself to tell myself 'you are beautiful'.
>
> MARQUINA, 26 February 2011

Two other participants indicated that they felt more in touch with their needs, more powerful and more capable of effecting changes after participating in these workshops (Galindez and Chavez, 31 January 2011). The choice to take time for themselves and treat their bodies with care was seen as a necessary form of self-love, which was needed as a means of recognizing themselves as independent subjects worthy of attention. Women were invited to take care of their bodies, and to take time for themselves to discover their own needs and priorities, in order to avoid relations of dependency in the future (Chirix 2003).

In the third phase of this workshop, women link their personal insights about how they have internalized, embodied and experienced their oppression back to their work in the public domain. Kaqla stressed that the therapeutic work-shops are the cardinal point of their work, but uses the third phase to discuss with women how to translate their insight about their personal processes to their public work (Mendoza 2007). On the basis thereof, the group of partici-pants drafts a type of manual on how to proceed in the future, and several women indicated that they meet up with other participants regularly in between workshops. This way, women do not only gain a firmer sense of own-ership over their own processes, but also facilitate similar changes amongst other women. This again underlines the permanent character of the transfor-mation process.

In conclusion, these workshops affected women both in their private lives and in their public roles. This linking of personal processes on the one hand with professional and societal processes on the other hand was strongly valued by participants, both by my own interviewees and by those cited in Mendoza (2007: 32). As one participant to the program expressed:

> I had no idea that my personal process was so intimately bound up with my work. [...]. Now I see how much this therapeutic process has taught me about my own oppression, and how much of this I can use in my daily work and my everyday life.[...] I value this program not just because it helped me to gain control over parts of my life and to feel more at ease with myself, but also in a very pragmatic way, because now I can do my job better.
>
> CHAVEZ, 31 January 2011

This testimony suggests that Kaqla has found a relevant way to pursue its goal of contributing to the formation and empowerment of community leaders. As their mission statement reads, Kaqla wants to "contribute to the formation of social therapists, i.e. people who can act as guides and who contribute to the creation of healthy and efficient organizations with functioning strategies which acknowledge the reality of oppression in an integral way. This starts with providing them with the basic tools to do so, starting with what they learn from their own process" (Palencia 2010: 76). In the next section I explore this link between personal processes and social change in more detail.

Feedback between the Process of *Sanación* and Work in the Public Domain

Social change is the most important long-term goal of both Kaqla and Actoras de Cambio. Both organizations use an experience-based approach, revolving around women's personal processes of empowerment as a precondition for their work in the public domain however. They thereby aim to avoid the pitfalls of both an overly politicizing approach and those of an overly psychologizing approach. Below, I explore whether and how this approach can contribute to the structural goal of changing the societal structures which lead to women's oppression.

Unlike many women's organizations which only touch upon the role of experience, emotion and affection in the fringes of their public work, these actors have premised their actions on the belief that an exploration of women's inner worlds is a precondition for their empowerment. The personal level was not only prioritized because this was seen as a means to genuinely empower women from the bottom up, but also because engaging in a personal process, entails the advantaged that women were not dependent on the benevolence of – political – actors to foster change. Kaqla and Actoras have used these personal experiences of women as the building blocks for their work in the public realm because of the supposition that "oppression goes beyond the political, cultural, social and economic conditions, that it affects our authentic being, our potential, our emotional and spiritual being; and that, to deal with these effects and traumas, it is not sufficient to make a theoretical or political analysis, but that we also have to turn to our own hearts to change our own histories' (Chirix 2003: 56).

The fact that Kaqla and Actoras see *sanación* as a precondition to genuine empowerment does however not mean that they see work in the public domain as marginal. Their premise is that the abstract and generalized discourse on oppression which is dominant in the public domain, should be complemented with an experience-based component where possible, so as to allow women to link general insights on oppression back to their own lives in a direct way. On the one hand both organizations have a tiered approach to pressing for change in the public domain, in the sense that they either work with community leaders or stimulate women to take on public roles after finishing the empowerment program. Explicit attention to the public domain runs through all phases of the personal empowerment programs. Moreover, these women are offered tools to also apply an experience-based approach to empowerment in their work with women. They for example learn to facilitate similar workshops themselves, or to establish networks (*"tejidos"*) for exchanging experiences with other women. Hence even though both initiatives only reach about twenty-five women per workshop, their work goes well-beyond individual healing or psychotherapeutic assistance, because women are taught to pass on insights from the workshops, in order to facilitate processes of experience-based awareness-raising amongst other women as well.[10] Thereby the work with personal processes of a small group of women feeds back into the collective level.

Next to this indirect influence on society, Kaqla and Actoras also have numerous activities in the public domain themselves such as the publication of research volumes, the organization of community debates, work with local groups, research into the societal causes of oppression, joining demonstrations and filing lawsuits on violence against women. This means that it acknowledges the value of work in the public domain.

Especially in terms of publishing, both organizations have been particularly active. For Kaqla, publications mainly consist of reports and research volumes on the societal and individual structures of oppression (see Chirix 2003, Bercian 2004 and Kaqla 2007, 2008 and 2009). These volumes are critical reflections on Mayan culture, but also studies of Kaqla's emotion- and body-based work with indigenous women, and aim to make this method more widely available to other actors in the field. It was the second book which received most attention, both positive and negative. This book is an analysis of women's rejection of oppressive elements from their own culture and their interpretation of the roles assigned to them. The book is thus about women who have transgressed the roles and spaces ascribed to them in terms by indigenous culture, on the basis of this indigenous culture. It thereby proposes new and alternative identities for indigenous women, and is written in a coherent and clear manner, so as to reach a large number of women (in terms of language, lay-out, distribution, et cetera). In the debate following the publication of the book, indigenous leaders themselves had an ambivalent attitude towards the approach, because even though Kaqla fostered a renewed ethnic awareness, it was critical of several aspects of Mayan tradition which are unfavorable to women and which require rethinking to allow for women's empowerment. This criticism was especially controversial because it came from activists who themselves strongly identify with their indigenous identity, and actively use elements of it as a resource. All interviewees at Kaqla affirmed that to them, their ethnic belonging was more important than other identities like being feminist, lesbian or activist. Álvarez, one of the founders of Kaqla, stated this most explicitly. 'I am lesbian. I am a woman. I am a feminist. But what is more fundamental, I come from an indigenous community. That defines how I see life more than these other identities' (14 February 2011). Feminist organizations

---

10   Kaqla's scheme of three-day meetings with twenty to twenty-five women four times per
      year, means that one facilitator can train 380 to 525 community leader per year in this way,
      who can themselves then adopt this approach.

and general public opinion on the other hand did not express a strong – positive or negative – reaction to Kaqla's publications.

On the contrary, the main publication of Actoras, was so well received by a large audience that it had to be reprinted soon after its initial publication. Both other members of other NGOs and the media referred to the "Tejidos que lleva el alma" publication on several occasions, indicating their support for this program which brought women back into the writing of their own history.

This links to yet another way in which both Actoras an Kaqla are engaged with the collective level, namely by trying to install a new form of rationality and a new discourse on women's oppression. Both organizations aim to facilitate a new way of thinking about uneven ethnic and gender relations, beyond the constraints of the existing discourse. Their work is thus not only about personal healing or about women becoming visible political subjects, but also about proposing new approaches to how women's rights and needs are commonly defined and defended. They thereby challenge the hegemony of rational knowledge and technical skills in the public realm, since these are often incompatible with the needs and resources which indigenous women themselves prioritized during the workshops (Palencia Prado 1999). Members and participants of Kaqla and Actoras who are also active in other organizations thereby aim to establish a dialogue between their new forms of knowledge based on the aforementioned *senti-pensar*, and the more accepted forms of knowledge in the public domain.

Kaqla and Actoras' role in the public domain is thus pinned on the bridges which they build with other organizations of civil society and with indigenous communities, as well as on the lobbying and awareness-raising efforts at the societal level and on its outreach programs for families and communities of participants. The mission statements of both organizations show that also their work in the public realm has a strong bottom-up approach, wherein work at that community level is in many cases prioritized over work at the national level, because participants can potentially feel more agency to instil changes in their immediate surroundings than at the national level (Chirix 2003). All of their work in the public domain, is based on the dynamics and discourse which arose from its experience-based work with women. Society is addressed on the basis of women's own individual experiences and through their own voices. Thereby Actoras and Kaqla also aim to introduce an element of subjectivity in their public strategies, and to pin these strategies on the logic of *senti-pensar* as well, because this is considered to reflect women's realities and needs more adequately through a purely rights-based approach. By discursively creating distinctive spaces for themselves in this way, the organizations and their participants aim to bring about a more genuine form of social and personal change on the basis of women's own experiences.

The organizations' choice to refrain from a purely rights-based approach and instead work with personal empowerment processes on the basis of culturally relevant techniques, has demonstrated positive results, both in women's lives and at the community level. Apart from giving testimony about feeling more empowered, women who participated in the programs were more active in different kinds of public activities in their communities in which they could contribute to the community development, such as agro-ecological projects (Sieder and MacLeod 2009: 9).

Despite these merits, the approach of Kaqla and Actoras de Cambio is not an absolute ideal because it also presents difficulties, both at a theoretical and at a practical level. On a theoretical level, the view of Kaqla and Actoras could be called essentialist, both with regards to how they approach gender identities and with regards to how they approach ethnic identities, because it reinforces the association of women with those activities and characteristics with which they have traditionally been associated with and revalues traditional gender roles. It thereby runs the risk of buttressing already existing limiting representations. It is relevant to remark though that the approach reinterprets and revalues 'the feminine' on its own terms, in a way which can disrupt hegemonic masculinity by exposing its limits (Irigaray 1985: 162). In other words, instead of trying to break the association of femininity with certain characteristics, they revalue these characteristics as signs of value and agency. They challenge the hegemony of characteristics which are typically linked to masculinity rather than making the argument that women can also possess these characteristics – an affirmation which feminists have often made in the past, and which is not usually questioned anymore. Rather than being essentialist, the organizations' focus on women's bodies and emotions thus constitutes an attempt to develop a new kind of rationality than the one reigning the public realm.

Another set of criticisms concerns the practical side of the approach. Balancing goals in the public and private domain complicates the daily work, both on an organizational level and for those women involved. On an organizational level, new forms of organizing workshops are needed. On a personal level, as one of the members of Kaqla argued, it is difficult to keep an eye on one's societal focus if one is at the same time caught up in a personal process. Engaging in a personal process and rethinking one's cardinal assumptions and concepts is a demanding undertaking. This, she argued, does not justify abandoning one in favor of the other however, since both are crucial to women's empowerment (Alvarez, 14 February 2011). Only through an experience-based approach can the terms of the societal debate be altered and can personal transformation processes be facilitated. Mainstream feminist organizations remain crucial to guaranteeing women's public rights, but organizations like

Kaqla can play a role in empowering and supporting both ordinary women and activists, and in influencing the discourse surrounding the issue of violence against women.

Concluding Remarks

The discussion of these two organizations is not intended as a generalization or as a recommendation of how a feminist approach should be conceptualized in Guatemala. Rather, it is an exploration of the conceptual and practical implications of such an approach for how we think about emancipation, and what strategies are deemed relevant to that end.

Both Kaqla and Actoras explore the potential of an experience-based approach rooted in indigenous belief systems to bring about social change (Fulchirone 2009: 371). They combine an experience-based approach with work in the public domain, both in a direct and an indirect way, amongst others by facilitating the personal empowerment process of community leaders. Kaqla and Actoras thus envision an integrated change in women's personal lives and their communities. Therefor, they complement their long-term goal of social change with a more direct approach which holds the promise of more direct results, both in women's personal lives as at the community level. This can be more empowering than only pursuing goals which appear as a distant horizon and for which mobilization does not have a perceivable short-term pay-off.

Their conceptualization of personal empowerment is pinned on an approach which focuses on the body, emotions and spirituality as means to raise awareness about existing attitudes and to deconstruct embodied beliefs regarding women's oppression. This approach revolves around direct experience, immediacy and sentiment, and acknowledges personal subjectivities, strengths, and needs. This can be used as a complement to feminist programs with a focus on the public domain. By taking agency in their own lives, from their own points of view, as individuals, as women and as indigenous people, the women of Actoras and Kaqla propose new relations and structures at the societal level and construct their own discourse on oppression, discrimination, emancipation and empowerment. This can be seen as a remedy to the ventriloquism of many emancipation programs today (Méndez 2010). Through this approach, the organizations have been particularly effective in creating what they call 'contenidos situados', i.e. they have taken common feminist topics but inserted these ideas into the local tradition – and vice versa – by referring to Mayan spirituality, cosmovision, rituals and gender complementarity (Pessar 2001). The approach of these two organizations thereby has the potential to install a debate on current approaches to women's emancipation because of the multiplicity of questions it triggers. Their approach presents a new view on rationality, on knowledge, on oppression and on women's rights. As Suárez Navaz and Hernández Castillo (2008) argue, this is important because it also implicitly questions the discourses currently dominating the debate on women's empowerment, such as the rights discourse, which are not per sé the most encompassing discourses in these contexts.

The work of Actoras de Cambio and Kaqla deviates from the approach of most feminist organizations in Guatemala and Nicaragua. Yet, despite these differences, these organizations can be seen as part of the feminist movement because they actively seek to change the structural conditions which contribute to women's oppression. To generate these changes, Actoras de Cambio and Kaqla aim for more than political and legislative changes however. They also envision structural change in women's personal lives. To bring about both types of change, these organizations combine a public approach with an experience-based approach, and thus incorporate women's personal processes into their empowerment programs. On the basis of the fieldwork, I argued that such an approach has immediate empowering effects for participants and also supports the goals in the public realm which Kaqla and Actoras set themselves, such as raising awareness and mobilizing for social change. This, interviewees argue, is because women who feel more empowered in their personal lives, also experience more agency in the public realm.

This chapter therefore argues that an experience-based approach rooted in indigenous culture fits the social movement paradigm better than it fits the psychotherapeutic framework. While the approach of these two organizations differs genuinely from that of mainstream feminist organizations, goals of both types of organizations show strong overlaps. Moreover, through their work with community leaders and the constant linking of personal and societal processes in the workshops, they also aim to integrate changes at the personal and collective level. This approach moreover invites for a reassessment of traditional – public – approaches to social change, and by extension, of the role of rationality and subjectivity in this process.

In conclusion, the theories and practice on gender and ethnicity developed by these two organizations are rooted in the search for a specific approach to indigenous women's empowerment, on the basis of their own culture. Such an experience-based approach pinned on indigenous traditions is promising, since it invites a new interpretation of empowerment which complements a conventional rational logic with an emotional and perceptive dimension. This is needed to address issues which are not easily expressed in a rationalistic discourse but which can play an important role in women's everyday lives

(Butler 2005, Das 1996). Kaqla and Actoras themselves therefore link personal processes to public ones to develop a new discourse and a new type of rationality, which Kaqla refers to as the *senti-pensar*. Growing self-esteem is of little use in a context where women have no formal rights, just like formal rights have little impact on women on women's daily lives if the attitudes of women and society at large do not change. Therefore work on both levels (the personal and the collective), and through both approaches (rationalistic and experience-based) is needed for women's empowerment. The approach of Kaqla and Actoras is thus different from that of other feminist organizations, but can feed back into it. This is illustrated by the fact that these organizations also set themselves goals in the public domain and use their experience-based work to support these goals.

Some organizations however, see an exclusive focus on personal processes as a sufficient means to empower women. One of these organizations is *Q'anil*. The next chapter asks whether *Q'anil's* approach is relevant for mainstream feminist organizations, and where an actor like this is to be located in the organizational landscape of feminist organizations. The chapter also assesses the role of ethnicity in facilitating this type of approach, as Q'anil does not explicitly work with indigenous women, but uses techniques which are strikingly similar to the ones of Actoras and Kaqla.

CHAPTER 7

The Socio-Political Value of an Experience-Based Approach

Rethinking Strategies of Collective Action

> There is a lot of activism that doesn't deal with empowerment, and you
> have to empower yourself in order to be relevant to any type of struggle.
> TALIB KWELI, 2013

The organization discussed in this chapter focuses on women's personal empowerment process. It differs from the organizations discussed in the previous chapter however, in the sense that it sees a focus on personal empowerment as a sufficient means to emancipate women, and therefore has no programs in the public realm. So whereas Actoras and Kaqla explore how attention to women's personal process can support the goal of social change, the organization discussed in this chapter focuses solely on individual empowerment. I consider whether, in the absence of a clear public goal, an experience-based approach which only focuses on women's personal processes, can still be socially relevant. This topic is explored on the basis of a case study of Q'anil, an organization which argues that empowering women through an experience-based approach also has direct effects at the societal level, because it makes women more aware of the impact of oppressive structures on their own lives and more self-confident about their ability to act in public. Q'anil itself pays no explicit attention to public aspects of women's emancipation and empowerment in its program. Can it, in the absence of goals or strategies in the public realm still be seen as an actor of civil society? Is this type of organization a part of the feminist movement? Can it facilitate structural changes to the oppression of women? And which assumptions on women's movements and empowerment does it challenge?

To answer these questions, I first present an analysis of the daily work of Q'anil. On the basis thereof, the next section discusses the social value of a purely personal approach and contrasts this with the work of Actoras and Kaqla. Consequently, I discuss how other feminist organizations and international donors assess this type of empowerment program. I conclude the chapter with a discussion of whether organizations proceeding exclusively through such an approach should be seen as actors of the feminist movement or as organizations for psychological assistance, and what this means for their position in civil society.

Q'anil: Empowering Ladinas through an Experience-Based Approach

To answer questions about the meaning and relevance of Q'anil's approach, it is important to understand its goals, working methods and organizational embedding.

Audience, Objectives and Organizational Ties of Q'anil

Q'anil emerged from the Actoras de Cambio program and started to work as an independent centre for healing, investigation and education in 2009. While Actoras de Cambio was aimed at recovering the memory of indigenous women who had experienced violence during the armed conflict, Q'anil only works with Ladina women.[1] This decision was made because Ladina women were often overlooked in post-war initiatives aimed at women's recovery and emancipation (Aguilar, 1 February 2011).[2] Following the armed conflict, there was a ubiquity of initiatives working with indigenous women because this group had been a major victim of the armed conflict, and because its history had been characterized by a high degree of discrimination and violence (Duggan et al 2008: 193). This fostered the understanding that special attention needed to be paid to the recovery and emancipation process of this group. Ladinas, on the other hand, were overlooked in some emancipation programs, because of the impression that they were less affected by oppressive structures than indigenous women who faced double oppression on the basis of both their gender and their ethnicity. Moreover, Ladina women did not face structural persecution during the armed conflict and were more present in public life. This buttressed the idea that Ladinas as a group were less affected by wartime violence and more liberated, and did thus not need specific emancipation or empowerment programs aimed at them. This oftentimes positioned Ladinas 'below the radar' of local and international agencies working for women's empowerment (Garrard-Burnett 2001:12). According to Aguilar (1 February 2011) however, it should not be ignored that also Ladinas live under patriarchal conditions,

---

1   The word Ladino – not to be confused with 'Latino' – in Guatemala officially refers to a distinct ethnic group (MINEDUC 2008) However, in popular use, it refers to non-indigenous Guatemalans, and especially mestizo people (mixed – European and native american – origin) from the middle class whose primary language is Spanish.

2   This is also reflected in the large number of academic publications on the identity formation process of indigenous women in Guatemala in the late 1990s (See for example Stern 1998, Little Siebold 2001, Choi 2002). Publications on the identity formation process of Ladina women on the other hand are scant (search in major social science databases).

which genuinely affect the way in which they perceive themselves and the way in which they think and act. Q'anil therefore aimed to raise self-awareness and facilitate the formation of an empowered identity amongst this group of women as well, by offering them the tools to embark on a process of self-reflection.

Not only the target group, but also the principal objective of Q'anil differs from that of Kaqla and Actoras de Cambio. Kaqla and Actoras' strategy of link-ing gender empowerment to ethnic empowerment, inspired a focus on the col-lective and societal level, also in their personal empowerment programs. Goals at the societal level were formally absent from Q'anil's mission statement up until mid-2011. Initially, Q'anil focused only on facilitating a process of healing, self-transformation and self-awareness, through collective forms of psycho-therapeutic, psychosocial and corporeal work. While Yolanda Aguilar, founder and facilitator at Q'anil, emphasized her belief in the need for social change, Q'anil had no formal strategies in the public domain, because social change was perceived as a logical consequence of personal change. As Aguilar explains, '[...] we all have something that needs healing, and this personal healing is a process everyone needs to go through for themselves first, before they can really stand their ground in interactions with others' (Aguilar, 4 February 2011). Q'anil's work is thus premised on the idea that strategies for women's empow-erment should also address issues which are not addressed through a tradi-tional public approach. These, according to Aguilar, can be a crucial element of women's empowerment, since they can facilitate access to the authentic self and enable genuine empowerment. In practice, this means that Q'anil focuses on women's inner worlds and psyche, rather than taking external systems (such as the legal, judicial or health rights of women) as the focus of its empow-erment program. Nevertheless, the goal of social change is becoming more vis-ible in Q'anil's work. On the new website, which was launched in the summer of 2011, Q'anil explicitly mentions the goal of social transformation, and spe-cific programs in this domain are proposed.[3] This creates the impression that Q'anil is growing closer to Kaqla and Actoras de Cambio regarding its goals. Future research can shed light on the future development and reasons for this evolution.

At present the attention for social and public objectives remains limited however, and has not yet led Q'anil to seek more structural relations with other

---

3   The mission statement now reads that 'Qanil is a space which contributes to the regeneration of the Guatemalan social fabric on the basis of experiential, exploratory and training pro-cesses, with men and women who are willing to embark on a process of self-healing and who are committed to personal and social transformation' (Q'anil 2011).

women's organizations which envision similar changes. Notwithstanding its positive attitude towards, and good contacts with, other women's and feminist organizations, Q'anil explicitly sets itself apart from these organizations, and sees itself as unique in the spectrum of women's and feminist organizations because it approaches the issue of women's empowerment in a genuinely different way (Aguilar, 11 February 2011). It therefore closely scrutinizes the relationships it enters into, in order to protect its own organizational identity and working methods. Relationships with other organizations are mostly informal and ad hoc, because, as Aguilar remarked, this allows Q'anil to preserve its specific identity. In the next section I explore several potential negative consequences of this strategy, such as the potential for mutual learning which is hampered.

To preserve its identity, Q'anil also closely monitors its relationship with international donors. When asked about this topic, Aguilar vigorously starts her reply with 'This is not an NGO, you know" (1 February 2011).[4] Funding mainly comes from private donors rather than multilateral or bilateral development aid agencies. This means that there is more flexibility in terms of priorities and working methods because, as Aguilar argues, these smaller donors do not have the same strict conditions for collaboration as their more influential counterparts, and are open to discussion about the terms and conditions of the funding, sometimes giving complete *carte blanche*. While, Q'anil has managed to create a niche for itself in this way, the strategy of only working with smaller and more flexible donors is not an option for most feminist organizations because the amount of money available in these alternative circuits is considerably smaller than the amount of money made available through bodies such as USAID, the Spanish Cooperation, the different programs of the United Nations and bilateral cooperation for example. Moreover, finding these smaller donors requires high investments of time, skills and resources which women's organizations do not always have.[5] Moreover, Q'anil itself depends on fees paid by participants, because the amount of money which it has been able to secure from these donors is inferior to its actual working costs.

---

4   While an NGO refers to any not-for-profit organization which is organized at the local, national or international level, amongst my interviewees, it often had the connotation of a project which was set up and administered by international donors and run by local activists, with an element of dependency.

5   Interviews with the founder of Q'anil suggest that the personal relationships which she established during her stay in Europe for example, have been decisive in helping to identify potential donors.

This means that the vast majority of women's organizations will continue to be dependent on larger international donors which do not always express an interest in alternative approaches (Cabrera Peréz-Armiñan 2009). This means that the case of Q'anil suggests that at present women's organizations have the choice between, on the one hand, relations with donors who provide sufficient funding but who require a substantial degree of compromise from women's organizations, or, on the other hand, entering into relations with donors who allow for more flexibility, but who cannot provide sufficient resources to operate.

Q'anil's Work in Practice

Q'anil's practical work is inspired by its historical affiliation with ECAP in the Actoras de Cambio project on the one hand (see chapter 6) and on the other hand by the training of its founder as an alternative therapist in Valencia (Spain) in the 1980s. Q'anil adapted ECAP's working methods to its own objectives because ECAP's methods were shaped to the needs of people involved in the exhumation programs, and were not developed for women-only groups or aimed at women's empowerment. Q'anil soon experienced that the dynamic which occurred in an all-female group was markedly different from that of ECAP groups, because women raised other issues, interacted in a different way and had other needs. This required that methods were applied in a flexible way and tailored to the needs of participants. The new therapeutic dynamic which arose was more focused on women's issues and women's own input. This entailed for example an emphasis on creating a safe setting and on working with the body (Meoño Magarin, 3 June 2010, facilitator at ECAP). Working with the body seemed less relevant for ECAP's focus group, but Aguilar's experience suggested that this was crucial to facilitate self-awareness and self-transformation in these all-women's groups aimed at empowerment. Aguilar approached this issue on the basis of techniques which merged elements from her – European – training with culturally relevant elements which appeal to the women whom she worked with (Aguilar, 1 February 2011). The next section presents the modalities of this approach, on the basis of a period of participatory observation, in which I participated in Q'anil's workshops and talked to many participants.

Participants

Most empowerment programs at Q'anil are organized as a series of workshops which are spread over a period of ten months to one year, with groups either meeting two evenings or one full day every month. These extended programs are possible because participants make a financial contribution to participate in the workshops. They pay an equivalent of 30 euro for a cycle of workshops, or alternatively, 5 euro for one workshop. Given these relatively high fees, Q'anil mainly attracts middle class women, who, in practice, often have jobs in the formal economy or hold a position in a social organization. This means that these women have the option of linking insights obtained on the basis of their personal process back to other realms of life, and more specifically to their roles in public life. This is something which Aguilar strongly encourages in an informal way. While there is no formal moment during the workshop when women sit together and discuss how they can turn to their personal process to bring about social change, I witnessed on several occasions how Aguilar – during coffee breaks, before or after the workshop – purposefully guided the conversation in such a way as to discuss the work and social situations of these women, and let them tell themselves how they see their personal changes fit in there. One of my interviewees described how she felt more capable of conducting her work with another women's organization after a series of workshops with Q'anil. When asked why this was, she commented:

> The difference between what we do here and what other empowerment programs do, cannot be captured in words, it is a difference of another kind, a difference of senses. In many organizations, there is a lot more talking and action, but at the same time nobody really feels connected to others or to their cause, because they only talk about facts, not about experiences or feelings. [In these other programs] we talk about our experiences as if they were a newspaper article. Whereas here, emotions are placed at the centre and language is made subordinate to it, not the other way around.
>
> LAPENNA, 4 February 2011

This suggests that despite Q'anil's experience-based approach and the absence of public goals or strategies from its program – at the time of the fieldwork – it still had the potential to affect the public realm to some extent, in the sense of changing the way in which women act in their public roles. As the section below shows, the first focus is on women's personal processes however.

Linking Body, Mind and Emotions

A typical Q'anil workshop starts with a short meditation during which the facilitator invites women to feel their bodies, become aware of the present moment, and allow their minds to step out of the turmoil of everyday life.

This exercise is used because it offers women the possibility to take a step back from their everyday concerns and to take time for themselves. This moment of taking time for oneself can in itself be transgressive in a context where women often see themselves as 'being for others'. After this brief meditation, exercises are done which serve a threefold goal, firstly, to explore their own feelings regarding oppression, secondly, to vocalize these, and thirdly, to link these insights and processes to daily life.

In the first place, exercises aim to illustrate the link between the body, the mind and emotions, and emphasize the way in which the body can be used as a tool to access the mind, emotions and memory. An example is an exercise whereby the facilitator invites women to think of a particular experience entailing a certain feeling – sadness, anger, fear, joy, et cetera – and to think of the corporeal sentiments this caused, and to identify and describe these very specifically. This exercise is aimed at fostering more awareness of their own bodies and psyches. The usefulness of exercises to create awareness of the body and emotions is acknowledged in theoretical literature on the topic. Meyers (1994: 34) for example stresses the importance of acknowledging certain feelings in one's own life, in order to be able to feel empathy towards others experiencing them, and to develop coping mechanisms.

Another example of exercises used by Q'anil, is an exercise whereby women are asked to make a drawing of how they feel at the present moment, then how they felt at the happiest time of their lives, the saddest time and the way in which they would want to feel. After doing so, women discuss their drawings, which often have a highly symbolic value and which often shed light on the dynamics which reign women's lives. Several women mentioned they were unaware of the recurring patterns in these drawings and in their lives, until they drew and started to explain them. When women cannot say much about their drawings or link them back to their present life, the facilitator asked questions about what the colors, forms, composition, et cetera, meant for the participant. The aim is to render women more aware of the different unconscious dynamics that influence them. After this, exercises are given which help women make sense of what they just expressed and to integrate this into their lives. These are often movement exercises or exercises with a partner, aimed at making women feel how this sentiment manifested itself in their bodies, and how it influences their interactions with other people. This way, Aguilar argues, women can make their feelings more tangible and concrete, and work with them in a more direct way (11 February 2011). Movement exercises also have the additional advantage of allowing women to come to know and enjoy their own bodies in a safe environment. As one participant argued:

For me, moving is a way to feel my body again, to feel where and how it is keeping me down, and which parts are strong. By moving, I feel the restrictions which I normally experience unconsciously. Moving my pelvis, or letting someone touch it, was very difficult for a long time, because it felt promiscuous. Now I don't feel so shy about this anymore, because I see it as a valuable part of myself and I realize that my shyness was foisted onto me; not only regarding this issue, but also regarding other issues.

TORRES, 4 February 2011

After making women familiar with the idea that the body, thoughts and emotions are intimately related to one another, exercises further explore how these elements are linked in practice. Examples of exercises here are an exercise whereby participants construct rag dolls which symbolize themselves. They shape the rag doll according to what they see as their strengths and weaknesses, to visibilize and become aware of how they see themselves. In another exercise, women would listen to the story of another woman, and then literally walk in her shoes and try to put themselves in the position of the woman in that particular situation which was just described, to see how she reacts to this, what the other person can learn from this reaction, what she herself can learn from this reaction, etc.

These exercises are common in therapeutic settings (Comas-Diaz 1987, Walker 1994, Clinton 2006), but should they also be acknowledged in feminist empowerment programs? Das et al (2000) and Meyers (1994) strongly believe they should, because there is an intricate relationship between the perception of one's own subjectivity, the process of identity formation and the likeliness of experiencing violence.[6] Therefore, working with this subjectivity, by letting women experience their and other points of view through concrete exercises can be seen as a decisive way to raise awareness amongst women of their own situation and of that of other women. This, according to Meyers, contributes to the formation of an empowered identity. The above exercises envision to raise awareness and to provide tools to express this. In a next stage, exercises are aimed at linking insights from the workshops back to women's daily lives.

The techniques used to this end are diverse, but most exercises are group exercises, which emphasize the relationship with other humans (Q'anil 2009). Unlike psychotherapeutic processes which only work with the individual, the approach of Q'anil thus builds on the way in which group dynamics and the

---

6   Das et al describe 'subjectivity' as the felt interior experience of the person, that includes his or her positions in a field of relational power (2000: 1).

individual experience influence each other. In this manner – even in the absence of a clear goal in the public domain – Q'anil contributes to an exploration of the link between the individual and the collective level, and facilitates an awareness amongst participants of how these different levels of experience interact. As a participant to one of the workshops illustrated:

> I always find the exercises very interesting, but I find it very difficult to take the floor in a group discussion afterwards. I make myself small and invisible and hope that no one will notice me. One day Yolanda confronted me with this, and we talked about why I did this [...] I still find it difficult to take the floor, but now I understand why I behave like this in a group and what the consequences thereof are. So when I really want to share something, I take a deep breath and claim my position in the centre of the attention.
>
> LAPENNA, 4 February 2011

Later in the interview, this interviewee stated how she also saw this pattern in her daily life, for example during meetings at work where she seldom took the floor. She also stated that this exercise made her think about how difficult she found it to make herself heard, and what caused this. Her experience also links back to another crucial aspect of Q'anil's approach, namely the role of group discussions and more specifically, of language.

The Role of Language

Throughout Q'anil's program, talking and rhetorical exercises are contained to a minimum. As Aguilar explains:

> I tried this [counseling techniques based on a rhetorical approach] as well, but what I noticed is that when women try to capture their experience in words, they feel shyer because of how taboo-laden some words are, they repeat the existing narrative or, more commonly, they remain silent. When working in this way [body-based work], a whole different dynamic arises. The group feels more like a group, women feel safer, and you obtain remarkable results much faster.
>
> AGUILAR, 1 February 2011

Moreover, most exercises are concluded with a brief moment of silence or meditation. The goal thereof is to allow women to feel what the exercise has brought them. Women first make sense of this for themselves, without anyone telling them how to interpret their experience. Afterwards there is a group reflection during which women share their experiences, and during which the facilitator further explores women's experiences through questions aimed at providing women with more insights on their personal process and eventually, with a new perspective on their own reality. This group reflection is a key component of the approach because it links the individual experience back to the experiences of others, and links the workshop experience back to daily life through questions designed to this end. It thereby allowed for further insights on dynamics underlying women's personal experiences of oppression, as well as teaching women to talk about their experiences in a language which feels right for them, thereby breaking the taboo which often surrounds these issues in a supportive way. Thus women first get the chance to reflect on their experience for themselves, and only then share this with other women, and maybe reinterpret it in the light of that exchange. They are not first presented with the views of others, which could keep them from arriving at their own interpretation of their experience.

During one of the workshops in which I participated in February 2011, an exercise in pairs was followed by such a group reflection about what every person had experienced. One of the participants was unable to say anything about herself, and answered every question with an interpretation of how she thought her companion had felt, and how she interpreted the actions of other members in the group. Noticing this, the facilitator tried to delve deeper into this experience by each time asking open questions about how the woman herself had felt. Insisting on this, and asking the same question – in different wording – several times, this woman eventually started to refer to herself and her own feelings and experiences in her answer. This way, no one was correcting her for the way in which she answered the question, no one was telling her what to feel, or telling her that her answers reflected the internalization of oppressive ideas. Instead she suggested this herself through guided questions, which showed her how hard she found it to think and talk about herself.

The language which women used to talk about themselves and to reflect on their experiences was moreover not directive or colonizing because it was not a traditional linear discourse with a stable external referent, but rather a language which was pinned on women's own subjective experiences. This was apparent for example in the fact that women constantly referred back to their bodies, replaced some words with gestures where they felt that words failed to express their feelings, and told stories which were often far from complete or coherent by traditional standards, but which seemed to make sense for the women in the group regardless. Specifically, women narrating on their experiences, or on how these linked back to their daily lives, often did not find the words to describe a certain feeling and simply omitted this word from their narrative, replacing it with a sound, gesture or facial expression: closed eyes, hand movements, certain ways of breathing, all seemed to replace that which women were unable to capture in words – and were understood and validated by the other participants. This should not be overlooked, because these instances of non-linear and non-verbal communication in which parts of women's psyche – other than a linear and discursive rational ones – were appealed to, were important for these women, in the sense that, even without having the words for it, they could express something which they felt, and something which they had lived through, and create a sense of mutual recognition and understanding with other women who had similar experiences, which would not have been possible through a standardized linear discourse, according to participants.

Facilitators contribute to the creation of this shared site of understanding by encouraging that women explore these non-verbal, non-linear and non-rational ways of expressing themselves. They do this, for example, by emphasizing the link between the stories which women are telling and their own bodies and feelings. For instance, by constantly asking women about what happens in their body while they are narrating something, facilitators purposely steer the dynamic of the reflection process away from rhetorical interpretations and towards a more experience-based language. They do so by interrupting the verbal narrative discourses for moments of looking inward and feeling what is happening in the women's bodies. This is not only done with the methodological/theoretical aim of facilitating the occurrence of a new language, but also has an immediate practical relevance because it draws the attention to how women have internalized oppressive discourses and how these discourses play out in their body, for example by creating feelings of guilt or by not allowing them to actually turn to themselves and experience their bodies.

Also in other settings, social organizations have obtained positive results by turning to a similar approach of language. McDonald's interviewees (2002: 121), all members of social movements in the domain of anti-globalization, describe how it was through "embodied communication, communication achieved through senses, emotion and passion" that they found their space in the movement, which allowed them to create a collective identity. These anti-globalists experimented with new forms of communication and of relating to one another in the context of their social protests, These experiments are comparable to those carried out by Q'anil in its therapeutic workshops, i.e. revolving around direct communication on the basis of emotion, embodied rather than discursive communication, the use of bodily movement as a means to express oneself, etc. McDonald further describes how this type of communication and interaction allowed for much more fluid structures which, in turn, allowed for acknowledging subjectivity and for achieving an experience of being grounded and an emotional connection to the issue (2002: 121).

This research thus suggests that the experience-based approach or the development of a new language of Q'anil is not *per se* limited to therapeutic workshops, but has a broader applicability. Moreover, the experiences described by McDonald's interviewees, show important overlaps with the experiences which participants at Q'anil describe. In both contexts, interviewees report an augmented sense of a shared identity and of feeling more grounded. As Torres, a participant in one of the workshops, remarked:

> Coming here, I feel more *conectada a tierra* each time, connected with myself as well. I no longer feel paralyzed by grief. I no longer see my body as a burden. I no longer feel as if these problems are so vast that there is nowhere to begin. We do things little by little, and it works fine for me.
>
> TORRES, 4 February

Closing Ritual

Every session is concluded with a short ritual, which is meant for women to establish a connection with one another in which they feel support, and on which they can fall back when trying to bring their new insights into practice. This way, non-rational methods are used as a means to establish a new reality, which better reflect the experience of these women. As one participant to a workshop reported:

> [These exercises] gave me the feeling I could breathe again- for the first time in my life maybe. Here it's not compulsory to see the way forward as going out, having a job and fighting for your rights. Here I can decide for myself what feels good and empowering, and if that which feels good for me is not the same as what Yolanda [facilitator] had in mind, we can still proceed. I don't need to grow by abiding to the ideals which someone else has in mind for me [...]. The rituals help me discover what feels good for me, who I want to be.
>
> RODRIGUEZ, 4 February 2011

The closing ritual provides women with an opportunity to give their own interpretation to the workshop, and carry with them those elements which were most relevant to them, which can be different for everyone. Acknowledging this multiplicity of interpretations and experiences is much harder to achieve through a rhetorical strategy in which women are presented with one narrative which is presented as a fact, but which may not apply or appeal to them in their situation (Meyers 2002: 27). On the other hand, closing a workshop with a ritual, may seem to have less practical relevance in the context of an empowerment program, because it does not allow facilitators to present women with a discursive conclusion in which they highlight those elements which they find most relevant. Nevertheless, non-directive and non-narrative strategies can potentially be more empowering precisely because they allow women to think for themselves about their own path towards empowerment in the way which is most relevant to them, rather than leaving them dependent on the interpretation of a facilitator.[7]

Unlike Kaqla or Actoras de Cambio's workshops, Q'anil does not offer follow-up workshops on how women can implement insights from the workshop in their professional roles. The idea that an experience-based approach to empowerment will logically bring about other forms of empowerment is thus pushed to the limit here. However, as mentioned above, informal attention to how these new insights can help women to empower other women, or how they can feed back into their professional roles for example, is ample and also formal attention is growing since mid-2011. Below, I assess what the usefulness of an approach focusing only on women's personal empowerment process can be for feminist organizations.

The Socio-Political Value of a Purely Personal Approach: Short and Long-Term Benefits

This section asks whether an approach which turns only to women's personal processes to foster empowerment can still be classified as feminist, and whether organizations adopting such an approach should be seen as actors of civil society. The answers to both questions are interrelated.

Several characteristics speak against defining Q'anil as an actor of civil society: the limited number of participants, the relatively high fees, the absence of explicit strategies to change the social conditions which contribute to women's oppression, and the fact that they do not envision to mobilize large sections of society for social change. Yet, Q'anil has the same objective as most mainstream feminist organizations – which are all seen as actors of civil society – namely to change the situation of women's oppression and to empower women. It thus

---

7   Also see Gross (1981) on how exercises without words can be less colonizing and therefore more empowering.

envisions the same goals as most feminist organizations, but uses a different strategy to arrive at this. One could thus argue that the organization can indeed be seen as feminist, because it has the aim of structurally changing the situation of women's oppression. However, whether an organization like Q'anil which only envisions this change by turning to women's personal processes, can also be defined as an actor of civil society, is more controversial, because of their working methods but also, because they do not work with men. This means that they do not only provide women with agency, but also, implicitly, lay the responsibility for their own situation with women.

The way in which Q'anil's exclusive focus on women's personal processes makes it a relevant factor in civil society is twofold. Firstly, through applied exercises aimed at creating more self-confidence and more self-awareness, Q'anil stimulates a sense of agency which impacts upon women beyond their private lives, and also influences the way in which they fulfill their public roles, for example in organizations of civil society (Benson 1994, Mackenzie 2000, Worrell 1992). Moreover, an increased awareness of the dynamics reigning their own life also fosters an awareness of other societal dynamics affecting them, such as the dynamic of oppression (Bermúdez 2001, Field Belenky 1997). Secondly, Q'anil's approach can feed back into the public realm because of the group discussions that follow the exercises and meditation. These group discussions link women's concrete experience back to everyday life, and link the individual experience to the experience of others, thereby adding a sense of mutual recognition and a practical relevance to the exercise. During these discussion women are also confronted with group dynamics and their role in these group dynamics, i.e. how a group influences them, and how they, in turn, can influence the dynamic of the group. These insights can also be applied to their position within other groups and interactions. Furthermore, these group discussions invite women to talk about their experiences in a language which feels right for them, and encourages them to find a new language which better reflects their own experiences (see for example Das 2000).

Organizations like Q'anil can thus to some extent be seen as facilitators of civil society activism, even if they may not be actors of civil society themselves. Organizations with a purely personal experience-based approach to women's empowerment could thus be seen as an intermediate tier between the personal lives of women and their social activism, facilitating an engaged and genuine form of activism as well as being a valuable form of empowerment in their own right. The latter should not be overlooked, as some participants indicated that their participation in Q'anil's workshops made them feel more in control of their personal lives, meaning that the program of Q'anil does not only constitute a stepping stone towards social activism, but that it also has direct effects on a personal level which are important in themselves. It is precisely this multi-layeredness which participants appreciated. As a group of participants argued, this allowed them to take what was relevant for them, to use this in the way most relevant to them. Of this group of participants, one woman indicated that she had no ambition to take on a public role in the women's movement, and that the program just helped her to cope with her daily situation, whereas two others stressed the importance of these workshops in their own work at different types of social organizations (Torres et al, 4 February 2011).

Yet, fostering social change or becoming more proficient in their work as social activists was usually not the first motivation of interviewees to participate in these workshops. From interviews with the participants, it appeared that none of these women attended Q'anil's workshops with the primary goal of changing the public realm. Their first goal was changing their own lives in the sense of becoming a more empowered person, getting to know themselves, and working through issues from their past which kept them down. Only in a later stage did they start to combine this with their public work to foster social change. These women talked about their empowerment struggle as an inherently intimate and personal one, as a struggle of working through personal processes in order to grow and become the master and protagonist of their own lives, rather than a struggle for rights based on leveling public action. These are two genuinely different struggles, they argued. But at the same time, their personal empowerment processes helped them in their struggle for women's emancipation – i.e. to overcome structural barriers to their empowerment in the public realm – and vice versa. So while the societal process of women's emancipation and women's personal empowerment are two different matters, participants considered both as necessary elements for women's emancipation. As Lapenna, a participant to the workshop and member of development agency, noted:

> I come here for me, for myself. This has nothing to do with my work. At work no one even knows I come here. I need this, in my life, to feel I am in charge of my own life. [...] It helps me in my work as well, but in an implicit way. I am more self-confident, I believe more strongly in what I do, and I feel that I have even become more efficient. But that's not my reason for coming here.
>
> LAPENNA, 4 February 2011

This suggests that facilitating women's personal empowerment struggle also supports them in their public roles. It could therefore be argued that taking personal processes out of the realm of oblivion where they have long lingered in the work of many feminist organizations, could potentially reinforce existing empowerment programs and give an impetus to civil society activism. The skepticism of feminist organizations *vis-à-vis* a purely personal approach is justified though because also structural changes in the public realm are crucial for women's emancipation, and focusing too much on women's personal processes risks a societal standstill and a depoliticization of the issue of oppression which shifts the responsibility away from powerholders, especially if such programmes do not work with men or decision-makers. Yet, precisely in a context where there is so little willingness at the political level to enforce women's rights, complementary strategies of empowerment could be a valuable resource.

My fieldwork suggests however that the potential of an experience-based approach focusing on women's personal processes is mainly relevant for women's empowerment when it is combined with elements and strategies which have their roots in the public realm and which also includes men. In the absence of such efforts, the approach of organizations like Q'anil risks to sand in purely psychological assistance which shifts all attention away from the societal factors leading to women's oppression and lays the unique responsibility for ending this situation with women themselves. This example thus illustrates the difficult balancing act between an overly politicized approach which overlooks women's personal processes altogether by focusing solely on the societal and policy level, and, on the other hand, a psychological approach which risks depoliticizing the issue of women's empowerment. The next section attempts to explore where an equilibrium between both approaches could lay.

Balancing Different Strategies

Several studies suggest a link between collective action and personal empowerment (see for example Bayard 2004 and 2006, Blumberg 1998 and Sardenberg 2008). What participants to the Q'anil workshops argued was that the insights about themselves, which they gained during these sessions, also helped them in their public work. As one participant who works with another civil society organization, illustrated:

> I had fought against patriarchal organizing and structures which oppressed us in all of the work I did, but I only did so in words. [...] I had never felt what this situation does to me personally, how it affected the way I think, the way I feel, the way I treat my dear ones, the way I look at my body. Now I am more aware of these things, and more capable of bringing my message across, because I know what I am talking about. I have felt why it is important to change these things, how they limit my choices and how they influence everything I do. When I feel demotivated about my work, I think about how I was before [participating in the Q'anil

workshops] and how I feel now, and I know how important it is to do the work I am doing.

TORRES, 4 February 2011

This testimony hints at the shortcomings of a – public – strategy which does not explicitly link oppression to how it plays out in women's bodies and minds. Q'anil, Kaqla and Actoras de Cambio avoid this by linking the abstract and theoretical discourse on social transformation to women's personal lives in an experience-based manner. They thereby enable a lived understanding of feminist ideas, and confront participants in a direct way with the effect of oppression and the need for social change in their own lives. This means that women can connect with the changes feminism advocates in a direct way, which none of them said to have experienced before. Kaqla and Actoras, but also Q'anil, thereby go beyond prompting a change in women's personal lives and also affect the way in which participants fulfill their public roles. Several interviewees at Kaqla and Q'anil confirmed how they needed this step of personal empowerment and of looking at their personal lives in order to be able to conduct more useful work in the public domain (for example Galindez and Delmorales 31 January 2011; Lapenna et al, 4 February 2011). As one of the participants to the Q'anil workshops put it:

I used to believe in the work I did [at a local feminist organization] but still I came home to a difficult situation every night. During the day I fought for women's [...] right to decide over their own lives, and in the evening I came home to a situation where very little had changed. I continued to do the whole household on my own, as if this was the cross I had to bear for being a woman. Participating in the healing circles showed me that a lot remained to be done in my own life, in the way I thought about it, in the way I experienced it, in the way I managed it. Sorting that out first, gave me more energy to start the working day with a clear mind and to do more [for the organization and for its participants]. The healing circles showed me that I could at least make a change in my own life. [...] No matter how small the steps forward were, they made me believe that women whom I work with too could take these small steps, and that I could help them with that. It is so much more rewarding to incite someone to take a small step, and then see that happening, than it is to campaign every day with no reward. [...]. I can now give women more appropriate advice, and I now believe what I advise them to do. I mean *really* believe. I have felt it. I have lived it; and I had someone helping me

make sense of it, someone who brought me back in touch with my own
life. That's the person I want to be for others too.

RODRIGUEZ, 4 February 2011

This testimony underlines the importance of Q'anil's workshops in terms of
helping women to apply theoretical concepts of feminism to their own lives.
This way participants realized that the theoretical concepts which they use are
not only abstract concepts, but that they run through their daily lives and corporal experience, and that, therefore, they mean something different for everyone. Q'anil thereby managed to break the limiting ascription of an oppressed
identity to women. This identity of 'the oppressed woman' who has to fight
against a Brobdingnagian patriarchal social structure, is paralyzing and limiting, notably so, because it offers very few niches in which women can indeed
accomplish change. As Meyers (1994) argues, this ascription of an oppressed
identity becomes so convincing that it becomes normative and prompts a
further internalization of the oppressive discourse. She argues that the matter-
of-fact presentation of evidence about this situation of oppression will not
empower women who are in the grip of a *figuration*[8] which supports these
norms. She argues that what is needed is an innovative counter-figuration
which facilitates the de-internalization of norms and images, and fosters wom-
en's abilities as agents (Meyers 1994: 55 and 2002: 27).

The work of Q'anil, Kaqla and Actoras serves precisely this purpose of
creating a felt awareness about the internalization of oppressive discourses,
and at the same time offering a compelling counter-figuration rather than only
presenting women with facts. These organizations' aim of facilitating the
integration of women's social, corporeal and emotive experiences – in a way
that makes sense to them – can facilitate their process of self-discovery,
self-definition and self-directions, and thereby their sense of autonomy and
self-value, which are needed for taking up roles in public life (Meyers 2002 and
1994, Benson 1994). It moreover offers women insights about the niches that
exist to challenge oppressive schemes – for example in the intimate domain –
and offers them the tools to bring about change there. An experience-based
approach can therefore be more inspiring and stimulating for women than an
approach rooted in the dynamics of the public realm, and can help them to

---

8   In the work of Meyers, figuration can be seen as the deep internalization of norms due to
    their entwining with prevalent cultural imagery. These norms are encoded in captivating
    forms that condense complex behavioral and psychological imperatives into memorable,
    emotionally compelling forms, called *figurations* (Meyers 2002: 25).

also see the active and constructive element in their identity as women. It is thereby a valuable complement to a purely rights-based approach.

What is important in this approach moreover, is that Q'anil, Kaqla and Actoras reinterpret and revalue 'the feminine' on its own terms, in a way which participants find relevant. To do this, they work with unexplored parts of women's identity. This can in itself challenge the current social order because it provides women with the counter-figuration which Meyers (2002) describes. This emphasis on and exploration of the characteristics which are traditionally ascribed to women is not *per se* limiting or conservative because these organizations explore where the empowering potential of those otherwise oppressive identities lies. The counter-figuration then lies precisely in the fact that women seek a new interpretation of the existing identities commonly ascribed to them (Schwarz 2004: 5).

Several characteristics which are seen as 'typically feminine' in the Guatemalan context are renounced by feminist organizations and other organizations which work in the public domain, because they are thought to be inherently limiting. The idea that women are more emotional for example is contested by mainstream feminists because this assumption allegedly denies that women can be rational as well. These mainstream feminist organizations see an expansion of the rationalistic utilitarian logic which reigns the public realm as the only appropriate path to women's emancipation and empowerment. Actoras, Kaqla and Q'anil on the other hand do not solely rely on this Cartesian rationality, but also on the concept of *senti-pensar*. Instead they probe for those characteristics which participants see as key to their female identity, acknowledge these – also if they do not fit the dominant frame of Cartesian rationality – and work with them in a way which is allegedly empowering for women. This way their approach remains consistent with the daily realities of women and gives them a sense of agency. They thereby reinterpret the way in which femininity is commonly represented and create new images and representations that expose the limits of the common understanding of femininity, which is also common amongst most feminist organizations. Instead of subscribing to the representation of women as passive and castrated (in psychoanalytical sense, see for example Irigaray 1985a: 162 on this topic), these organizations emphasize the symbolic correlation of femininity with a – dangerous – fluidity that has the potential to reform and dissolve form and order (See for example Lloyd 1984: 3, Grosz 1994: 203). By creating awareness amongst women of how traits which are commonly ascribed to them, can be interpreted in a positive manner and applied in the struggle for their cause, these organizations offer a critical revaluation of traditionally feminine roles. This can facilitate autonomy by increasing self-awareness and self-trust, and by opening up new domains within which women can be active (Schwarz

2004: 6). These organizations incorporate elements of difference feminism to revalue certain domains and characteristics which they see as crucial to women's lives, rather than envisioning the 'old dream of symmetry' (Irigaray 1985b: 11). However, their radical openness to work with whatever comes up during the therapeutic process also allowed them to explore identity components which women found important and which did not fit the traditional conception of a female identity. They found that acknowledging that there may be differences between women and men, does not mean that women's identities have to be constricted to typically female identities such as the mother-identity. They also explore how women reacted to working with characteristics typically attributed to men in Guatemala. This prevented them from becoming restrictive and limiting. Instead, turning to difference feminism and indigenous principles of complementarity allowed them to acknowledge different realities and explore a new form of rationality which reflected the personal realities of these women more adequately. In doing so, the organizations constantly seek to balance premises of difference feminism and indigenous beliefs in complementarity on the one hand, with a radically open interpretation of gender constructs on the other hand.

In this way, the approach of Actoras, Kaqla and Q'anil invites for the rethinking of a number of prevailing feminist assumptions on social change and political mobilization. All three have tried to use transformative healing experiences to re-script cultural narratives, i.e. to change the way in which women's empowerment and gendered identity is commonly conceived. They do so by challenging common interpretations of female identity, of women's emancipation and empowerment strategies and of the way in which the personal and the political are related. In doing so, they aim to restore the value of the personal sphere and its specific dynamics, and to integrate these into their public program where appropriate. This way, they are trying to supplement the idea of politics of collective action with a new dimension, namely with elements from the personal realm. For these organizations, collective action refers to a wider spectrum of human activity than only public protest. These organizations turn to collective and group-based processes, but apply them in a way which is uncommon amongst social organizations, namely through psychotherapeutic, corporeal and emotion-based work. These activities are not commonly included in strategies of collective action. The approach of this organization thus invites for a broader interpretation of what constitutes collective action, and of what means are appropriate to foster social change. Their concept of collective action does not approach every problem which women face as a political problem with a solution in the public realm, but instead explicitly includes personal issues in its social activism. Doing so, they demonstrate both an awareness of the socio-political component of many of the problems that women face, as well as of the potential of an experience-based approach to influence this.

This difficult balancing act has allowed them to take into account the everyday lives of women more directly. The work of organizations like Kaqla and Actoras can thus be an important resource for, and complement to, the work of the feminist movement. The place of an organization like Q'anil in civil society is more ambiguous, as its reluctance to engage in any form of direct social activism or with men makes it debatable whether they are an actor of civil society. While the organization can seemingly contribute to a more healthy civil society, it should probably not be seen as a member of civil society itself because of its lack of a social action.

Relevance of an Experience-Based Approach for Other Social Actors

Above, I analyzed the potential of an experience-based approach – whether combined or as a stand-alone strategy – to contribute to change in the public domain. This section evaluates how organizations proceeding through an experience-based approach relate to other feminist organizations and the donor community.

Organizational Interfaces

Having established the potential merit of combining different approaches to women's empowerment, this section considers how organizations focusing on women's personal empowerment are perceived by other feminist organizations, and how relations are between both types of organizations.

In this context, it is important to consider where the Guatemalan women's and feminist movement finds itself at present and under what conditions it is operating. The first part of the book illustrated how the women's and feminist movement in Guatemala today largely finds itself in a defensive position trying to maintain itself in the face of an unfavorable political regime, and that it is trying to establish its identity as a respected social actor. These factors led to the adoption of a rights-based public approach. Yet, several interviewees working in mainstream feminist organizations expressed their dissatisfaction with this approach and expressed an interest in complementary strategies. As Cubillo, member of the legal department at Ixchen, commented:

> I only help women with the legal aspect of their situation. My colleague helps her with the health aspect, in case of abuse. Other colleagues organize workshops to raise awareness amongst women of their own situation [...] It's all quite fragmented. [...] often see the same women coming back. [...It would be more useful if...] we could help women in their

daily lives, before things get out of hand. Learning them that they are capable of changing things in their own life, even if the state or society is not supporting them.

CUBILLO, 24 April 2010

This statement shows that activists themselves are to some extent dissatisfied with the current approach, and suggests that an experience-based approach could meet the aspirations of these activists. But how do interviewees assess the concrete possibility of engaging with an experience-based approach and of focusing more heavily on women's personal empowerment process?

The opinions of interviewees on this topic can be grouped into three categories. A first, relatively small group rejected the relevance of personal processes for feminist organizations working on women's empowerment, and advocated a unique focus on socio-political and structural issues. They thereby *de facto* substituted the idea of personal empowerment with that of public emancipation. This group of respondents did not see organizations proceeding through a purely experience-based approach as part of the feminist movement if they do not prioritize change in the social structures themselves. While even these interviewees would not deny the relevance of an experience-based approach and personal processes altogether, the idea that these had little socio-political relevance shone through in their answers. One member of a women's organization in the capital was not *per se* against the idea of a experience-based approach to empowerment, but at the same time her rejection of the relevance of such an approach for the feminist project was perceptible when she argued:

> I think we ought to explore the potential of such strategies indeed. It would be wrong for us, as feminists, to be blind to any form of action that has the potential to change the situation of women. And if these organizations obtain good results, we can only encourage them. But I personally don't see it fit to approach the issue of women's empowerment (*empoderamiento*) as if this were something which women themselves have to sort out. Such an approach reduces the issue to a psychological one.
>
> ASENCIÓ, UNAMG, 24 May 2010

The importance of this belief, according to the interviewee, meant that her organization would not establish any professional links with organizations only focusing on women's personal empowerment, because of the risk that this would lead to a strategy of blame-shifting. This closes the door for collaboration with organizations which subscribe to a different logic. This opinion is inspired by the belief that a psychologization of women's empowerment, stands in contrast to a political approach which envisions changes in the social structures.

A second group of respondents avoided the *a priori* exclusion of an experience-based approach from the feminist movement's strategies, by – reticently – acknowledging the value of an experience-based approach for women's empowerment. While seeing psychosocial assistance as a crucial part of women's empowerment, these respondents did not envision the incorporation of an experience-based approach into their own organizational structure, because of time and financial constraints, different foci, and the requirement of different skills and training. Arguments about insufficient resources were dominant in explaining why their organizations would probably not turn to an experience-based approach in the near future. One interviewee from a feminist organization in the capital argued:

> ...we have no one here who is an expert on that topic, and recruiting someone with this purpose is not within our financial reach. Also developing and implementing programs in this domain is too costly for now. We are dependent on the limited budget of funding we receive and it is important to choose priorities in accordance.
>
> MORALES, Tierra Viva, 1 June 2010

This statement illustrates the extent to which donors can impact on the selection of priorities of feminist organizations, and the fact that this triggers the choice of objectives and programs with an immediate and measurable pay-off. This interviewee suggested that because of priorities of donors and their demands to see results, organizations focus more strongly on strategies which have an immediate result. In practice, this leads to the prioritization of work in the public domain, through actions and campaigns, which can be documented and presented more easily. Yet, respondents in this group suggested that both public and private emancipation and empowerment strategies were needed, but that they were two different undertakings. These interviewees thus did not subscribe to the view which says that social structures can only be changed by means of social struggle, or that pursuing women's empowerment through an experience-based approach by definition entailed a de-politicization of the issue. Yet, there was a degree of reservation and a number of practical concerns withholding them from incorporating elements from an experience-based approach themselves or establishing structural relations. They did have difficulties though conceiving of a practical reciprocity between both approaches – due to organizational constraints – and therefore tended to continue prioritizing public work in practice. However, they were open to more structural relations with organizations adopting a different approach.

A last – smaller – group of respondents acknowledged and expressed an explicit interest in the work of feminist organizations adopting an experience-based approach, as well as a desire to incorporate elements of this strategy into their own working methods. Specifically, references to the body, which have been important in feminist discourse throughout, are now being complemented with a discourse focusing on women's personal and bodily experiences. This is for example visible in the campaigns of the Nicaraguan feminist movement, which draws the attention to women's concrete experiences and interpretations, and to the element of enjoying their own bodies (also see Tierra Viva 2010, Cumes 2009: 106, Nelson 2006). This campaign at the same time makes the link with the social value of such a strategy, so as to render it compatible with the goals of the feminist struggle.

Yet, apart from a number of dispersed initiatives in both countries, most feminist organizations' discourse on the body remains either functionalist by depicting the body as an instrument in the struggle for emancipation, or notoriously one-sided by depicting the body as something surrounded with pain, danger and negative feelings – violence, rape, murder, abortion, guilt and shame. This approach risks reducing women's bodies to an instrument in the public struggle for emancipation, rather than seeing the body as something constituting women's personal sense of self. The extent to which mainstream feminist discourses link the body to emotions, affection, spirituality and enjoyment is limited, and these topics tend to be filtered out of the discourse of Guatemalan feminists altogether. This is remarkable, because such a discourse could be subversive on different levels, i.e. by linking its theoretical explanations with women's personal experiences or by allowing women to explore a realm of positive feelings which is often shielded from them (Fulchiron 2004: 48, also see campaign MFN supra). As a whole, the Guatemalan feminist movement has thus not managed to turn to the body as a domain in which empowerment can happen from the bottom-up.

Mainstream feminist activists are still unfamiliar with many of the efforts which alternative feminist organizations are undertaking in this domain. This can partially be attributed to organizational constraints, in which maintaining a coherent policy of alliance with organizations working on the basis of an experience-based approach was not a priority. This leads to a discussion of the role of donors in facilitating the building of bridges between different approaches.

Impact of the Donor Community on the Appreciation of Experience-Based Approaches

When considering the way in which an experience-based approach focusing on women's personal processes could be useful for feminist organizations in practice, the influence of the donor community is crucial, because financial donors structurally affect the programmatic choices and priorities of women's and feminist organizations.

Both Kaqla and Q'anil have a different relationship with their financial donors than most other feminist organizations. Both organizations were established by women who had gone through a process of convalescence themselves. These women vigorously insisted on making this process the cornerstone of their organizations. Initially both benefitted from a predisposition towards securing psychological assistance for victims of the armed conflict. Their strategy did however not resonate with the changing priorities and demands of most prominent donor agencies, which adopted a rights based approach since the early 2000s. This meant that both organizations had to find alternative sources of funding (Álvarez 14 February 2011, Aguilar 1 February 2011). In addition to this, securing funding became increasingly difficult because of a decreasing interest in Latin America as a region on the side of the international donor community (Interviews with C. Álvarez, member of Kaqla, 21 February 2011 and Neirynck, fieldworker, 28 april 2010).

While this leads to a precarious situation in terms of securing funding, which challenges the continuity of the work of these organizations, it has at the same time incited them to systematically seek out donors who give them the space to develop their own identity and working methods. In this way, both organizations have been relatively successful in adhering to their own programs and limiting the influence of international donors. Interviewees from both organizations – like most of my interviewees at women's organizations – were firm in denying that donors had any influence on their programs at all (Aguilar, Q'anil, 4 February 2011, Lopez, Kaqla, 16 February 2011). This is unlikely to be the case, because in an interaction between donors and NGOs, adaptations of some kind are likely to occur (Klandermans 1992). However, the extent to which this has happened seems to be limited indeed, considering that both organizations continue to focus on issues and working methods which fall outside of the realm of donor priorities.

Part of the reason why Kaqla and Q'anil have been able to stick to their priorities in the current environment, and have not had to transform drastically, but only to accommodate some elements of the donors' priorities, is precisely their uncompromising attitude when it comes to their psychotherapeutic and corporeal experience-based approach. This position, which did not allow them to obtain funding from the bigger funding agencies which favored rights-based programs, pressured them to attract smaller donors who were more open to their priorities and organizational identity. The scarcity of funding thus benefited them in the long run in the sense of helping them to preserve their identity.

Despite their success in singling out these smaller donors and entering into more equal relations with them, the cases of Kaqla and Q'anil also illustrate an overall lack of interest on the side of the donor community for topics and methods which do not fit a traditional feminist discourse or rights-based approaches (Morales 1 June 2010, Aguilar 26 May 2010, S. Álvarez 21 February 2011). In general terms, donors continue to fund, on the one hand, women's organizations who work with women's practical gender needs, but which have no goal of social transformation or empowerment, or, on the other hand, feminist organizations which envision women's empowerment and struggle for their rights through a rights-based approach, but do not work with women's everyday and tangible experiences. On the side of the donors, there is a seeming lack of interest in empowerment strategies that challenge commonly accepted feminist strategies and envision women's empowerment in an alternative way. This means that financial donors are not creating an impetus for local organizations to collaborate with such initiatives. The unfamiliarity on the side of the donors thus reinforces unfamiliarity with such strategies amongst local feminist organizations. As Sarah, a member of directorate at Kaqla, remarked:

> A lot of the knowledge and insights which were created in the immediate after-war have gone lost, because there was only an interest in changing the political structures [...] we [referring to the indigenous population] for one have our own system, which may not be Cartesian, and thus meets with a lot of resistance, but which has helped us a lot. The pressure to depart from it and adopt a more mainstream approach is growing though. This is trying, because we learnt by doing that this type of rationality is not the thing which tends to help us in our work with women. Affection is.
>
> ÁLVAREZ, 14 February 2011

Another interviewee at Kaqla also criticized the extent to which local-level dynamics were determined by the priorities of the most prominent international donors, to the detriment of an experience-based approach and complementary approaches to women's empowerment. She raised this question in relation to the issue of giving Western names to the local approaches and ideas, arguing that organizations do this:

...to have them valued, to have others see that they are important, to have others listening to us – not to understand ourselves. It is all about showing others that we too share their culture, that we are important. And in order not to have to face the confrontation with ourselves, we gladly go along with this. Instead of convincing ourselves of our own worth, we try to convince them. "Look at us. Here we are. We are worthy. We have rights." But does this strategy really help us? Does it really serve us as a point of reference in our own lives?

MENDOZA, 31 January 2011

This statement hints at the large gap that continues to exist between the methods and priorities imposed by the international donor community and the needs of smaller local women's organizations. The existence of this gap is also fostered by the fact that most donor organizations do not have local offices, yet give relatively little room to the expertise which local organizations may have in determining adequate empowerment strategies. Validating the input of smaller local organizations which break new ground and work with culturally relevant methods may present a complement to the current public focus. For this to happen a willingness at mutual learning is needed. In practice, this would mean paying due attention to the methods of these smaller organizations. This acknowledgment would give rise to the revaluation of women's personal empowerment processes.

Concluding Remarks

Organizations focusing only on women's personal processes are experimenting with alternative paths to empowerment. By exploring from the bottom-up what women's needs are and which aspects of their lives are most important to them, these organizations are developing a new discourse and new programs, which may contain elements which can be relevant for organizations adopting a more mainstream approach of women's empowerment. However, rather than seeing these approaches as the new way forward which all women's organizations should envision, this chapter presents a more moderate view. In this view, the insights which these organizations may bring to traditional empowerment programs are acknowledged, but at the same time, the potential pitfalls of this approach are stressed. In particular the approach of Q'anil should be considered with caution. Unlike Actoras de Cambio and Kaqla, Q'anil shies any type of social mobilization. The psychologizing approach of organizations like Q'anil is relevant in the sense that empowerment touches upon issues of identify formation, and that women's personal processes should probably be incorporated in any approach aiming to influence this. Yet, on the other hand, uniquely stressing personal processes, can entail the depoliticization of the issue of women's oppression and empowerment. This means that a balanced approach is needed which incorporates both the personal processes of women and the societal dynamics influencing these.

Organizations like Actoras, Kaqla and Q'anil can arguably be seen as instances of *possibilism* (Hirschman 1971), in the sense that they seek manageable alternatives to the grand changes propagated by many feminist organizations. Yet, these seemingly modest goals, have inspired them to conceptualize change in a new way. While having their roots in the revolutionary struggle, these organizations incorporate feminist psychotherapy in their attempts to change gender relations. Both psychotherapeutic work and social analysis are seen as crucial elements to empower women and to counter women's internalization of injustice and oppression (Meyers 1994: 62).[9]

In their work, Actoras, Kaqla and Q'anil consider the fact that women may have other priorities and require different working methods than those which are dominant amongst feminist organizations at present. They moreover consider the possibility that the personal domain is characterized by a different dynamic than the public one, and explore what this may look like. They therefore go beyond a discursive strategy to denounce the colonization of women's bodies as the core of their oppression. The idea is that a discursive strategy does not consider the sensory aspects of oppression and does not necessarily provide women with a sense of ownership over their bodies. Instead, it is argued, a mere discursive denunciation of the effects of oppression on women's bodies, hijacks women's bodies for the feminist struggle, rather than returning them to women themselves. An approach focusing on women's personal processes on the other hand, aims to bring women back in touch with their own bodies and emotions so as to generate personal and concrete experiences of what oppression does with them, and to take back the ownership over their bodies, thoughts and emotions. They thereby link theoretical propositions to women's personal experiences. Participants in these programs stressed how they have been able to build on these tangible experiences in the workshops to gain a sense of agency in their own lives.

While many feminist activists whom I talked to acknowledged the potential value of such an approach, Q'anil's exclusive focus on personal processes, left it rather isolated from other women's organizations and financial donors.

---

9 While Q'anil did not engage in public strategies or social action itself, it acknowledges the importance thereof.

The founder of Q'anil emphasized that this position of relative isolation allowed Q'anil to preserve its own identity and guaranteed its independence. Yet, at the same time, it also has more ambiguous consequences, in the sense of limiting the potential for collaboration or for tapping into the social relevance of its approach. Realizing this, Q'anil itself started to focus more on working with social leaders who can incorporate elements from the Q'anil workshops into their own work in order to contribute to a paradigm shift in mainstream feminist organizations as well.

In conclusion, Q'anil, like Actoras de Cambio and Kaqla, is exploring alternatives for women's empowerment, in a situation where feminist organizations have not managed to bring about the profound changes which they themselves aspired. Q'anil, Actoras and Kaqla's work is pinned on the idea that creating change is not something which necessarily consists of vast social changes, but that it can also consist of small changes in women's personal lives, which can feed back into the societal realm. The value of these organizations lies precisely in their attempt to foster more attention for small-scale bottom-up processes which place women's personal experiences at the centre of empowerment. This does not mean that their approach is to be considered an ideal per se. The case of Q'anil illustrates precisely the danger of foregoing all types of social activism, namely that the social dimension of oppression is overlooked, which also renders structural change more difficult. Therefore an argument can be made in favor of organized activism for women's emancipation as it is advocated by the feminist movement today, as there is no evidence from the fieldwork that an approach which focuses only on women's personal processes constitutes a valid alternative for rationalistic approaches to women's empowerment. Q'anil's case moreover suggests that organizations which only work with women's personal processes should probably not be considered as actors of civil society as such. Even if they can contribute to a more healthy civil society by facilitating women's healing process, and even if the positive results which they obtain can feed back into the public realm, Q'anil itself rather seems to be a case of psychological assistance, as long as it does not pay more explicit attention to the social structures underlying women's oppression and empowerment or to working with men. Thus, while Q'anil is decidedly relevant for women's empowerment and supports the feminist goals and even feminist activism, it can at present not be seen as an actor of civil society because of its lack of a social dimension.

Programs like those of Actoras de Cambio and Kaqla which combine an experience-based approach with attention to the social dimension of empowerment, seem more promising because they explicitly link changes in women's personal lives to their potential for activism in other social organizations and their role in society. The case can thus be made for creating spaces for dialogue in which a two-track approach can be developed in which both women's personal experiences and the need for socio-political change can be acknowledged. My research confirms the role which donors can potentially play in this, because they inspire much of the priority structure of the feminist movement. In summary, in these two countries with significant structural barriers to women's emancipation, public and rights-based approaches continue to play a vital role for the feminist movement as an actor of civil society, but experience-based approaches can potentially complement these strategies and can help to redefine the concept of women's mobilization and empowerment.

Conclusion
New Perspectives for Female Mobilization

> I'm not as idealistic as I used to be. My experience as an organizer is that
> we don't know how to make things change. I think people who debate in
> elaborate theories on how to create change are not at all involved in
> trying to make those theories work. I believe strongly that theory and the
> best strategies emerge out of trying things out, actually trying to make
> them happen at all and then being reflective on that to figure out what
> you've learnt.
>
> CHARLOTTE BUNCH, 1983, cited in Ryan 1992: 79

The book's central theme is how the history of the Guatemalan and Nicaraguan
women's movements influenced their current approach to women's empowerment. This question arises from several overlapping puzzles. How is it that, in
two countries with such vocal women's and feminist movements, such high
levels of violence against women persist and so few changes in gender norms
are visible? If women's mobilization during conflict has indeed benefited their
post-war social activism, then how come women's organizations remain so
dependent on international donors? And what explains why two countries
which are similar in many respects, yielded women's movements which are
very different in some crucial respects? Underlying all these issues, is the question of how – dynamics related to – the armed conflict influenced the newly
emerging women's movements, and what the impact of these dynamics is on
the current women's movements.

The first part of the book considered the impact on women's mobilization
of several factors related to the armed conflict, such as the influence of wom-
en's revolutionary mobilization, the influence of international actors and
donors who entered both countries during the armed conflict and post-war
reconstruction, and the influence of political polarization in the post-conflict
period. These factors can explain many similarities between both women's
movements, such as the dependence on international donors, the fragmentation and NGOization of the movement, and the preference for rights-based
approaches on the one hand or service-provision on the other hand. A last factor indirectly related to the armed conflict which the book considered, is ethnicity. I argue that this factor has been activated by the armed conflict in the
sense that in Guatemala the targeted persecution of indigenous people and
consequent attention for their recovery on the side of international donors,
fostered a growing ethnic awareness. This factor can help to explain important

differences between the Guatemalan and Nicaraguan women's movements, as is illustrated below. All four elements continue to have an influence on the present day women's movement through mechanisms of individual and organizational learning and adaptation, and through narrative construction and activation by those actors involved.

This question on the influence of conflict moves to the background in the second part of the book, which analyses alternative strategies to women's empowerment used by some indigenous organizations. Yet, as this conclusion will highlight, their strategies are also directly related to the legacy of the armed conflict, notably so, in the sense that the armed conflict created an increased ethnic awareness which inspired this approach.

In this conclusion, I summarize the main arguments of the book and consider the implications thereof for other social movements operating in different social contexts. I thereby aim to link academic and policy-relevant findings in a culturally relevant way.

Revolutionary Mobilization, Ethnicity and Empowerment

The book traced how several factors related to the armed conflict have over time influenced the development of the women's movement. This analysis challenges the commonsensical idea that women's revolutionary mobilization or the presence of international donor agencies has prompted a viable form of women's mobilization in the post-conflict period. Several reasons for this are cited.

Firstly, the revolutionary roots of the women's movement inspired a focus on political goals, which did not always accurately reflect women's gendered needs and meant that women sometimes mobilized around demands which were not entirely theirs, but which had a more general societal importance. This also meant that certain topics which were not easily formulated as political goals, for example topics related to women's personal lives, received little or no attention from mainstream feminist organizations. The focus on political goals also meant that the women's movement was heavily influenced by the polarization which increasingly characterized the political landscape, especially in Nicaragua. Next to a focus on political goals, the revolutionary roots of the movement also influenced the way in which organizations aspired to achieve these goals. In specific traditional forms of public protest and awareness-raising, such as protest marches and handing out pamphlets, remained important. These traditional forms of protest, which were often set up in a confrontational way, reinforced the situation of polarization, both within the movement and *vis-à-vis* government. These public protest and awareness-raising campaigns were complemented with a strong reliance on a rights-based approach.

The choice for a rights-based approach is also related to the role of international donor agencies who entered both countries in the immediate post-conflict period. Also the extent to which these played a constructive role in the development of a balanced women's movement is called into question in this book. While their financial, logistical and moral support gave an important impetus to civil society activism immediately after the armed conflict, I emphasize the way in which their politics inadvertently nurtured fragmentation within the women's movement. On the one hand, they – often unintentionally – riveted existing ideological divides between organizations, such as Nicaraguan pro-FSLN and anti-FSLN women's organizations. On the other hand, they created a situation in which women's organizations had to compete with one another to obtain funding. This way small women's initiatives became competitors in the struggle for funding, rather than only being compatriots in the struggle for women's emancipation. This dynamic was reinforced by the fact that donor agencies entered both countries at a time when the young women's organizations did not yet have a solid organizational identity, which made them more reliant on, and open to, the priorities of donors.

Today's women's movements in both Guatemala and Nicaragua thus have significant shortcomings, such as one-sided political and public goals, methods imposed by donors or in reaction to the political constellation, heavy reliance on foreign money, fragmentation, and the adoption of an unsettled and submissive identity. These factors hamper their development towards a self-determined and influential social actor. My cross-national comparison shows that these tendencies are less prominent in the Guatemalan women's and feminist movement, which is remarkable given the fact that the Guatemalan armed conflict lasted longer (1960-1996), was more violent, and led to more intense repression of civil society actors (Jalón, staff AHPN, 15 May 2010). This more balanced development of the Guatemalan women's movement can partially be explained by the fact that international funds were allocated and monitored in a more structural way. The overarching issue of historical clarification and reconciliation (CEH) meant that there was attention for creating cross-organizational networks and spaces for interlocution between different expressions of the women's movement, while at the same time deviant programs and indigenous practices to achieve this aim were encouraged. This minimal agreement between different actors of civil society was not present in the Nicaraguan case to the same extent, where the defeat of the FSLN triggered very diverse reactions from civil society, because there was no common topic which all actors could identify with.

The book thus also challenges the implicit assumption of many actors of the Guatemalan women's movement that ethnicity is a factor complicating the development of the women's and feminist movement. Activists in Guatemala often lamented the fact that the existence of separate indigenous and Ladina organizations created a division in the movement which kept them from speaking with one voice. While this is undoubtedly a relevant observation, I argue that ethnicity has also been a positive factor for progress and diversification of the women's movement in the Guatemalan case. It triggered organizations to turn to the daily realities of their target group, and organize on the basis thereof. Amongst these indigenous organizations, we see a willingness to experiment with alternative approaches to women's empowerment, precisely on the basis of these indigenous cultures. Because of their emphasis on women's daily lives, these organizations are also not as easily drawn into the political dynamics of polarization as their mainstream feminist counterparts.

Ethnic diversity in Guatemala thus made the women's movement there more diverse in terms of priorities and approach, without being divided or carved up along political dividing lines as was the case in Nicaragua. Groups organizing around indigenous principles were encouraged by donors who saw the need to acknowledge the multiplicity of initiatives with a culturally specific approach and priorities. Turning to traditional indigenous principles – which are often regarded as conservative by actors in the field – has contributed to the development of a less dogmatic and politicized women's movement, and to the creation of several smaller women's organizations which link empowerment back to women's personal experiences. They have thus developed a new approach to the issue of women's empowerment, which combines a focus on public action with an emphasis on women's personal experiences and the dynamics of their private lives. As a result, in the Guatemalan peace process as well as in the current women's movement, there has been more attention for the impact of violence and oppression on women's psyche and everyday actions, and not only to the public dimension of violence and oppression. This dynamic is unseen in Nicaragua, where the ethnic factor is largely absent.

In short, the book challenges the assumption that women's revolutionary mobilization and the influx of international aid have had an unequivocally positive impact on women's organizing in the post-conflict period (see, for example, Kampwirth 2004a and 2004b, Chinchilla 1990). A careful examination shows that neither revolutionary mobilization, nor foreign funding, nor the way in which both interplay, have incontestably advanced the formation of an influential women's movement in either of these two countries. In line with Hulme and Edwards (1997: 278), I argue that the interplay of these two factors has in fact made women's organizations 'more bureaucratic and less prone to take risks or bear the cost of listening to those who they seek to assist'. The influence of women's revolutionary mobilization, and especially of external funding agencies, thus needs to be carefully considered with regards to their effect on duplication, fragmentation and competition within the movement. Equally so, the research invites for a reconsideration – by scholars and practitioners – of the idea that ethnic diversity complicates female mobilization. In contrast, the presence of ethnic diversity has balanced the ambivalent influence of revolutionary mobilization and donor priorities in Guatemala.

Deviant Paths towards Women's Empowerment – Psychoanalytical and Corporeal Feminism

While the first part of the book established how war-related dynamics can accurately explain both similarities and differences in the development of the women's movement in both countries, the second part turned to the outcomes of this evolution and established that there is a fair amount of dissatisfaction amongst feminist activists themselves on the current strategies. Revolutionary mobilization of women and the presence of international donors prompted a strong preference for public approaches and priorities in the public domain – such as a focus on democratization – amongst current women's and feminist organizations.

Activists' dissatisfaction with these approaches are subtle, but during interviews they often mentioned the rising number of cases of violence against women, or the absence of significant changes in terms of gender norms. This dissatisfaction either triggered organizations to fight more fiercely against a common enemy who was to blame – usually government – or in other cases, to conceive of alternative and complementary approaches to women's empowerment. The second part of the book focused on organizations – Actoras de Cambio, Kaqla and Q'anil – which developed an unconventional approach to women's empowerment. I refer to this approach as an experience-based approach, because it emphasizes the personal lives and experiences of women. In practice these organizations work with small groups, which explore the value of women's experiences and of 'feminine' identities commonly ascribed to women. They work on the basis of psychotherapeutic and corporal feminism,[1] and incorporate insights from difference feminism which reflect

---

1   For an elaboration on these two strands of feminism, see Grosz (1994: ix) who defines corporeal feminism as the form of feminism that refigures the body so that it moves from the

indigenous beliefs. On the basis of this, they seek to empower women from the bottom-up, without seeking validation at a public level. Their working methods are rooted in Mayan *cosmovision*,[2] psychotherapeutic counseling and group therapy.[3] They work with emotions, bodily perception, and spirituality – all elements which are not easily incorporated in the discourse and dynamic of a rationalistic public approach. However, these organizations do not see their work as an alternative to public strategies or rights-based approaches, but rather as being complementary. Two of them – Actoras de Cambio and Kaqla – have an explicit public approach which complements their experience-based work (publication of methodologies, lobbying, outreach projects, et cetera), and a third – Q'anil – is gradually starting to incorporate this public focus into its work as well.

My research shows that these initiatives were created in a period when there was a lot of attention and funding for psychotherapeutic and psychosocial assistance – both by local actors of civil society and by the international donor community. They took attention to the topic of war-related trauma, and broadened it to the everyday lives of women, which were often characterized by violence and oppression. These organizations argued that by bringing women in touch with their emotions, experiences and trauma, they would become more defensible in their everyday lives. This means that for Actoras de Cambio, Kaqla and Q'anil, women's psychosocial needs are central in their empowerment process. They tailored their methods and their goals to the everyday experiences of women and thereby provided participants with more possibilities to define for themselves the issues which they find most relevant for their empowerment, on the basis of their everyday experiences – also if this meant that they would turn to parts of their identities commonly seen as

---

periphery to the centre of analysis; see Meyers (1994: 11) who defines psychoanalytic feminism as the form of feminism which exhibits emotional significance of gender, while at the same time probing gender and relational capacities that have traditionally been associated with women, but that have usually been dismissed. Meyers also warns for the pitfalls of this strand of feminism (overlooking differences between women and economic and material realities) and proposes a solution to them: to use it as a theory on the nature of subjectivity and the meaning of gender, rather than as a complete theory eclipsing other forms of social analysis.

2 Using for example the medicine wheel (a traditional Mayan representation of the universe, time, individuals, nature, etc, which can be applied to the life of a person), ritual cleansing and bonfires, and the Nawal.

3 such as bio-energetics (a body-oriented psychotherapy that combines psychological analysis, active work with the body and relational therapeutic work, Klopstech 2008) and movement therapy (the use of movement and dance for emotional, cognitive, behavioral and physical conditions, Payne 2006).

conservative or oppressive. These programs elicit a number of questions about traditional feminist thinking and practice in the domain of empowerment, and hint at the need to reconceptualize what is needed for women's empowerment.

The vast majority of participants (between ten and forty for each workshop) at Actoras, Kaqla and Q'anil assess their participation as positive – even if sometimes psychologically confronting – arguing that both their personal healing process and their activism in other women's organizations benefited from their participation in these programs. In mainstream, second-wave feminist organizations[4] few of the women whom I interviewed could easily translate their work in the public domain – or what they knew about patriarchy and oppression – back to their own lives, emotions and psyche. This is illustrative of the blind spot which these organizations have for an essential part of their members' and activists' lives. The majority of these women at mainstream feminist organizations expressed a vigorous fervor and eagerness when defending their cases, but at the same time could not veil an undertone of despondency and pessimism about the potential for bringing about genuine change. Kaqla's strategy of working with women who are active in other women's organizations, can be exceptionally useful in this context, because it bridges the gaps between both types of women's initiatives. The approving attitudes of members of mainstream Guatemalan women's organizations on the work of Kaqla, constitutes a background against which Kaqla could take up this bridging function.

Participants and facilitators in Actoras, Kaqla and Q'anil emphasized the importance of working with sentiments and corporeality – also for allegedly public issues – to avoid the mere politicization of women's personal lives, and to begin a process of genuine change in their everyday lives. This avoids making empowerment dependent on third parties, in the political or legal domain for example. More importantly however, these organizations challenge the commonsensical equation of women's empowerment with their stronger presence in the public domain or with the expansion of their formal rights. Organizations which set public participation of women as a key goal, often overlook that women enter the public realm with a comparative disadvantage – i.e on externally imposed conditions such as the dominance of a certain concept of rationality – at best with the aim of changing these conditions afterwards (Bourdieu 2001, Welsch 2001). Complementary strategies may be useful in that context.

---

4   Second-wave feminism here refers to a set of priorities and approaches which revolve around official legal inequalities, sexuality, family and reproductive rights, and which focuses much of its attention on legal reform (Mansbridge 1986). Since these organizations are most common in Guatemala and Nicaragua, I refer to them as mainstream feminist organizations.

In specific, interviewees at Kaqla for example suggest that it is important to work on both levels in parallel. They argue that their participation in the experience-based workshops also impacts upon the way in which they carry out their public work because they felt more agency and felt more confident, both on a personal and on a professional level.

In what ways do these three organizations then provide new perspectives for the feminist movement? As they articulate new and different goals in the domain of empowerment, they challenge some of the fundamental ideas on which feminist thinking has been based for a long time. Actoras, Kaqla and Q'anil articulate the need for a different – complementary – conceptualization of women's empowerment and offer practical means to achieve this. They thereby also touch upon issues which have been discussed for a longer time within feminist movements, such as the need for a new language which better expresses women's daily experiences of oppression. The way in which these organizations work with women can be a means to develop such a language; and thus offers a practical opportunity to complement mainstream feminist discourse and practice.[5]

Juxtaposing the approach of mainstream feminist organizations with the work of feminist organizations adopting an experience-based approach which builds on corporeal and psychoanalytic feminism invites for a reflection on the concepts of empowerment and mobilization and for an assessment of the relevance thereof for other social – women's – organizations.

Empirical, Theoretical and Policy Implications of the Research

The case studies in this book contribute to several discourses and have implications beyond Nicaraguan and Guatemalan feminist organizations.

First, the book offers new empirical data. It compiles and analyses in detail the structures and approaches of the women's and feminist movement in Nicaragua and Guatemala, and more specifically, it presents data on the working methods of several smaller organizations which have not been subject of detailed research and analysis before. This research thereby for the first time maps the complete landscape of women's organizations in Guatemala and

---

5   Also see Herman (1997) and Butler (1997), who challenge the usefulness of a discursive linear language, and propose a new language which allows for deviation from the norm of linearity and the *narrative imperative, i.e.* the imperative to tell and be heard; an imperative which can never bring satisfaction in the case of trauma. Also see Laub (1995: 63) on the "imperative to tell" , despite the "impossibility to tell" such stories.

Nicaragua, and their historical and organizational embedding; thereby also considering organizations which are not usually seen as members of the women's movement. This broadens our understanding of the mechanisms through which armed conflicts, donor policies and ethnic relations can influence social movements, and of the outcomes thereof, as well as providing empirical data on organizations which have responded to these influences in an unconventional way.

Second, the book has policy relevance, for local women's movements and their financial donors, but also more broadly for women's movements working in other contexts and social movements working on related topics. By delving into the way in which the current policies of women's organizations are shaped, the book contributes to a greater awareness of how the historical origins of the movement feed into its policy choice and on the importance of women's personal experiences for empowerment programs. This allows for the creation of more pertinent working methods in which more aspects of women's lives are actively integrated.

For feminist organizations in Nicaragua and Guatemala, the discussion of different approaches to empowerment is valuable because in both countries efforts to improve the situation of women – through collective mobilization, economic assistance programs, new legislation, and an expanding number of women's organizations – have only had limited effects on women's daily lives. Both statistical indicators (see for example Ellsberg 2000) and interviewees suggest that the amount of positive changes which have occurred, both in terms of reducing violence against women and in terms of changing gender norms, has not been proportional to the amount of energy invested by women's and feminist organizations. As Norma Cruz, founder of Sobrevivientes, expressed, 'the efforts [are] strenuous, payback limited, and we're not spared from regular setbacks' (20 May 2010). This statement hints at the relevance of new complementary forms of action, which work on a different level and in a genuinely new way.

The research also showed that experience-based approaches have the potential to fulfill this role and to install a climate for change from the bottom-up, because they make women more defensible and aware of their own needs. This makes an experience-based approach relevant to consider in any empowerment program. The research findings are especially important in the Nicaraguan context of political hostility against civil actors. An experience-based strategy focusing on women's personal processes can help to bring about change in this context because it is less susceptible to political control by the state. This is because it is not necessarily visible in the public domain at first, even though in the long run it can bring about changes in attitudes and political culture because it installs change from the bottom-up. Yet, feminist organizations adopting an experience-based approach were non-existent in Nicaragua at the time of the fieldwork (2010-1011). Instead, feminist organizations reacted to the political polarization and the hostilities against them by also taking on a more politicized stance themselves. Interviews also demonstrated the important role of the donor community in this context. To change and develop in a different direction, women's organizations need permission and stimuli from their benefactors. At this level as well, a rethinking of what is seen as emancipation and empowerment, has the potential to diversify the landscape of women's activism. The particular contribution of organizations adopting an experience-based approach is that they stress a bottom-up approach, and in that way encourage the type of grassroots activism which had become institutionalized in the immediate post-conflict period.

A focus on women's private lives and personal experiences as part of a strategy of empowerment also opens up new perspectives and possibilities for women's organizations in other countries. This way, the case studies in this book speak to many debates. Already in 1971, Alinsky hinted at the need for more pragmatic strategies which can be easily incorporated into people's daily lives, to bring about radical transformation, because these actions cannot easily be repressed by an external force. This also hints at the relevance of an integrated approach consisting of public and private elements – for a number of other issues which today mainly lead to public mobilization.

Thirdly, the book contributes to theoretical-conceptual debates. By structurally developing the concept of an experience-based approach to women's empowerment, I enter new ground, and the case study findings call into question some taken for granted feminist parameters of empowerment The book thus invites empowerment programs to engage with women's private lives in a new way. The cases of Actoras, Kaqla and Q'anil offer new theoretical and conceptual perspectives on three basic assumptions underlying much feminist activity. These assumptions are related to the concept of an empowered identity, the language in which this is discussed, and the definition of a women's movement and mobilization. I single out these three issues, because they ran through many interviews and because the experience-based approach of these organizations sheds new light on these issues. They are reconceptualized as having an important experience-based component as well, and not just as issues which are defined in and by the public realm.

With relation to how an experience-based approach focusing on personal processes challenges feminist interpretations of an empowered identity, the first question which arises is what such an identity looks like. This issue has elicited vehement discussions among academics and activists alike.

My fieldwork showed that in Guatemala and Nicaragua, feminism's stress on the equality of men and women has de facto erased characteristics traditionally seen as female from the concept of an emancipated identity for women. The stress on equality has in practice come to mean that women's emancipated gender identity has become a copy of a traditional male identity. Women enter the public sphere and take on roles formerly deemed male, without much attention for their specific identity as women. This is inherently limiting, because it denies the value of characteristics linked to women's gender identities and private roles, and because it pushes women to participate in the public domain on the reigning conditions. Instead of being truly liberating, this concept thus becomes a new straightjacket for women which denies their daily realities.

By contrast, Actoras, Kaqla and Q'anil, explore the premises of difference feminism which are compatible with indigenous beliefs of complementarity and with women's daily lives, namely that there may be certain characteristics which women can on average identify with more strongly. The de facto existence of differential gender identities is thus acknowledged and used as a stepping stone to explore the characteristics which women themselves define as typical for women and as empowering. This way, women are given the chance to actively and consciously participate in their own process of collective identity formation, and to leave behind those aspects of their identity which are imputed to them, either by patriarchy or by mainstream feminist conceptions. Participatory observation and interviews showed that this process of exploring which elements of their identity could facilitate their empowerment, was a radically open one, based on the input of those women involved, i.e. there was a willingness to explore both the value of characteristics which are excluded by mainstream feminists because they are seen as conservative – such as the mother role – and the value of characteristics which are excluded from women's traditional identities – such as the role of breadwinner. The approach thereby allows for the emergence of a genuinely empowering and self-defined identity.

This issue of self-determination versus heteronomy[6] is also at the core of the second issue which these case studies problematize, namely the issue of which language is appropriate to discuss women's empowerment process. The research exposed the preference of mainstream Guatemalan and Nicaraguan feminist organizations for a traditional narrative linear discourse held in the public domain. As Butler (1997), Herman (1997) and Das (1996) argue however, such a language is ill-suited to give voice to cumulative or sub-traumatic experiences and to private experiences, since these have a different logic, which is

---

6   or more accurately, *fremdbestimmung* in German (or *ser dirigada por otros* in Spanish).

not linear.[7] My findings suggest that traditional feminist organizations impose externally-defined linguistic structures onto women's personal experiences. This is the case for example with the way in which traditional feminist concepts and constructs – such as emancipation, oppression, gender – are transposed to the local context and the extent to which feminists still place a higher value on typically male elements, such as the public realm or a rational discursive strategy. The three organizations in the second part of the book on the contrary work with women to develop new and more adequate forms for expressing their realities, by using their emotions, bodies and rituals as a point of reference. This effort to create something new which is theirs, rather than toiling to adapt and adopt old forms, contains the core of women's empowerment (Butler 2004).

This issue of language, and how different social actors deal with it, also links back to the third issue which is brought up by acknowledging the value of an experience-based approach, namely the question of whom we see as actors of civil society in general, and as part of the feminist movement in particular. The book suggests that organizations proceeding only through an experience-based approach are not in themselves actors of civil society – even if they contribute to civil society activism – because they are not active in the public or political sphere. On the contrary, I argue that organizations pinning their public work on an experience-based approach are an integral part of civil society and of the feminist movement for two main reasons.

Firstly, these organizations do not turn women's personal empowerment into an absolute and isolated goal, but instead link this personal empowerment to how women can change the societal conditions of their oppression. These societal dysfunctions are also the focus of the therapeutic process, during which women are offered tools to interpret the impact of structural conditions of oppression on their own life. In the workshops, these organizations focus on personal empowerment as a resource for improving the – structural – conditions in which women live. These organizations thus interpret personal empowerment as a goal in its own right – and not as a derivate of emancipation. While their first aim is to make women stronger and more confident, and to give them a sense of control over their own lives, they also link this to social, political and legal change. This approach emphasizes how women's daily realities and own experiences interact with larger societal dynamics. The priorities of these organizations thus overlap with those of other local feminist organizations who see structural change at the societal level as a key

---

7   See Khan 1963 on the notion of cumulative trauma and Kira 2001 on the notion of sub-traumatic condition.

to women's emancipation, but they avoid the almost exclusive focus on public hurdles to women's empowerment which other feminist organizations have.

Secondly, organizations proceeding on the basis of an experience-based approach challenge the traditional concept of a women's movement because of how they work. It has been common in academic literature (Klandermans 2007, Snow 2004, and Poletta 2001) and in the field alike, to think of – women's – social movements as visible public and political forces which operate in the public domain by means of collective action and mobilization. The consequence thereof has been that many women's organizations have adopted methods and goals – which did not *per se* reflect their daily realities – in order to be acknowledged as a social actor and receive funding. The cases of Actoras, Kaqla and Q'anil offer a new perspective on social activism. These organizations have managed to work with women on the issue of empowerment in a way which eluded the dominant dynamic in the feminist movement of 'going public' (Davis 1999: 20). Instead they developed alternative and complementary methods to women's empowerment in a joint effort with the women they work with. Even though these organizations proceed in a different way, and do not always revolve around being a visible public force, they can still be seen as a significant player in the feminist movement because of the similar goals which they set themselves. Moreover their work is based on group processes rather than individual assistance, which also illustrates their social component.

The book discloses the need to rethink what the terms 'empowerment' and 'emancipation' mean, and questions what constitutes a social movement and how it operates. I suggest that non-conventional forms of action and activism in the personal domain should not be overlooked as avenues to women's empowerment, even if they are not forms of social activism by standard definitions. As long as the dominant idea is that a feminist social movement only needs to act in public and have a socio-political project, its goals and methods as well will remain predominantly political and public, and will overlook women's personal lives. Hence, the sort of empowerment likely to follow from this is also one in the public domain rather than in the personal domain. Only when considering the potential of, and need for, attention to the dynamics of women's personal experience and emotions, can personal empowerment be structurally enshrined in the working programs of women's organizations.

Concluding Remarks

Women's and feminist movements have long been conceptualized as those forms of women's action which manifest themselves in the public domain (see for example Taylor 1989, Waylen 1993, Beckwith 2000). As a consequence, for an organization to be defined as a member of the feminist movement, it is supposed to have a public or rights-based focus and to use traditional forms of public action, such as protest marches, awareness-raising campaigns and lobbying. The reality on the ground in both Guatemala and Nicaragua has however revealed two shortcomings of such a conceptualization. Firstly, programs of organizations which work along these public lines, did not always find their way into women's personal lives and could not always integrate the dynamics of women's personal lives into their program. Secondly, a strong emphasis on the public domain led to a high degree of politicization in these two countries which was not always beneficial to women's causes. Therefore, there is a need to rethink what we see as relevant strategies for women's emancipation and empowerment, in such a way that also takes into account the relevance of the daily lives and experiences of women for their empowerment process.

On the basis of the above discussion, I conclude that organizations adopting an experience-based approach – especially those which also have a public working axis – can be seen as important actors of change in the feminist movement. This approach has showed its merit, not only in changing the lives of participants, and supporting the work which these women do with other organizations of the women's and feminist movement, but also in inviting for a reconceptualization of what is commonly seen as an appropriate strategy for women's empowerment. They thereby invite for the acknowledgment of non-political and non-public forms of action as legitimate complementary strategies to change the situation of women's oppression.

In order for such a paradigm shift to take place, however, feminist organizations have to deal with the legacy of the past. My research has contributed to a reassessment of how dynamics related to the armed conflict feed back into the current policies and priorities of women's and feminist organizations through a process of individual and organizational learning. This questioned the assumed causal relation between popular mobilization and efficient social mobilization afterwards (See for example Booth 1998, Pearce 1998, Serra Vázquez 2007). I also reassessed the role of ethnicity for the emergence of a more diverse women's movement, arguing that the presence of ethnic diversity in Guatemala has helped to balance the influence of foreign funding, and made women's organizations less dogmatic. By locating and analyzing the niche-players who emerged from this dynamic, the book invites for a reassessment of the concept of women's empowerment, and the avenues to arrive at this, in a way which acknowledges women's personal experiences.

The case studies in this book thus have several implications. For both academia and involved actors, they invite for a new perspective on social movements and social action; one which goes beyond a public paradigm and considers the value of an experience-based approach. Findings show that both organizations which cater to women's immediate practical gender needs and feminist organizations which push for socio-political and legal change are needed, but that both may in themselves be insufficient to facilitate women's genuine empowerment. This means that new complementary forms of action are needed, which go beyond public conceptions of women's empowerment, and work on the basis of women's own experiences and sentiments. This requires the acknowledgement – by financial donors, local actors and academia alike – of the existence of three types of women's initiatives with equal value: organizations for direct practical assistance, organizations for legal and socio-economic change, and organizations for empowerment in the personal realm.

Appendix
Alphabetical Overview of Interviewees

Interviewee	Function/position	Place and date of interview
Aguilar, Camila	Ex-guerrillera in Central Guatemala	Rabinal El Quiché, Guatemala, May 17, 2010
Aguilar, Yolanda	Founder and member of Actors of change (Actoras de Cambio), founder and president of Q'anil, academic researcher, spokesperson of the feminist movement, member of several smaller women's initiatives	Guatemala City, May 26, 2010 and February 4, 11 and 18, 2011
Alfaro, Lilia Espinoza, Thelma	President and first secretary of the women's movement Luisa Amanda Espinoza (AMNLAE)	Managua, April 30, 2010
Arellano, Eva, Durán, Jacinda	Former participants to one of the workshops of Actoras de Cambio	Antigua, Guatemala, February 17, 2011
Aróstegui Sanchez, Nancy	Former feminist activist from Nicaragua	Managua, April 29 2010
Asenció, Jeanette	Coordinator of the program for no violence and the construction of peace at the Guatemalan National Union for Women (UNAMG), and member of Actoras de Cambio for UNAMG	Guatemala City, May 24, 2010
Astorga, Nora	Member of the Casa de la Mujer in Granada	Granada Nicaragua, March 22, 2010
Azucena, Evelyn	Coordinators for the training programs of the defense group for indigenous women (DEMI)	Guatemala City, June 7, 2010

---

* For the reasons of anonymity, not all names are the real names of interviewees, i.e. names in italics are made up.

(*Continued*)

Interviewee	Function/position	Place and date of interview
Álvarez, Carmen	Founding member of Kaqla	Guatemala City, February 21, 2011
Álvarez, Ceci	Organizing member of the Guatemalan network of no violence (REDNOVI)	Guatemala City, June 2, 2010
Álvarez, Sara	Former founding member of Kaqla	Guatemala City, February 14 and 21, 2011
Barrios-Klee, Walda	Academic, member of UNAMG, advisor to Actoras de Cambio	Guatemala City, January 26, 2011
Berlanga, Mariana	Member of Actoras de Cambio	Guatemala City, February 24, 2011
Blandón, Martha	Representative for the think-tank for the decriminalization of therapeutic abortion (grupo estrategico por la despenalización del aborto terapeutico)	Managua, April 29, 2010
Cabrera, Luisa	Head of the psychosocial program at Actoras de Cambio	Guatemala City, February 15, 2011
Cabrera, Norma	Executive member of the Guatemalan National Union for Women (UNAMG) and member of the institute for international women's studies (Instituto Internacional de Estudios de la Mujer, Universidad de San Carlos Guatemala)	Guatemala City, May 27, 2010
Canil Gave, Maria	Director of the National coordinator of Guatemalan women (CONAVIGUA)	Guatemala City, May 26, 2010
Casagrande, Ana	board member of the Guatemalan Council of Mayan Women (CMMG)	Guatemala City, May 23, 2010
Cassisi, Rita	Program developer at the headoffice of the Women and local economic development program of the UNDP (MyDEL)	Guatemala City, May 21, 2010

(Continued)

Interviewee	Function/position	Place and date of interview
Castañeda, Patricia	Advisor to Actoras de Cambio	Guatemala City, February 12, 2011
Castro, Alina	Member of the feminist Grupo Venancia	Managua, Nicaragua, March 2, 2011
Consuelo, Mrs.	Representative for the Council of indigenous people and of the FSLN in the North of Nicaragua (Deputada del Consejo de los pueblos Indigenas)	Mozonte, Nicaragua, April 26, 2010
Cruz, Norma	Founder of Fundación Sobrevivientes foundation, foundation for survivors of intra-family violence	Guatemala City, May 20 and June 7, 2010
Cubillo Rivas, Reyna	Member of the legal department of the women's centre of Ixchen	Managua, April 24, 2010
Delgado, Violeta	Board member of the Reformist Sandinista Party of Nicaragua (MRS)	Managua, April 13, 2010
Declerck, Xavier	Director North program Oxfam Solidarity	Brussels, November 26, 2012
Desgranges, Eli	Fieldworker reproductive health program Guatemalan National Union for Women (UNAMG)	Antigua, May 12, 2010
Diez, Andrea	Psychologist and former staff of Actoras de Cambio	Guatemala City, February 16, 2011
Erazo, Judith	Director of the Organization for community studies and psychosocial assistance (ECAP)	Guatemala, City, January 25, 2011
Espinoza, Argentina	Head of women's rights department at IXCHEN	Managua, May 3, 2010
Eugenia, Maria Reyes, Christina, Gutierrez, Maria F.	Mothers of fallen FSLN combatants working at the museum for heroes and martyrs (museo de las madres de héroes y martires)	Estelí, Nicaragua, April 26 2010

(Continued)

Interviewee	Function/position	Place and date of interview
Ferrín, Martha	Member of the Collective for the Defense of Women's rights (CODEFEM)	Guatemala City, June 10, 2010
Flores, Evelyn	Head of the training department at the Puntos de Encuentro Foundations (Fundación Puntos de Encuentro)	Managua, April 20, 2010
Galindez, Sara, Chavez, Irina, Delmorales, Maria	Former participants to a workshop of Kaqla	Guatemala City, January 31, 2011
Galvez, Guadaloupe	Head of a small feminist NGO in Guatemala	Guatemala City, February 12, 2011
García Hernández, Maria Guadalupe	Long-standing member of Mama Maquín	Guatemala City, January 26, 2011
García, Glenda	Academic and member of Myrna Mack Foundation	Guatemala City, May 13, 2010
García, Olga	Individual activist for women's rights	Rivas, Nicaragua, 19 april 2010
Gonzalez, Juana Moreno, Elvira	Ex-guerrilleras in the North of Guatemala	Huehuetenango, Guatemala, May 14, 2010
Grandison Samuel, Débora	Counsellor for women of the Council for the defense of human rights (Procuradora de las mujeres de la Procuraduría para la Defensa de los Derechos Humanos)	Managua, April 21, 2010
Green, Ingrid	Director's assistant in the Nicaraguan Institute for women (INIM)	Managua, April 29, 2010
Gutierrez, Luisa	Ex-guerrillera, no longer active in the women's movement	Transvaal, Guatemala, May 17, 2010

(Continued)

Interviewee	Function/position	Place and date of interview
Hernandez, Elisa	Member of the Presidential secretary for women (SEPREM)	Guatemala City, June 11, 2010
Jalón, Carlos	Staff at the National Historical Police Archive (AHPN)	Guatemala City, May 15, 2010
Jiménez, Giovanni (group interview with ten other members of the association present)	President of the men's association against violence (Asociación de hombres contra la violencia)	Managua, April 29, 2010
Jiménez, Juanita	Executive member of the Autonomous Women's Movement(MAM)	Managua, April 13, 2010
Lemus, Karla	Head of the legal department of the Guatemalan Women's Group (GGM)	Guatemala City, May 5, 2010 and June 2, 2010
Lopez Mejía, Angelica	Facilitator and advisor at the Community Improvement Association (ASDECO)	Chichicastenango, Guatemala, February 8, 2011
Lopez, Angélica	Researcher for Actoras de Cambio, member of Kaqla	Guatemala City, February 16, 2011
Martinez, Patricia Garcia, Edita, Rivera, Anna, Mendoza, Jacqueline	Ex-guerrilleras during the FSLN revolutionary struggle	Puerto Sandino, Nicaragua, April 27, 2010
Mendoza, Marta	Member of Kaqla	Guatemala City, January 31, 2011
Meneses, Virginia	Responsible for the political action program of the Network of women against violence (Red de mujeres contra la violencia)	Managua, April 19, 2010
Meoño Magarín, Leonel	Board member at the Organization for community studies and psychosocial assistance (ECAP)	Guatemala City, June 3, 2010

(Continued)

Interviewee	Function/position	Place and date of interview
Meza, Ivanía	Coordinator of the León office of Program developer at the head office of the Women and local economic development program of the UNDP (MyDEL)	León, Nicaragua, April 7, 2010
Méndez, Luz	Coordinator of Actoras de Cambio 2005-2008, member of Actoras de Cambio for UNAMG	Guatemala City, February 18, 2011
Montenegro, Sofia	President and founder of the Centre for communication research (CINCO), journalist, researcher, writer, co-founder of the Barricada revolutionary newspaper and of MAM, spokesperson of the feminist movement	Managua, May 2, 2010
Monzón, Ana Silvia	Sociologist, radio journalist and spokesperson of the women's movement	Guatemala City, May 21, 2010
Morales, Evelyn	Organizing member of Tierra Viva	Guatemala City, June 1, 2010
Neirynck, Heleen	Fieldworker for the Belgian cooperation's program for agricultural projects women (projects with UNAM)	Ocotál, Nicaragua, April 28, 2010
Ortiz-Martinez, Fabiola	Executive director of the National Coordinator for the prevention of violence against women (CONAPREVI)	Guatemala City, June 1, 2010
Pedrosa, Elizabeth	Organizing member at the Group for mutual support (GAM)	Guatemala City, June 3, 2010
Pena, Blanca	Former member of the Guerrilla army of the poor (EGP)	Guatemala City, June 2, 2010

(Continued)

Interviewee	Function/position	Place and date of interview
Perez, Valentina Ruiz, Filipa	Non-combatants during the Guatemalan armed conflict	Huehuetenango, Guatemala, May 14, 2010
Ramirez, Gabriela	Former member of the Guatemalan National Revolution Unit (URNG), former member of a women's organisation, no longer active	Guatemala City, May 22, 2010
Reyes, Gabriela, Herrera, Nelia	Mothers of fallen FSLN combatants	Estelí, Nicaragua, April 28, 2010
Rivas, Olga	Staff at the Presidential secretary for women (SEPREM), and founder and director of the Women's group for the amelioration of family life (GRUFEPROMEFAM)	Guatemala City, May 27, 2010
Romero, Beatriz, Muñoz, Belinda, Castro, Marta	Ex-guerrilleras during the FSLN revolutionary struggle	Managua, April 27, 2010
Rowland, Karen	Member of Bead Amigos, Christian organization for the empowerment of poor families	Chinandega, Nicaragua, April 23, 2010
Say, Claudia, Galvez, Jenny	Members of the Guatemalan Women's Group (GGM), legal section	Guatemala, February 8, 2011
Socorro, Beltrán	Commissioner for women and children - third district of Managua (Comisaría de la mujer y de la niñez - distrito tres)	Managua, April 30, 2010
Torres, Luz Marina	President of the collective of the 8th of March (Colectivo 8 de Marzo)	Managua, April 21, 2010
Torres, Sindy, Rodriguez, Marina, Lapenna, Camila	Participants to a Q'anil workshop	Guatemala City, February 4, 2011

(*Continued*)

Interviewee	Function/position	Place and date of interview
Trejo, Alba	Presidential commissioner against femicide (Comisionada presidencial contra el femicidio)	Guatemala City, May 31, 2010
Tuyuk, Rosalina	Organizing member of the coordinating body of indigenous war-widows (CONAVIGUA)	Guatemala City, June 7, 2010
Valderrama, Lidia, Marquina, Juliana	Participants to the workshop 'affection and the power of our bodies' (Afección y el poder de nuestros cuerpos) by Kaqla, and members of other women's organizations	Guatemala City, February 26, 2011
Valenzuela, Angélica	Director of the Centre for investigation, training and support of women (CICAM)	Guatemala City, June 3, 2010
Van Vuuren, Saskia	Representative of Rotary International and founder and director of El Arbol, NGO working with young women on foresting projects	Chinandega, Nicaragua, April 22, 2010
Vargas, Maria, Valdez, Heloisa, Ruiz, Veronica	Indigenous women from the capital, non-combatants during the armed conflict	Guatemala City, May 20, 2010
West, Ronald	Missionary for Amigos por Christo	Chinandega, Nicaragua, April 22, 2010

Bibliography

Aasen, B. (2009). Aid for women's empowerment and gender equality – what do we know? In Norwegian Institute for Urban and Regional Research (Ed.). Oslo: NIBR.

Abu-Lughod, L., and Lutz, C.A. (1990). Introduction: emotion, discourse and the politics of everyday life. In C.A. Lutz and L. Abu-Lughod (Eds.), language and the politics of emotion (pp. 1–23). Cambridge: Cambridge University Press.

Actoras de cambio. (2006). Rompiendo el silencio: Justicia para las mujeres víctimas de violencia sexual durante el conflicto armado en Guatemala. Guatemala: ECAP, UNAMG.

Adams, M.L. (1989). There is no place like home: feminism and identity politics. feminist review, 31, 23–33.

Aguilar T., A.L. (1997). Un movimiento de mujeres embrionario. Guatemala. In Aguilar T. Ana Leticia, B.E. Dole, M. Herrera, S. Montenegro, L. Flores and L. Camacho (Eds.), Movimiento de mujeres en Centroamérica (pp. 83–168). Managua: La Corriente.

Aguilar T., A.L. (2006). Femicidio. La pena capital por ser mujer. Boletina GGM, 3.

Aguilar T., A.L., Dole, B.E., Herrera, M., Montenegro, S., Flores, L., and Camacho, L. (1997). Introducción. In Aguilar T. Ana Leticia, B.E. Dole, M. Herrera, S. Montenegro, L. Flores and L. Camacho (Eds.), Movimiento de mujeres en centroamérica. Managua La Corriente.

Aguilera, G., and Beverly, J. (1980). Terror and violence as weapons of counterinsurgency in Guatemala. Latin American perspectives, 7(2/3), 91–113.

Aldama, A.J. (2003). Violence, bodies and the color of war. In A.J. Aldama (Ed.), Violence and the body: race, gender and the state (pp. 1–18). Bloomington: Indiana University Press.

Aldama, A.J. (2003). Violence, bodies and the color of fear. In A.J. Aldama and A. Arteaga (Eds.), Violence and the body: race gender and the state (pp. 1–15). Bloomington: Indiana University Press.

Alsop, R. (1993). Whose interests? Problems in planning for women's practical needs. world development, 21(3), 367–377.

Alvarez, S.E. (1990). Engendering democracy in Brazil. Princeton: Princeton University Press.

Alvarez, S.E. (1999). Advocating feminism: the Latin American feminist NGO 'Boom'. International feminist journal of politics, 1(2), 181–209.

AMNLAE. (n.d.). The advances achieved by the Nicaraguan Women's movement. Managua: AMNLAE.

Anazaldúa, G. (2002). Now let us shift... the path of conocimiento...inner work, public acts. In G. Anazaldúa and A. Keating (Eds.), This bridge we call home: radical visions for transformation (pp. 540–578). New York: Routledge Press.

Antrobus, P. (2004). The Global Women's Movement: Origins, Issues and Strategies. New York: Zed Books.

Ardón, P. (1999). Post-War reconstruction in Central America: Lessons from El Salvador, Guatemala and Nicaragua. In O.W. Papers (Ed.), Post-War reconstruction in Central America. Oxford: Oxfam International.

Ariès, P., and Duby, G. (1990). From the Fires of Revolution to the Great War (Vol. IV). Paris: Editions du seuil.

Asdeco. (2005). El arte de aprender de sí misma y de las crisis. Paper presented at the módulo de formación humana, Chichicastenango.

Avila, E., and Parker, J. (1999). Woman Who Glows in the Dark: A Curandera Reveals Traditional Aztec Secrets of Physical and Spiritual Health. Putnam.

Ayres, R.L. (1998). Crime and violence as development issues in Latin America and the Caribbean. Washington D.C.: World Bank.

Babb, F. (1997). Negotiating spaces: gender, economy, and cultural politics in post-sandinista Nicaragua. Identities: Global studies in culture and power, 4(1), 45–70.

Babb, F.E. (2001). After the revolution: mapping gender and cultural politics in neoliberal Nicaragua. Austin University of Texas Press.

Barnard, C.I. (1938). Functions of the Executive. Cambridge: Harvard University Press.

Barrett, L.F. (2005). Feeling is perceiving: Core affect and conceptualization in the experience of emotion. In L.F. Barrett, P.M. Niedenthal and P. Winkielman (Eds.), Emotion and Consciousness. New York: Guilford.

Bayard de Volo, L. (2001). Mothers of Heroes and Martyrs: gender identity politics in Nicaragua, 1979–1999. Baltimore: Johns Hopkins University Press.

Bayard de Volo, L. (2003). Analyzing politics and change in women's organizations: Nicaraguan mothers' voice and identity. International feminist journal of politics, 5(1), 92–115.

Bayard de Volo, L. (2006). the non-material long-term benefits of collective action: empowerment and social capital in a Nicaraguan women's organization. Comparative politics, 38(2), 149–167.

Bayat, A. (2007). Islamism and the politics of fun. Public culture, 19(3), 433–459.

Bayat, A. (2010). Life as politics: how ordinary people change the Middle East. Stanford: Stanford University Press.

Beckwith, K. (2000). Beyond compare? women's movements in comparative politics. European journal of political research, 37(3), 431–468.

Benkler, Y. (1999). Free as air to common use: First amendment constraints on enclosure of the public domain. New York University Law Review, 74(2), 354–446.

Bercian, A. (2004). La palabra y el sentir de las Mujeres Mayas de Kaqla. Guatemala: Cholsamaj.

Berger, S.A. (2003). Guatemaltecas: the politics of gender and democratization. In S. Eckstein and T.P. Wickham-Crowley (Eds.), Struggles for social rights in Latin America. New York: Routledge.

Berger, S.A. (2006). Guatemaltecas: the women's movement, 1986–2003. Austin: University of Texas Press.

Berlant, L. (2000). The Subject of True Feeling: Pain, Privacy, Politics. In S. Ahmed, J. Kilby, C. Lury, M. McNeil and B. Skeggs (Eds.), Transformations. Thinking through feminism. New York: Routledge.

Bermúdez, J.L. (2001). Bodily self-awareness and the will: reply to Power. Minds and machines, 11(1), 139–142.

Bernstein, M. (2008). Celebration and suppression: the strategic uses of identity by the lesbian and gay movement. In J. Reger, D. Myers and R. Einwohner (Eds.), Identity work in social movements. Minneapolis: University of Minnesota Press.

Bickham Mendez, J. (2002). Organizing a Space of their Own? Global/Local Processes in a Nicaraguan Women's Organization. Journal of developing societies, 18(2-3), 196–227.

Bickham Mendez, J. (2002). Creating alternatives from a gender perspective: transnational organizing or maquila workers' rights in Central America. In N.A. Naples and M. Desai (Eds.), Women's activism and globalization: linking local struggles and transnational politics (pp. 121–135). London and New York: Routledge.

Biekart, K. (1999). The politics of civil society building: European private aid agencies and democratic transitions in Central America. Utrecht: Transnational institute.

Blumberg, R.L. (1998). Climbing the Pyramids of Power: Alternative Routes to Women's Empowerment and Activism. In P.H. Smith, J.L. Troutner and C. Hunefeldt (Eds.), Promises of Empowerment: Women in East Asia and Latin America. Lanham: Towman and Littlefield.

Blumberg, R.L. (2001). Risky Business: What happens to gender equality and women's rights in post-conflict societies? Insights from NGO's in El Salvador. International Journal of Politics, 15(1), 161–173.

Booth, J.A. (1998). Civil Society and Political Context in Central America. American Behavioral scientist, 42(1), 33–46.

Bradshaw, S. (2004). Is the rights focus the right focus? Nicaraguan responses to the rights agenda. Third World Quarterly, 27(7), 1329–1341.

Brass, D.J. (1984). Being in the right place: A structural analysis of individual influence in an organization. Administrative science quarterly, 29(4), 518–539.

Broughton, J. (1978). Development of the concepts of self, mind, reality and knowledge. New directions for child and adolescent development, 1, 75–100.

Bruner, J. (1991). The narrative construction of reality. Critical inquiry, 18(1), 1–21.

Buechler, S.M. (1990). Women's movements in the United States: Woman Suffrage, equal rights and beyond. New Brunswick: Rutgers University Press.

Bujard, O., and Wirper, U. (2010). La revolución es un libro y un hombre libre. Managua: Instituto de Historia de Nicaragua y Centroamérica de la Universidad Centroamericana.

Burr, V. (1995). An introduction to social constructionism. London: Routledge.

Butler, J. (1993). Bodies that matter: on the discursive limits of 'sex'. New York and London: Routledge.

Butler, J. (2004). Precarious life: powers of mourning and grieving. London and New York: Verso.

Butler, J. (2005). Giving an account of oneself. New York: Fordham University Press.

Cabrera Perez-Armiñan, L.M. (2009). Mapeo de organizaciones de sociedad civil en el tema violence contra las mujeres en Guatemala Guatemala: CORDAID ASO-SEPRODI.

Caliskan, S., and Griese, K. (2006). Women fighting violence in war-torn societies. development, 48(1), 127–131.

Cartwright, D. (1965). Influence, Leadership, Control. In J.G. March (Ed.), Handbook of organizations. Chicago: Rand McNally.

Caruth, C. (1995). Trauma: explorations in memory. Baltimore: The Johns Hopkins University Press.

Caruth, C. (1996). Unclaimed experience: trauma, narrative and history. Baltimore and London: Johns Hopkins University Press.

Castillo, E.L. (2007). Las mujeres retornadas en el conflicto y processo de pacificacion en Guatemala (1980–2005) ¡luchar para retornar, retornar para luchar! Universia. Retrieved from http://biblioteca.universia.net/html_bura/ficha/params/title/mujeres-retornadas-conflicto-proceso-pacificacion-guatemala-1980-2005-luchar-retornar/id/30798637.html

Castro, G. (1990). American feminism: a contemporary history. Paris: Presses de la fondation nationale des sciences politiques.

CEDAW. (2002). Nicaragua: Research and statistical data Retrieved 9 december 2009, from http://webapps01.un.org/vawdatabase/countryInd.action?countryId=962#cat5

CEDAW. (2005). Consideration of reports submitted by States parties under article 18 of the Convention on the Elimination of All Forms of Discrimination against Women – Nicaragua. In C. o. t. E. o. D. a. Women (Ed.), Periodic reports of state parties Geneva: Convention on the elimination of all forms of discrimination against women.

CEDAW. (2008). Encuesta Nacional de salud familiar Retrieved 9 december 2009, from http://webapps01.un.org/vawdatabase/uploads/Guatemala%20-%20FESAL2008-violencia%20de%20pareja.pdf

Chejter, S. (2007). Feminismos latinoamericanos. Madrid: Acsur – Las Segovias.

Chinchilla, N. (1990). Revolutionary Popular Feminism in Nicaragua. Gender and society, 4(3), 370–397.

Chinchilla, N.S. (1991). Marxism, feminism, and the struggle for democracy in Latin America. Gender and Society, 5(3), 291–310.

Chirix García, E.D. (2003). Alas y raices – Afectividad de las mujeres mayas. Guatemala: Grupo de mujeres Mayas Kaqla.

Choi, J. (2001). The role of language in ideological construction of Mayan identities in Guatemala. Paper presented at the Texas Linguistic Forum, Austin.

CINCO Centro de Investigación de la Comunicación. (2006). La busqueda de un liderazgo autónomo. Managua: CINCO Centro de Investigación de la Comunicación.

CLADEM Comité de América Latina y el Caribe para la defensa de los derechos de la mujer. (2000). Cuestion de vida. Lima: CLADEM.

Clinton, A. (2006). Seemorg Matrix Work: A new transpersonal psychotherapy. Journal of transpersonal psychology, 38(1), 95–116.

Coalición Nacional de Mujeres. (1996). Agenda Minima. Managua: Coalición Nacional de Mujeres.

Colker, R. (1989). Feminism, theology and abortion: toward love, compassion and wisdom. California Law Review, 77(5), 1011–1075.

Comas-Diaz, L. (1987). Feminist therapy with mainland Puerto Rican women. Psychology of women quarterly, 11(4), 461–474.

Comisión para el Esclarecimiento Histórico (CEH). (1999). Guatemala: memoria del silencio. Informe de la Comisión para el Esclarecimiento Histórico. Ciudad de Guatemala: CEH.

Cook, J., and Fonow, M.M. (1986). Knowledge and women's interests: feminist methodology in the field of sociology. Sociological Inquiry, 56(1), 2–29.

Cooperaccio. (2009). Mujeres libre de violencias Retrieved 12 November 2011, from http://www.cooperaccio.org/que-hacemos/mujeres-libres-de-violencias/proyectos-cooperacion-internacional/proyecto/?id=397.

Craske, N. (1999). Women and politics in Latin America. New Brunswick: Rutgers University Press.

Criquillon, A. (1995). The Nicaraguan Women's Movement: Feminist Reflections from Within. In M. Sinclair (Ed.), The Politics of Survival: Grassroots Movements in Central America (pp. 209–238). New York: Monthly Review.

Cuadra Lira, E., and Jiménez Martinez, J. (2009). The women's movement and the struggle for their rights in Nicaragua. Paper presented at the Social Movements and Citizenship in Central America Managua.

Dalton, D. (2007). Building National Campaigns: Activists, Alliances, and How Change Happens. Oxford: Oxfam.

Das, V. (1996). "Language and Body: Transactions in the Construction of Pain. Daedalus, 125(1), 67–91.

de Cicco, G. (2009). Uneté para poner fin a la violencia contra las mujeres. AWID derechos de las mujeres.

de Vignemont, F. (2007). Habeas corpus: the sense of ownership of one's own body. Mind and language, 22(4), 427–449.

Della Porta, D. (2006). Globalization from below: transnational activists and protest networks. Minneapolis: University of Minnesota Press.

Della Porta, D., and Diani, M. (2006). Social Movements: an introduction (1999 second ed.). Oxford: Blackwell.

Delli Carpini, M.X. (2004). Mediating democratic engagement: the impact of communications on citizens' involvement in political and civic life. In L.L. Kaid (Ed.), Handbook of political communication research. New Jersey: Lawrence Erlbaum Publishers.

DePuy, W. (2006). A History and A Hope: El Proyecto Chico Mendez and the Sowing and Dawning of Community Development and Cultural Empowerment in a K'iche' Maya Town.

Destrooper, T. (2012). The reshaping of gender in wartorn societies: women's movements in Guatemala and Nicaragua 1980–2010. (PhD), European University Institute, Florence.

Deutsch, F. (2007). Undoing Gender. Gender and society, 21(1), 106–127.

Devos, T., and Banaji, M.R. (2003). Implicit self and identity. Annals of the New York Academy of Sciences, 1001(The self from soul to brain), 177–211.

DiCarrie, N. (2007). Agency and embodiment: performing gestures/producing culture. Cambridge, Mass.: Harvard University Press.

Dietz, M. (1985). Citizenship with a feminist face: the problem with maternal thinking. Political Theory, 13(1), 19–37.

DNSA. (2010). Database on Guatemala Retrieved 24-02-2010, from https://ezproxy .library.nyu.edu/login?url=http://nsarchive.chadwyck.com/

Dore, E. (2006). Myths of Modernity: Peonage and Patriarchy in Nicaragua. Durham: Duke University Press.

Doyle, K. (2009). Operation Sofia: documenting genocide in Guatemala K. Doyle (Ed.) National Security Archive Electronic Briefing Book No. 297.

Dubois, E.C. (1978). Feminism and Suffrage: The Emergence of an Independent Women's Movement in America 1848–1869. Ithaca: Cornell University Press.

Duggan, C., Paz, C., Bailey, P., and Gullerot, J. (2008). Reparations for Sexual and Reproductive Violence: Prospects for Achieving Gender Justice in Guatemala and Peru. International Journal of Transnational Justice, 2(2), 192–213.

Duncan, J. (1978). Organizational behaviour. Boston: Houghton Mifflin.

Duncker, C. (2006). Kritische Reflexionen das ideologie Begriffes: zur bedeutung der Ideologien für den Menschen. London: Turnshare.

Dzodzi, T. (2004). The Rights-Based Approach to Development: Potential for Change or More of the Same? Capetown: Community Development Research Association.

Edkins, J. (2003). Trauma and the memory of politics. Cambridge: Cambridge University Press.

Edwards, M., and Hulme, D. (1996). Too Close for Comfort? The Impact of Official Aid on Nongovernmental Organizations World development, 24(6), 961–973.

Ehrenreich, B. (2007). Dancing in the streets: a history of collective joy. New York: Metropolitan Books.

Ekman, P. (2003). Emotions revealed. New York: Times Books.

Ellsberg, M., Liljestrand, J., and Winkvist, A. (1997). The Nicaraguan network of women against violence: using research and action for change. Reproductive health matters, 5(10), 82–92.

Ellsberg, M., Peña, R., Herrera, A., Liljestrand, J., and Winkvist, A. (2000). Candies in hell: women's experiences of violence in Nicaragua. Social science and medicine, 51(11), 1595–1610.

Elshtain, J.B. (1979). Feminists against the family, The Nation.

Elshtain, J.B. (1981). Public man, private woman: women in social and political thought. Princeton: Princeton University Press.

Epstein, S. (1994). Integration of cognitive and psychodynamic unconscious. American psychologist, 49(8), 709–724.

Erickson, R.J. (1995). The importance of authenticity for self and society. Symbolic interaction, 18(2), 121–144.

Escobar, A. (2008). Territories of difference: place, movement, life, redes. Durham: Duke University Press.

Escobar Sarti, C. (2011, 05/03). Yo no soy culpable, Prensa Libre.

Esparza, M. (2005). Post-war Guatemala: long-term effects of psychological and ideological militarization of the K'iche Mayans. Journal of genocide research, 7(3), 377–391.

Evans, S. (1979). Personal politics: the roots of women's liberation in the civil rights movement and the new left. New York: Vintage Books.

Ewig, C. (1999). The strengths and limits of the NGO women's movement model: Shaping Nicaragua's democratic institutions. Latin American research review, 34(3), 75–102.

Fairclough, N., and Wodak, R. (1997). Critical discourse analysis. In T. Van Dijk (Ed.), Discourse as Social Interaction. London, New Delhi and Thousand Oaks.

Ferree, M.M., and Miller, F. (1985). Mobilization and meaning: Some social-psychological contributions to the resource mobilization perspective on social movements. Social inquiry, 55, 38–61.

Fischer, A. (1993). Sex-differences in emotionality: fact or stereotype? Feminism and Psychology, 3(3), 303–318.

Flood, M., and Pease, B. (2009). Factors influencing attitudes to violence against women. Trauma, violence and abuse, 10(2), 125–142.

Flores-Ortiz, Y. (2003). Re/memberingthe body – latina testimonies of social and family violence. In A.J. Aldama and A. Arteaga (Eds.), Violence and the body: Race gender and the state. Bloomington: Indiana University Press.

Fordham, M.H. (1998). Making women visible in disaster: problematizing the private domain. Disasters, 22(2), 126–143.

Franceschet, S. (2003). "State feminism" and the women's movements: the impact of Chile's Servicio Nacional de la Mujer on Women's Activism. Latin American Research Review, 38(1), 9–40.

Franceschet, S. (2004). Explaining Social Movement Outcomes Collective Action Frames and Strategic Choices in First – and Second-Wave Feminism in Chile. Comparative Political Studies, 37(5), 499–530.

Franco, J. (1998). The Long March of Feminism. NACLA Report on the Americas, 31(4).

Franzoni, J.M., and Voorend, K. (2011). Who cares in Nicaragua? A care regime in an exclusionary social policy context. General and introductory development studies, 42(4).

Fraser, N. (1990). Rethinking the Public Sphere: A Contribution to the Critique of Actually Existing Democracy. Social Text, 25(26), 56–80.

Fredrickson, B. (1998). What good are positive emotions? Review of general psychology, 2(3), 300–319.

Fredrickson, B. (2000). Cultivating positive emotions to optimize health and well-being. Prevention and Treatment. Prevention and Treatment, 3(1), 1–25. Retrieved from http://psycnet.apa.org/journals/pre/3/1/1a/.

Fredrickson, B., and Losada, M. (2005). Positive affect and the complex dynamics of human flourishing. American psychologist, 60(7), 678–686.

Freedom House. (2010). Countries at the Crossroads 2010 – Nicaragua. Refworld UNHCR. Retrieved from http://www.refworld.org/docid/4be3c8d00.html

Freeman, J. (1972). The tyranny of structurelessness. Berkeley Journal of Sociology, 17, 151–165.

Friedman, E. (1995). Women's human rights: the emergence of a movement. In J. Peters and A. Wolper (Eds.), Women's rights, human rights: international feminist perspectives. New York: Routledge.

Fromm, E. (2005). The fear of freedom.

Frühling, H., Tulchin, J.S., and Golding, H.A. (2003). Crime and violence in Latin America: citizen security, democracy, and the state. Baltimore: Johns Hopkins University Press.

Fukuyama, M., and Sevig, T. (1999). Integrating spirituality into multicultural counseling. Thousand Oaks: Sage publications.

Fulchirone, A. (2009). Tejidos que lleva el alma : memoria de las mujeres mayas sobrevivientes de violación sexual durante el conflicto armado. Guatemala: ECAP and UNAMG.

Gagnon, J. (2004). An interpretation of desire: essays in the study of sexuality. Chicago: University of Chicago Press.

Garcia Santiago, I. (2007). Informe estadistico de la violencia en Guatemala. Guatemala: PNUD.

Garrard-Burnett, V. (2000). Aftermath: Women and gender issues in postconflict Guatemala. In U. A. f. i. development (Ed.), working paper 311. Washington: Center for Development and Evaluation.

Gaulin, S., and McBurney, D.H. (2003). Evolutionary psychology. Upper Saddle River: Prentice Hall.

Gavetti, G., Levinthal, D., and Ocasio, W. (2007). Neo-carnegie: the carnegie school's past, present, and reconstructing for the future. Organization science, 18(3), 523–536.

Gilpin, R. (1981). War and change in world politics. Cambridge: Cambridge University Press.

Giulianotti, R., and Robertson, R. (2007). Forms of Glocalization: Globalization and the Migration Strategies of Scottish Football Fans in North America. Sociology, 41(1), 133–152.

Goffmann, E. (1963). Stigma: notes on the management of spoiled identity. Englewood Cliffs: Prentice Hall.

Gomáriz Moraga, E., and Jovel, R. (2007). Evaluación de la política nacional de promoción y desarollo de las mujeres Guatemaltecas y plan de equidad de oportunidades 2001–2006. Guatemala: Secretaria presidencial de la mujer.

Gross, R. (1981). Feminism from the perspective of buddhist practice. feminism and buddhist practice.

Gross, R. (1981). Buddhism from the Perspective of Women's Bodies. Buddhist Cristian Studies, 1, 72–82.

Grosz, E. (1994). Volatile bodies: Towards corporeal feminism. Bloomington: Indiana University Press.

Guatemalan Human Rights Commission. (2009). Guatemala's femicide law: progress against impunity? Washington: The Guatemalan Human Rights Commission.

Guatemalan National Revolutionary Unit. (1982). Declaration of Revolutionary Unity in Guatemala. Latin American perspectives, 9(3), 115–122.

Habermas, J. (1989). The Structural Transformation of the Public Sphere: An Inquiry into a Category of Bourgeois Society. Cambridge, Mass: MIT Press.

Hajer, M.A. (2006). Doing discourse analysis: coalitions, practices and meaning. In M. Van den Brink and T. Metze (Eds.), World matters in policy and planning. Discourse theory and method in the social sciences. Utrecht: Koninklijk Nederlands Aardrijkskundig genootschap.

Halperin, S. (2004). War and social change in modern Europe: The great transformation revisisted. Cambridge: Cambridge University Press.

Hamel, C.E. (2008). Surviving Slavery: Sexuality and Female Agency in Late Nineteenth and Early Twentieth-Century Morocco. Historical Reflections 34(1), 73–88.

Hanish, C. (1969). The personal is political. In Redstockings of the Women's Liberation Movement (Ed.), Feminist revolution. New York: Random House.

Harris, S.G. (1994). Organizational culture and individual sensemaking: A schema-based perspective organization science, 5(3), 309–321.

Havens, L. (1985). A theoretical basis for the concepts of self and authentic self. Journal of the American Psychoanalytic Association, 34, 363–378.

Heidegger, M. (1962). Being and time (J. Macquarrie and E. Robinson, Trans.). New York: Harper and Row.

Hercus, C. (1999). Identity, emotion and feminist collective action. Gender and society, 13(1), 34–55.

Herman, J.L. (1997). Trauma and recovery: the aftermath of violence – from domestic abuse to political terror. New York: BasicBooks.

Hernández, L., and Krajewski, S. (2009). Crossing cultural boundaries: taboo, bodies and identities. Newcastle upon Tyne: Cambridge Scholars.

Heyes, C. (2007). Self transformations: Foucault, ethics, and normalized bodies. Oxford and New York: Oxford University Press.

Hill, P.C. (2003). Advances in the Conceptualization and Measurement of Religion and Spirituality Implications for Physical and Mental Health Research American psychologist, 58(1), 64–74.

Hill, P.C., Pargament, K.I., Hood, R.W., Mcculough, M.E., Swyers, J.P., Larson, D.B., and Zinnbauer, B.J. (2000). Conceptualizing Religion and Spirituality: Points of Commonality, Points of departure. Journal for the theory of social behaviour, 30(1), 51–77.

Hirschman, A.O. (2002). Shifting involvements: private interest and public action. Princeton NJ: Princeton University Press.

Hochschild, A.R., and Ehrenreich, B. (2003). The commercialization of intimate life: notes from home and work. San Francisco: University of California Press.

Holland, D., Fox, G., and Daro, V. (2008). Social movements and collective identity. Anthropological quarterly, 81(1), 95–126.

Holmes, M. (2010). The emotionalization of reflexivity. Sociology, 44(1), 139–154.

Hooks, M. (1993). Guatemalan women speak. Washington DC: EPICA.

Hulme, D., and Edwards, M. (1997). NGO's states and donors, too close for comfort. New York: St. Martin's Press.

Human Rights Watch. (2004). In War As In Peace: Sexual Violence and Women's Status. World Report 2004 Retrieved 16 March 2010, from http://hrw.org/wr2k4/15.htm.

IIARS. (2009). Actoras de Cambio Retrieved 16 november 2011, from http://www.iiars.org/dbiniciativas/Organizacion_detalles.php?idorganizacion=29.

Indreiten, L.E. (1994). Mamá Maquin: a case study of a women's organization amongs repatriated refugees in Guatemala. (Master of Philosophy), University of Dublin, Dublin.

Inness, J.C. (1992). Privacy, Intimacy and Isolation. Oxford: Oxford University Press.

Instituto Nacional de Estadisticas (INE). (2002). Estadisticas de violencia intrafamiliar. Ciudad de Guatemala: INE.

Instituto Nacional de Estadisticas (INE). (2009). Estadisticas de hechos delictivos 2007. Ciudad de Guatemala: INE.

Isserman, M. (1987). If I had a hammer – : the death of the old left and the birth of the new left. New York: Basic Books.

Jackson, F. (1982). Epiphenomenal Qualia. The Philosophical Quarterly, 32(127), 127–136.

Jacobson, J.K. (1995). Much ado about ideas: the cognitive factor in economic policy. World Politics, 47, 283–310.

Jaggar, A. (1983). Feminist politics and human nature. Totowa, NJ: Rowan.

James, W. (1950). The principles of psychology (Vol. 1). New York: Dover.

Jenkins, J.H., and Karno, M. (1992). The meaning of expressed emotion: Theoretical issues raised by cross-cultural research. American Journal of Psychiatry, 149(1), 9–21.

Jocón Gonzáles, M.E. (2005). Fortalecimiento de la participación política de las mujeres mayas. Chimaltenango: Asociación Maya Uk'u'x B'e.

Johnson, S. (1989). Wildfire: igniting the she/volution. Albuquerque: Wildfire books.

Junta de gobierno de reconstrucción nacional. (1979). Programa de gobierno. Algún lugar de Nicaragua: Junta de Gobierno de reconstrucción nacional.

Kampwirth, K. (2003). Arnoldo Alemán takes on NGO's: antifeminism and the new populism in Nicaragua. Latin American politics and society, 45(2), 133–158.

Kampwirth, K. (2004). Feminism and the legacy of the revolution: Nicaragua, El Salvador, Chiapas. Ohio: Ohio University Press.

Kampwirth, K. (2006). Resisting the feminist threat: antifeminist politics in post-Sandinista Nicaragua. NWSA Journal, 18(2), 73–100.

Keating, A. (2005). Shifting perspectives: spiritual activism, social transformation and the politics of spirituality. In A. Keating (Ed.), Entre mundos/among worlds: new perspectives on Gloria E. Anzaldúa (pp. 241–254). New York: PalgraceMacMillan.

Khan, I. (2004). Está en nuestras manos. No más violencia contra las mujeres. Madrid: Amnistía Internacional.

Kim, D.H. (1993). The link between individual and organizational learning. Sloan management review, 35(1), 37–50.

Klopstech, A. (2008). Bioenergetic analysis and contemporary psychotherapy: further considerations. The clinical journal of the international institute for bioenergetic analysis, 18(1), 114–136.

Klugman, J. (2009). Human Development report: overcoming barriers: human mobility and development Human Development Report. New York: United Nations Development Programme.

Koch, J. (2008). Does gender matter in fragile states? Copenhagen: Danish Institute for International Studies.

Koelsch, L.E., Fuehrer, A., and Knudson, R. (2008). Rational or not: subverting understanding through the rational/non-rational dichotomy. Feminism and Psychology,
18(2), 253–259.

Kurtenbach, S. (2007). Context matters: violence in war, post-war and non-war societies. INEF. Hamburg.

Kweli, T. (2013, February 7). Social Justice and activism A talk with Talib Kweli: Ithaca
College.

Kwon, J.-H. (2010). Where Is the Sandinista Spirit?: Nicaraguan Women's NGOs and the
Return of Daniel Ortega (Undergraduate Honours), Duke University, Durham.

LaCapra, D. (2001). Writing history, writing trauma. Baltimore: Johns Hopkins
University Press.

Lagarde, M. (2001). Los cautiveros de las mujeres: madreposas, monjas, putas, presas y
locas. Mexico, D.F.: UNAM.

Lambach, D. (2007). Oligopolies of violence in post-conflict societies. Hamburg: GIGA
research programme: violence, power and security.

Lambek, M., and Antze, P. (1996). Introduction: forecasting memory. In P. Antze and
M. Lambek (Eds.), In Tense Past: Cultural Essays in Trauma and Memory
(pp. xi-xxxviii). New York: Routledge.

Lara, I. (2008). Latina Health Activist-Healers bridging body and spirit. Women and
therapy, 31(1), 21–40.

Laub, D., M.D. (1995). Truth and testimony: the process and the struggle. In C. Caruth
(Ed.), Trauma: explorations in memory (pp. 61–75). Baltimore: Johns Hopkins
University Press.

Laub, D. (2009). On holocaust testimony and its reception within its own frame, as a
process in its own right. History and memory, 21(1), 127–150.

Laufer, R.S. (1985). The serial self. In J.P. Wilson, Z. Harel and B. Kahana (Eds.), Human
adaptation to extreme stress: from the holocaust to Vietnam. New York: Plenum
Press.

Laufer, R.S. (1989). The aftermath of war: adult socialization and political development. In R.S. Sigel (Ed.), Political Learning in Adulthood: A Sourcebook of Theory
and Research. Chicago: University of Chicago Press.

Leonard, M. (2002). Country profiles from Latin America: Colombia, Guatemala,
Nicaragua. The reproductive health for refugees consortium, U.S. department of
state. New York.

Levine, E.L. (2010). Emotion and power (as social influence): Their impact on organizational citizenship and counterproductive individual and organizational behavior.
Human Resource management review, 20(1), 4–17.

Levine, P., and Frederick, A. (1997). Waking the Tiger: Healing Trauma. Berkeley: North
Atlantic Books.

Lichterman, P. (1996). The search for political community. Cambridge: Cambridge University Press.

Light, D. (1992). Healing their Wounds: Guatemalan Women as Political Activists. Women and therapy, 13(3), 297–308.

Lind, A. (1992). Power, gender and development. In A. Escobar and S.E. Alvarez (Eds.), The Making of social movements in Latin America : identity, strategy, and democracy. Boulder: Westview Press.

Lister, R. (1995). Dilemmas in engendering citizenship. Economy and society, 24(1), 1–40.

Little-Siebold, C. (2001). Beyond the Indian-Ladino Dichotomy: Contested Identities in an Eastern Guatemalan Town. Journal of Latin American Anthropology, 6(2), 176–197.

Lorde, A. (1984). Sister Outsider. Berkeley, CA: Crossing Press.

Luciak, I.A. (2001). After the revolution: gender and democracy in El Salvador, Nicaragua, and Guatemala. Baltimore: Johns Hopkins University Press.

Lupe, M. (1983). Guatemala: women in the revolution. Latin American perspectives, 3(1), 103–108.

Lustick, I.S. (1996). History, historiography, and political science: multiple historical records and the problem of selection bias. The American Political Science Review, 90(3), 605–618.

MacKinnon, C. (2005). Women's lives, men's laws. Cambridge: Belknap Press of Harvard University Press.

Maier, G.W., Prange, C., and von Rosenstiel, L. (2003). Psychological perspectives of organizational learning. In M. Dierkes, A. Berthoin, J. Child and I. Nonaka (Eds.), Handbook of organizational learning (pp. 14–34). Oxford and New York: Oxford University Press.

Makar, F. (2011). 'Let Them Have Some Fun': Political and Artistic Forms of Expression in the Egyptian Revolution. Mediterranean Politics, 16(2), 307–312.

MAM Movimiento Autonomo de Mujeres. (2009). Politico y ciudadanía de las mujeres. Movimiento Autonomo de Mujeres. Managua. Retrieved from http://www .movimientoautonomodemujeres.org/downloads/47.pdf.

Mansbridge, J. (1986). Why we lost the ERA. Chicago: University of Chicago Press.

March, J.G., and Simon, H.H. (1958). Organizations. New York: John Wiley and Sons.

Marcos, S. (2009). Mesoamerican women's indigenous spirituality: decolonizing religious beliefs. Journal of feminist studies in religion, 25(2), 25–45.

Markus, H.R. (1977). Self-schemata and processing information about the self. Journal of personality and social psychology, 35(1), 63–78.

Martin, T.L., and Doka, K., J. (2000). Men don't cry... women do. Philadelphia: Taylor and Francis.

Marx Ferree, M., Gamson, W.A., Gerhards, J., Rucht, D., and Suzanne, S. (2002). Shaping abortion discourse : democracy and the public sphere in Germany and the United States. New York and Cambridge: Cambrdige University Press.

McAdam, D. (1988). Freedom Summer. New York: Oxford University Press.

McAdam, D., McCarthy, J.D., and Mayer, N.Z. (1996). Alternative perspectives on social movements: political opportunities, mobilizing structures and cultural framings. Cambridge and New York: Cambridge University Press.

McDonald, K. (2002). From solidarity to fluidarity: social movements beyond 'collective identity' – the case of globalization conflicts. Social movement studies, 1(2), 109–128.

McKinney, K. (2007). "Breaking the conspiracy of silence": testimony, traumatic memory, and psychotherapy with survivors of political violence. Ethos, 35(3), 265–299.

McLeod, M. (2010). Drawing the Connections: Mayan Women's Quest for a Gendered Spirituality. In S. Marcos (Ed.), Women and indigenous religions. Santa Barbara Calif: Praeger.

Mead, G.H. (1964). The social self. In A. Reck (Ed.), Selected writings: George Herbert Mead (pp. 142–149). Chicago: University of Chicago.

Medicos Descalzos. (2005). Informe diagnóstico a traves de usuarios: Médicos, Mayas y servicios de salud. Caractrización de elementos culturalmente accesibles y aceptados para la presentación de servicios de salud. In P.P. GUA (Ed.). Chinique: PNUD.

Melucci, A. (1996). Challenging Codes: Collective Action in the Information Age. Cambridge: Cambridge University Press.

Menchú, R. (1994). Me llamo Rigoberta Menchú y así me nació la conciencia. México: Siglo Veintiuno.

Méndez, G. (2010). ¿El fin de la ventriloquia? Los cuestionamientos a las capacitaciones a mujeres indígenas. Paper presented at the Congress of the Latin American Studies Association Toronto.

Méndez, L. (2006–2008). Informe psicosocial: Documentos de trabajo de Consorcio Actoras de Cambio y informes semestrales a IDRC. Metodologías de abordaje del acompañamento psicosocial y del proceso de fromación-sanación. ECAP. Guatemala.

Mendez, L., and Morán, S. (2006). Las mujeres a diez años de los acuerdos de paz. Guatemala: Consejo Nacional de los Acuerdos de Paz.

Mendoza, M. (2007). Reconociendo la memoria y poder de nuestros cuerpos. Kaqla Guatemala. Guatemala City.

Metoyer, C.C. (2000). Women and the state in post-Sandinista Nicaragua. Boulder: Lynne Rienner Publishers.

Meyer, D.S., and Whittier, N. (1994). Social movement spillover. Social Problems, 41(2), 277–298.

Meyers, D.J. (2008). Ally identity: the politically gay. In J. Reger, D.J. Myers and R. Einwohner (Eds.), Identity work in social movements. Minneapolis: University of Minnesota Press.

Meyers, D.T. (1989). Self, society and personal choice. New York: Columbia University Press.

Millán Moncayo, M. (2006). Indigenous women and zapatismo. New horizons of visibility. In S. Speed, R. Hernández Castillo and L. Stephen (Eds.), Dissident women and cultural politics in Chiapas. Austin: University of Texas Press.

MINEDUC. (2008). Reflexiones sobre el mestizaje y la identidad nacional en Centroamérica: de la colonia a las Républicas liberales. Guatemala: MINEDUC.

Miranda, R., and Ratliff, W. (1993). The Civil War in Nicaragua: inside the Sandinistas. Transaction publishers: New Brunswick and London.

Moberg, S. (2005). El movimiento de mujeres y el estado Nicaraguënse: La lucha por la autonomía. ISP Collection, 437.

Molyneux, M. (1985). Mobilization without emancipation. Women's interests, the state and revolution in Nicaragua. Feminist Studies, 11(2).

Montenegro, S. (1996). Mujeres, medios de comunicacion y elecciones. Managua: CINCO.

Montenegro, S. (1997). Un movimiento de mujeres en auge. Nicaragua. In Aguilar T. Ana Leticia, B.E. Dole, M. Herrera, S. Montenegro, L. Flores and L. Camacho (Eds.), Movimiento de mujeres en centroamérica (pp. 339–446). Managua: El Corriente.

Morales, L., and Morán, S. (2006). A diez años de la firma de la ¿paz? lo que sigue matando es al impunidad. Guatemala: Federación Luterana.

Morris, A., and Mueller, C.M.C. (1992). Frontiers in social movement theory. New Haven: Yale University Press.

Mosby, D.E. (2003). "The Erotic as Power": Sexual Agency and the Erotic in the Work of Luz Argentina Chiriboga and Mayra Santos Febres. Cincinati Romance Review, 30(winter), 83–98.

Moser, C. (1989). Gender planning in the third world: meeting practical and strategic gender needs. World Development, 17(11), 1799–1825.

Moser, C., and McIlwaine, C. (2006). Latin American Urban Violence as a Development Concern: Towards a Framework for Violence Reduction World Development, 34(1), 89–112.

Mumby, D.K., and Putnam, L.L. (1992). The politics of emotion: a feminist reading of bounded rationality. The academy of managemment review, 17(3), 465–486.

Munck, R. (2008). Deconstructing violence: power, force and social transformation. Latin American perspectives, 35(3), 3–19.

Munkres, S. (2008). Being 'sisters' to Salvadoran peasants: deep identification and its limitations. In J. Reger, D. Myers and R. Einwohner (Eds.), Identity work in social movements (pp. 189–212). Minneapolis: University of Minnesota Press.

Nakaya, S. (2003). Women and Gender Equality in Peace Processes: From Women at the Negotiating Table to Postwar Structural Reforms in Guatemala and Somalia Global Governance, 9(4), 459–477.

NAM institute for the empowerment of women. (2009). Guatemala. country profiles Retrieved 28 october 2010, from http://www.niew.gov.my/niew/en/download/doc_details/57-guatemala

NAM institute for the empowerment of women. (2009). Nicaragua. Country Profiles. Retrieved from http://www.niew.gov.my/niew/en/download/doc_details/58-nicaragua.

Nohlen, D. (2005). Elections in the Americas: A data handbook. New York: Oxford University Press.

ODI Overseas Development Institute. (1999). What can we do with a rights-based approach to development? In briefing paper 3 (Ed.). London: Overseas Development Insititute.

Ogrodnick, M. (1999). Instinct and intimacy: political philosophy and autobiography. Toronto: University of Toronto Press.

Olff, M., Langeland, W., Draijer, N., and Berthold, P.R. (2007). Gender differences in posttraumatic stress disorder. Psychological Bulletin, 133(2), 183–204.

Ortega Saavedra, D., Tirado Lopez, V.M., and Ortega Saavedra, H. (1979). Why the FSLN struggles in Unity with the people. Latin American perspectives, 6(1), 108–113.

Palencia Prado, T. (1999). Género y cosmovision maya. Guatemala: Saqil Tzij.

Palencia, T. (2010). Caminos para la plenitud de las mujeres mayas y nuestros pueblos. Guatemala: Mujeres Mayas de Kaqla.

Parsons, T., and Shils, E. (1951). Towards a general theory of action. New York: Harper and Row.

Pateman, C. (1983). Feminist critique of the public/private dichotomy. In S. Benn and G. Gaus (Eds.), Public and private in social life. New York: St. Martin's Press.

Pateman, C. (1988). The sexual contract. Stanford: Stanford University Press.

Paulson, S. (2002). Engaging ethnicity and gender in Bolivia. Practicing anthropology, 24(4), 5–10.

Payne, H. (2006). Dance movement therapy: theory, research and practice. Hove: Routledge.

Pearce, J. (1998). From Civil War to 'Civil Society': Has the End of the Cold War Brought Peace to Central America? International Affairs, 74(3), 587–615.

Peetz, P. (2008). Discourses on Violence in Costa Rica, El Salvador, and Nicaragua: Laws and the Construction of Drug – and Gender-Related Violence Hamburg: German Institute of Global and Area Studies.

Pereira, C. (2009). Interrogating Norms: Feminists theorizing sexuality, gender and heterosexuality. Development, 52(1), 18–24.

Pessar, P. (2001). Women's Political Consciousness and Empowerment in Local, National, and Transnational Contexts: Guatemalan Refugees and Returnees. Identities: global studies in culture and power, 7(4), 461–500.

Peterson, S.R. (1977). Coercion and rape: the state as a male protection racket. In M. Vetterling-Braggin, F.A. Elliston and J. English (Eds.), Feminism and philosophy. Totowa: Littlefield, Adams.

Piron, L.-H. (2005). Rights-based approaches and bilateral aid agencies: more than metaphor? IDS Bulletin, 36(1), 19–30.

Pisano, M. (1996). Un cierto desparpajo. Santiago de Chile: Ediciones Numero Critico.

Pizarro, A.M. (2000, 4 october). La ausencia de una perspectiva de salud integral de las mujeres. Paper presented at the Reformas al codigo penal de nicaragua. Primer foro de consulta.

Plummer, K. (2003). Intimate citizenship: Private decisions and public dialogues. Washington: University of Washington Press.

Poal Marcet, G. (1995). Reflexiones en torno a los aspectos psicosociales que inciden en la relación mujeres-mundo laboral Cuadernos de relaciones laborales, 6, 93–105.

Polletta, F. (2008). Culture and movements. The annals of the American Academy of Political and Social Science, 619, 78–96.

Polletta, F., and Jasper, J.M. (2001). Collective identity and social movements. Annual review of sociology 27, 283–305.

Polletta, F., and Lee, J. (2006). Is telling stories good for democracy? Rhetoric in public deliberation after 9/11. American sociological review, 71(5), 699–723.

Pontes, H. (2008). Critique of culture in the feminine – Crítica de cultura no feminino. Mana, 4(1).

Portocarrero, G. (2008). Transgression as a specific form of enjoyment in the criollo world Theory and event, 11(3), 245–270.

Pouliot, V. (2008). The logic of practicality: a theory of practice of security communities. International organization, 62(2), 257–288.

Prentice, D.A. (2002). What women and men should be, shouldn't be, are allowed to be, and don't have to be: contents of prescriptive gender stereotypes Psychology of women quarterly, 26(2), 269–281.

Prokhovnik, R. (1998). Public and private citizenship: from gender invisibility to gender inclusiveness. Feminist review, 60(1), 84–104.

Pupavac, V. (2004). International Therapeutic Peace and Justice in Bosnia. Social and Legal Studies, 13(3), 377–401.

Q'anil. (2009). Empoderarnos desde nuestra propia experiencia. Guatemala: Q'anil.

Q'anil. (2011). Centro de Sanación, Investigación y Formación Humanista y Traspersonal Q'anil Retrieved 26 november 2011, from http://centrosanacionqanil.blogspot .com/p/centro-qanil.html

Ramirez Horton, S.E. (1982). The role of women in the Nicaraguan revolution. In T.W. Walker (Ed.), Nicaragua (pp. 147–160). New York: Praeger.

Randall, M. (1980). La Mujer en la insureción. Nicarahuac, 1(July/August), 34.

Randall, M., and Yanz, L. (1981). Sandino's daughters: testimonies of Nicaraguan women in struggle. Vancouver: New Star Books.

Ray, R., and Korteweg, A. (1999). Women's Movements in the Third World: Identity, Mobilization, and Autonomy. Annual review of sociology, 25, 47–71.

Red de Mujeres contra la Violencia. (2000, 28 September). Porque queremos tanto a la vida, El nuevo diario.

Reilly, N. (2007). Seeking gender justice in post-conflict transitions: towards a transformative women's human rights approach. International Journal of Law in Context, 3(2), 155–172.

Reynolds, P. (2010). Disentangling privacy and intimacy: intimate citizenship, private boundaries and public transgressions. Human Affairs, 1, 33–42.

Robertson, R. (1994). Globalisation or glocalisation? Journal of international communication, 1(1), 33–52.

Rosenwasser, P. (2000). Tool for Transformation: Cooperative Inquiry as a Process for Healing from Internalized Oppression AERC 2000, 392–396. Retrieved from.

Rothman, J., and Friedman, V.J. (2003). Identity, conflict and organizational learning. In M. Dierkes, A. Berthoin, J. Child and I. Nonaka (Eds.), Handbook of organizational learning and knowledge (pp. 582–598). Oxford and New York: Oxford University Press.

Rowbotham, S. (1992). Women in movement: feminism and social action. New York: Routledge.

Rowbotham, S. (1993). To be or not to be: the dilemmas of mothering. Feminist Review, 31(spring), 82–93.

Rudder, C.E. (2008). Private governance as public policy: a paradigmatic shift. The Journal of Politics, 70(4), 899–913.

Ruppert, U. (2002). Global Women's Politics: Towards the "Globalizing" of Women's Human Rights? In M. Braig and S. Wölte (Eds.), Common ground or mutual exclusion? : women's movements in international relations. New York: Zed Books.

Ryan, B. (1992). Feminism and the women's movement: dynamics of change in social movements. New York and London: Routledge.

Safa, H.I. (1990). Women's movements in latin america. Gender and Society, 4(3), 354–369.

Saint-Germain, M. (1993). Paths to power of women legislators in Costa Rica and Nicaragua. Women's studies international forum, 16(2), 119–138.

Sanday, P.R. (1974). Female status in the public domain. In M.Z. Rosaldo, L. Lamphere and J. Bamberger (Eds.), Women, Culture and Society (pp. 189–206). Stanford, Calif.: Stanford University Press.

Sapiro, V. (1983). The political integration of women: roles, socialization and politics. Urbana: University of Illinois Press.

Scherer, K.R., and Tran, V. (2001). Effects of emotion on the process of organizational learning. In M. Dierkes, A. Berthoin, J. Child and I. Nonaka (Eds.), Handbook of organizational learning (pp. 369–394). Oxford and New York: Oxford University Press.

Schild, V. (2000). Gender equity without social justice: women's rights in the neoliberal age. NACLA report on the America's, 34(1), 25–28.

Schimmelfennig, F. (2001). The Community Trap: Liberal Norms, Rhetorical Action, and the Eastern Enlargement of the European Union. International Organization, 55(1), 47–80.

Schirmer, J.G. (1993). The seeking of truth and gendering of consciousness. In S.A. Radcliffe and S. Westwood (Eds.), "Viva": women and popular protest in Latin America. London and New York: Routledge.

Schmidt, V. (2008). Discursive Institutionalism: The Explanatory Power of Ideas and Discourse. Annual review of political science, 11, 303–326.

Schwarz, A. (2004). Autonomy, Figuration, Embodiment: Meyers and Irigaray. Paper presented at the Southern Society for Philosophy and Psychology, Boston.

Senge, P.M. (1990). The fifth discipline: the art and practice of the learning organization. New York: Doubleday.

Serra Vázquez, L.H. (2007). La Sociedad Civil Nicaragüense. Sus Organizaciones y sus relaciones con el estado. Managua: Friedrich Ebert Stiftung.

Shayne, J.D. (2004). The revolution question: Feminism in El Salvador, Chile and Cuba. New Jersey: Rutgers University Press.

SI Mujer – Servicios integrales para la mujer. (2006). Violencias Sexuales. Managua: SI Mujer.

Sieder, R., and MacLeod, M. (2009). Genero, derecho y cosmovisión Maya en Guatemala. Desacatos, 31(3).

Silverman, D. (2006). Interpreting qualitative data: methods for analyzing talk, text, and interaction. London, Thousand Oaks, New Delhi: Sage.

Simões, S., Reis, B.P.W., Biagioni, D., Fialho, F.M., and Bueno, N.S. (2009). The private motivations of public action: women's associational lives and political activism in Brazil. In V. Demos and M. Texler Segal (Eds.), Advances in gender research: perceiving gender locally, globally and intersectionally. Bingley: Emerald Group Publishing.

Snow, D.A., Rochford, B.E., Worden, S.K., and Benford, R.D. (1986). Frame Alignment Processes, Micromobilization, and Movement Participation. American Sociological Review, 51(4), 464–481.

Staggenborg, S. (1989). Organizational and Environmental Influences on the Development of the Pro-Choice Movement. Social Forces, 68(1), 204–240.

Staggenborg, S. (1991). The Pro-Choice Movement: Organization and Activism in the Abortion Conflict. Oxford: Oxford University Press.

Staten, C.L. (2010). The history of Nicargua. Santa Barbara California: Greenwood.

Stephen, L. (1997). Women and social movements in Latin America. Power from below. Austin: University of Texas Press.

Stern, M. (1998). In/securing identities. An exploration: ethnic and gender identities among Maya women in Guatemala. Anales nueva época, 1(1), 141–178.

Sternbach, N.S., Navarro-Aranguren, M., Chuchryk, P., and Alvarez, S.E. (1992). Feminisms in Latin America: from Bogota to San Bernard. Signs, 17(2), 393–434.

Stetlet, K., and Sharp, D. (2008). Beyond the Peace Table: Post-Conflict Gender Influence for Finding Security and Justice. Paper presented at the Women Peacemakers conference, San Diego.

Stillion, J.M., and Noviello, S.B. (2001). Living and dying in different worlds: gender and differences in violent death and grief. Illness, crisis and loss, 9(3), 247–259.

Suárez Navaz, L., and Hernández Castillo, R. (2008). Descolonizando el feminismo: teorías y practicas desde los márgenes. Madrid: Cátedra.

Tarrow, S. (1998). Power in movement: social movements and contentious politics. Cambridge and New York: Cambridge University Press.

Tetreault, M.A. (2000). Women and revolution in Vietnam. In B.G. Smith (Ed.), Global feminisms since 1945: a survey of issues and controversies (pp. 45–65). London and New York: Routledge.

Thayer, M. (1994). After the fall: The nicaraguan women's movement in the 1990s. Paper presented at the Lasa XVIII International Congress, Atlanta Georgia.

Tröger, A.M. (1986). Between rape and prostitution: survival strategies and chances of emancipation for Berlin women after World War II. In J. Friedlander (Ed.), Women in culture and politics: a century of change. Bloomington: Indiana University Press.

Turner, R.H. (1973). Determinants of social movement strategies. In T. Shibutani (Ed.), Human Nature and collective behaviour. New Brunswick: Transaction books.

Uvin, P. (2007). From the right to development to the rights-based approach: how 'human rights' entered development. Development in Practice, 17(4 and 5), 597–606.

Valdez Medina, J.L., and Gonzáles Arratia, N.I. (1999). El autoconcepto en hombres y mujeres mexicanos. Ciencia ergo sum, 6(3), 265–269.

Valdivia, A.N. (1991). Gender, press and revolutions: a textual analysis of three newspapers in Nicaragua's Sandinista period, 1979–1988. (PhD), University of Illinois: Urbana.

Valenzuela Sotomayor, M.D.R. (2001). Mujer y género en Guatemala. Guatemala: Edinter.

Veraeli Swai, E. (2006). Construction of womanhood in Africa: the case of women in rural Tanzania. (Doctoral), Pennsylvania State University, Ann Arbor.

Vince, R. (2002). The impact of emotion on organizational learning. Human resource development international, 5(1), 73–85.

Walker, A. (1983). In search of our mother's gardens. San Diego: Harcourt Brace Jovanovich.

Walker, L.E. (1994). Abused women and survivor therapy: A practical guide for the psychotherapist. Washington DC: American Psychological Association.

Ward, L.G., and Throop, R. (1992). Emotional experience in Dewey and Mead: Notes for the social psychology of emotion. In D.D. Franks and V. Gecas (Eds.), Social perspectives on emotions (Vol. 1). Greenwich, CT: JAI Press.

Weedon, C. (1999). Feminism, theory, and the politics of difference. Oxford: Blackwell Publishers.

Weick, K. (1974). Amendments to organizational theorizing. The academy of management journal, 17(3), 487–502.

Weismantel, M. (2004). Cities of women. In C. Brettell and C. Sargent (Eds.), Gender in Cross-cultural perspective. Englewood Cliffs: Prentice Hall.

Westwood, S., and Radcliffe, S.A. (1993). "Viva": women and popular protest in Latin America. London and New York: Routledge.

Whitehead, S. (2002). Men and masculinities: key themes and directions. Cambridge: Polity Press.

Widmaier, W., Blyth, M., and Seabrook, L. (2007). Exogenous Shocks or Endogenous Constructions? The Meanings of Wars and Crises. International Science Quarterly, 51(4), 747–759.

Wieschiolek, H. (2003). "Ladies, just follow his lead" Salsa, gender and identity. In N. Dyck and E. Archetti (Eds.), Sport, dance and embodied identities. New York: Oxford.

Williams, P. (1994). Dual Transition from Authoritarian Rule: Popular and Electoral Democracy in Nicaragua. Comparative Politics, 26(2), 169–185.

Wodak, R. (2008). Introduction: discourse studies, important concepts and terms. In R. Wodak and M. Krzyzanowski (Eds.), Qualitative discourse analysis in the social sciences. Basingstoke: Palgrave MacMillan.

Wölte, S. (2002). Claiming rights and contesting spaces: women's movements and international human rights discourse in africa. In M. Braig and S. Wölte (Eds.), Common ground or mutual exclusion? : women's movements in international relations. New York: Zed Books.

Yamin, A.E. (2009). Suffering and Powerlessness: The Significance of Promoting Participation in Rights-Based Approaches to Health. Health and Human rights, 11(1), 5–22.

Young, I.M. (2003). The logic of masculinist protection. signs, 29(1).

Zinnbauer, B.J., Pargament, K.I., Cole, B., Rye, M., Butter, E., Belavich, T., Kadar, J. (1997). Religion and spirituality: unfuzzying the fuzzy. Journal for the scientific study of religion, 36(4), 549–564.

Zuckerman, E., and Greenberg, M.E. (2004). The Gender Dimensions Of Post-Conflict Reconstruction: An Analytical Framework For Policymakers gender and development, 12(3), 70–82.

Index

www.ingramcontent.com/pod-product-compliance
Lightning Source LLC
Chambersburg PA
CBHW060027030426
42334CB00019B/2210

* 9 7 8 1 6 0 8 4 6 4 8 8 3 *